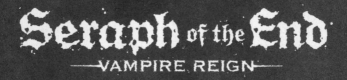

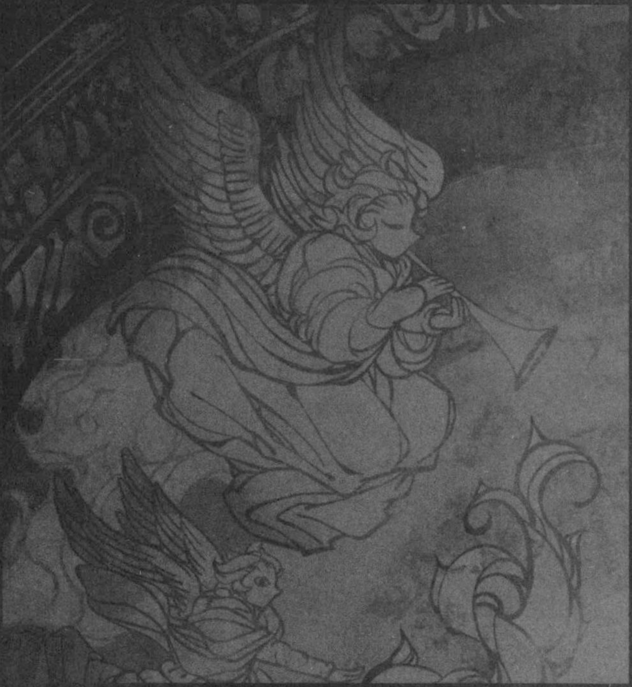

Seraph of the End

—VAMPIRE REIGN—

2

STORY BY **Takaya Kagami**
ART BY **Yamato Yamamoto**
STORYBOARDS BY **Daisuke Furuya**

CHARACTERS

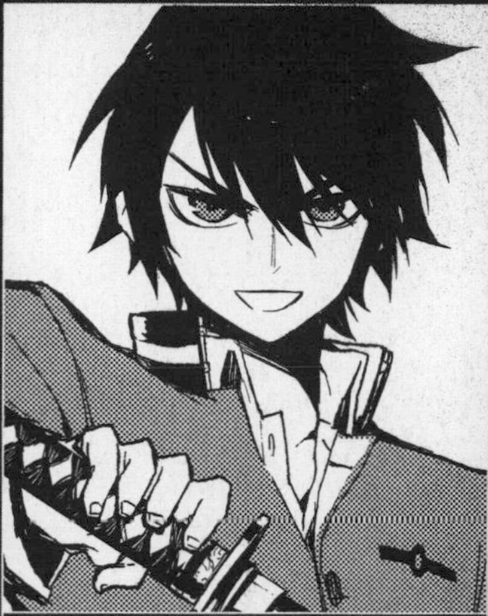

YUICHIRO HYAKUYA

A boy who escaped from the vampire capital, he has both great kindness and a great desire for revenge. Lone wolf.

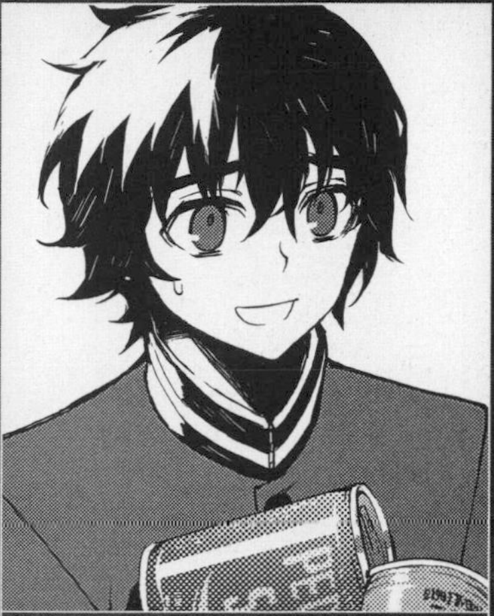

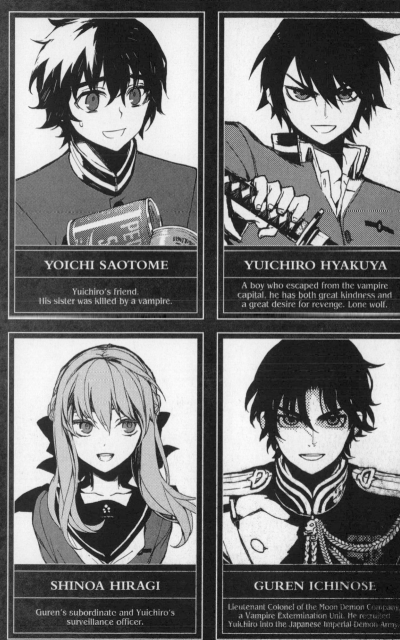

YOICHI SAOTOME

Yuichiro's friend.
His sister was killed by a vampire.

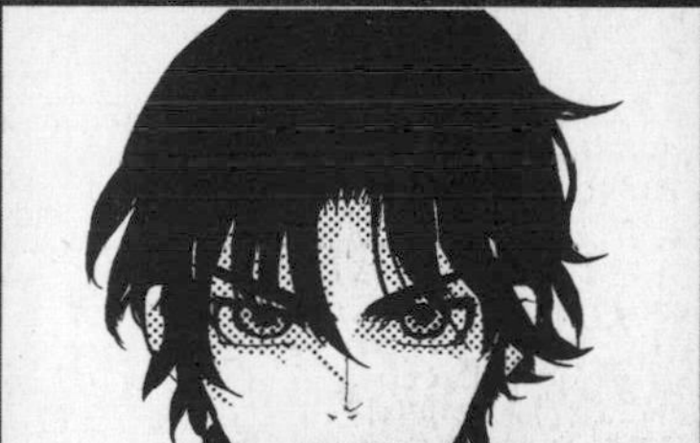

GUREN ICHINOSE

Lieutenant Colonel of the Moon Demon Company, a Vampire Extermination Unit. He recruited Yuichiro into the Japanese Imperial Demon Army.

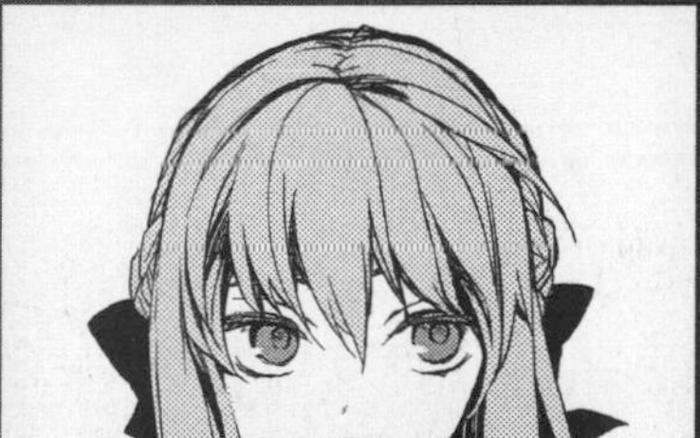

SHINOA HIRAGI

Guren's subordinate and Yuichiro's surveillance officer.

STORY

A mysterious virus decimates the human population, and vampires claim dominion over the world. Yuichiro and his adopted family of orphans are kept as vampire fodder in an underground city until the day Mikaela, Yuichiro's best friend, plots an ill-fated escape for the orphans. Only Yuichiro survives and reaches the surface.

Four years later, after Yuichiro swears revenge against vampires for the death of his family, he is accepted into the Moon Demon Company, a Vampire Extermination Unit in the Japanese Imperial Demon Army. He begins his training with Yoichi under the supervision of Shinoa and the command of Lieutenant Colonel Guren Ichinose.

Meanwhile, a boy looking much like a grown Mikaela shows up in the vampire city of Sanguinem. Has Mikaela joined the vampires?

Seraph of the End
—VAMPIRE REIGN—

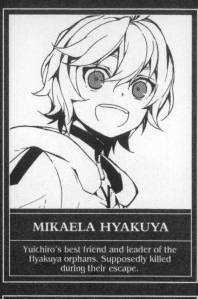

MIKAELA HYAKUYA

Yuichiro's best friend and leader of the Hyakuya orphans. Supposedly killed during their escape.

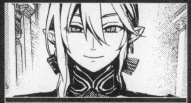

FERID BATHORY

A Seventh Progenitor vampire, he killed Mikaela.

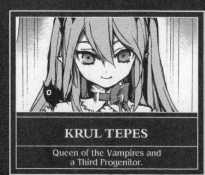

KRUL TEPES

Queen of the Vampires and a Third Progenitor.

Seraph of the End

VAMPIRE REIGN

2

CONTENTS

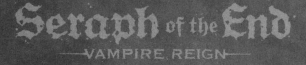

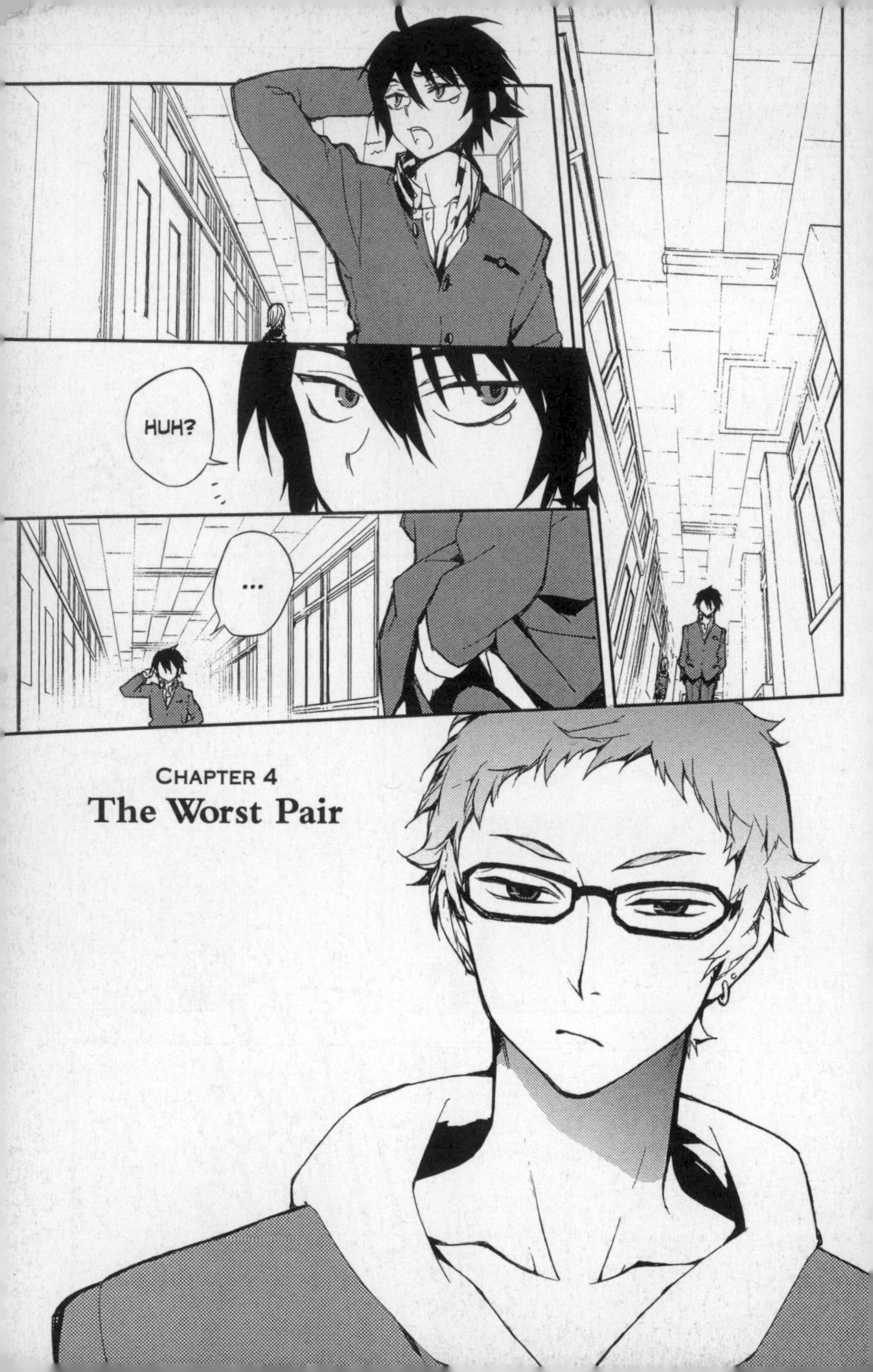
HUH?
...

CHAPTER 4
The Worst Pair

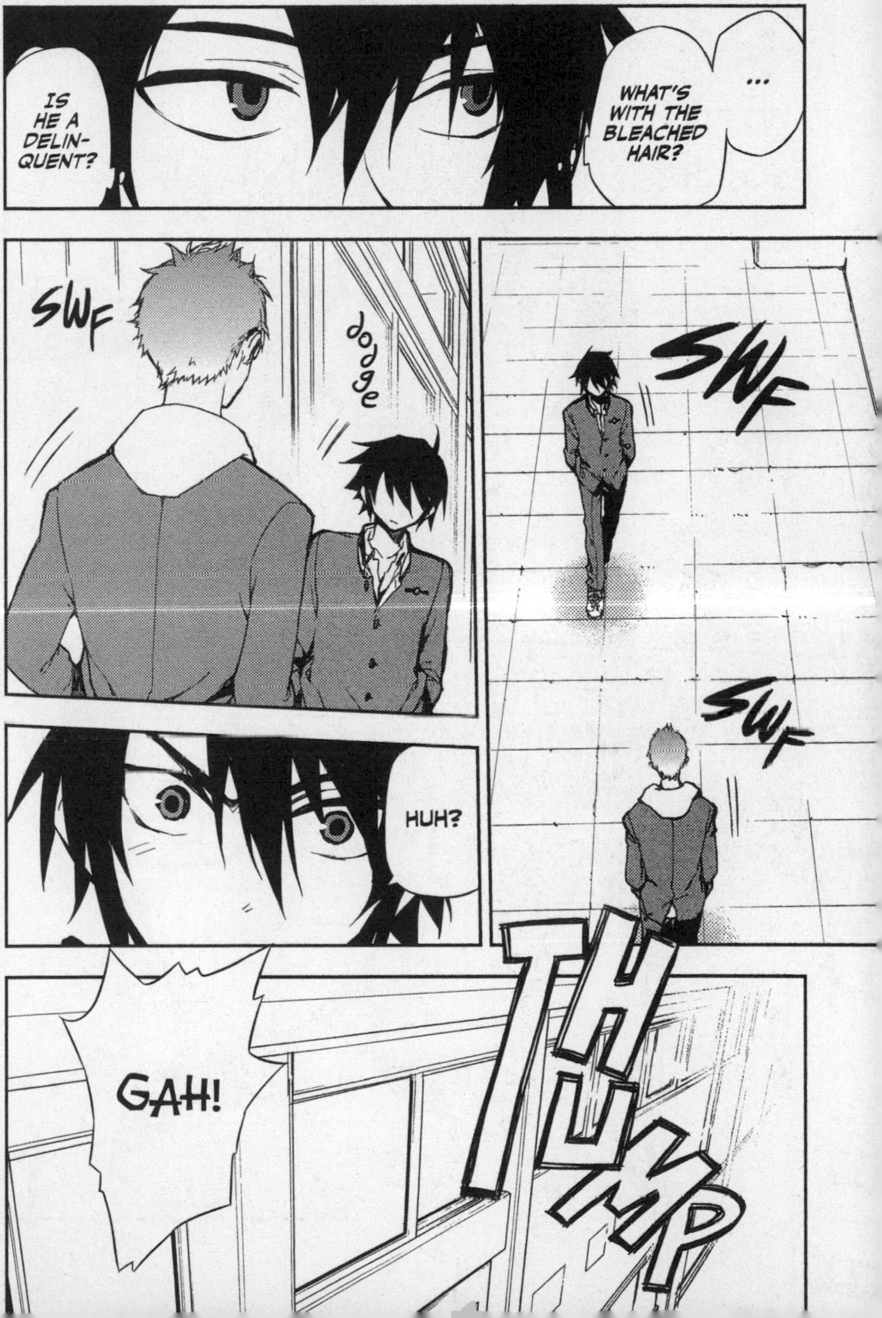
...
WHAT'S WITH THE BLEACHED HAIR?
IS HE A DELIN-QUENT?
SWF
SWF
dodge
SWF
HUH?
THUMP
GAH!

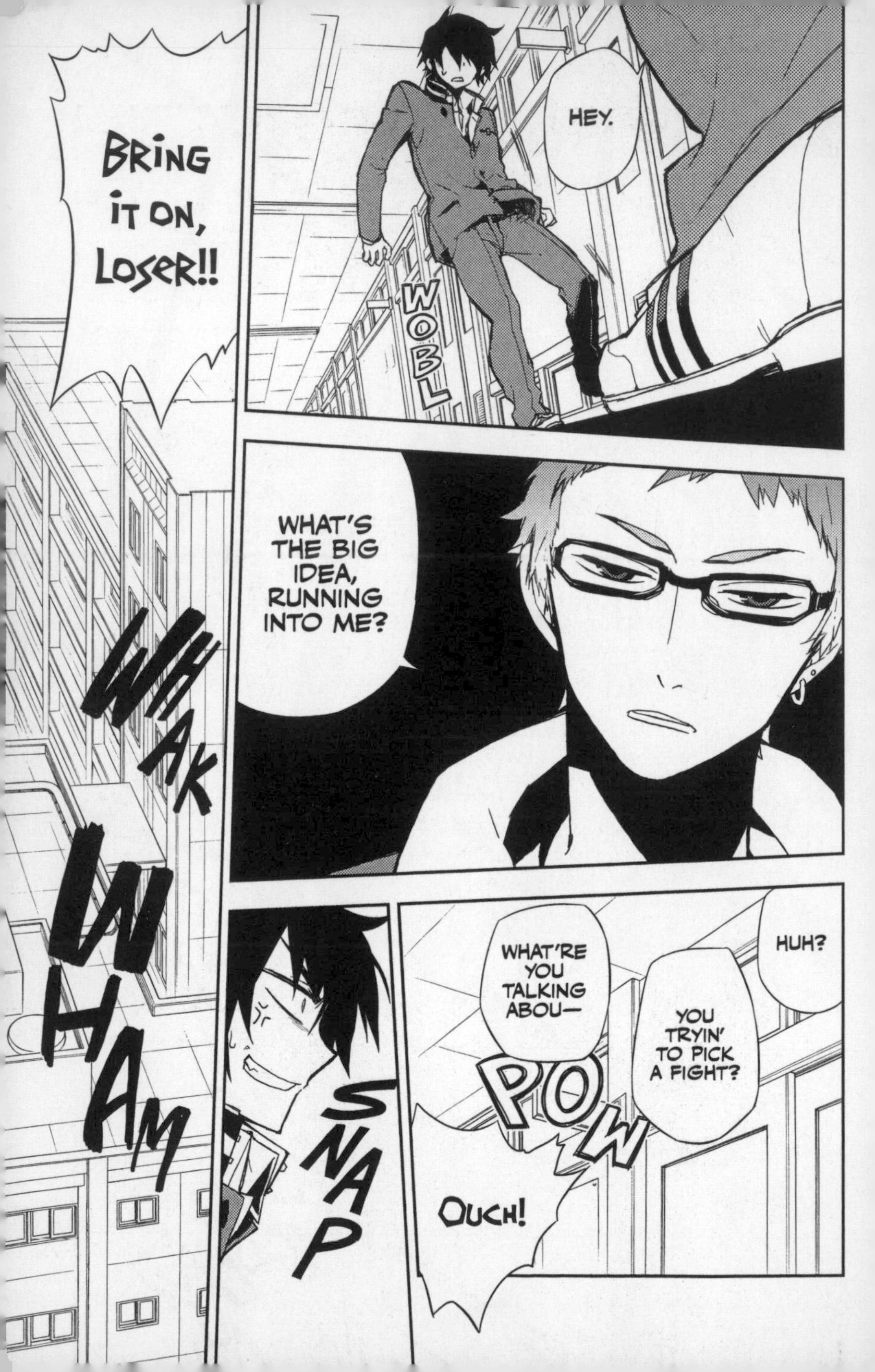
HEY.
WOBL
WHAT'S THE BIG IDEA, RUNNING INTO ME?
HUH?
YOU TRYIN' TO PICK A FIGHT?
WHAT'RE YOU TALKING ABOU—
POW
OUCH!
SNAP
BRING IT ON, LOSER!!
WHAK
WHAM

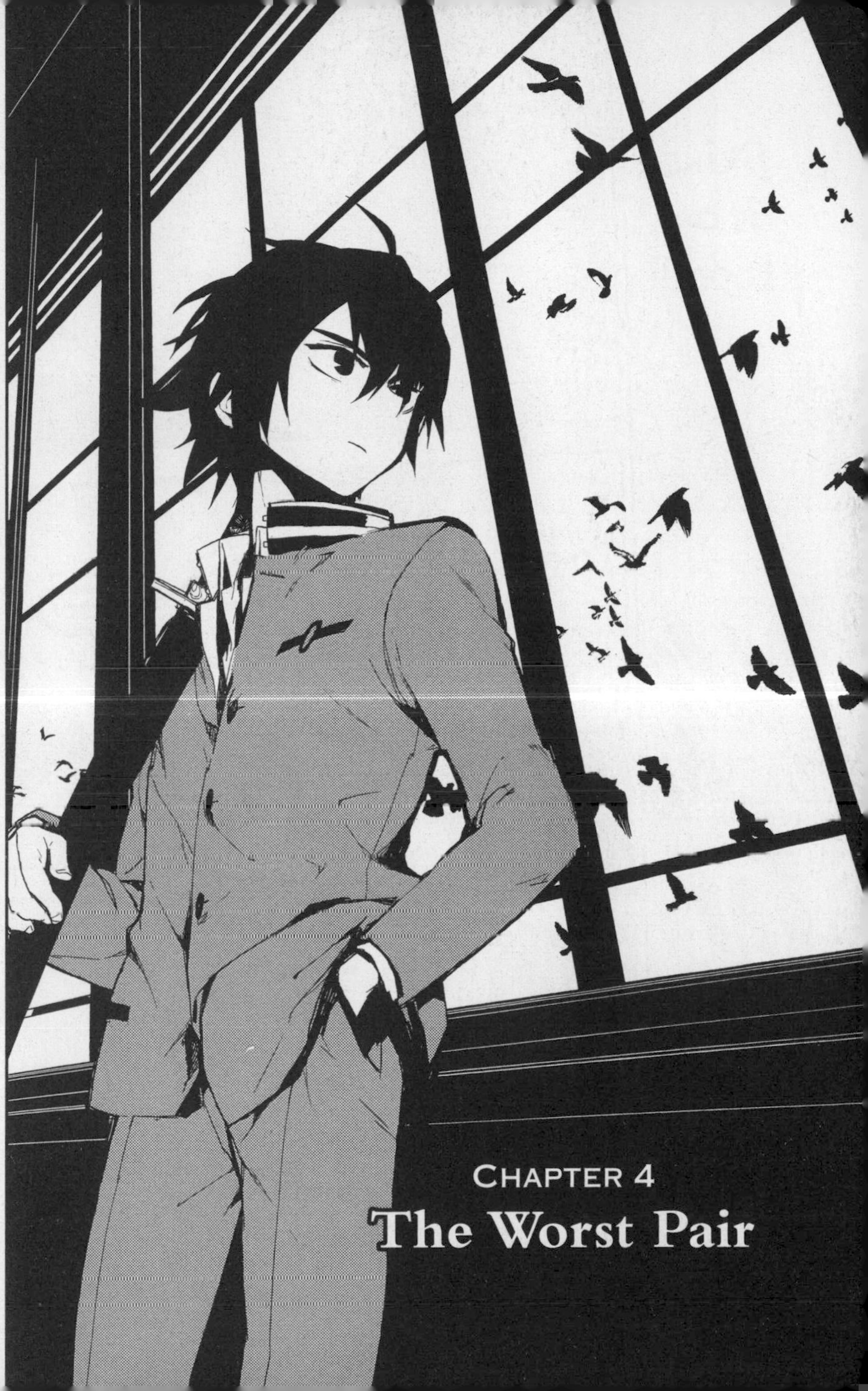

CHAPTER 4

The Worst Pair

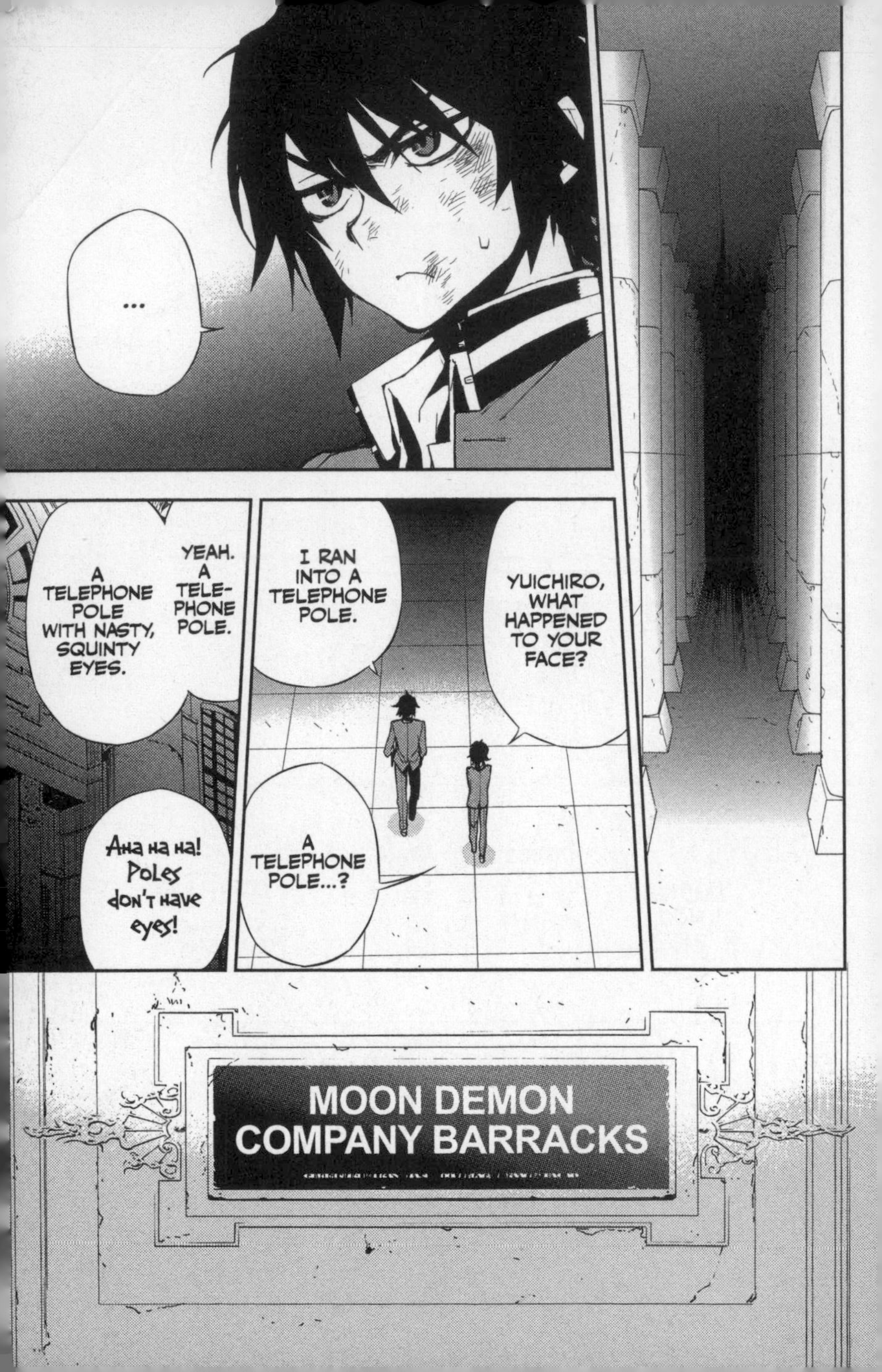
...
YUICHIRO, WHAT HAPPENED TO YOUR FACE?
I RAN INTO A TELEPHONE POLE.
A TELEPHONE POLE...?
YEAH. A TELE-PHONE POLE.
A TELEPHONE POLE WITH NASTY, SQUINTY EYES.
Aha ha ha! Poles don't have eyes!
MOON DEMON COMPANY BARRACKS

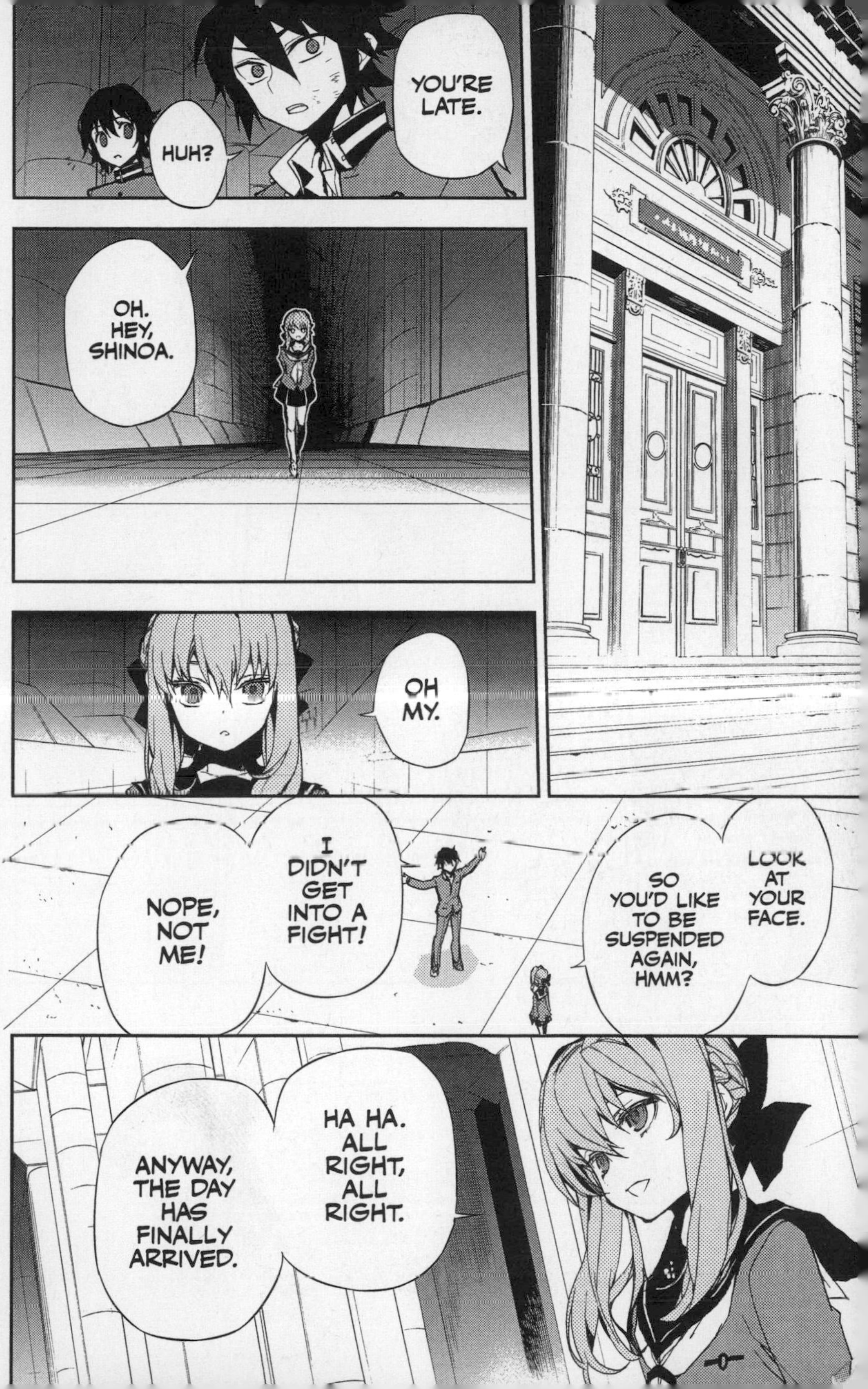
YOU'RE LATE.
HUH?
OH. HEY, SHINOA.
OH MY.
LOOK AT YOUR FACE.
SO YOU'D LIKE TO BE SUSPENDED AGAIN, HMM?
I DIDN'T GET INTO A FIGHT!
NOPE, NOT ME!
HA HA. ALL RIGHT, ALL RIGHT.
ANYWAY, THE DAY HAS FINALLY ARRIVED.

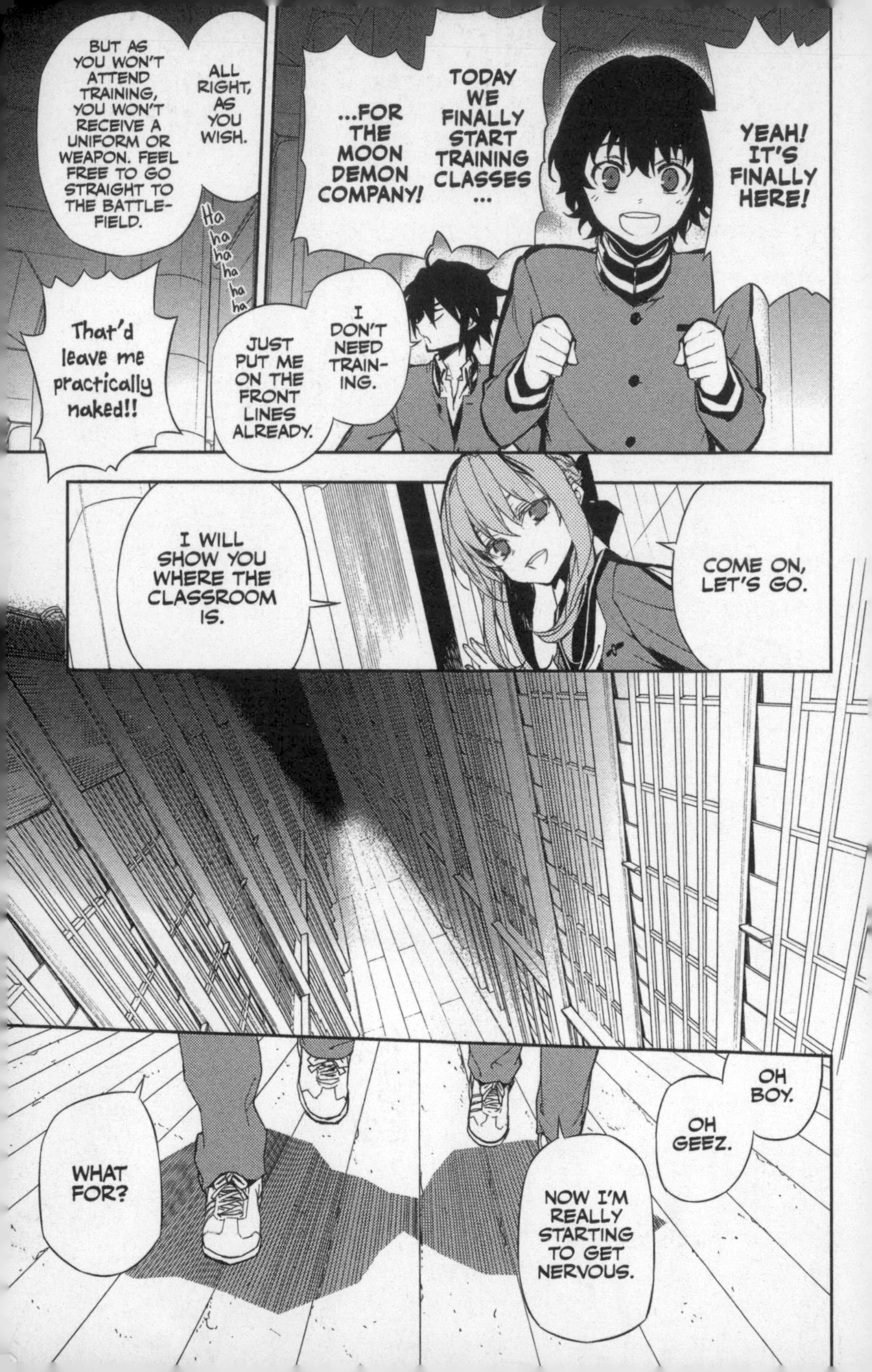
YEAH! IT'S FINALLY HERE!
TODAY WE FINALLY START TRAINING CLASSES ...
...FOR THE MOON DEMON COMPANY!
I DON'T NEED TRAINING.
JUST PUT ME ON THE FRONT LINES ALREADY.
ALL RIGHT, AS YOU WISH.
BUT AS YOU WON'T ATTEND TRAINING, YOU WON'T RECEIVE A UNIFORM OR WEAPON. FEEL FREE TO GO STRAIGHT TO THE BATTLE-FIELD.
Ha ha ha ha ha ha
That'd leave me practically naked!!
COME ON, LET'S GO.
I WILL SHOW YOU WHERE THE CLASSROOM IS.
OH BOY.
OH GEEZ.
NOW I'M REALLY STARTING TO GET NERVOUS.
WHAT FOR?

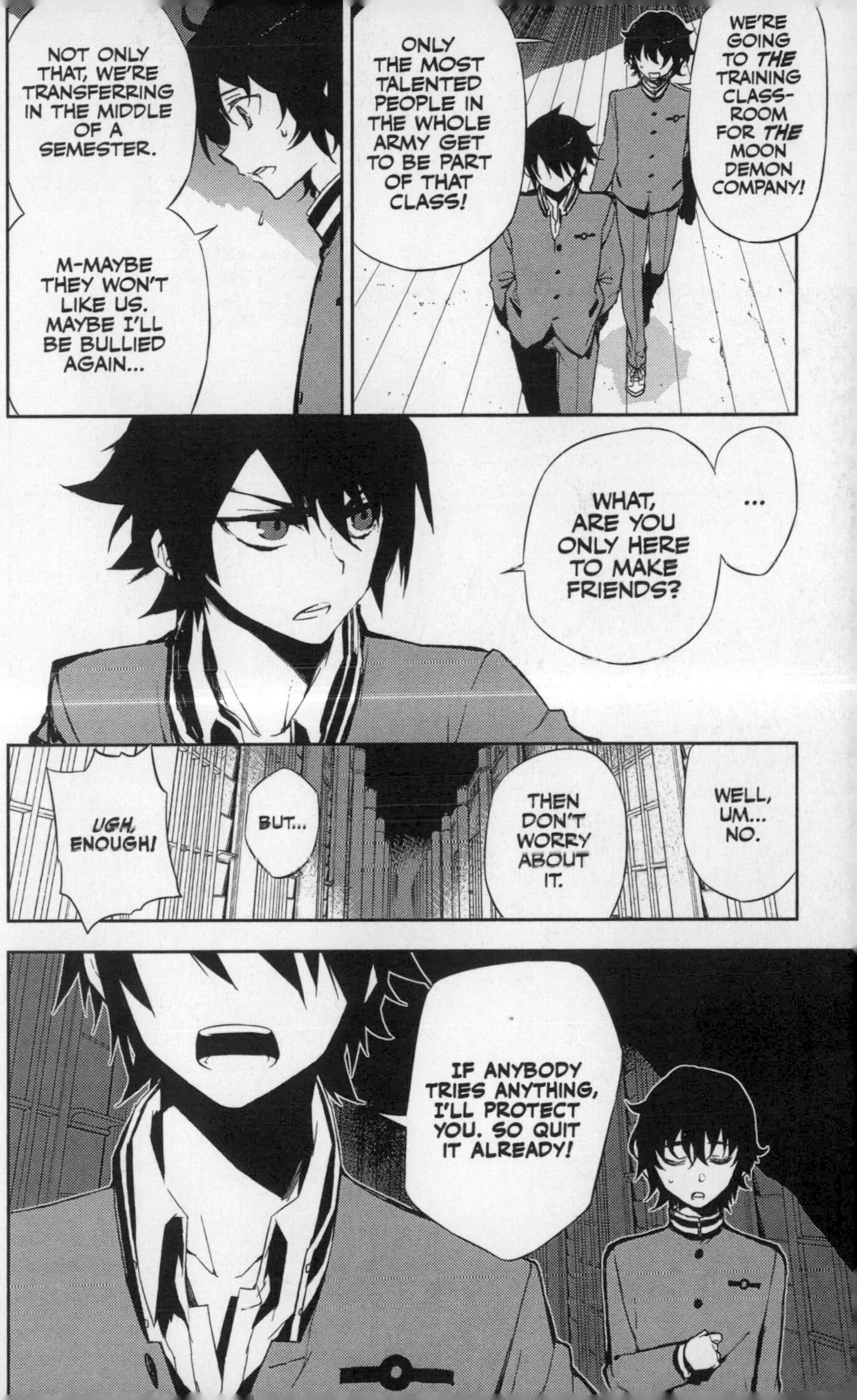
WE'RE GOING TO *THE* TRAINING CLASS-ROOM FOR *THE* MOON DEMON COMPANY!
ONLY THE MOST TALENTED PEOPLE IN THE WHOLE ARMY GET TO BE PART OF THAT CLASS!
NOT ONLY THAT, WE'RE TRANSFERRING IN THE MIDDLE OF A SEMESTER.
M-MAYBE THEY WON'T LIKE US. MAYBE I'LL BE BULLIED AGAIN...
...
WHAT, ARE YOU ONLY HERE TO MAKE FRIENDS?
WELL, UM... NO.
THEN DON'T WORRY ABOUT IT.
BUT...
UGH, ENOUGH!
IF ANYBODY TRIES ANYTHING, I'LL PROTECT YOU. SO QUIT IT ALREADY!

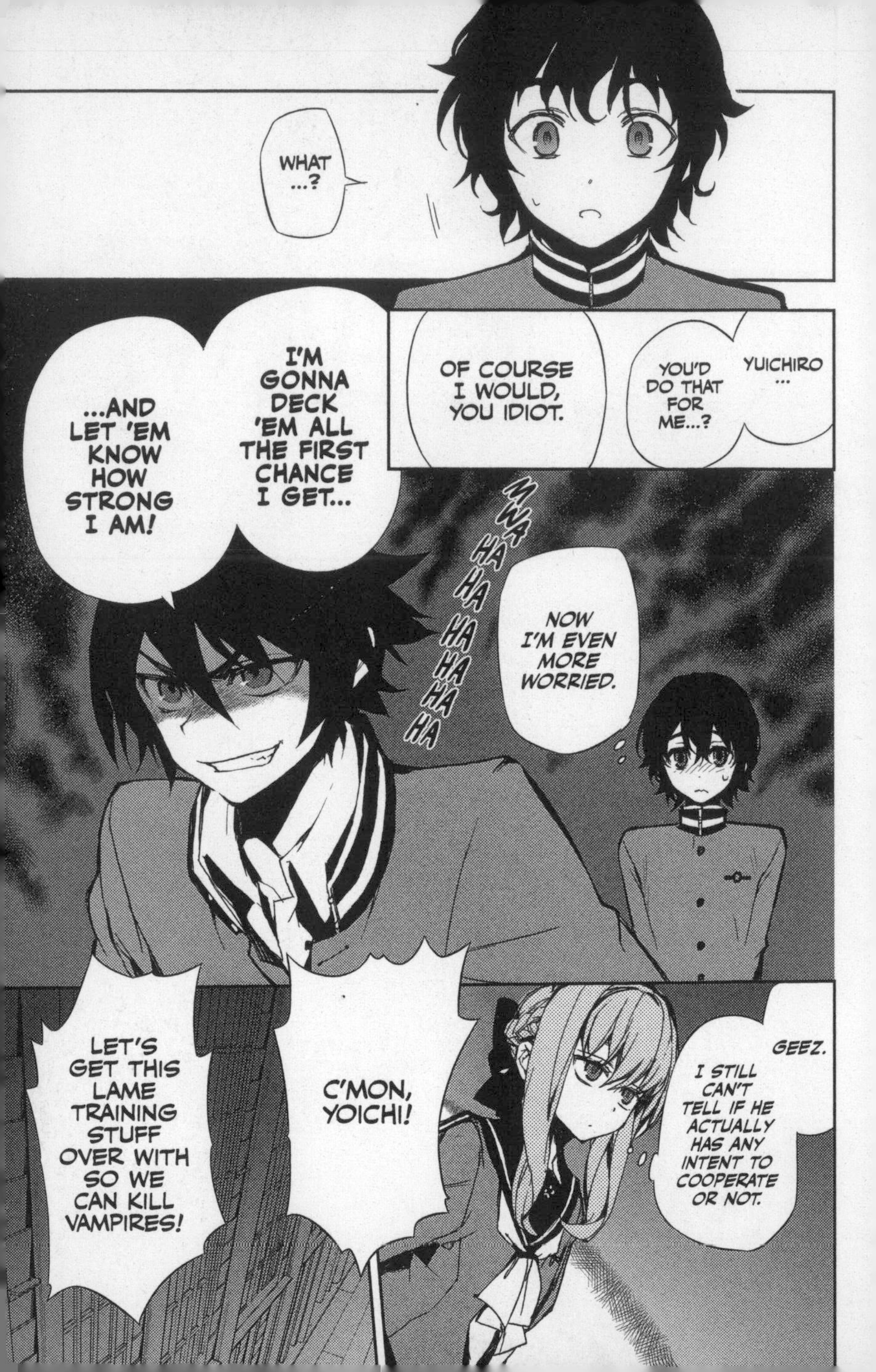
WHAT ...?
YUICHIRO ...
YOU'D DO THAT FOR ME...?
OF COURSE I WOULD, YOU IDIOT.
I'M GONNA DECK 'EM ALL THE FIRST CHANCE I GET...
...AND LET 'EM KNOW HOW STRONG I AM!
MWA HA HA HA HA HA HA HA
NOW I'M EVEN MORE WORRIED.
GEEZ.
I STILL CAN'T TELL IF HE ACTUALLY HAS ANY INTENT TO COOPERATE OR NOT.
C'MON, YOICHI!
LET'S GET THIS LAME TRAINING STUFF OVER WITH SO WE CAN KILL VAMPIRES!

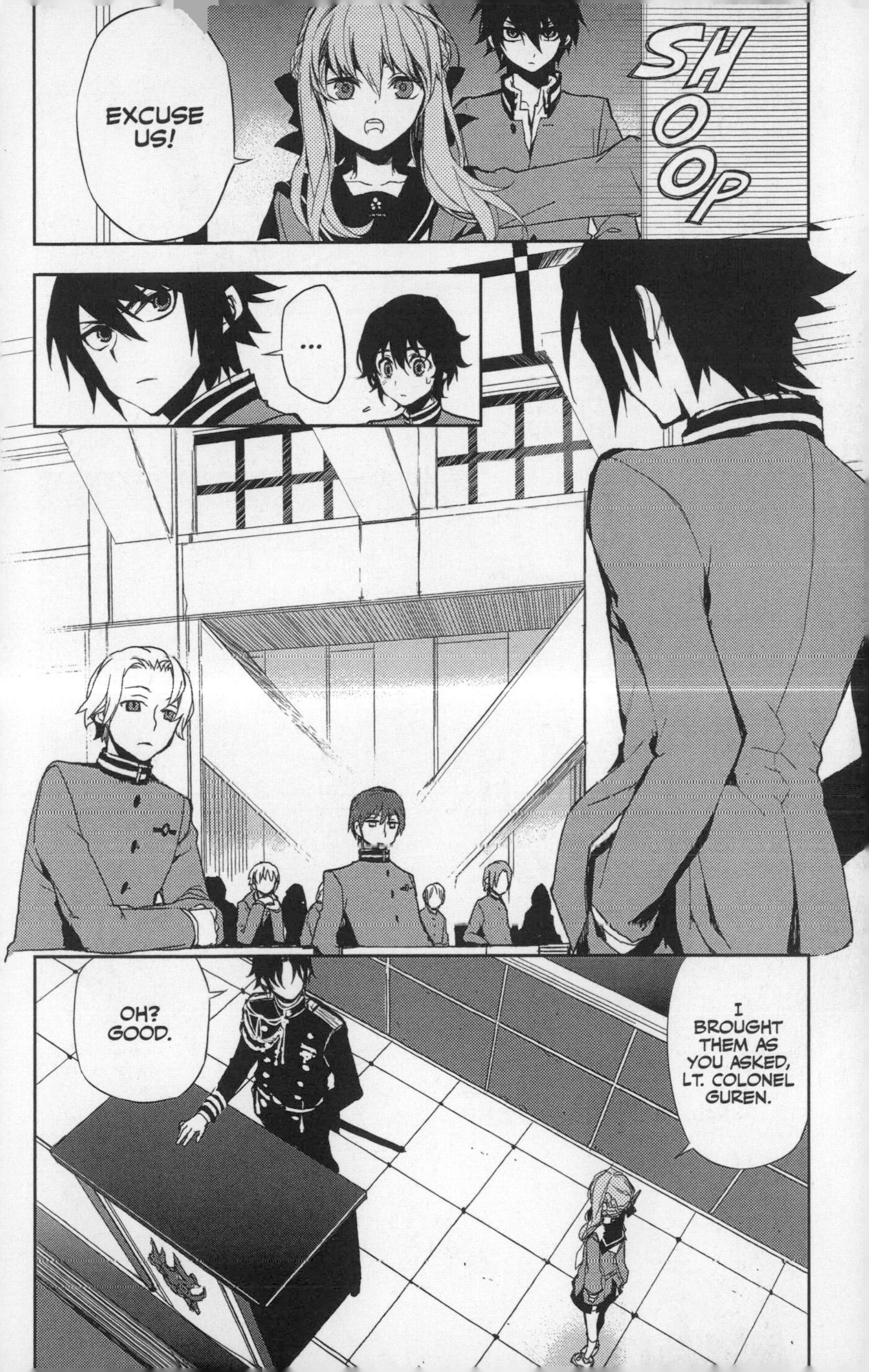
SHOOP
EXCUSE US!
...
I BROUGHT THEM AS YOU ASKED, LT. COLONEL GUREN.
OH? GOOD.

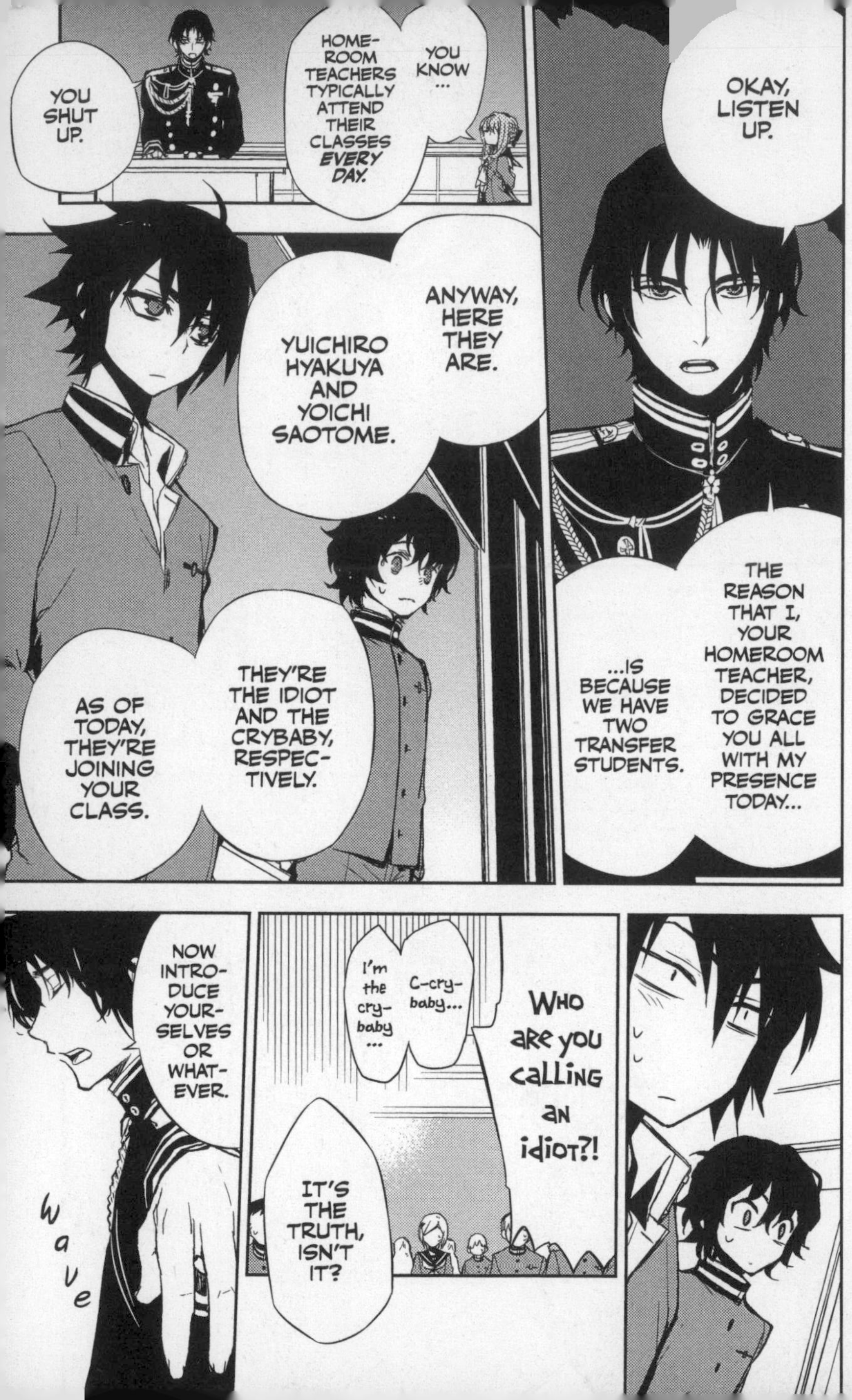
OKAY, LISTEN UP.
YOU KNOW...
HOMEROOM TEACHERS TYPICALLY ATTEND THEIR CLASSES EVERY DAY.
YOU SHUT UP.
THE REASON THAT I, YOUR HOMEROOM TEACHER, DECIDED TO GRACE YOU ALL WITH MY PRESENCE TODAY...
...IS BECAUSE WE HAVE TWO TRANSFER STUDENTS.
ANYWAY, HERE THEY ARE.
YUICHIRO HYAKUYA AND YOICHI SAOTOME.
THEY'RE THE IDIOT AND THE CRYBABY, RESPECTIVELY.
AS OF TODAY, THEY'RE JOINING YOUR CLASS.
Who are you calling an idiot?!
C-crybaby...
I'm the crybaby...
IT'S THE TRUTH, ISN'T IT?
NOW INTRODUCE YOURSELVES OR WHATEVER.
Wave

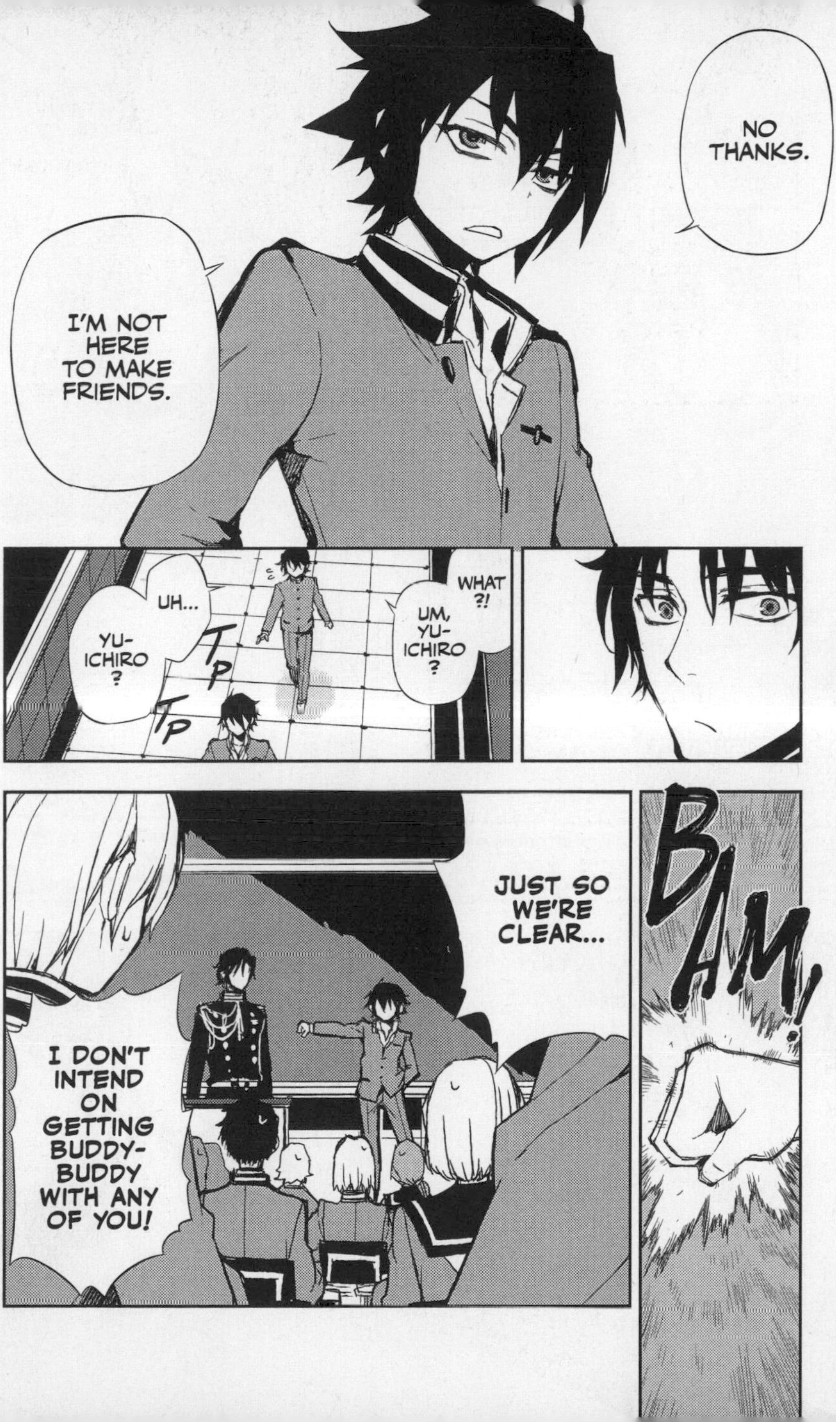
NO THANKS.
I'M NOT HERE TO MAKE FRIENDS.
WHAT?!
UM, YU-ICHIRO?
UH...
YU-ICHIRO?
TP
TP
BAM!
JUST SO WE'RE CLEAR...
I DON'T INTEND ON GETTING BUDDY-BUDDY WITH ANY OF YOU!

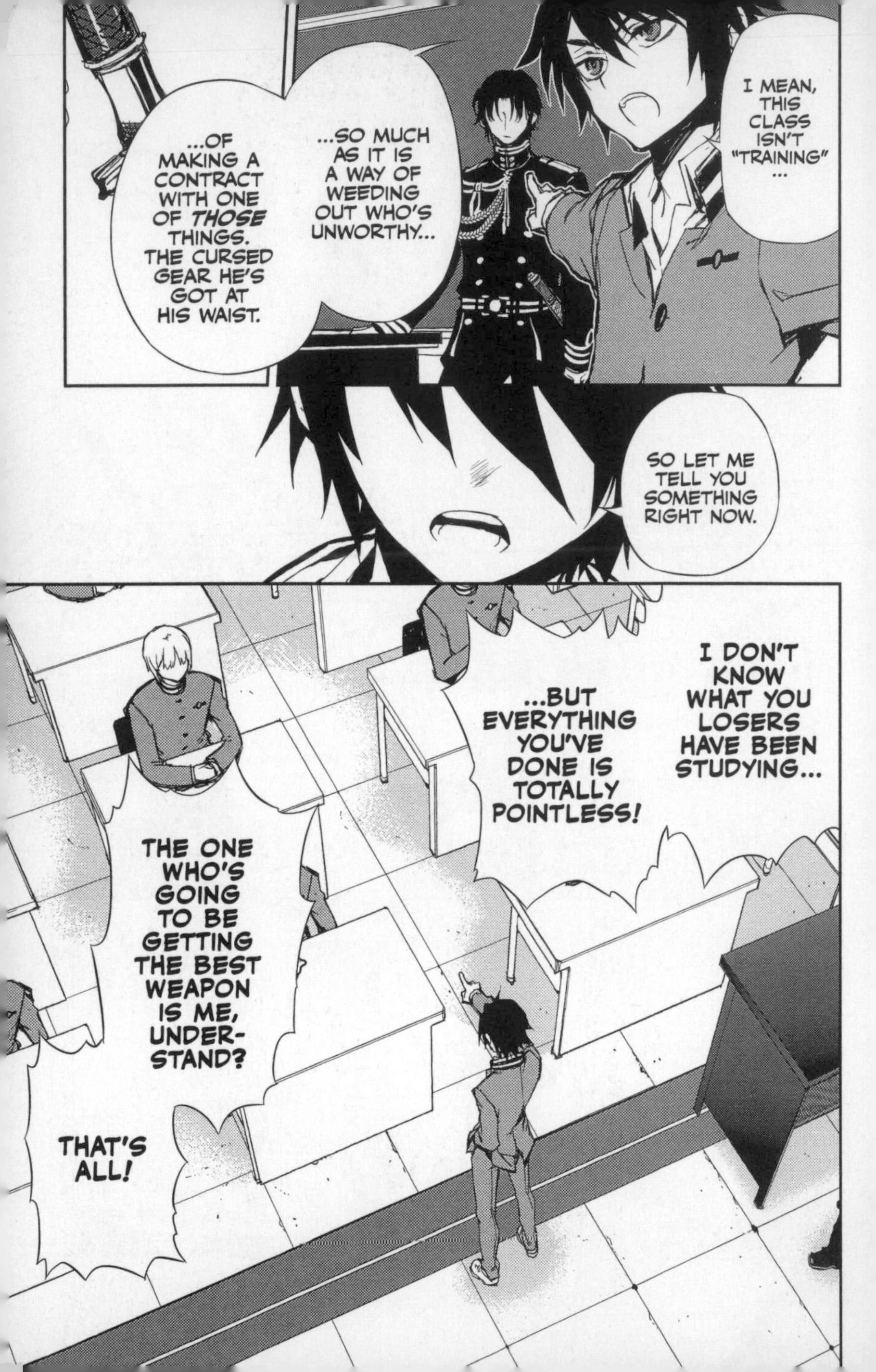
I MEAN, THIS CLASS ISN'T "TRAINING"...
...SO MUCH AS IT IS A WAY OF WEEDING OUT WHO'S UNWORTHY...
...OF MAKING A CONTRACT WITH ONE OF *THOSE* THINGS. THE CURSED GEAR HE'S GOT AT HIS WAIST.
SO LET ME TELL YOU SOMETHING RIGHT NOW.
I DON'T KNOW WHAT YOU LOSERS HAVE BEEN STUDYING...
...BUT EVERYTHING YOU'VE DONE IS TOTALLY POINTLESS!
THE ONE WHO'S GOING TO BE GETTING THE BEST WEAPON IS ME, UNDER-STAND?
THAT'S ALL!

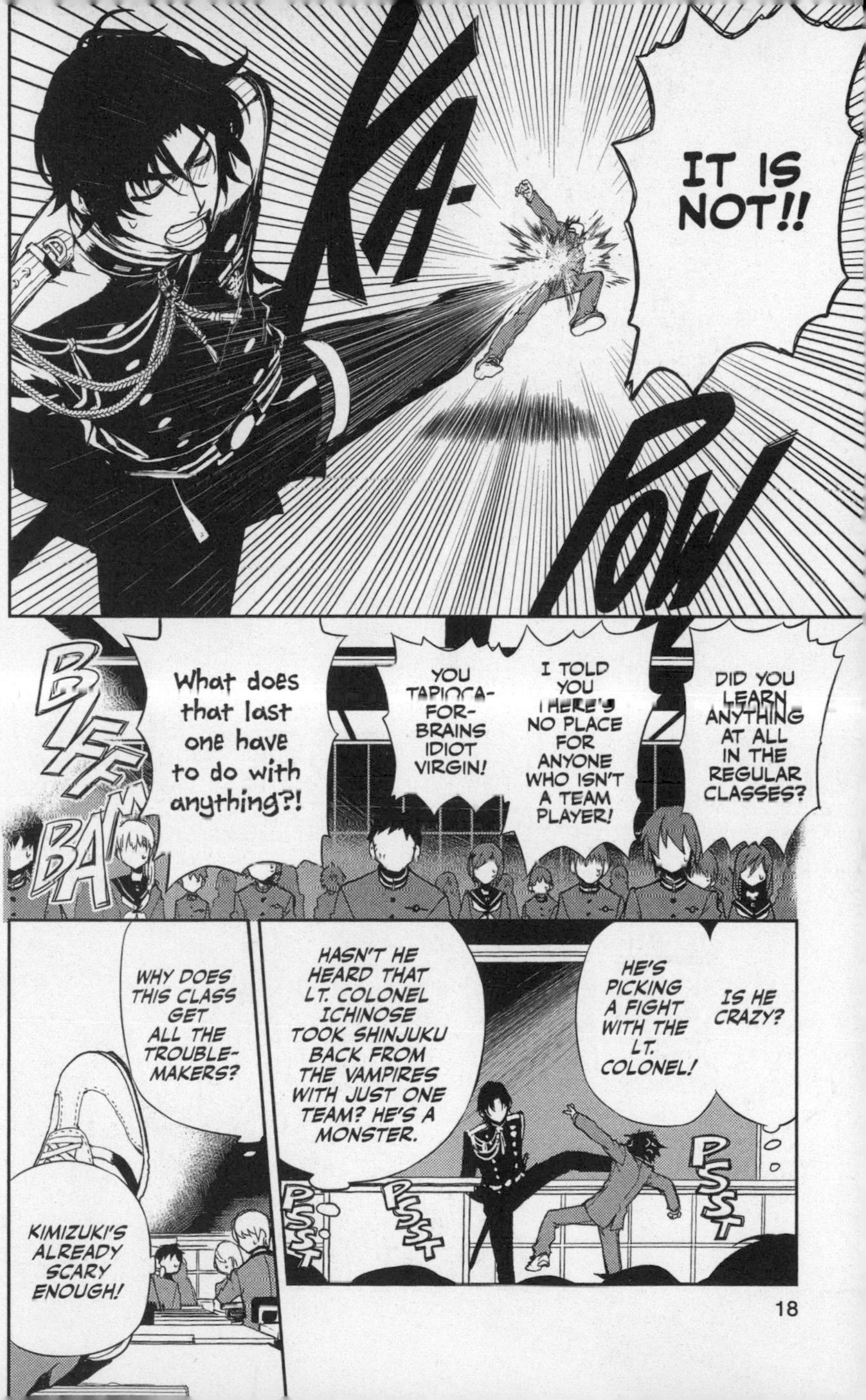
IT IS NOT!!
KA-POW
DID YOU LEARN ANYTHING AT ALL IN THE REGULAR CLASSES?
I TOLD YOU THERE'S NO PLACE FOR ANYONE WHO ISN'T A TEAM PLAYER!
YOU TAPIOCA-FOR-BRAINS IDIOT VIRGIN!
What does that last one have to do with anything?!
BIFF
BAM
BAM
IS HE CRAZY?
HE'S PICKING A FIGHT WITH THE LT. COLONEL!
HASN'T HE HEARD THAT LT. COLONEL ICHINOSE TOOK SHINJUKU BACK FROM THE VAMPIRES WITH JUST ONE TEAM? HE'S A MONSTER.
PSST
PSST
PSST
WHY DOES THIS CLASS GET ALL THE TROUBLE-MAKERS?
KIMIZUKI'S ALREADY SCARY ENOUGH!

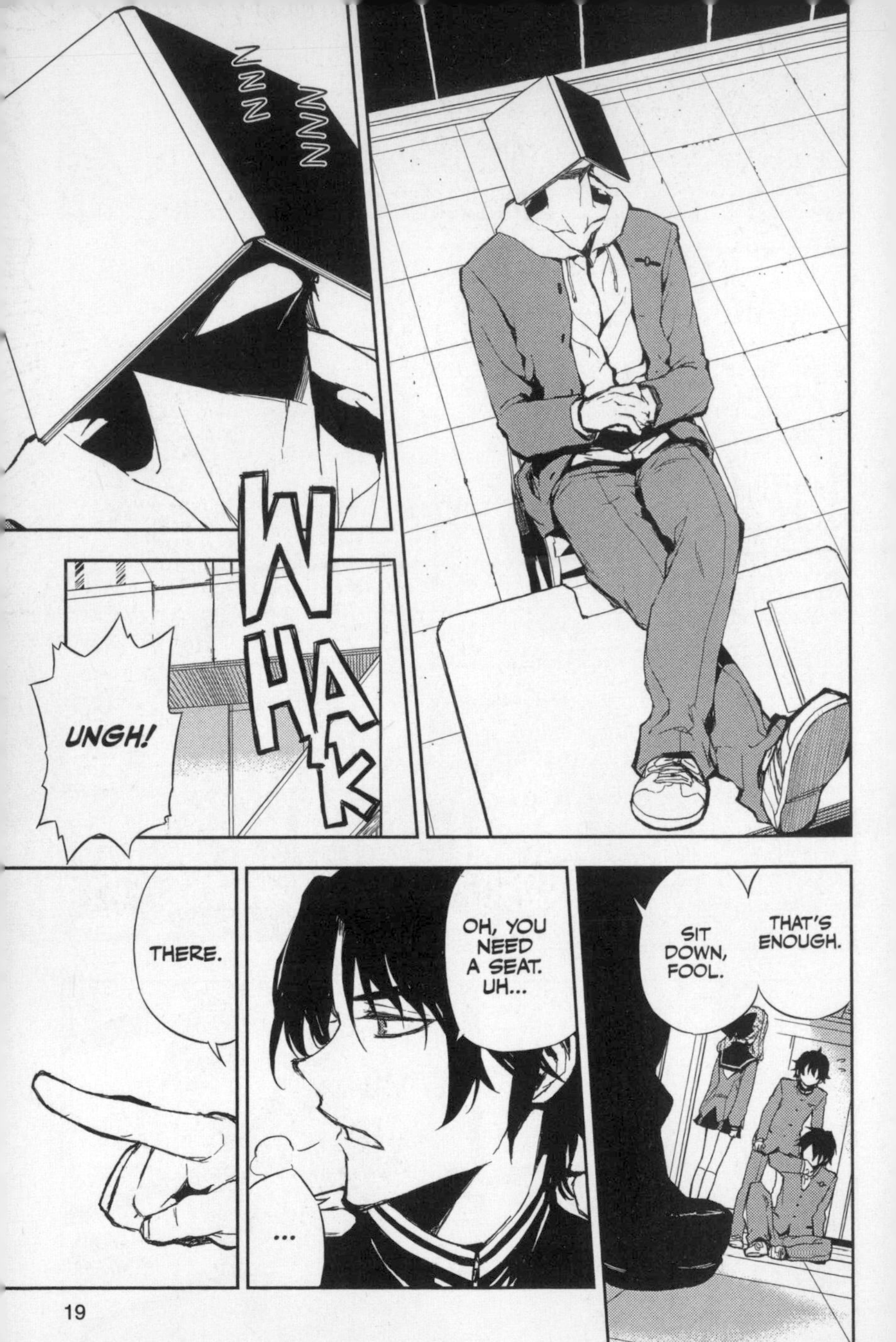
ZZZ
ZZZ
WHAK
UNGH!
THAT'S ENOUGH.
SIT DOWN, FOOL.
OH, YOU NEED A SEAT. UH...
...
THERE.

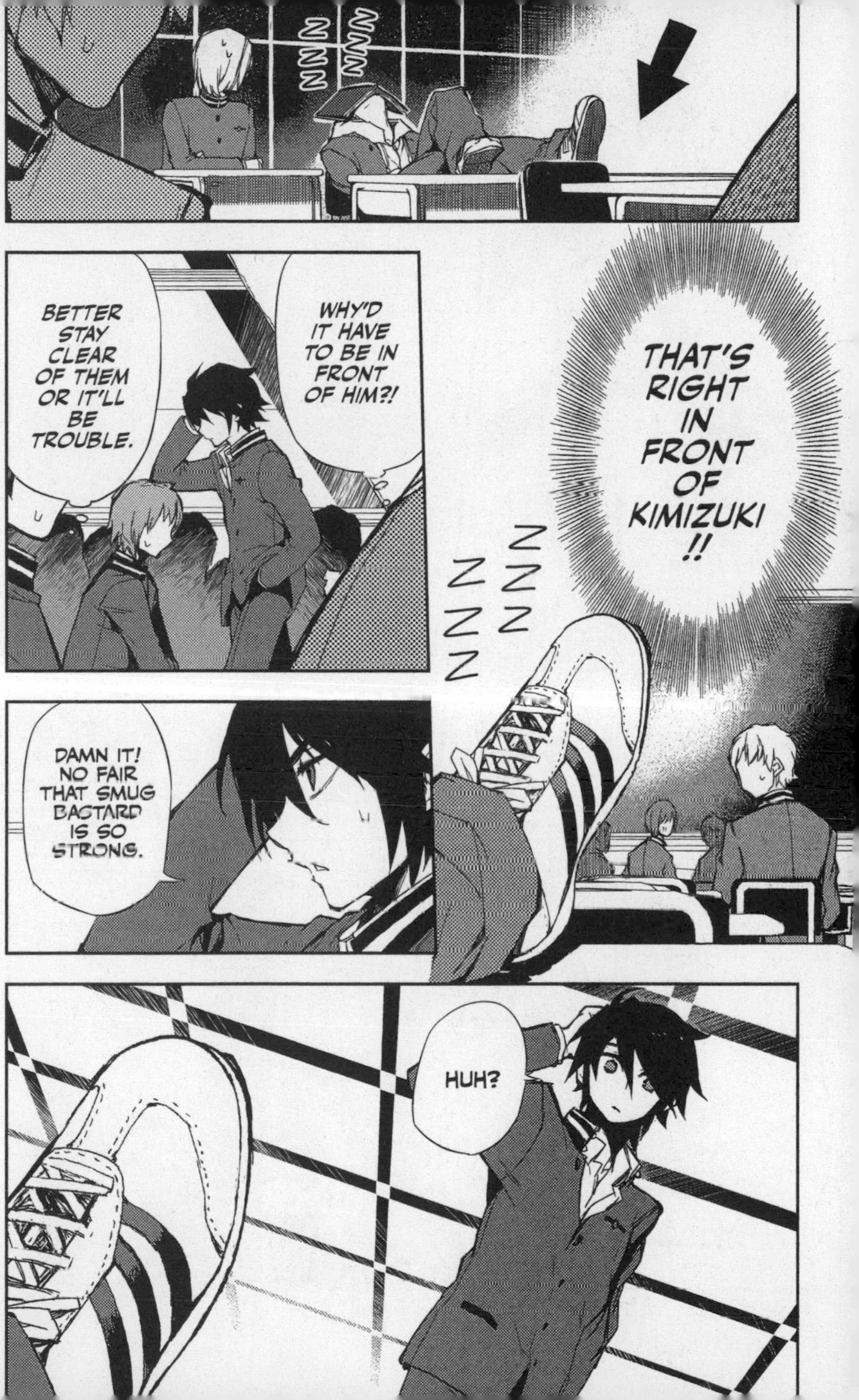
ZZZZ
ZZZZ
THAT'S RIGHT IN FRONT OF KIMIZUKI!!
ZZZ
ZZZZ
WHY'D IT HAVE TO BE IN FRONT OF HIM?!
BETTER STAY CLEAR OF THEM OR IT'LL BE TROUBLE.
DAMN IT! NO FAIR THAT SMUG BASTARD IS SO STRONG.
HUH?

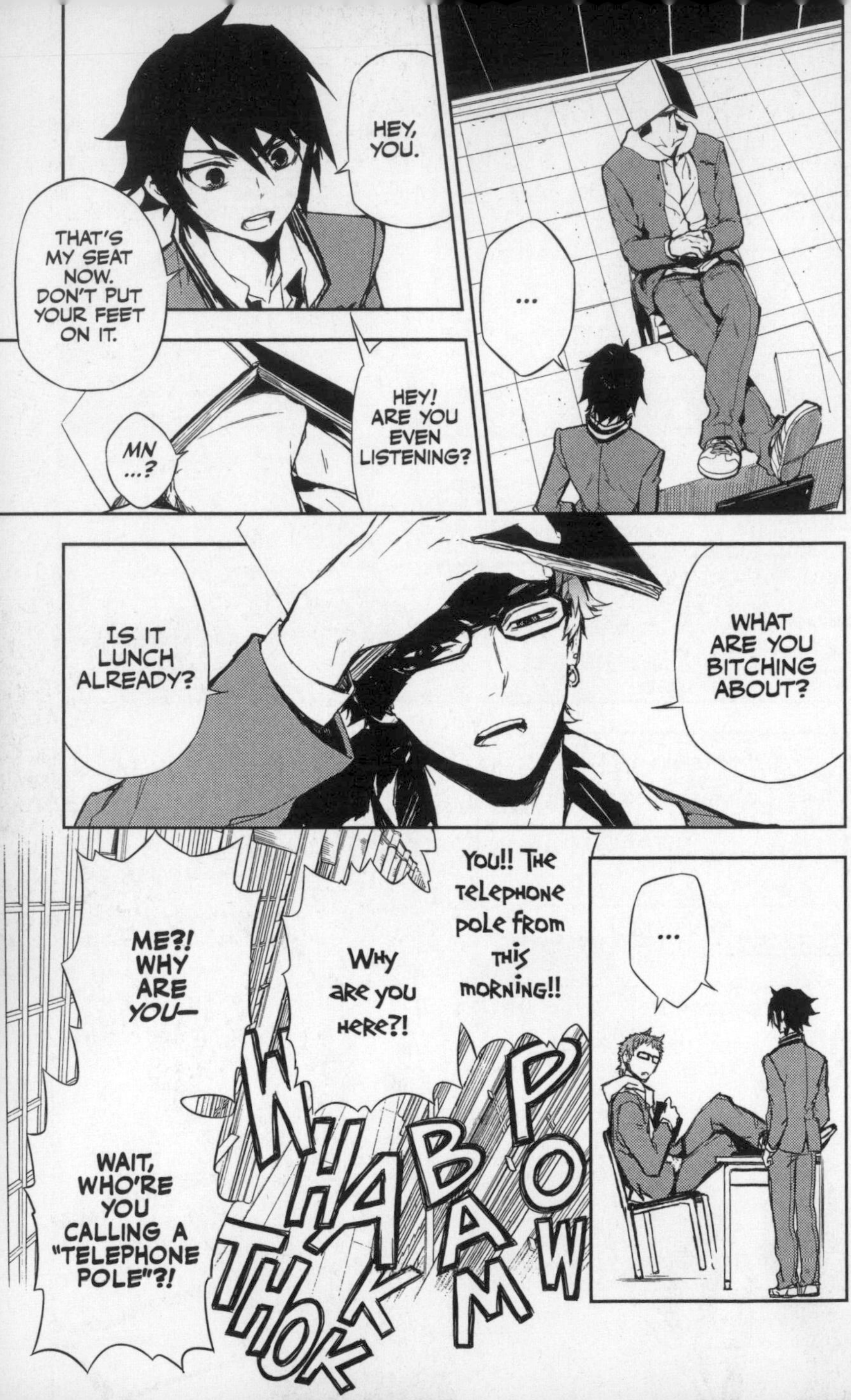
...
HEY, YOU.
THAT'S MY SEAT NOW. DON'T PUT YOUR FEET ON IT.
HEY! ARE YOU EVEN LISTENING?
MN ...?
WHAT ARE YOU BITCHING ABOUT?
IS IT LUNCH ALREADY?
...
YOU!! The telephone pole from this morning!!
Why are you here?!
ME?! WHY ARE YOU—
WHA
BAM
POW
THOK
WAIT, WHO'RE YOU CALLING A "TELEPHONE POLE"?!

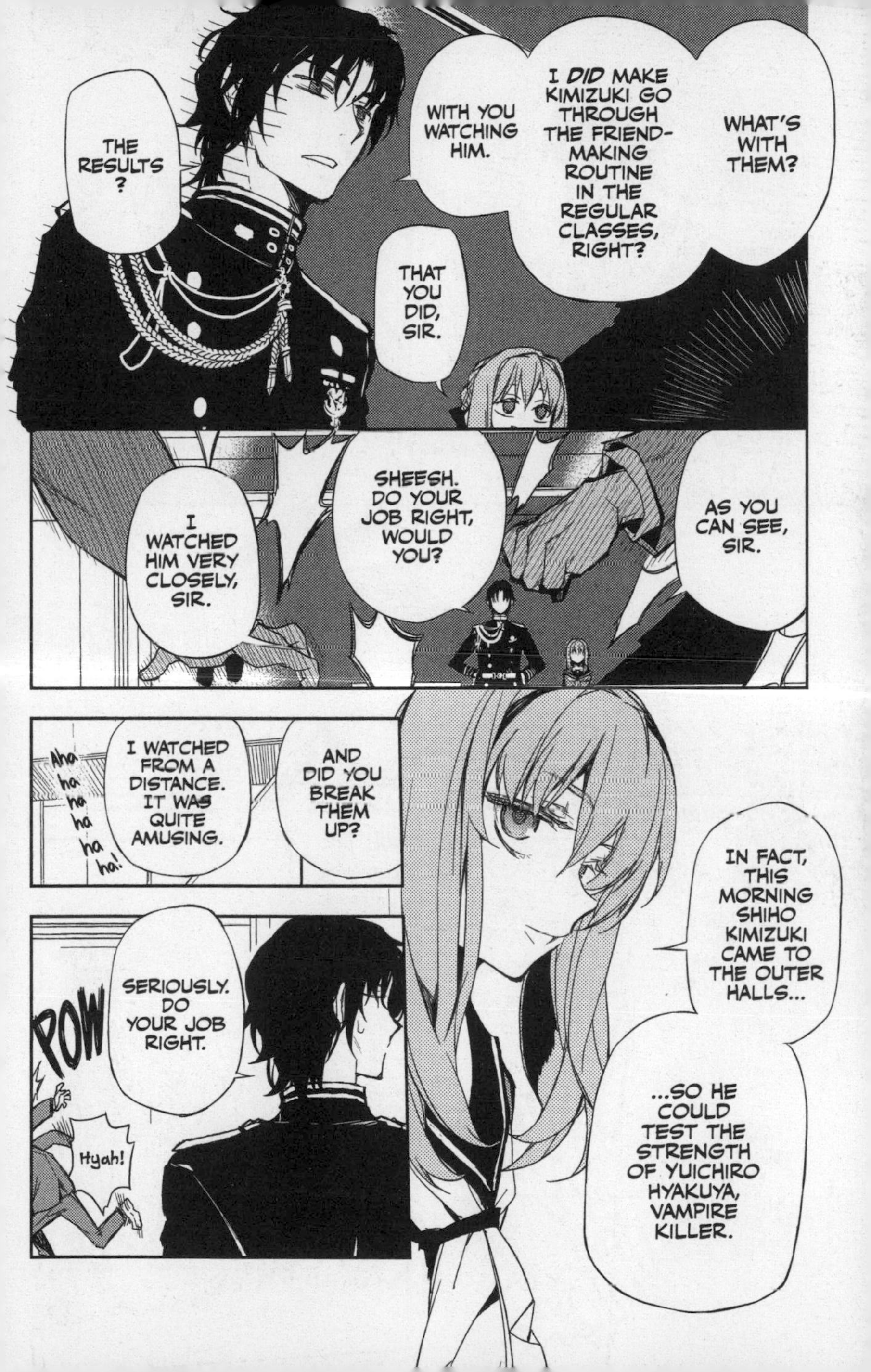
WHAT'S WITH THEM?
I *DID* MAKE KIMIZUKI GO THROUGH THE FRIEND-MAKING ROUTINE IN THE REGULAR CLASSES, RIGHT?
WITH YOU WATCHING HIM.
THAT YOU DID, SIR.
THE RESULTS?
AS YOU CAN SEE, SIR.
SHEESH. DO YOUR JOB RIGHT, WOULD YOU?
I WATCHED HIM VERY CLOSELY, SIR.
IN FACT, THIS MORNING SHIHO KIMIZUKI CAME TO THE OUTER HALLS...
...SO HE COULD TEST THE STRENGTH OF YUICHIRO HYAKUYA, VAMPIRE KILLER.
AND DID YOU BREAK THEM UP?
I WATCHED FROM A DISTANCE. IT WAS QUITE AMUSING.
Aha ha ha ha ha ha!
SERIOUSLY. DO YOUR JOB RIGHT.
POW
Hyah!

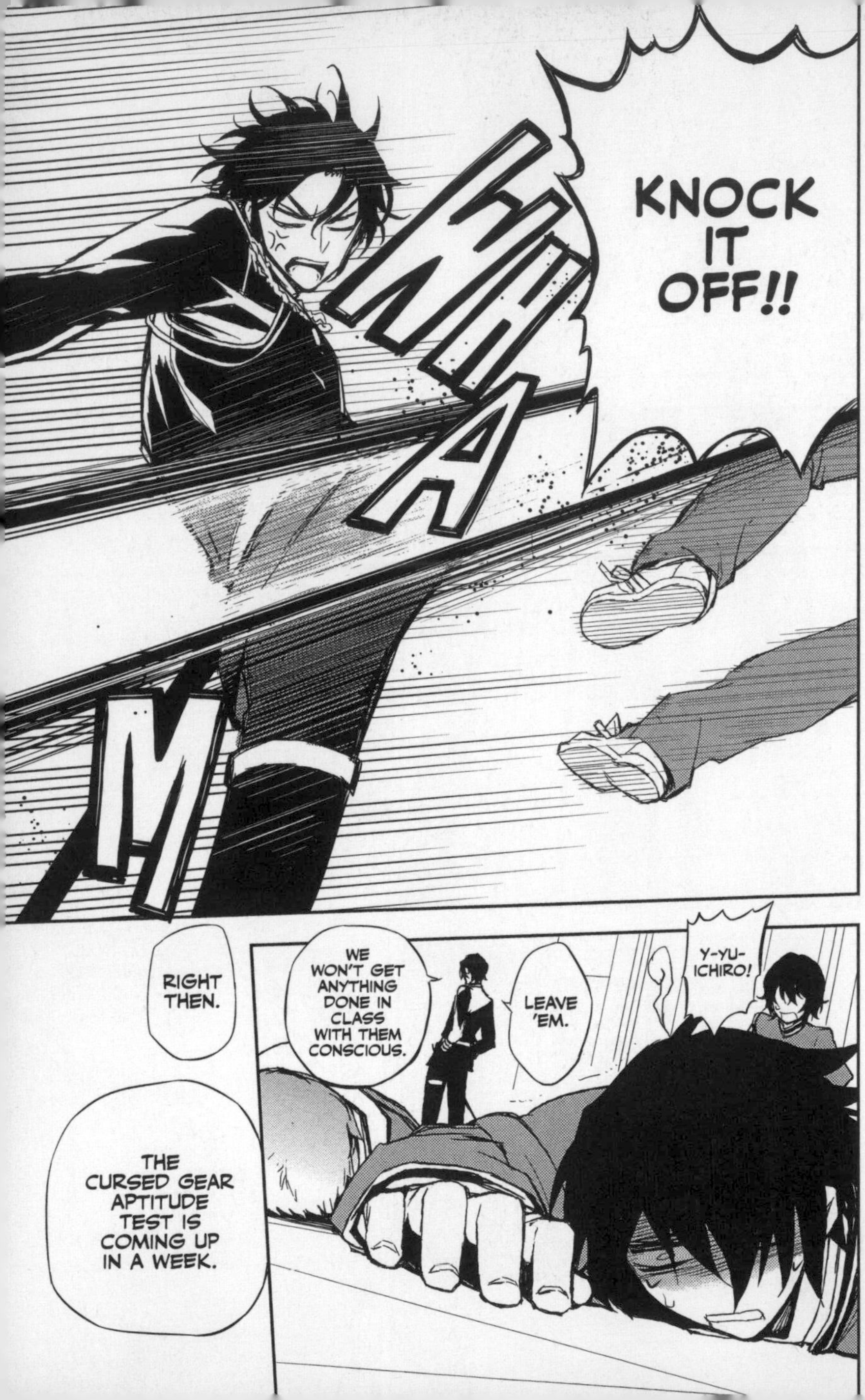
KNOCK IT OFF!!
WHAM
Y-YU-ICHIRO!
LEAVE 'EM.
WE WON'T GET ANYTHING DONE IN CLASS WITH THEM CONSCIOUS.
RIGHT THEN.
THE CURSED GEAR APTITUDE TEST IS COMING UP IN A WEEK.

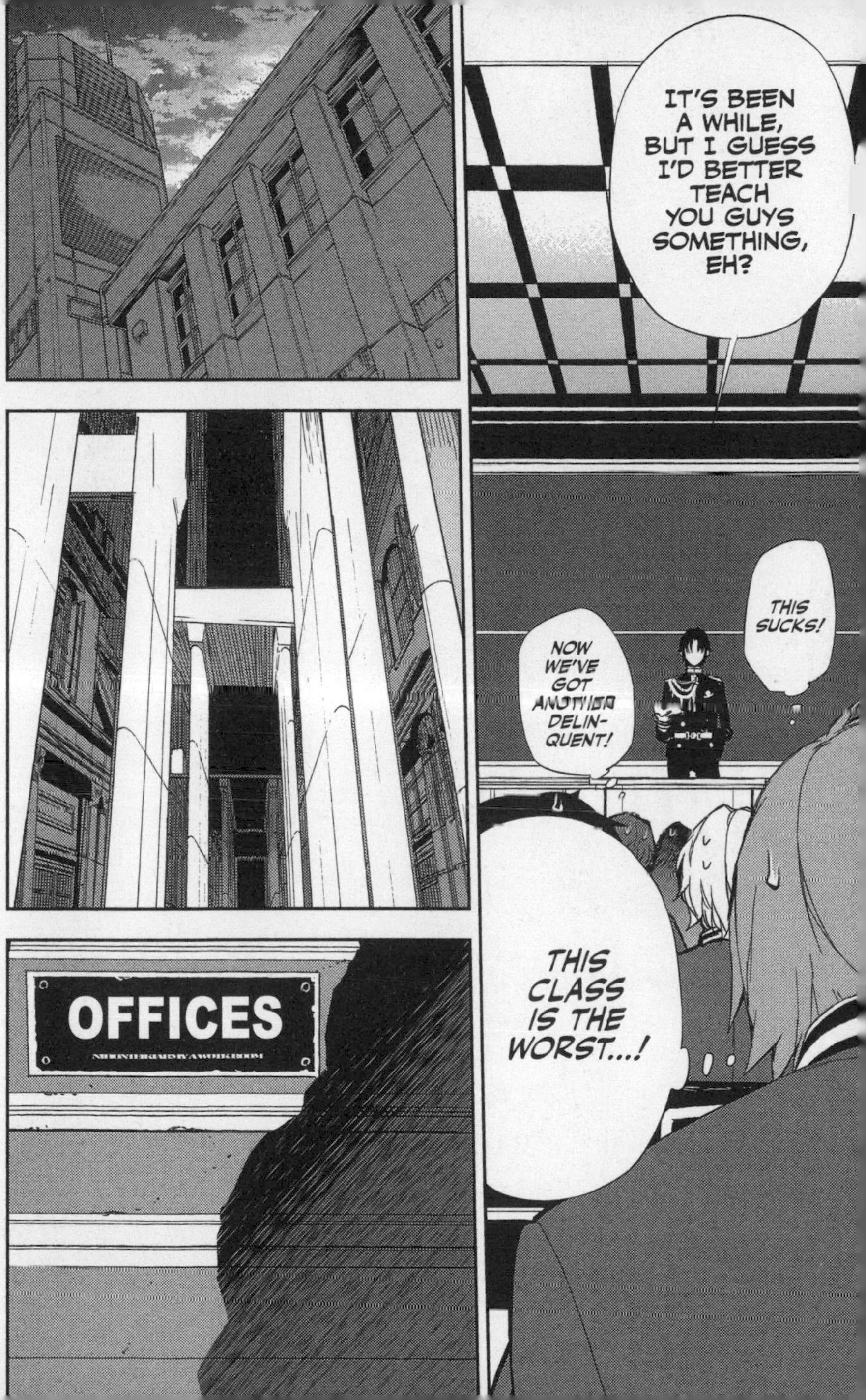
IT'S BEEN A WHILE, BUT I GUESS I'D BETTER TEACH YOU GUYS SOMETHING, EH?
THIS SUCKS!
NOW WE'VE GOT ANOTHER DELIN-QUENT!
THIS CLASS IS THE WORST...!
OFFICES

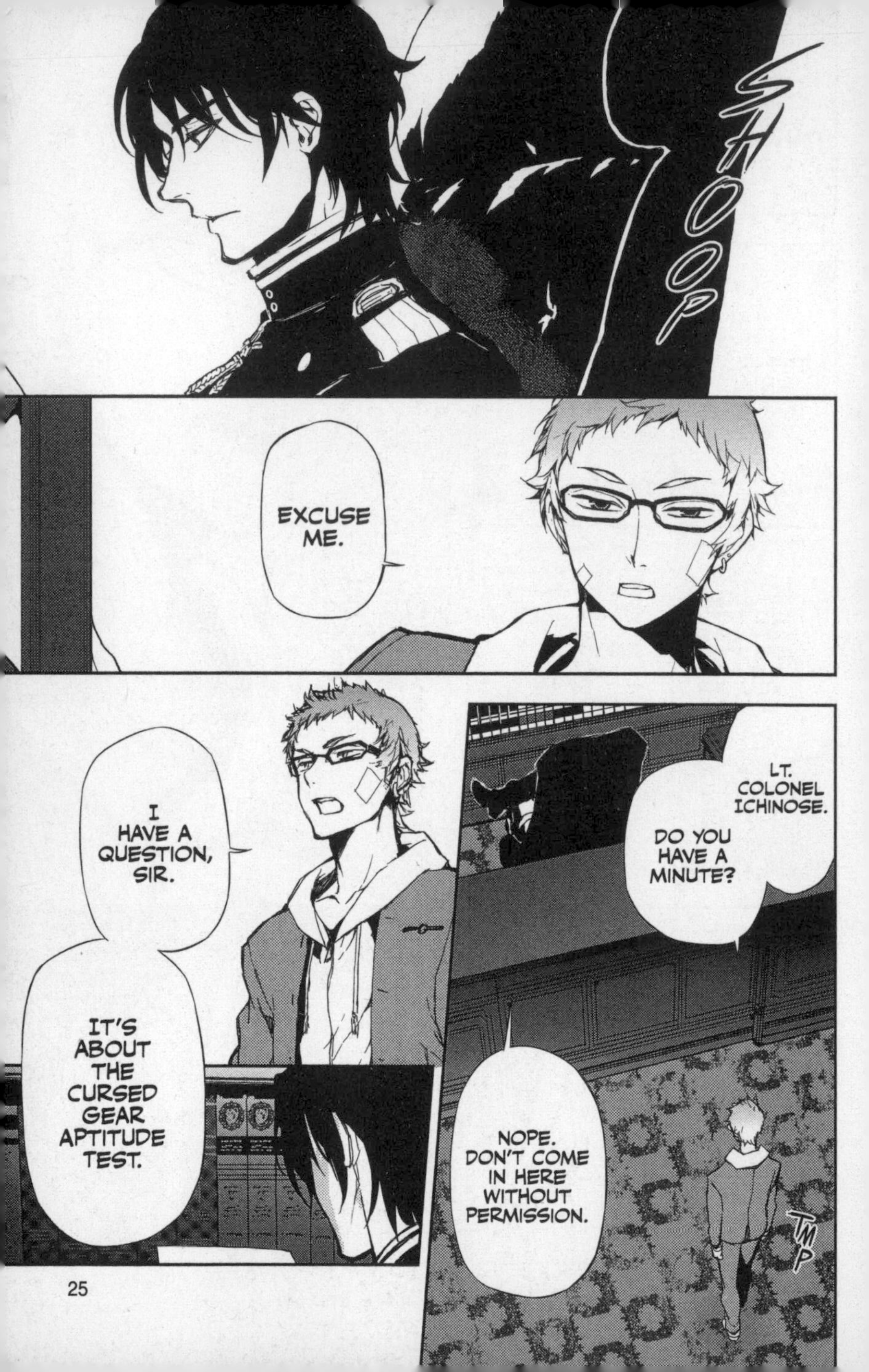
SHOOOP
EXCUSE ME.
LT. COLONEL ICHINOSE.
DO YOU HAVE A MINUTE?
NOPE. DON'T COME IN HERE WITHOUT PERMISSION.
TMP
I HAVE A QUESTION, SIR.
IT'S ABOUT THE CURSED GEAR APTITUDE TEST.

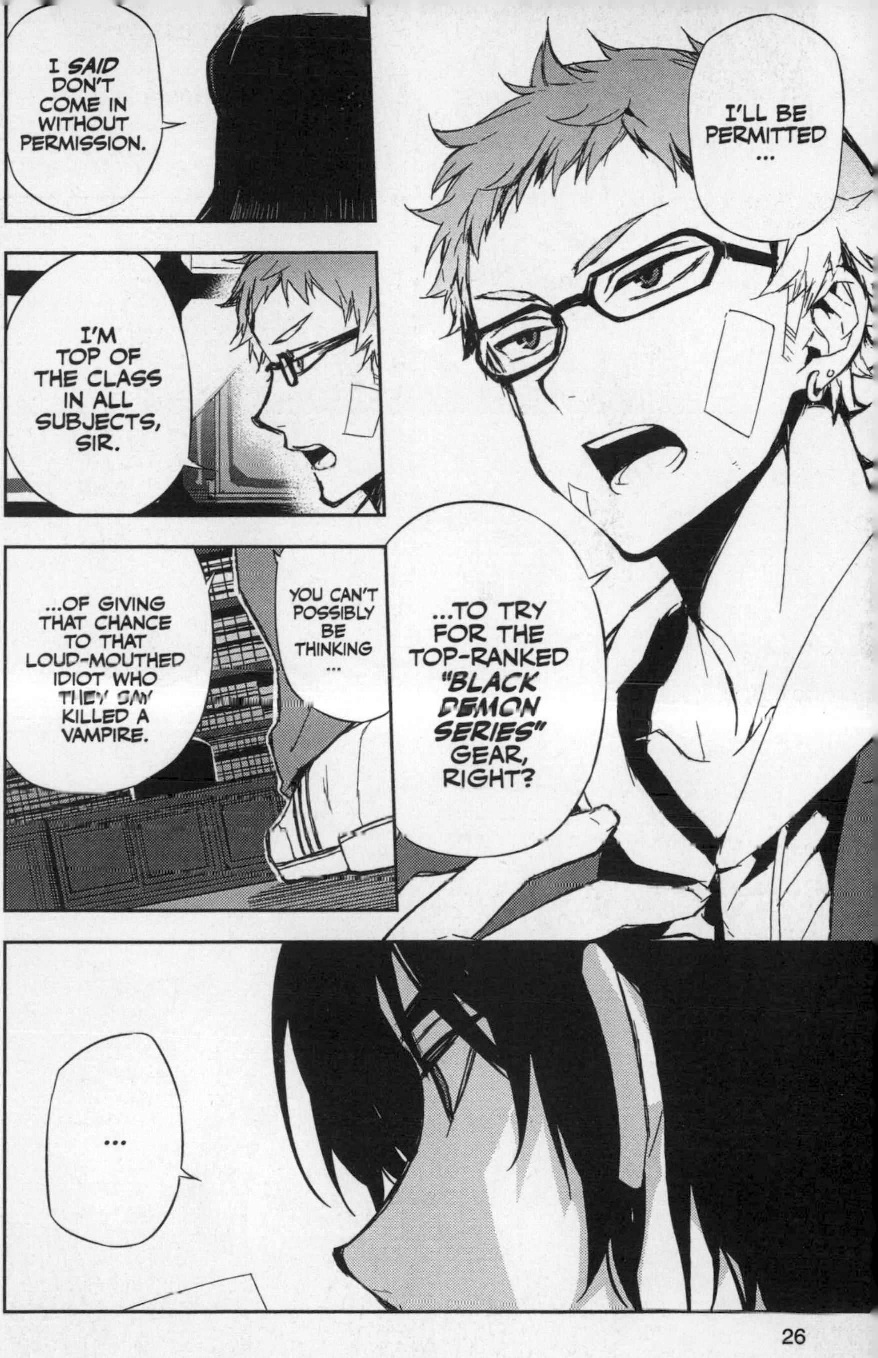
I'LL BE PERMITTED ...
...TO TRY FOR THE TOP-RANKED "BLACK DEMON SERIES" GEAR, RIGHT?
I SAID DON'T COME IN WITHOUT PERMISSION.
I'M TOP OF THE CLASS IN ALL SUBJECTS, SIR.
YOU CAN'T POSSIBLY BE THINKING ...
...OF GIVING THAT CHANCE TO THAT LOUD-MOUTHED IDIOT WHO THEY SAY KILLED A VAMPIRE.
...

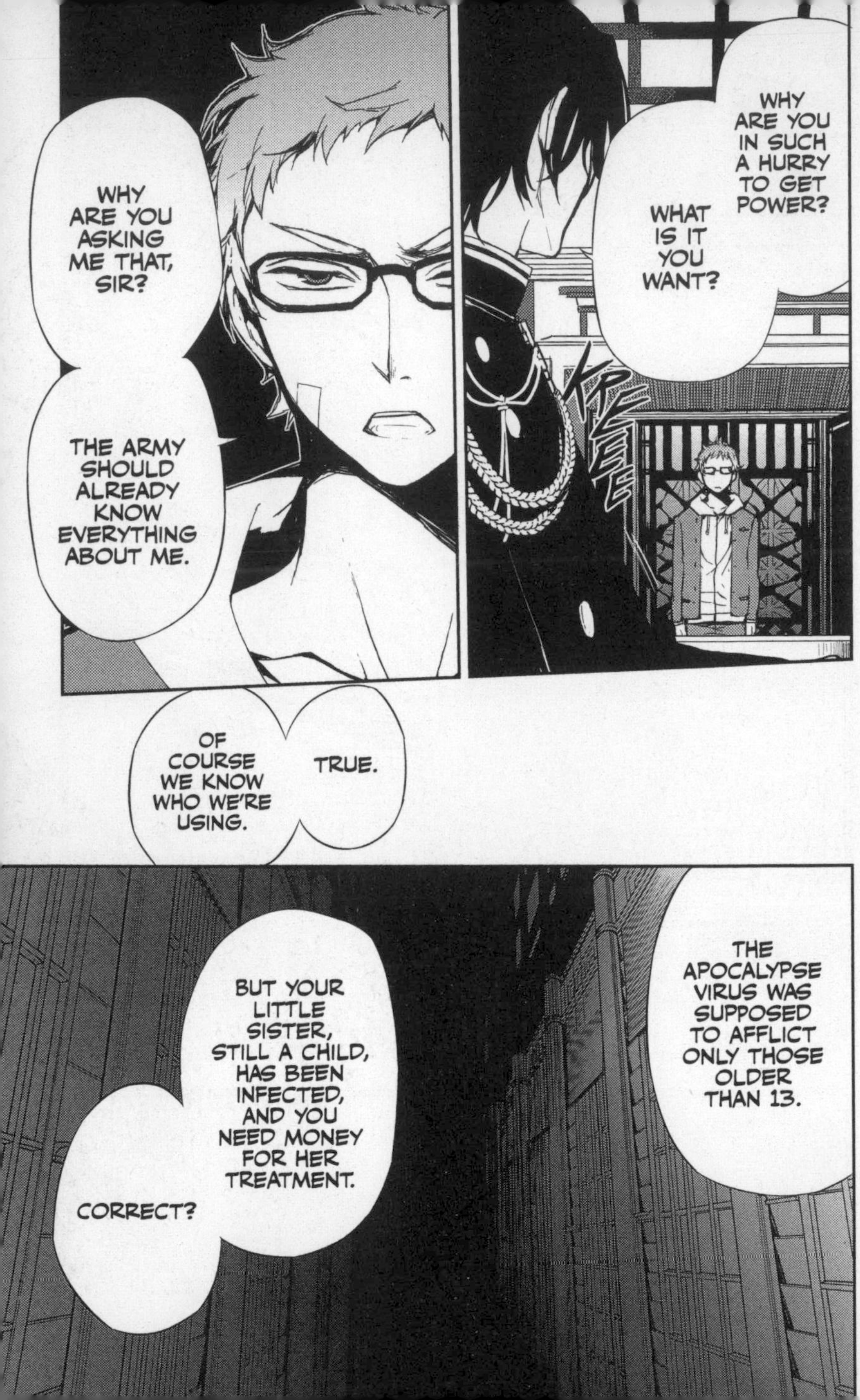
WHY ARE YOU IN SUCH A HURRY TO GET POWER?
WHAT IS IT YOU WANT?
KREEE
WHY ARE YOU ASKING ME THAT, SIR?
THE ARMY SHOULD ALREADY KNOW EVERYTHING ABOUT ME.
TRUE.
OF COURSE WE KNOW WHO WE'RE USING.
THE APOCALYPSE VIRUS WAS SUPPOSED TO AFFLICT ONLY THOSE OLDER THAN 13.
BUT YOUR LITTLE SISTER, STILL A CHILD, HAS BEEN INFECTED, AND YOU NEED MONEY FOR HER TREATMENT.
CORRECT?

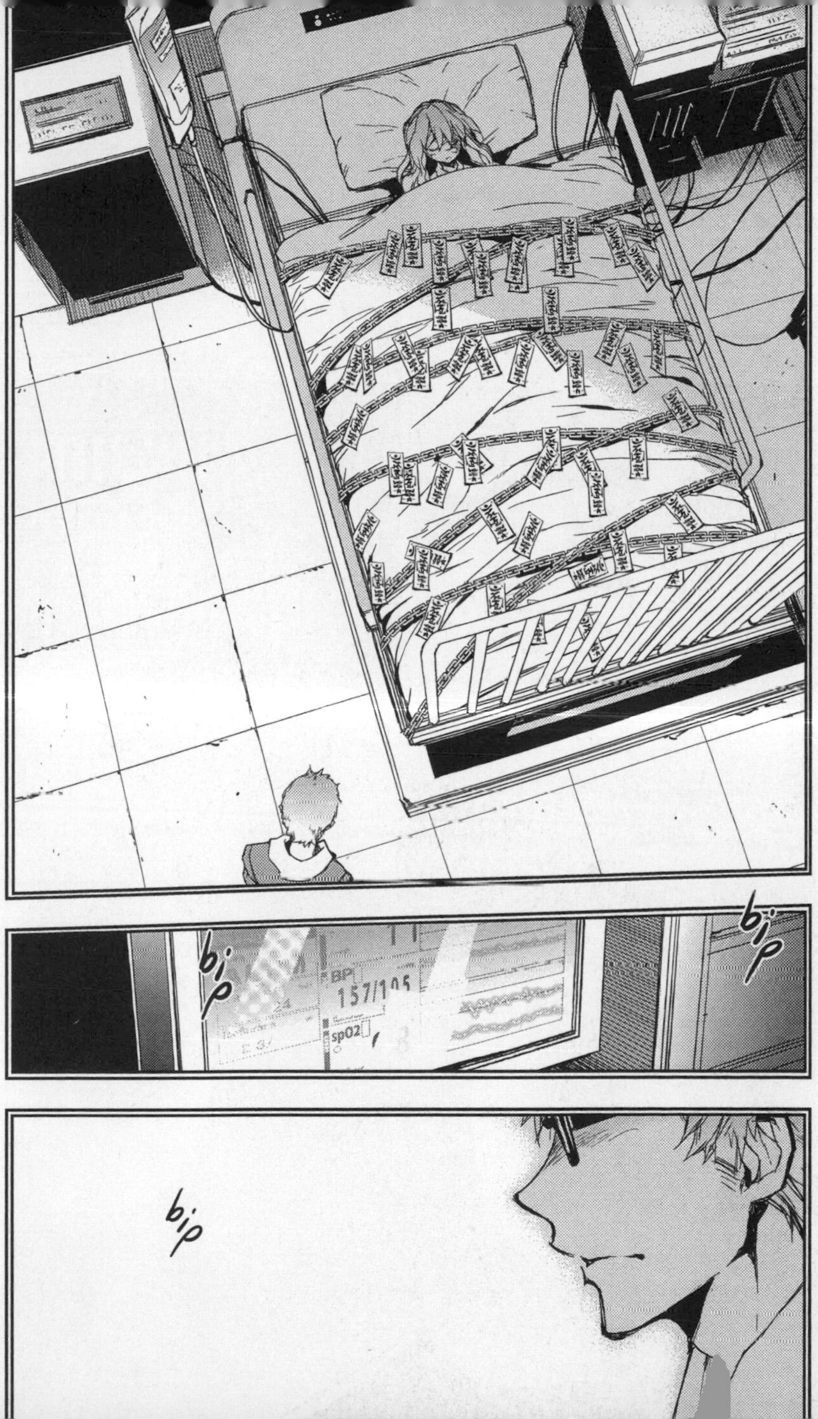
bip
bip
BP
157/105
bip

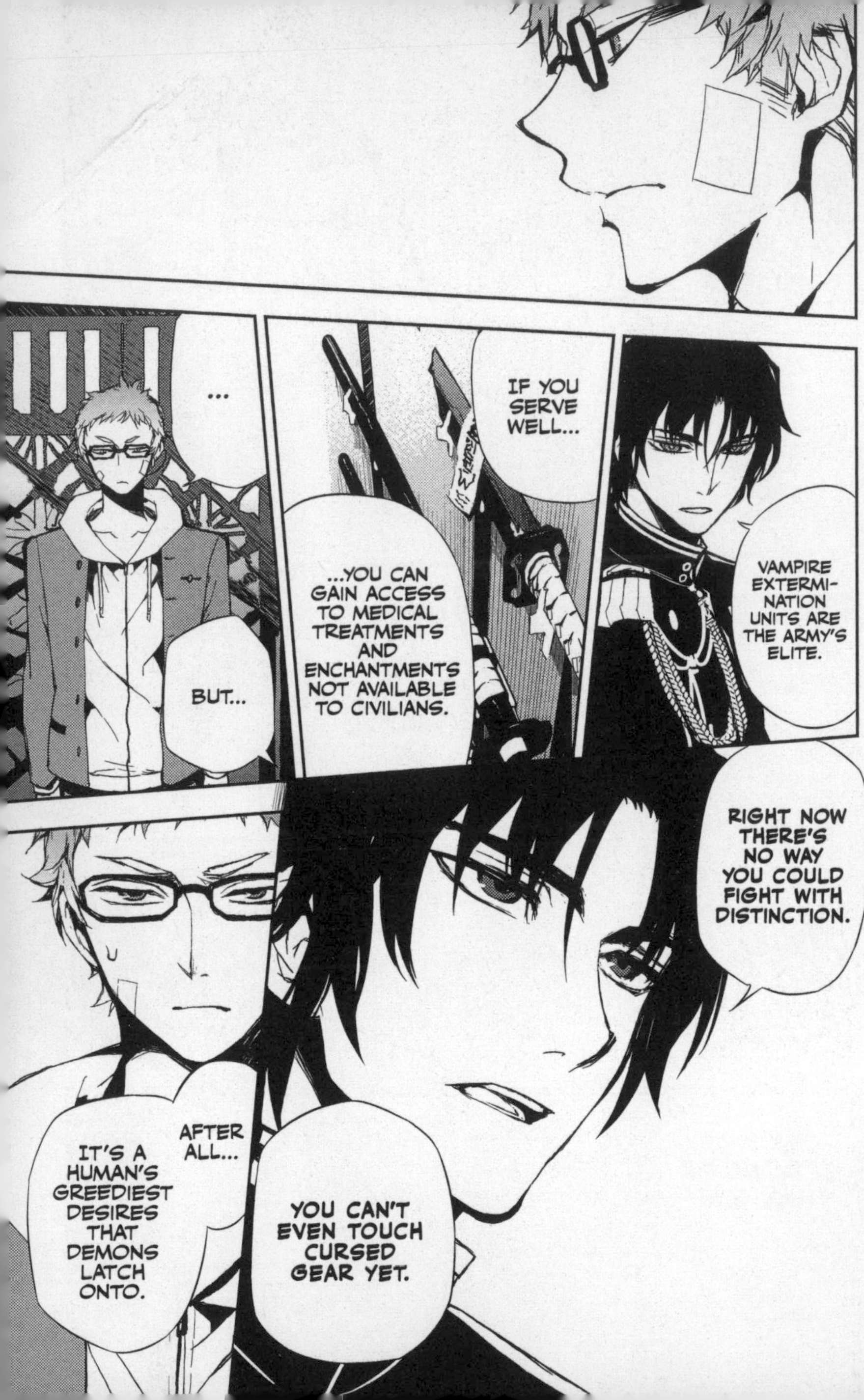
VAMPIRE EXTERMINATION UNITS ARE THE ARMY'S ELITE.
IF YOU SERVE WELL...
...YOU CAN GAIN ACCESS TO MEDICAL TREATMENTS AND ENCHANTMENTS NOT AVAILABLE TO CIVILIANS.
...
BUT...
RIGHT NOW THERE'S NO WAY YOU COULD FIGHT WITH DISTINCTION.
YOU CAN'T EVEN TOUCH CURSED GEAR YET.
AFTER ALL...
IT'S A HUMAN'S GREEDIEST DESIRES THAT DEMONS LATCH ONTO.

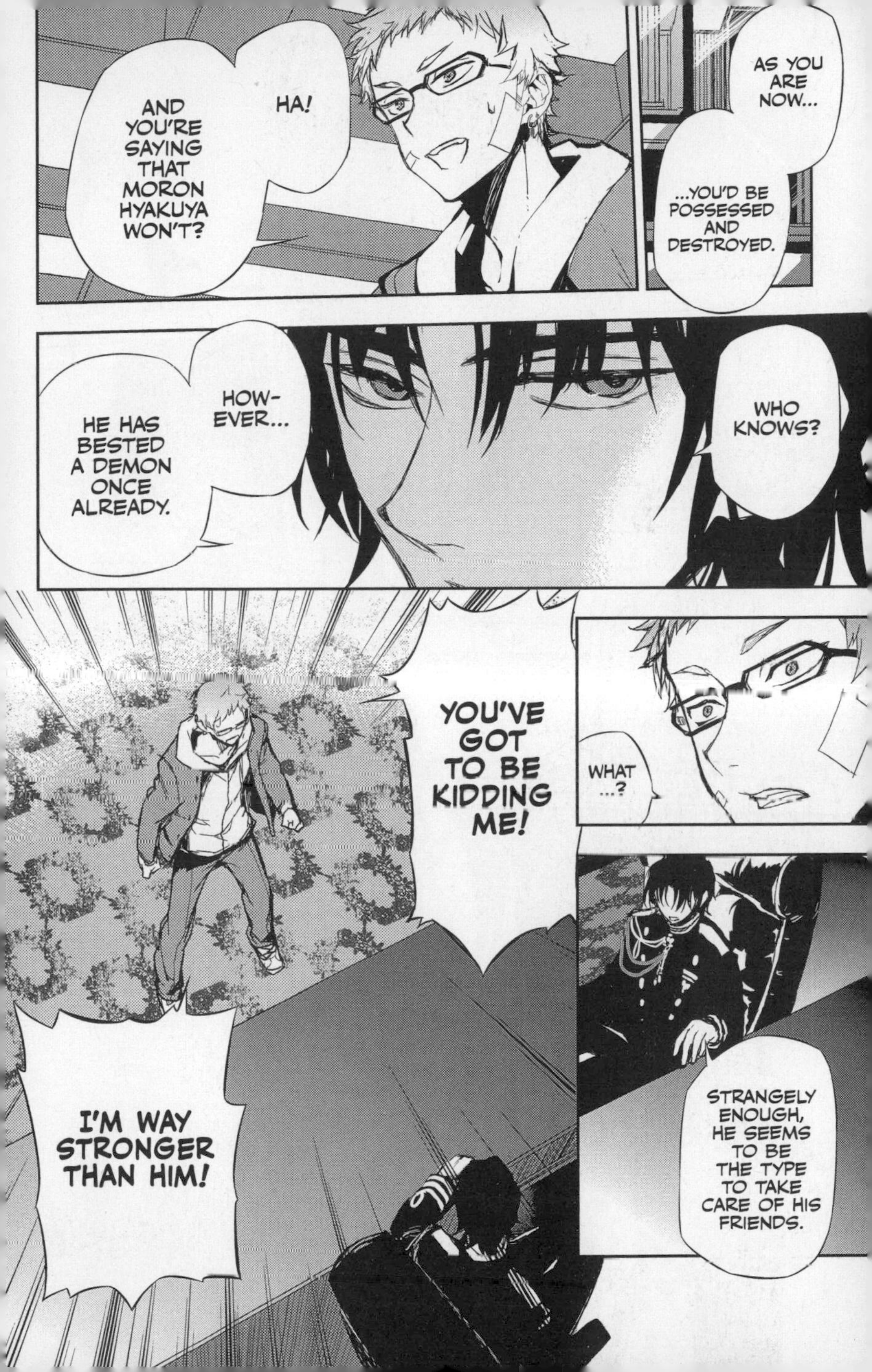
AS YOU ARE NOW...
...YOU'D BE POSSESSED AND DESTROYED.
HA!
AND YOU'RE SAYING THAT MORON HYAKUYA WON'T?
WHO KNOWS?
HOW-EVER...
HE HAS BESTED A DEMON ONCE ALREADY.
WHAT ...?
STRANGELY ENOUGH, HE SEEMS TO BE THE TYPE TO TAKE CARE OF HIS FRIENDS.
YOU'VE GOT TO BE KIDDING ME!
I'M WAY STRONGER THAN HIM!

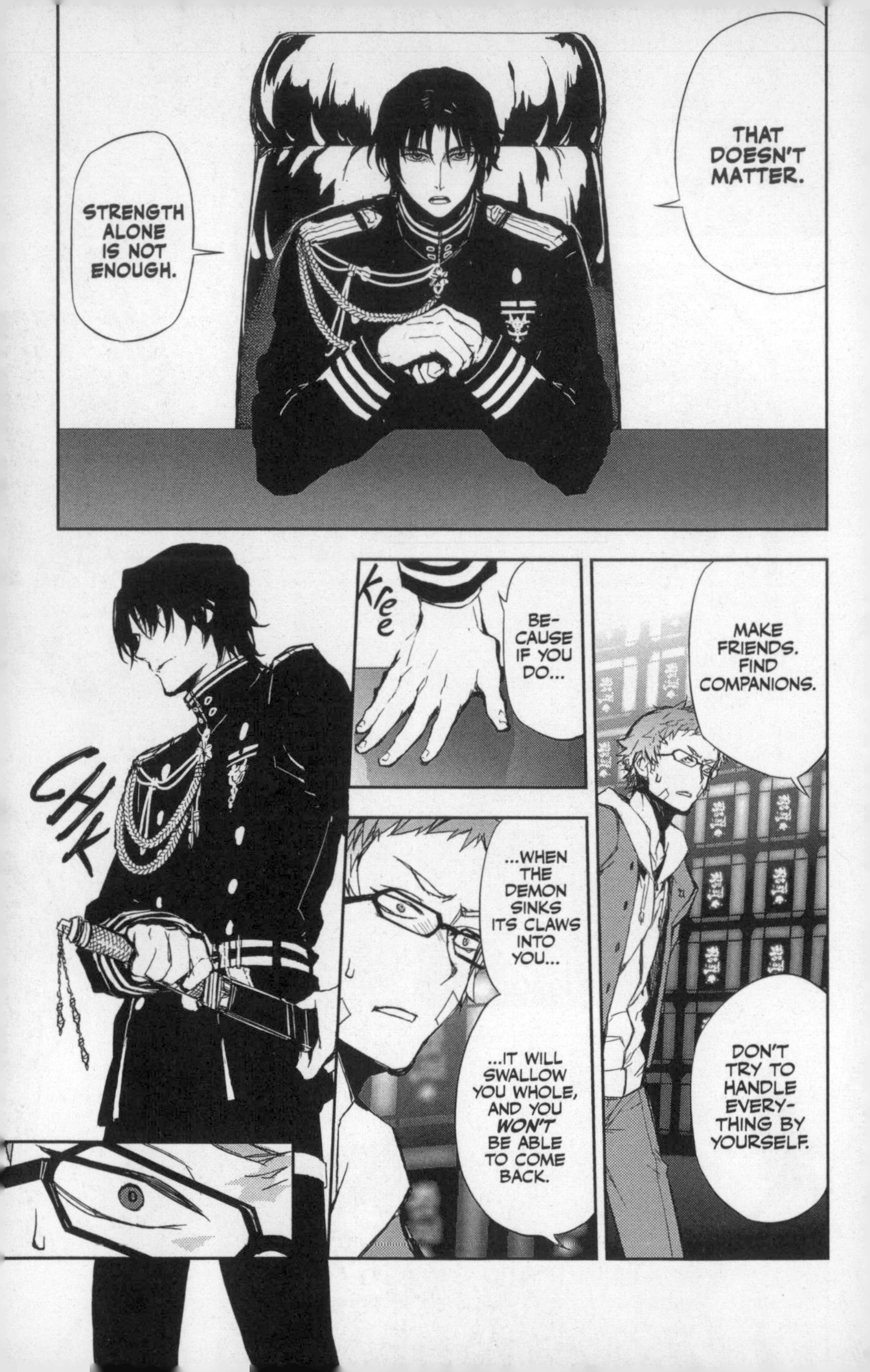
THAT DOESN'T MATTER.
STRENGTH ALONE IS NOT ENOUGH.
MAKE FRIENDS. FIND COMPANIONS.
DON'T TRY TO HANDLE EVERY-THING BY YOURSELF.
Kree
BE-CAUSE IF YOU DO...
...WHEN THE DEMON SINKS ITS CLAWS INTO YOU...
...IT WILL SWALLOW YOU WHOLE, AND YOU *WON'T* BE ABLE TO COME BACK.
CHK

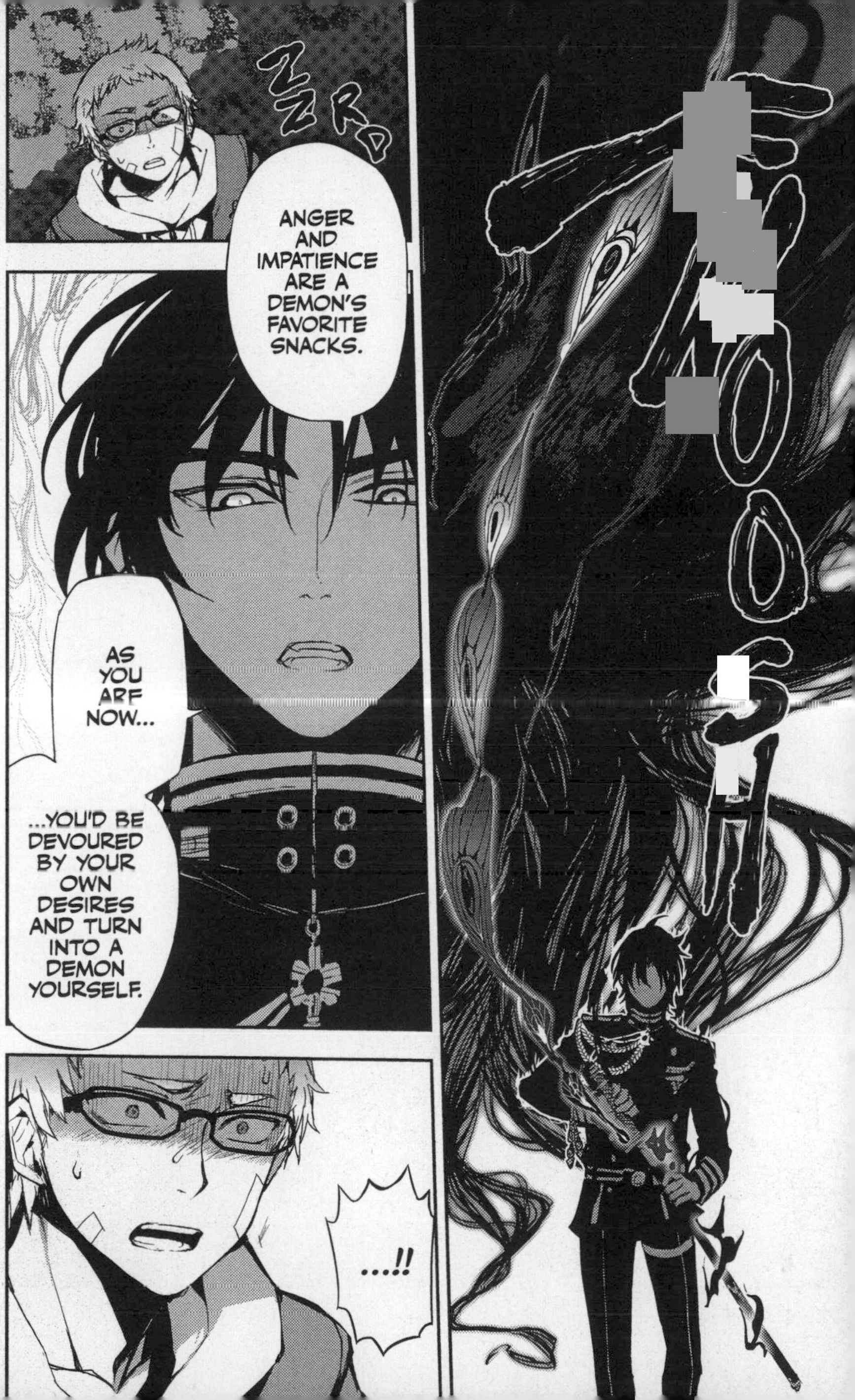

ZZRD
ANGER AND IMPATIENCE ARE A DEMON'S FAVORITE SNACKS.
AS YOU ARE NOW...
...YOU'D BE DEVOURED BY YOUR OWN DESIRES AND TURN INTO A DEMON YOURSELF.
...!!

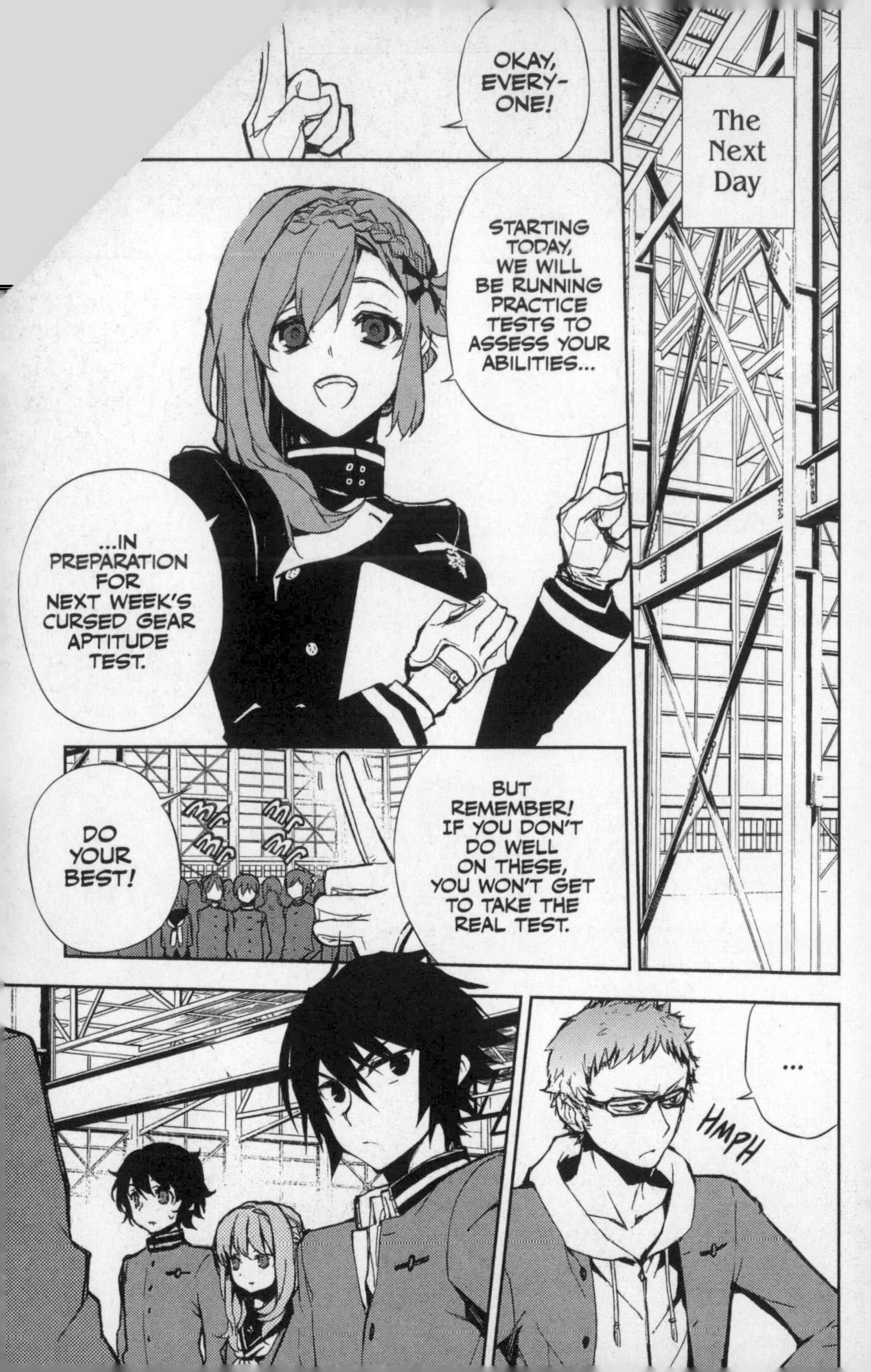
The Next Day
OKAY, EVERYONE!
STARTING TODAY, WE WILL BE RUNNING PRACTICE TESTS TO ASSESS YOUR ABILITIES...
...IN PREPARATION FOR NEXT WEEK'S CURSED GEAR APTITUDE TEST.
BUT REMEMBER! IF YOU DON'T DO WELL ON THESE, YOU WON'T GET TO TAKE THE REAL TEST.
DO YOUR BEST!
...
HMPH

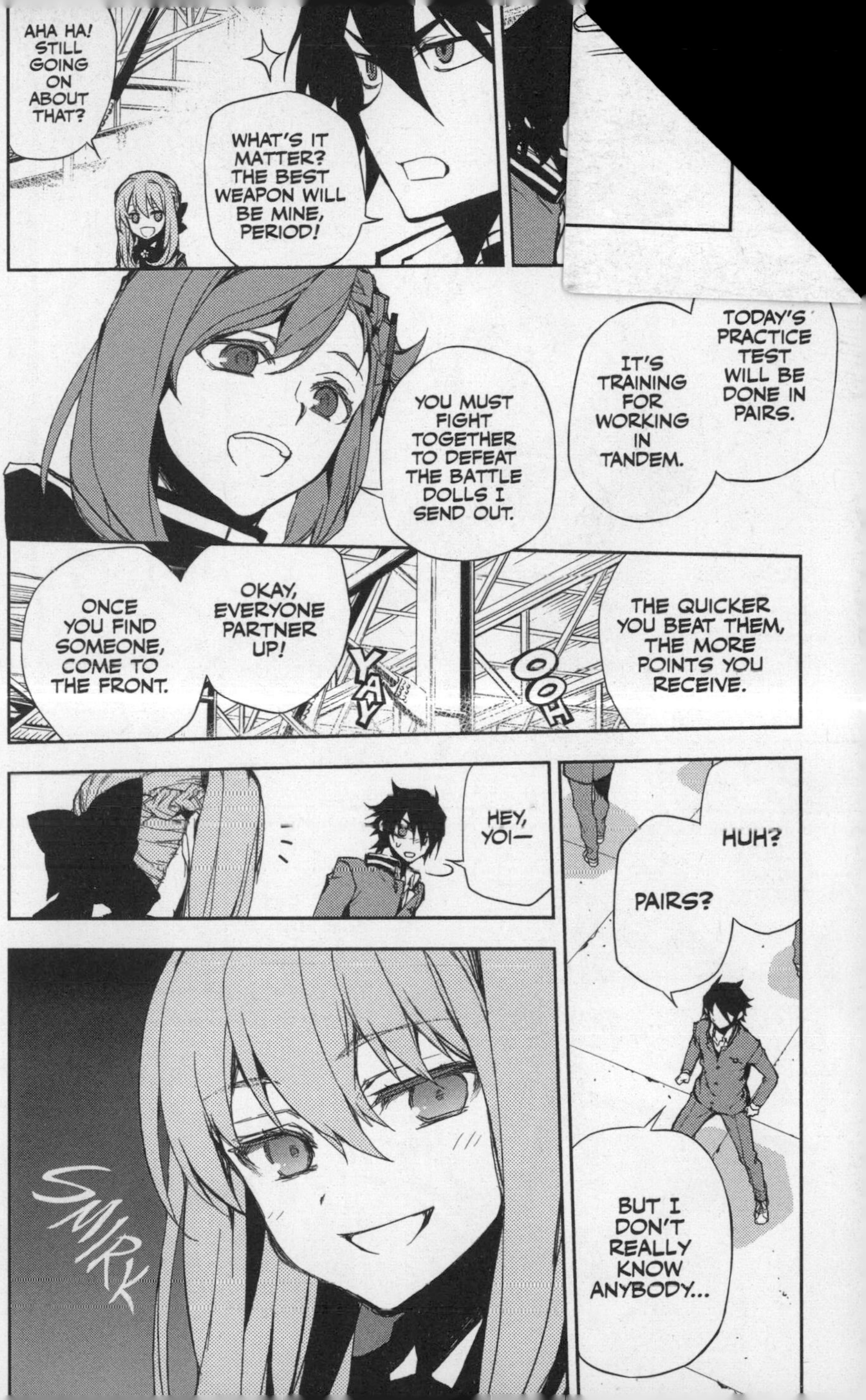
AHA HA! STILL GOING ON ABOUT THAT?
WHAT'S IT MATTER? THE BEST WEAPON WILL BE MINE, PERIOD!
TODAY'S PRACTICE TEST WILL BE DONE IN PAIRS.
IT'S TRAINING FOR WORKING IN TANDEM.
YOU MUST FIGHT TOGETHER TO DEFEAT THE BATTLE DOLLS I SEND OUT.
THE QUICKER YOU BEAT THEM, THE MORE POINTS YOU RECEIVE.
OOOH
YAY
OKAY, EVERYONE PARTNER UP!
ONCE YOU FIND SOMEONE, COME TO THE FRONT.
HUH?
PAIRS?
BUT I DON'T REALLY KNOW ANYBODY...
HEY, YOI—
SMIRK

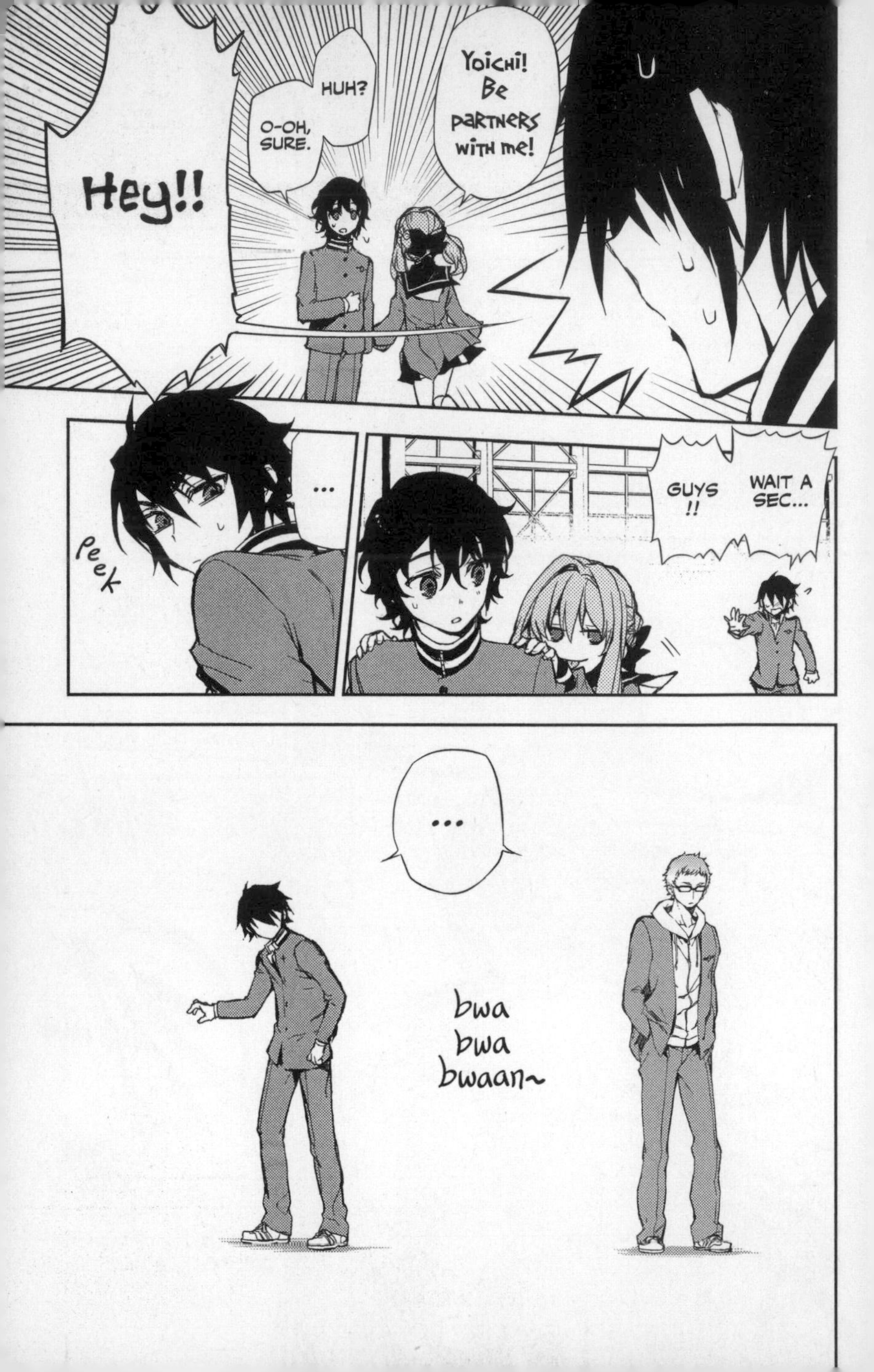
Yoichi! Be partners with me!
HUH?
O-OH, SURE.
Hey!!
WAIT A SEC...
GUYS !!
...
peek
...
bwa bwa bwaan~

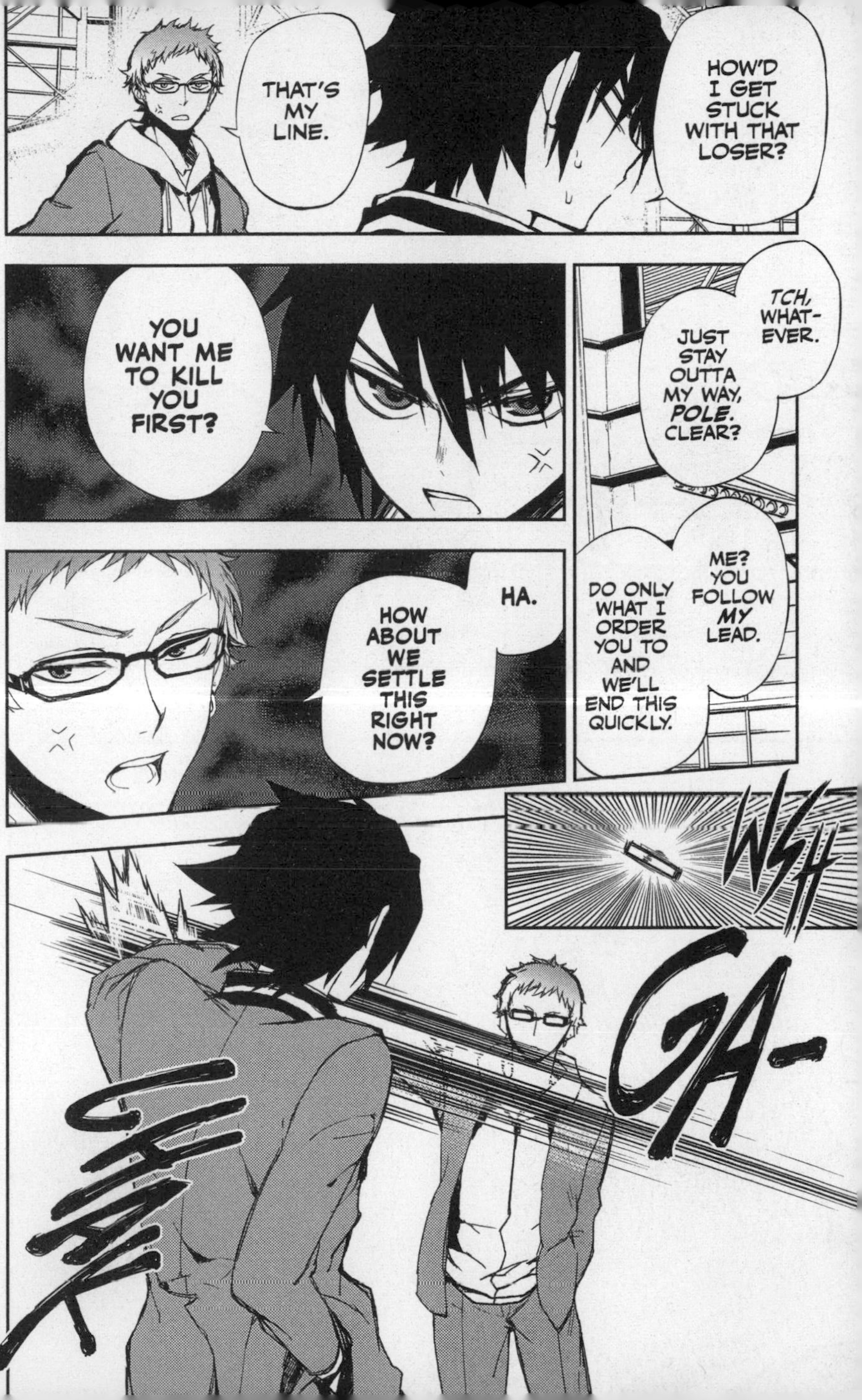
HOW'D I GET STUCK WITH THAT LOSER?
THAT'S MY LINE.
TCH, WHAT-EVER.
JUST STAY OUTTA MY WAY, *POLE*. CLEAR?
ME? YOU FOLLOW *MY* LEAD.
DO ONLY WHAT I ORDER YOU TO AND WE'LL END THIS QUICKLY.
YOU WANT ME TO KILL YOU FIRST?
HA.
HOW ABOUT WE SETTLE THIS RIGHT NOW?
WSH
GA-
CHAK

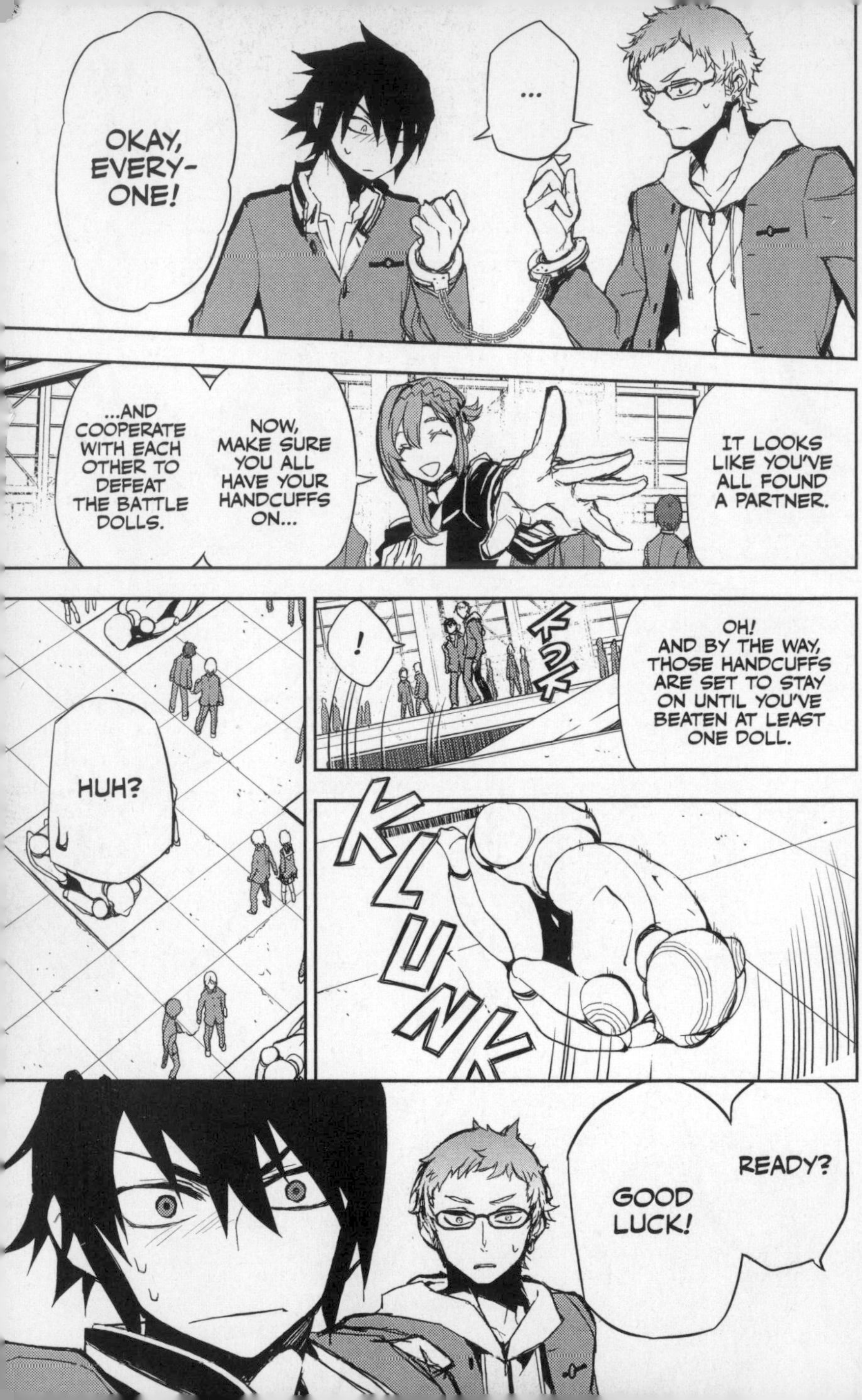
...
OKAY, EVERY-ONE!
IT LOOKS LIKE YOU'VE ALL FOUND A PARTNER.
NOW, MAKE SURE YOU ALL HAVE YOUR HANDCUFFS ON...
...AND COOPERATE WITH EACH OTHER TO DEFEAT THE BATTLE DOLLS.
OH! AND BY THE WAY, THOSE HANDCUFFS ARE SET TO STAY ON UNTIL YOU'VE BEATEN AT LEAST ONE DOLL.
!
KLUNK
HUH?
READY?
GOOD LUCK!

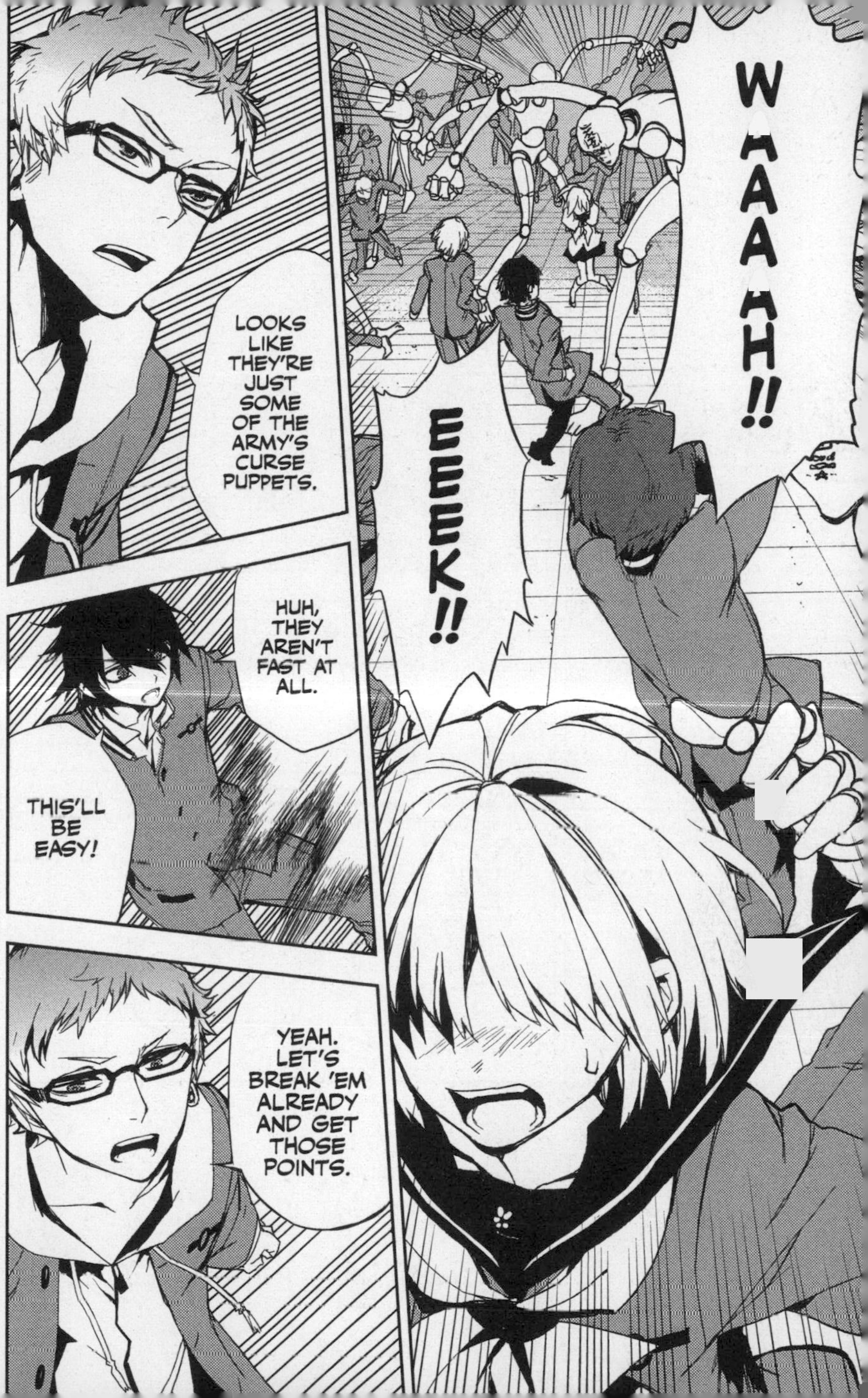
WAAAAH!!
EEEEK!!
LOOKS LIKE THEY'RE JUST SOME OF THE ARMY'S CURSE PUPPETS.
HUH, THEY AREN'T FAST AT ALL.
THIS'LL BE EASY!
YEAH. LET'S BREAK 'EM ALREADY AND GET THOSE POINTS.

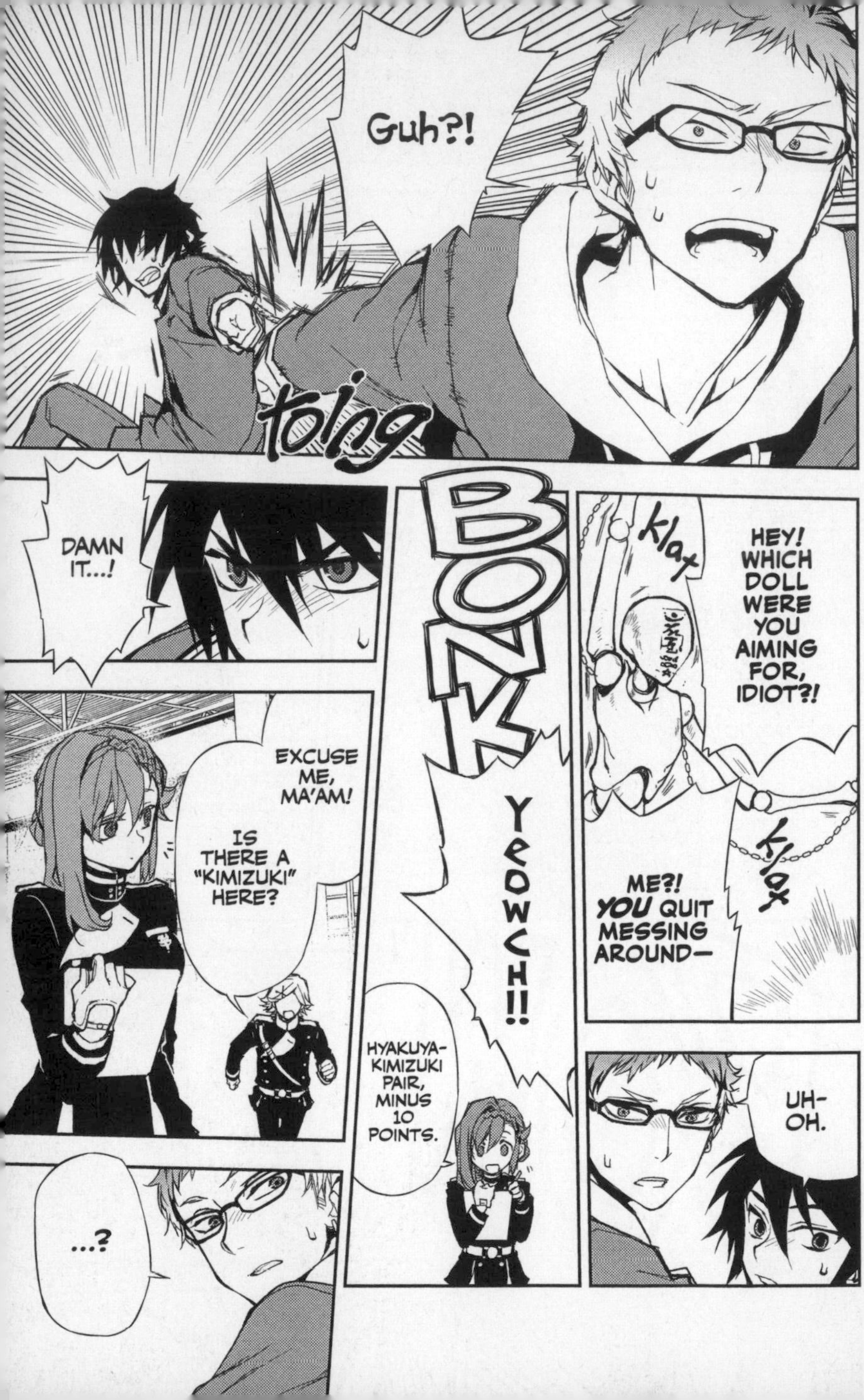

Guh?!
toing
klat
HEY! WHICH DOLL WERE YOU AIMING FOR, IDIOT?!
ME?! *YOU* QUIT MESSING AROUND—
klat
UH-OH.
BONK
YEOWCH!!
HYAKUYA-KIMIZUKI PAIR, MINUS 10 POINTS.
DAMN IT...!
EXCUSE ME, MA'AM!
IS THERE A "KIMIZUKI" HERE?
...?

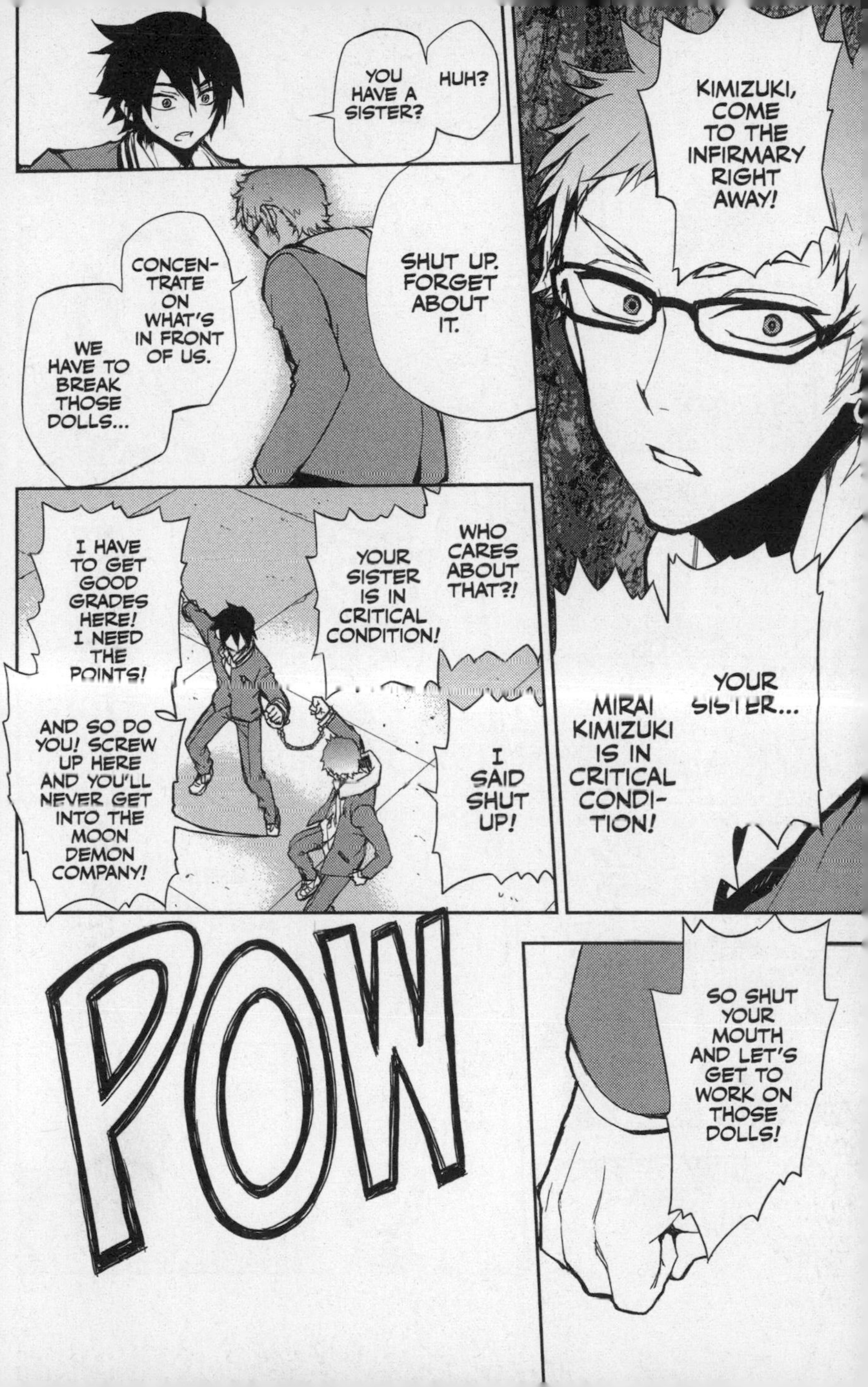
KIMIZUKI, COME TO THE INFIRMARY RIGHT AWAY!
YOUR SISTER...
MIRAI KIMIZUKI IS IN CRITICAL CONDITION!
HUH?
YOU HAVE A SISTER?
SHUT UP. FORGET ABOUT IT.
CONCEN-TRATE ON WHAT'S IN FRONT OF US.
WE HAVE TO BREAK THOSE DOLLS...
WHO CARES ABOUT THAT?!
YOUR SISTER IS IN CRITICAL CONDITION!
I HAVE TO GET GOOD GRADES HERE! I NEED THE POINTS!
I SAID SHUT UP!
AND SO DO YOU! SCREW UP HERE AND YOU'LL NEVER GET INTO THE MOON DEMON COMPANY!
SO SHUT YOUR MOUTH AND LET'S GET TO WORK ON THOSE DOLLS!
POW

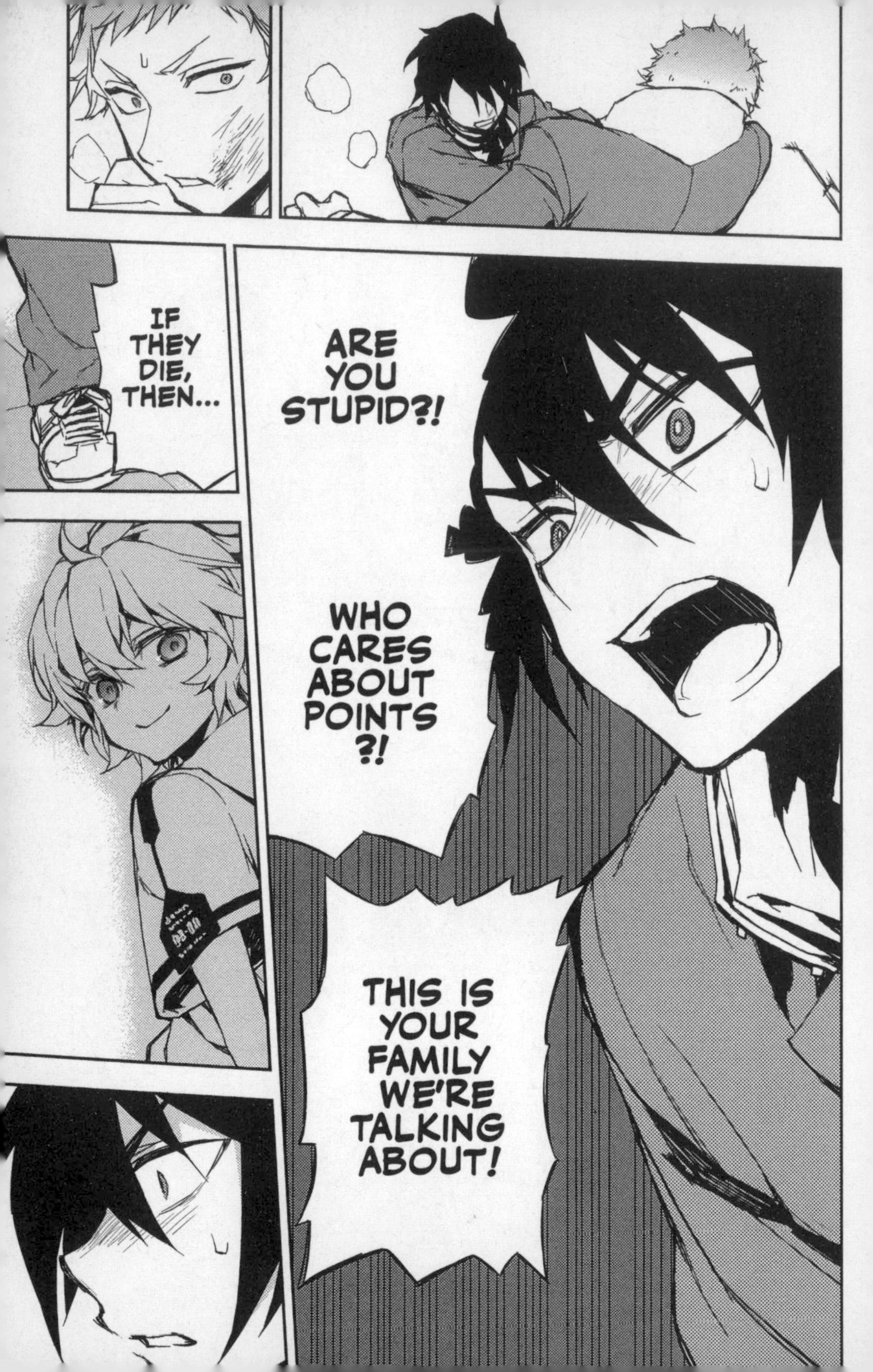
ARE YOU STUPID?!
WHO CARES ABOUT POINTS?!
THIS IS YOUR FAMILY WE'RE TALKING ABOUT!
IF THEY DIE, THEN...

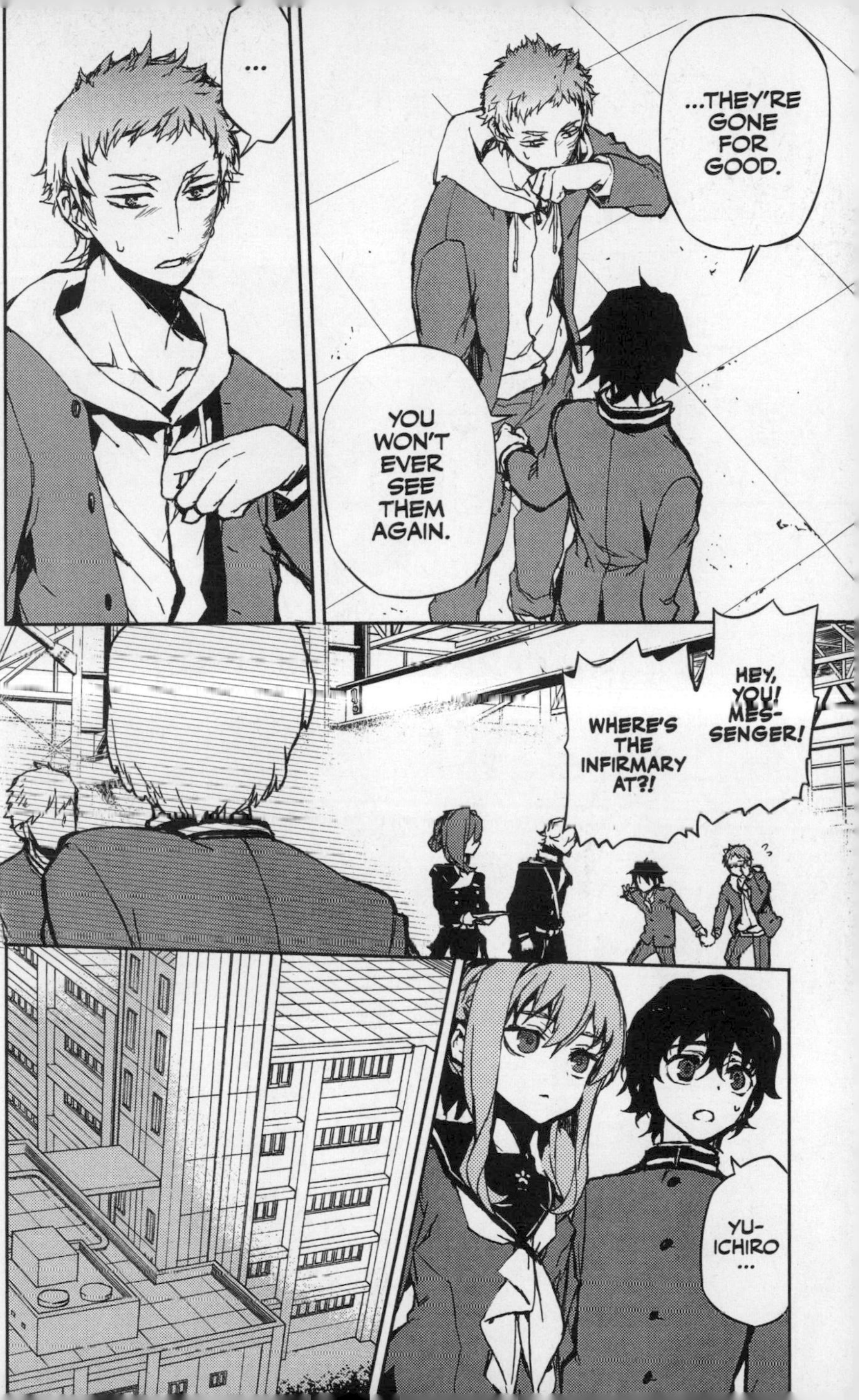
...THEY'RE GONE FOR GOOD.
YOU WON'T EVER SEE THEM AGAIN.
...
HEY, YOU! MES-SENGER!
WHERE'S THE INFIRMARY AT?!
YU-ICHIRO ...

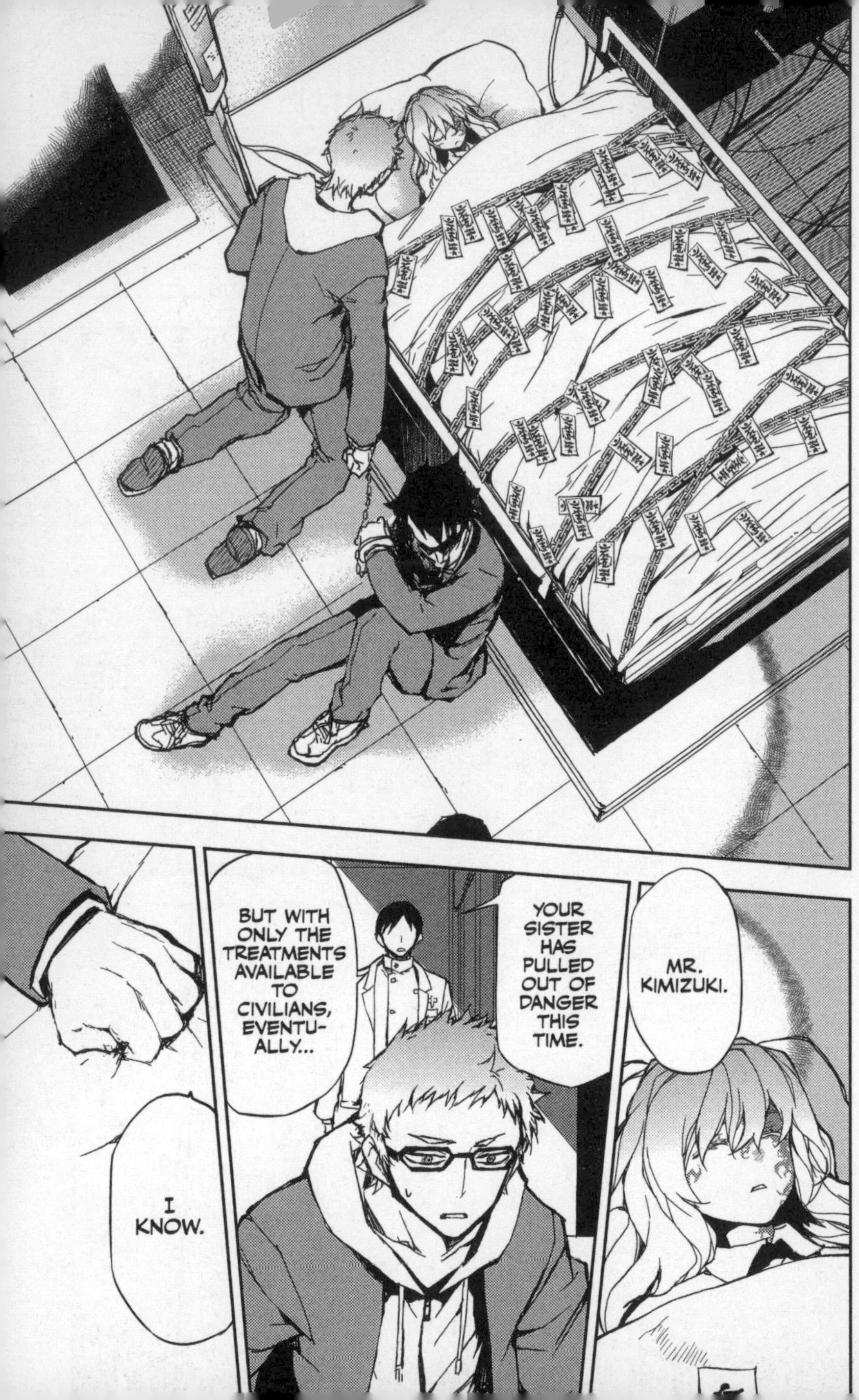
MR. KIMIZUKI.
YOUR SISTER HAS PULLED OUT OF DANGER THIS TIME.
BUT WITH ONLY THE TREATMENTS AVAILABLE TO CIVILIANS, EVENTUALLY...
I KNOW.

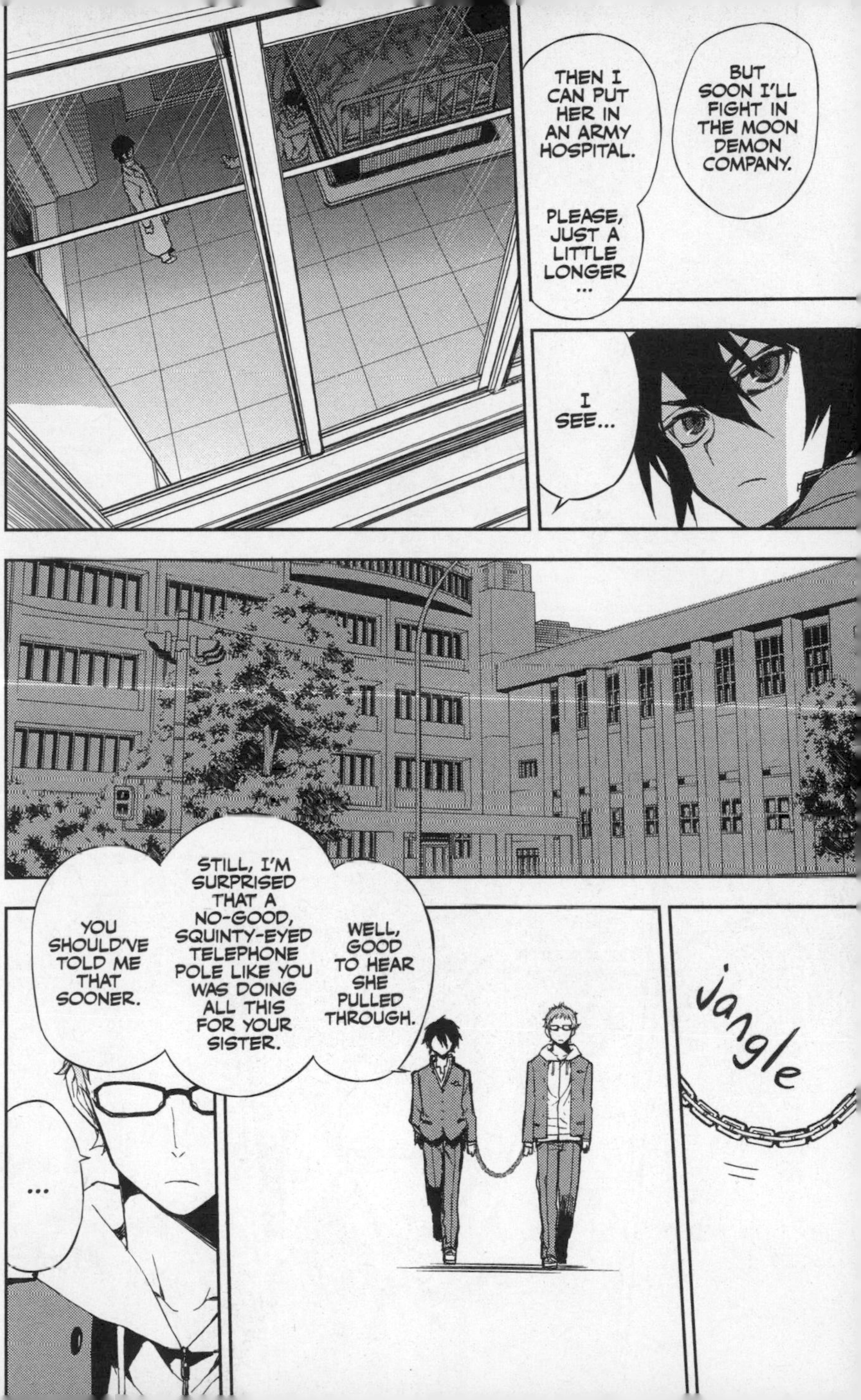
BUT SOON I'LL FIGHT IN THE MOON DEMON COMPANY.
THEN I CAN PUT HER IN AN ARMY HOSPITAL.
PLEASE, JUST A LITTLE LONGER ...
I SEE...
jangle
WELL, GOOD TO HEAR SHE PULLED THROUGH.
STILL, I'M SURPRISED THAT A NO-GOOD, SQUINTY-EYED TELEPHONE POLE LIKE YOU WAS DOING ALL THIS FOR YOUR SISTER.
YOU SHOULD'VE TOLD ME THAT SOONER.
...

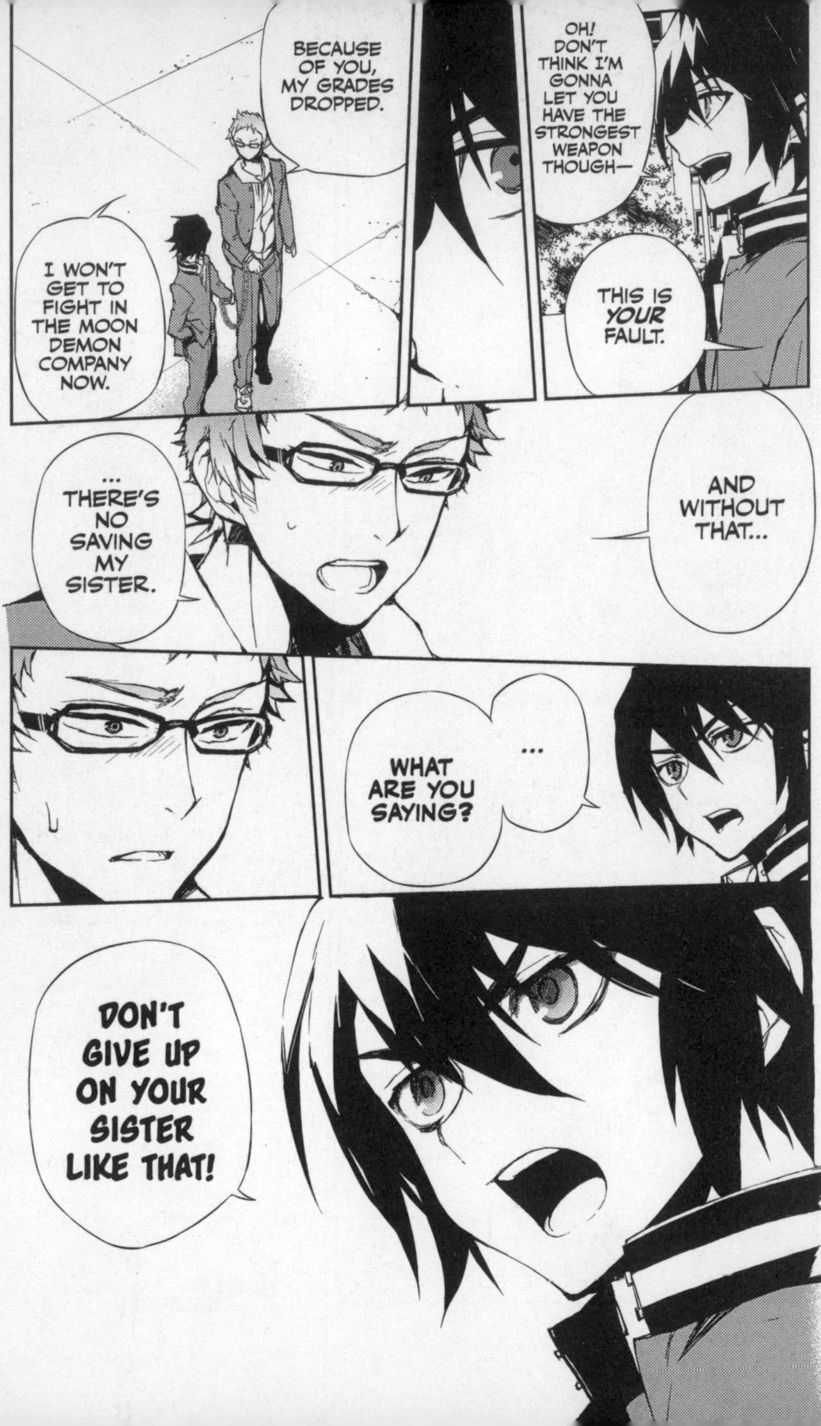
OH! DON'T THINK I'M GONNA LET YOU HAVE THE STRONGEST WEAPON THOUGH—
THIS IS *YOUR* FAULT.
BECAUSE OF YOU, MY GRADES DROPPED.
I WON'T GET TO FIGHT IN THE MOON DEMON COMPANY NOW.
AND WITHOUT THAT...
... THERE'S NO SAVING MY SISTER.
...
WHAT ARE YOU SAYING?
DON'T GIVE UP ON YOUR SISTER LIKE THAT!

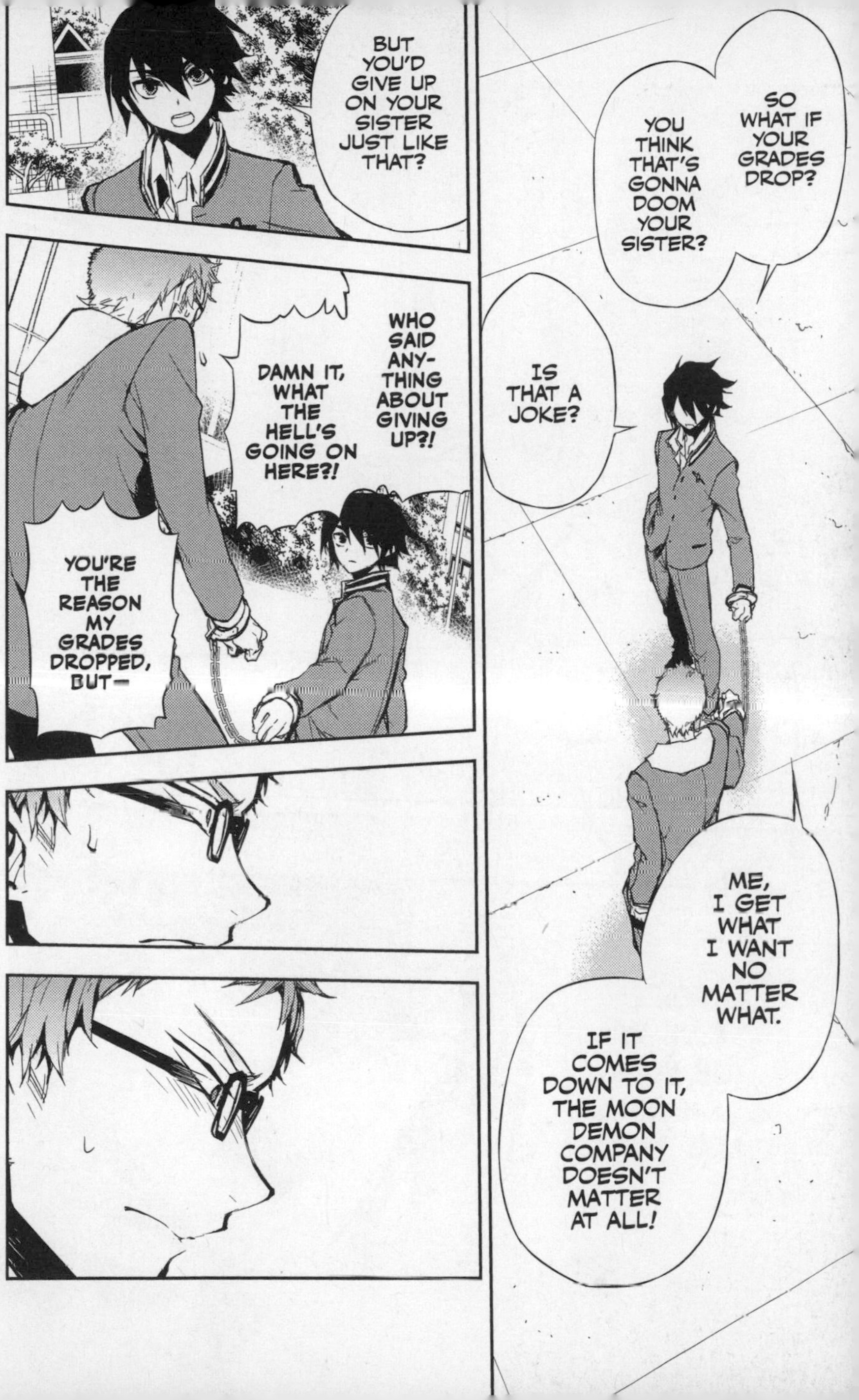
SO WHAT IF YOUR GRADES DROP?
YOU THINK THAT'S GONNA DOOM YOUR SISTER?
IS THAT A JOKE?
ME, I GET WHAT I WANT NO MATTER WHAT.
IF IT COMES DOWN TO IT, THE MOON DEMON COMPANY DOESN'T MATTER AT ALL!
BUT YOU'D GIVE UP ON YOUR SISTER JUST LIKE THAT?
WHO SAID ANYTHING ABOUT GIVING UP?!
DAMN IT, WHAT THE HELL'S GOING ON HERE?!
YOU'RE THE REASON MY GRADES DROPPED, BUT—

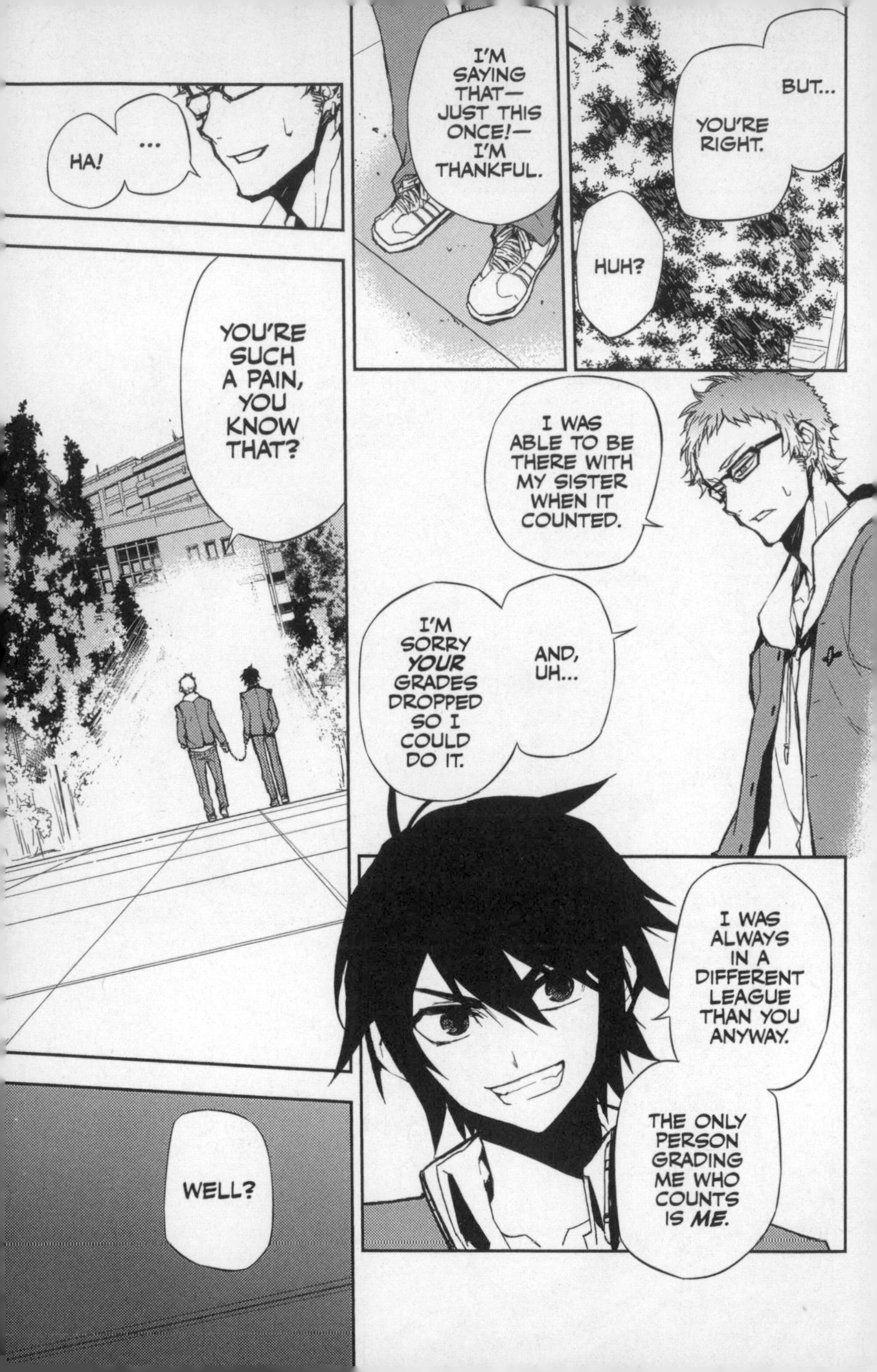
BUT... YOU'RE RIGHT.
HUH?
I'M SAYING THAT— JUST THIS ONCE!— I'M THANKFUL.
HA! ...
I WAS ABLE TO BE THERE WITH MY SISTER WHEN IT COUNTED.
AND, UH...
I'M SORRY *YOUR* GRADES DROPPED SO I COULD DO IT.
I WAS ALWAYS IN A DIFFERENT LEAGUE THAN YOU ANYWAY.
THE ONLY PERSON GRADING ME WHO COUNTS IS *ME*.
YOU'RE SUCH A PAIN, YOU KNOW THAT?
WELL?

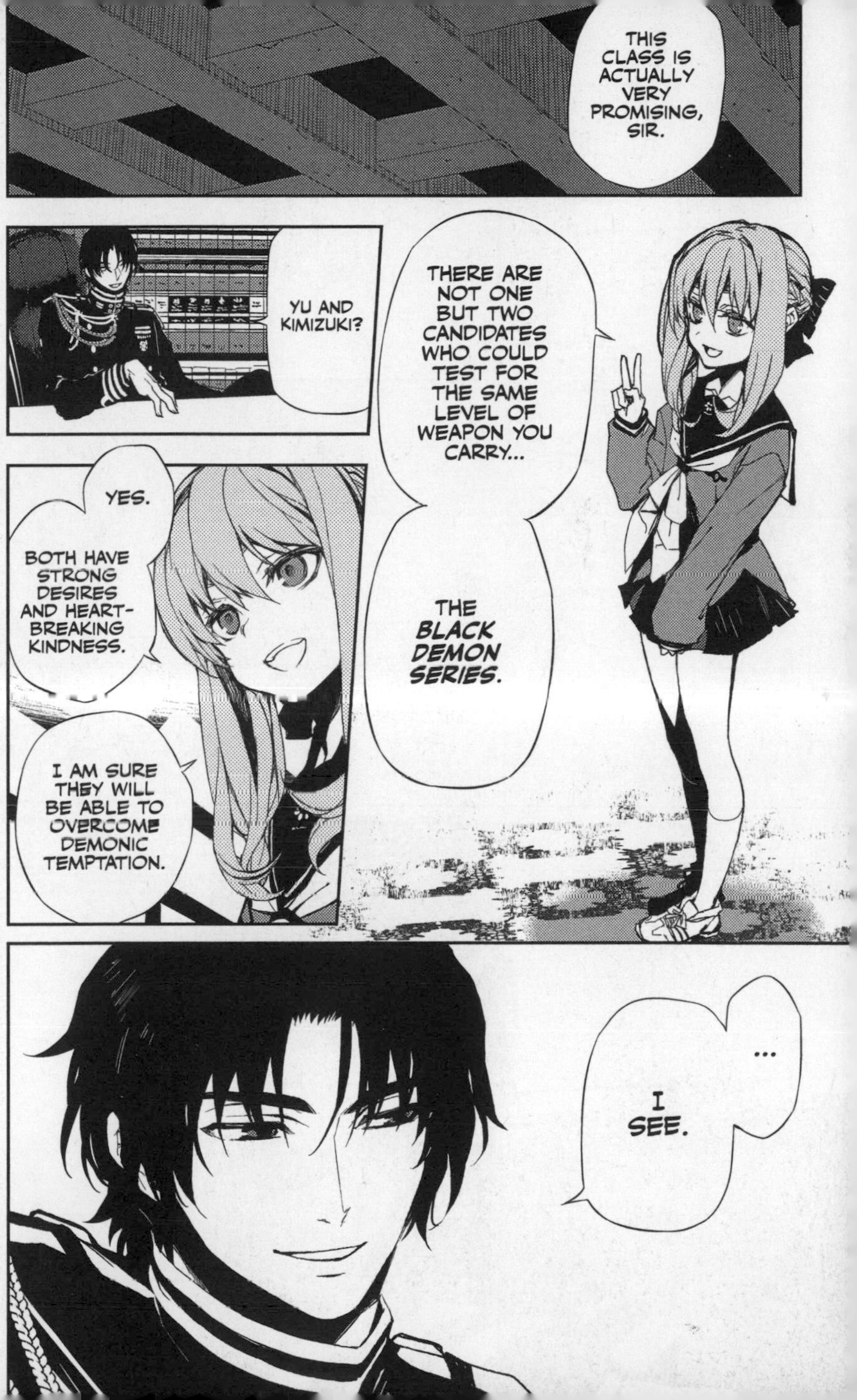
THIS CLASS IS ACTUALLY VERY PROMISING, SIR.
THERE ARE NOT ONE BUT TWO CANDIDATES WHO COULD TEST FOR THE SAME LEVEL OF WEAPON YOU CARRY...
THE *BLACK DEMON SERIES*.
YU AND KIMIZUKI?
YES.
BOTH HAVE STRONG DESIRES AND HEART-BREAKING KINDNESS.
I AM SURE THEY WILL BE ABLE TO OVERCOME DEMONIC TEMPTATION.
...
I SEE.

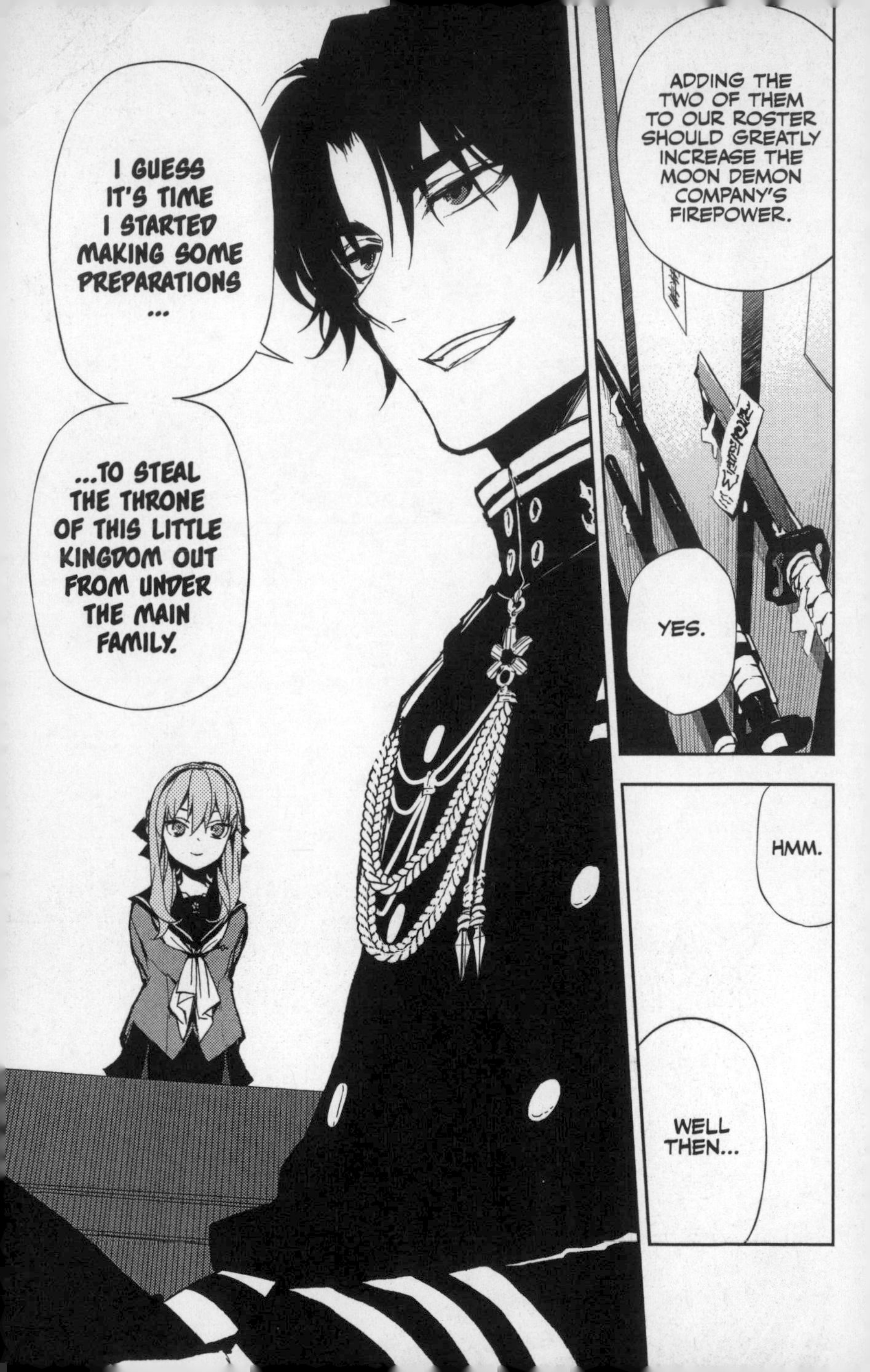
ADDING THE TWO OF THEM TO OUR ROSTER SHOULD GREATLY INCREASE THE MOON DEMON COMPANY'S FIREPOWER.
YES.
HMM.
WELL THEN...
I GUESS IT'S TIME I STARTED MAKING SOME PREPARATIONS ...
...TO STEAL THE THRONE OF THIS LITTLE KINGDOM OUT FROM UNDER THE MAIN FAMILY.

Seraph of the End

VAMPIRE REIGN

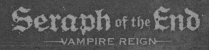

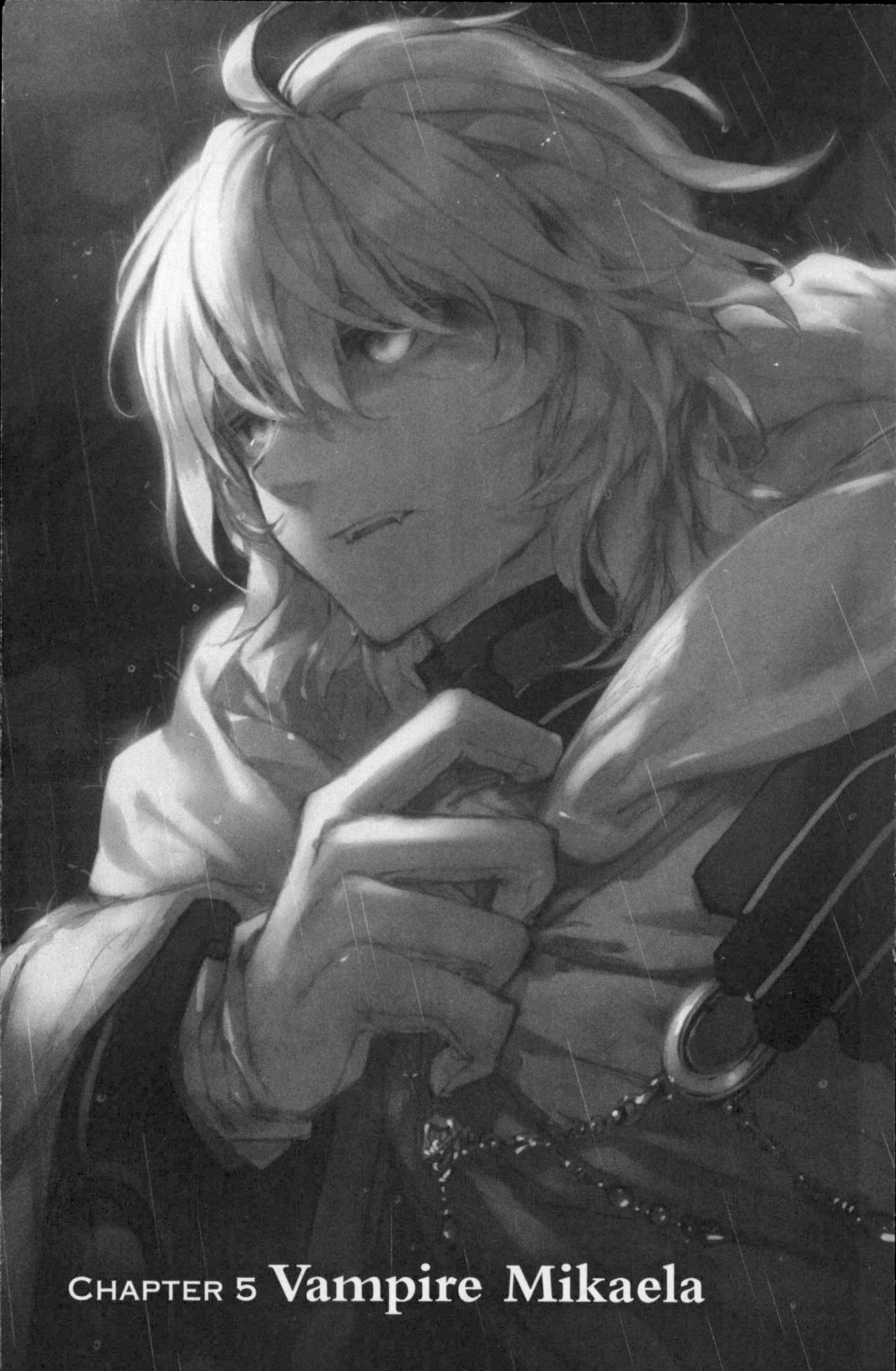

CHAPTER 5 Vampire Mikaela

Seraph of the End
VAMPIRE REIGN

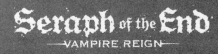

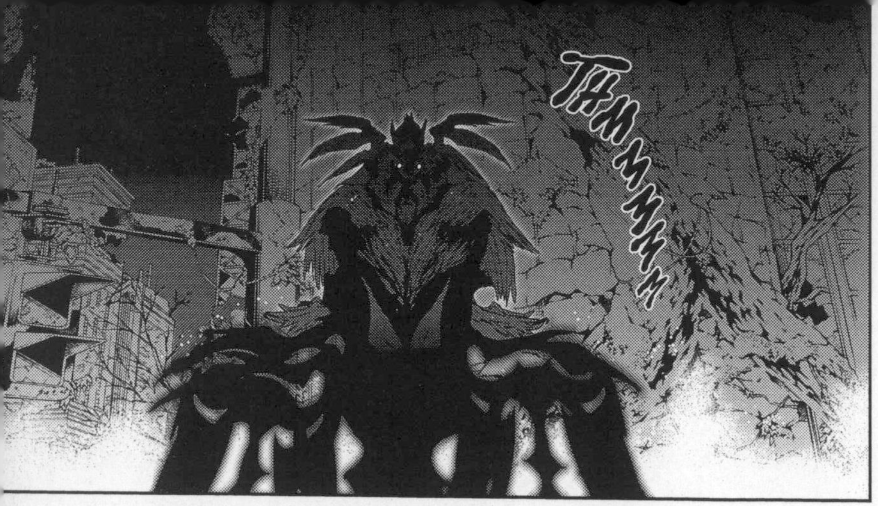
THMMMMMM

Sannomiya, Kobe

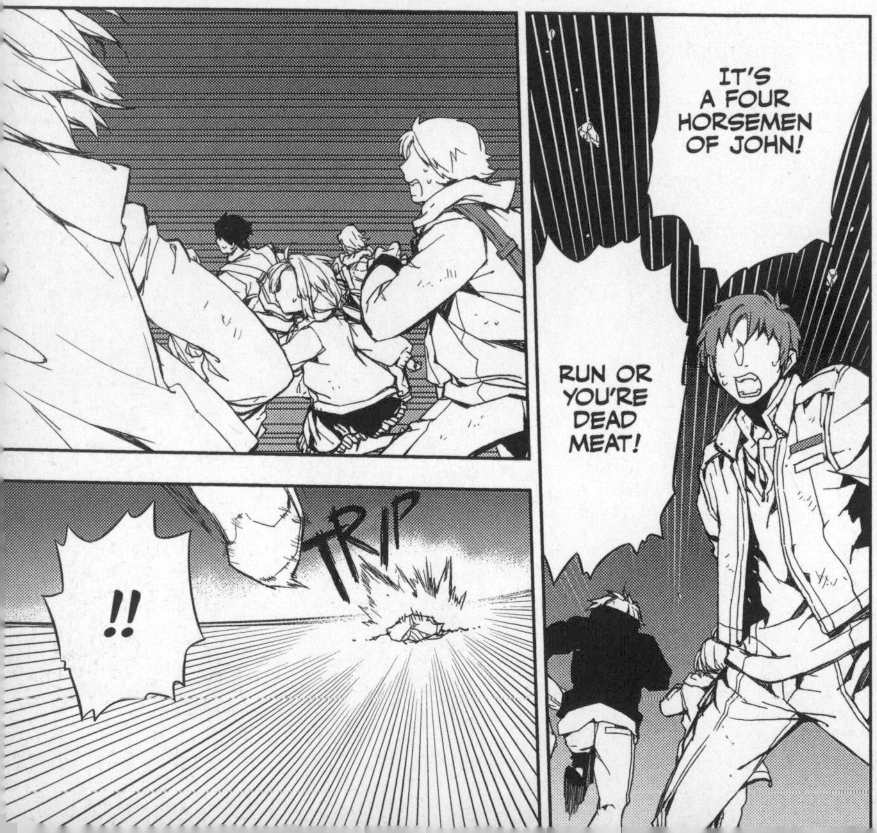
IT'S A FOUR HORSEMEN OF JOHN!
RUN OR YOU'RE DEAD MEAT!
TRIP
!!

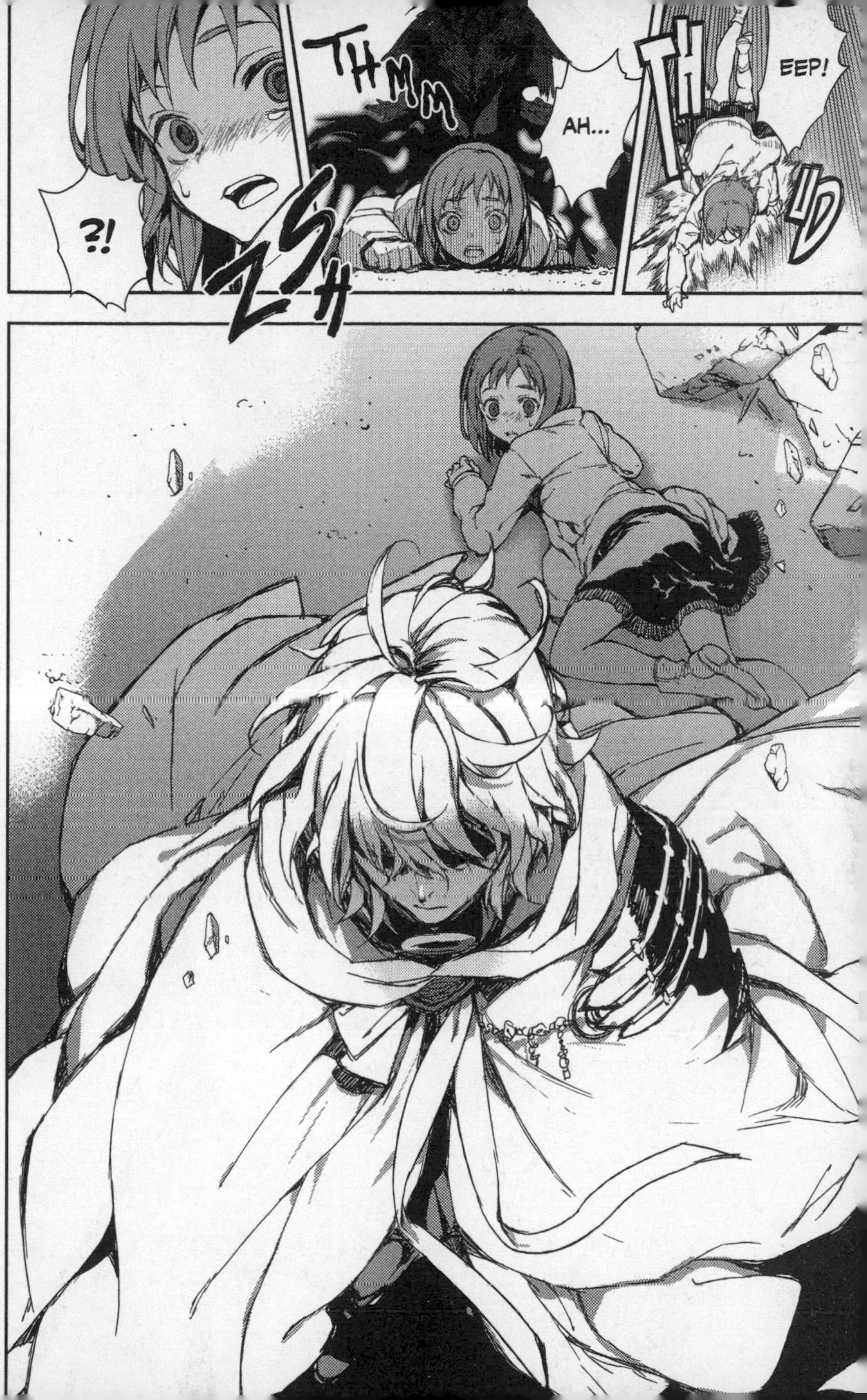
EEP!
THUD
THMM
AH...
?!
ZSH

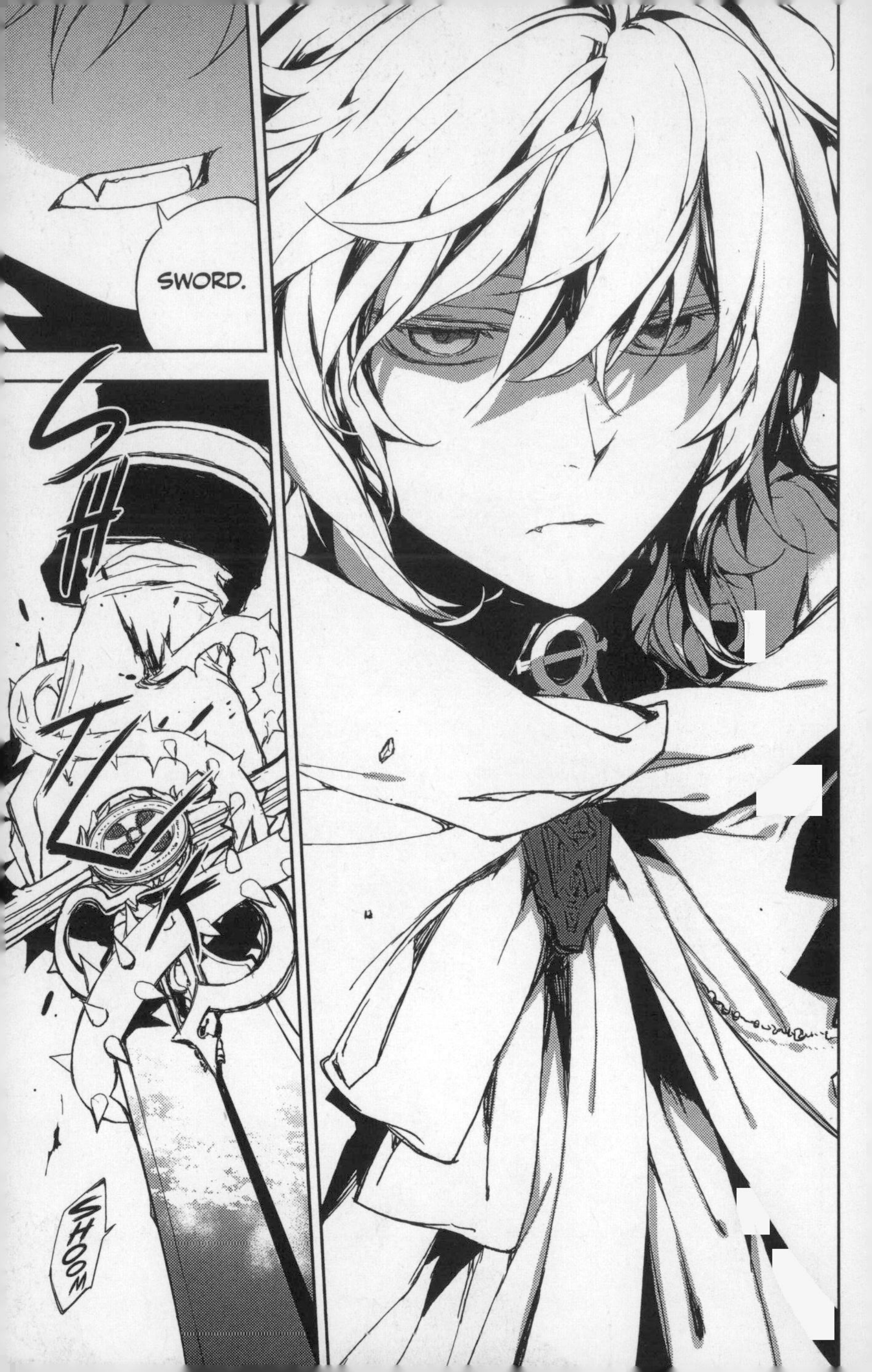
SWORD.
SHOOM

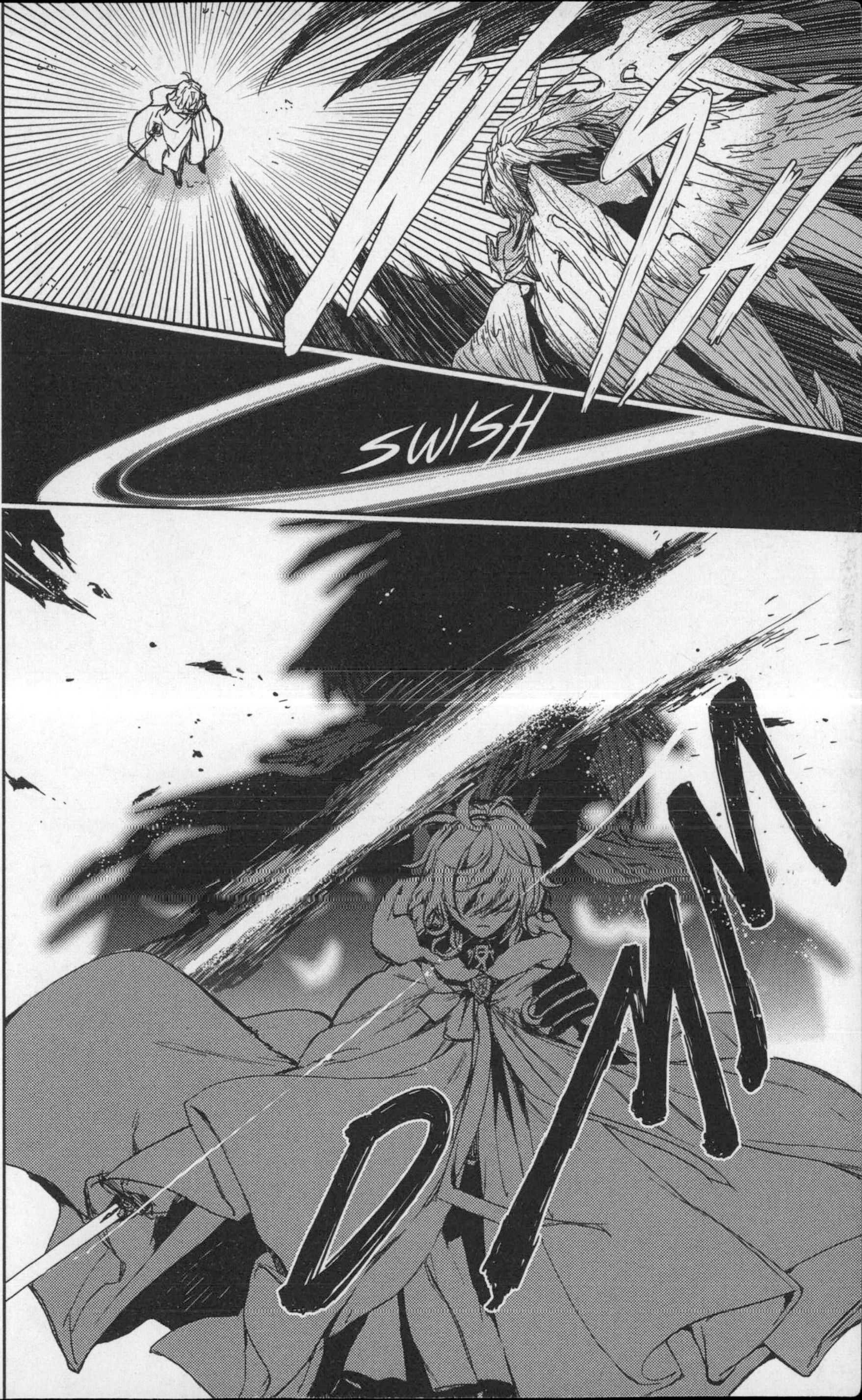
SWISH

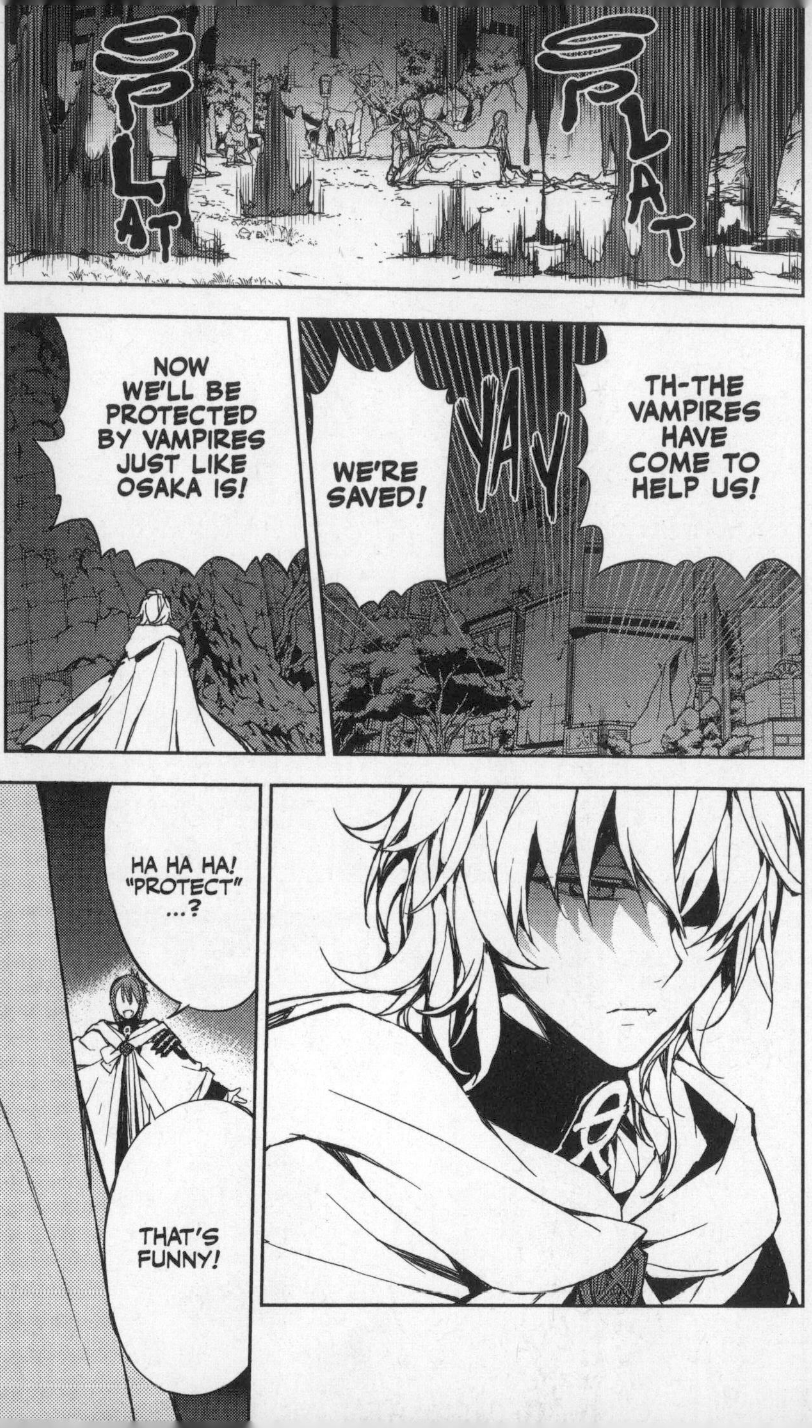
SPLAT
SPLAT
TH-THE VAMPIRES HAVE COME TO HELP US!
YAY
WE'RE SAVED!
NOW WE'LL BE PROTECTED BY VAMPIRES JUST LIKE OSAKA IS!
HA HA HA! "PROTECT" ...?
THAT'S FUNNY!

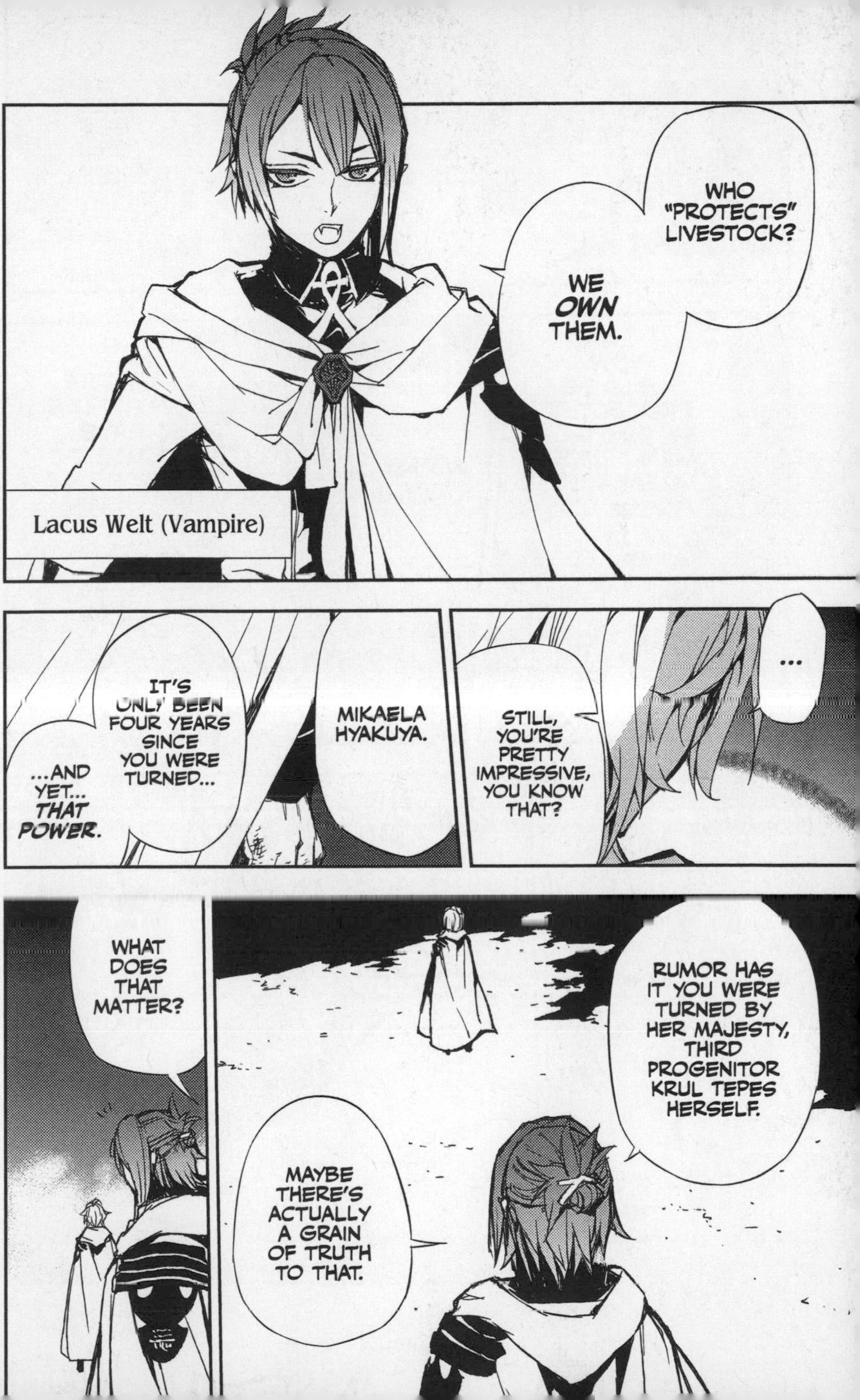
WHO "PROTECTS" LIVESTOCK?
WE OWN THEM.
Lacus Welt (Vampire)
...
STILL, YOU'RE PRETTY IMPRESSIVE, YOU KNOW THAT?
MIKAELA HYAKUYA.
IT'S ONLY BEEN FOUR YEARS SINCE YOU WERE TURNED...
...AND YET... THAT POWER.
RUMOR HAS IT YOU WERE TURNED BY HER MAJESTY, THIRD PROGENITOR KRUL TEPES HERSELF.
MAYBE THERE'S ACTUALLY A GRAIN OF TRUTH TO THAT.
WHAT DOES THAT MATTER?

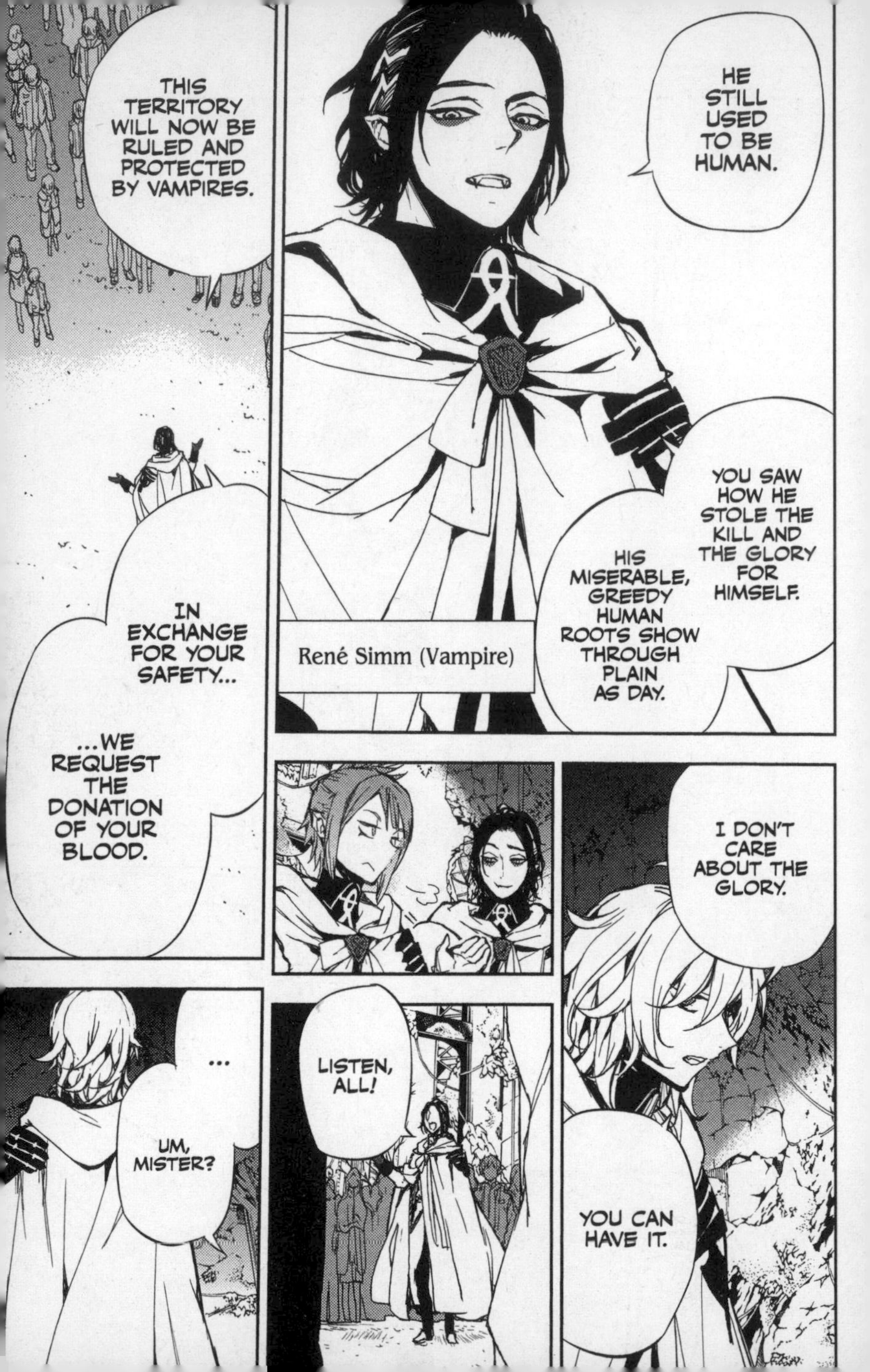
HE STILL USED TO BE HUMAN.
YOU SAW HOW HE STOLE THE KILL AND THE GLORY FOR HIMSELF.
HIS MISERABLE, GREEDY HUMAN ROOTS SHOW THROUGH PLAIN AS DAY.
René Simm (Vampire)
I DON'T CARE ABOUT THE GLORY.
YOU CAN HAVE IT.
LISTEN, ALL!
THIS TERRITORY WILL NOW BE RULED AND PROTECTED BY VAMPIRES.
IN EXCHANGE FOR YOUR SAFETY...
...WE REQUEST THE DONATION OF YOUR BLOOD.
...
UM, MISTER?

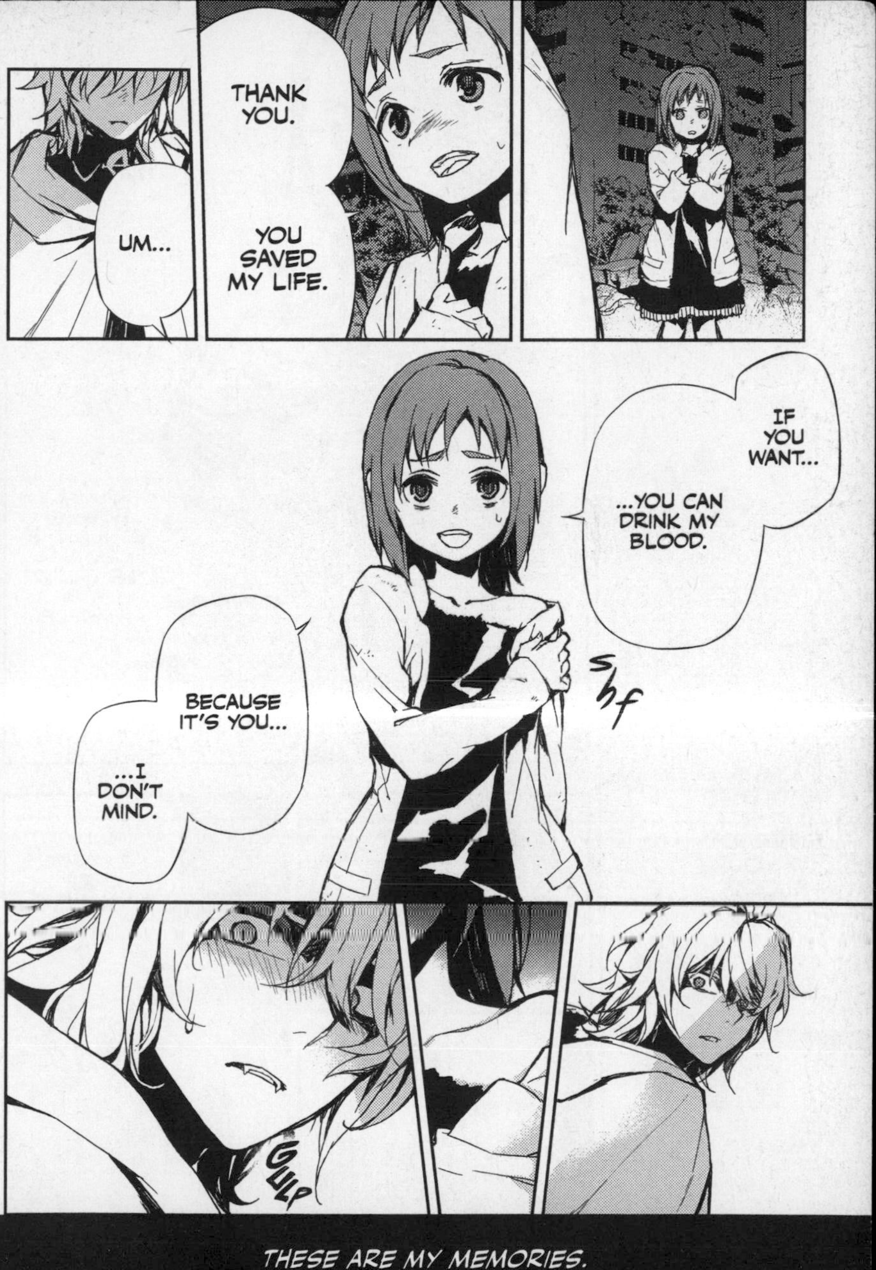
THANK YOU.
YOU SAVED MY LIFE.
UM...
IF YOU WANT...
...YOU CAN DRINK MY BLOOD.
SHF
BECAUSE IT'S YOU...
...I DON'T MIND.
GULP
THESE ARE MY MEMORIES.

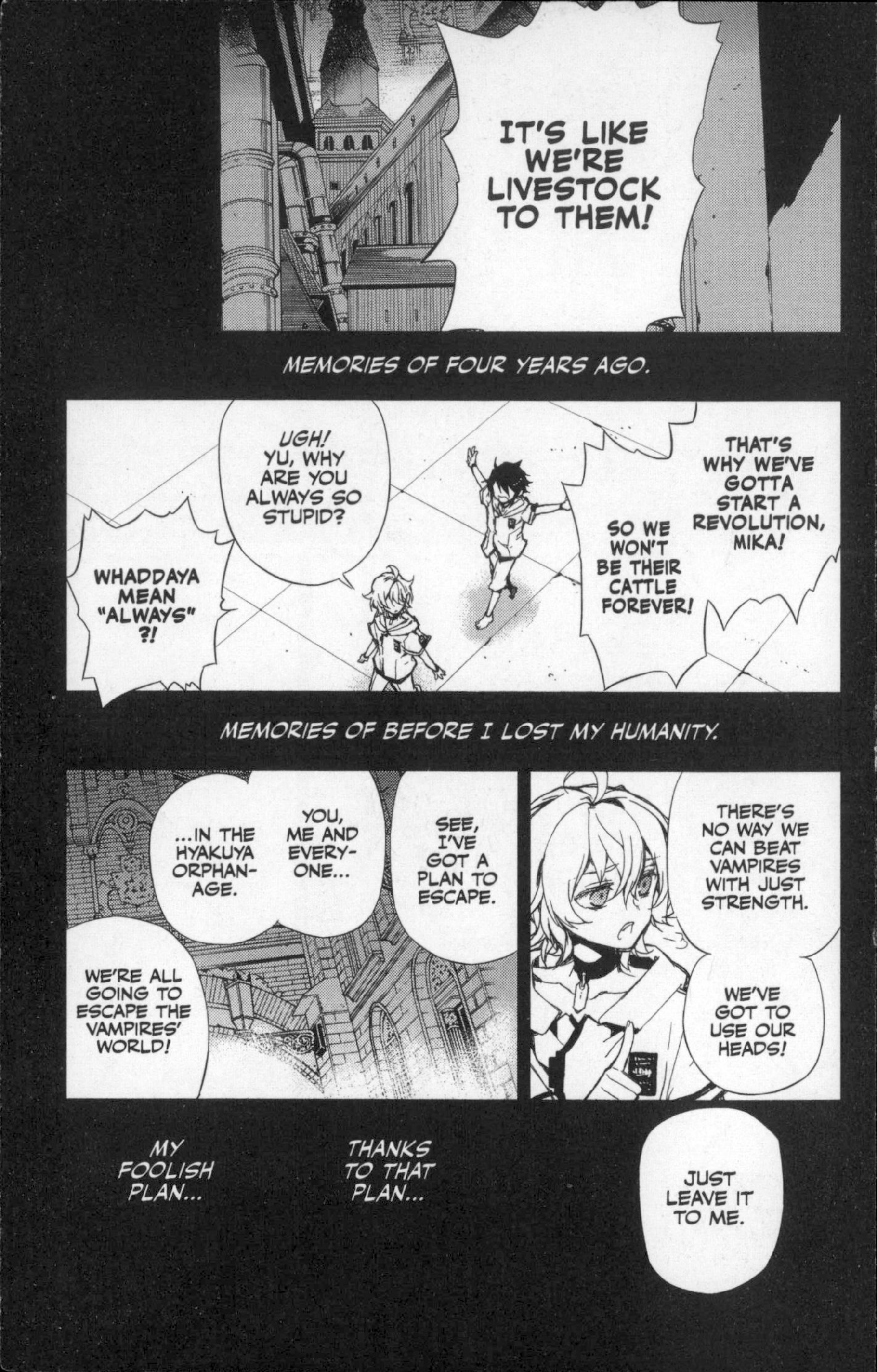
IT'S LIKE WE'RE LIVESTOCK TO THEM!
MEMORIES OF FOUR YEARS AGO.
THAT'S WHY WE'VE GOTTA START A REVOLUTION, MIKA!
SO WE WON'T BE THEIR CATTLE FOREVER!
UGH! YU, WHY ARE YOU ALWAYS SO STUPID?
WHADDAYA MEAN "ALWAYS"?!
MEMORIES OF BEFORE I LOST MY HUMANITY.
THERE'S NO WAY WE CAN BEAT VAMPIRES WITH JUST STRENGTH.
WE'VE GOT TO USE OUR HEADS!
SEE, I'VE GOT A PLAN TO ESCAPE.
YOU, ME AND EVERY-ONE...
...IN THE HYAKUYA ORPHAN-AGE.
WE'RE ALL GOING TO ESCAPE THE VAMPIRES' WORLD!
JUST LEAVE IT TO ME.
THANKS TO THAT PLAN...
MY FOOLISH PLAN...

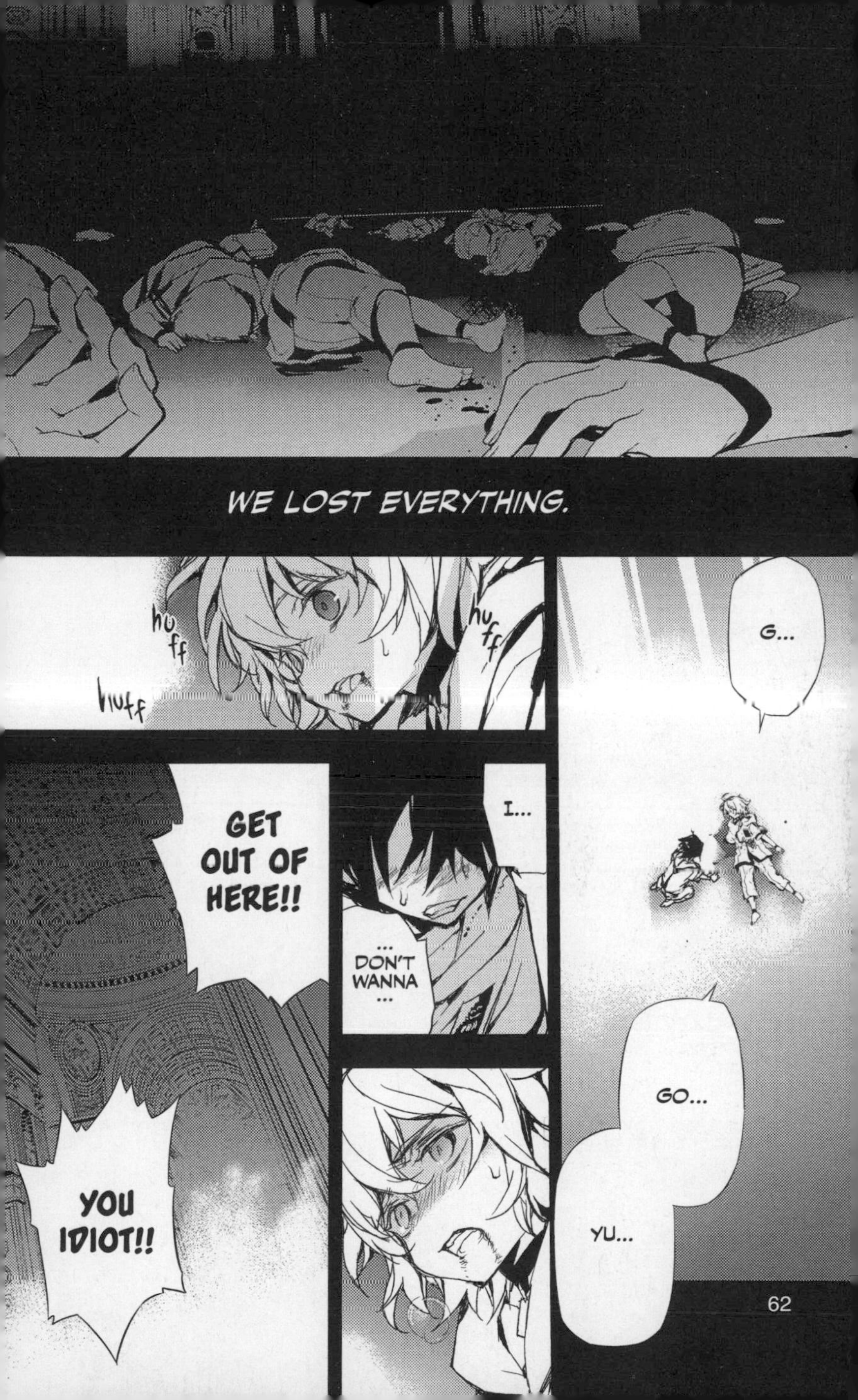

WE LOST EVERYTHING.
G...
GO...
YU...
huff
huff
huff
I...
... DON'T WANNA ...
GET OUT OF HERE!!
YOU IDIOT!!

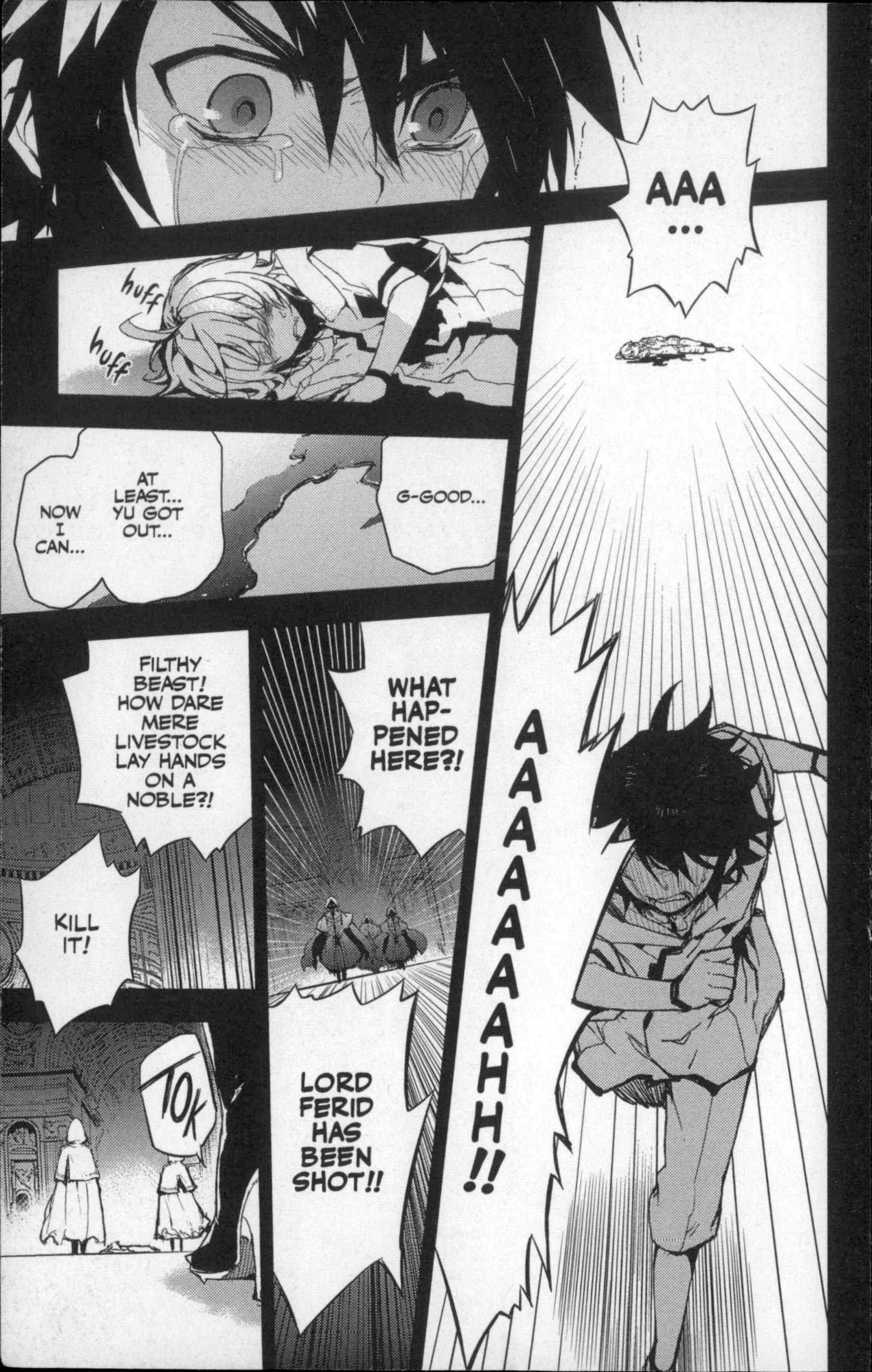
AAA ...
AAAAAAAAAHH!!
huff huff
G-GOOD...
AT LEAST... YU GOT OUT...
NOW I CAN...
WHAT HAP-PENED HERE?!
LORD FERID HAS BEEN SHOT!!
FILTHY BEAST! HOW DARE MERE LIVESTOCK LAY HANDS ON A NOBLE?!
KILL IT!
TOK

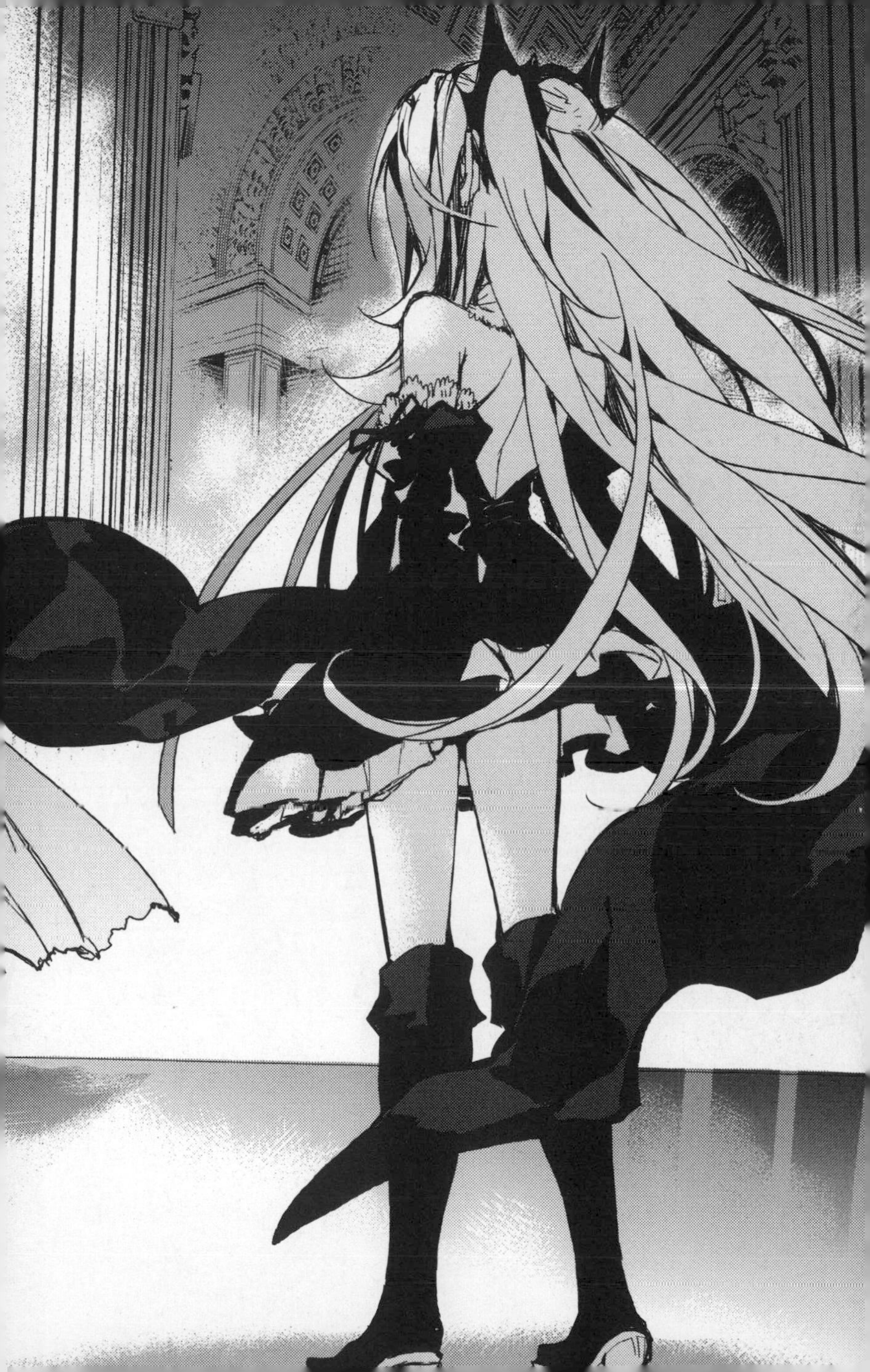

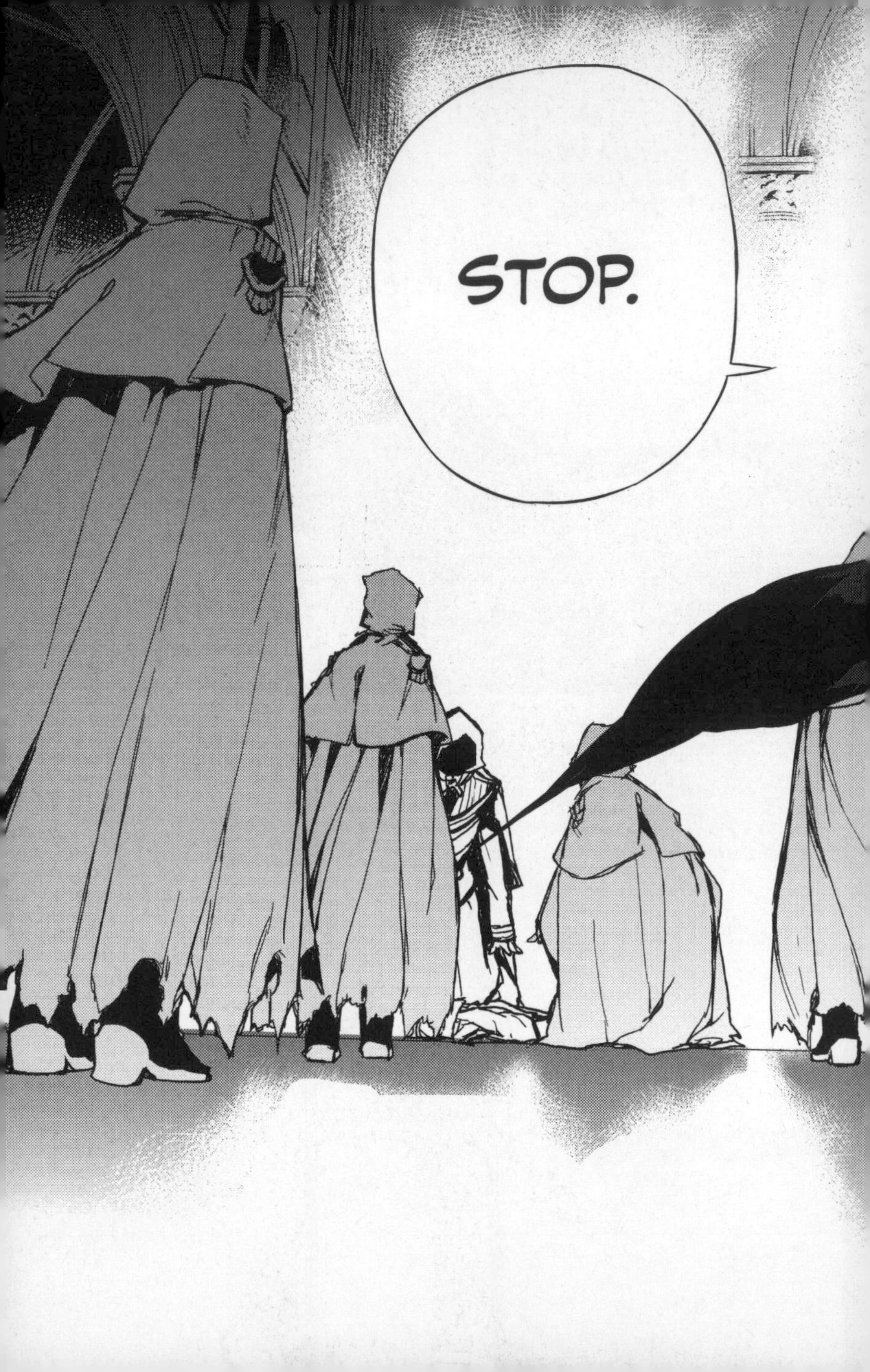
STOP.

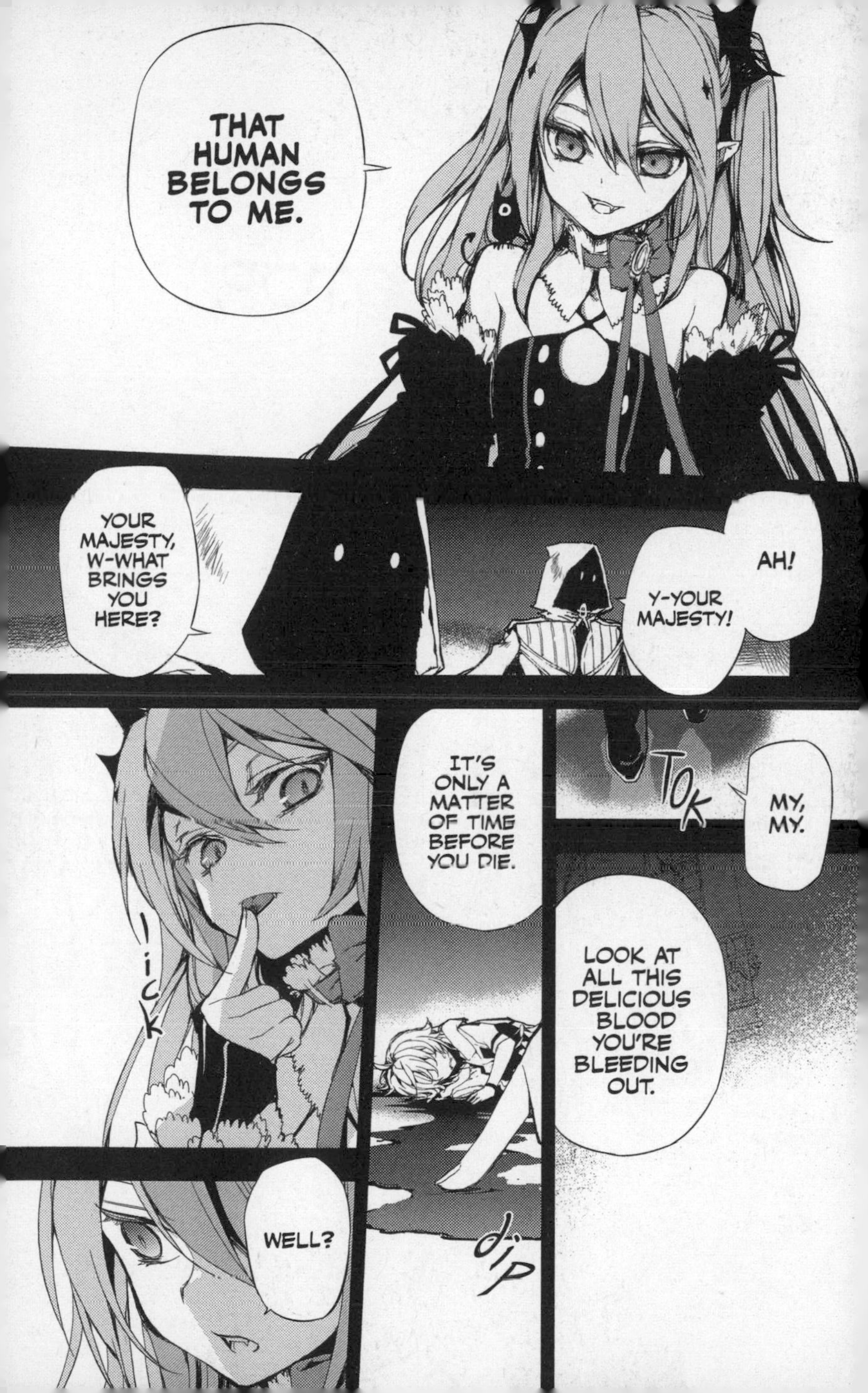
THAT HUMAN BELONGS TO ME.
AH!
Y-YOUR MAJESTY!
YOUR MAJESTY, W-WHAT BRINGS YOU HERE?
TOK
MY, MY.
LOOK AT ALL THIS DELICIOUS BLOOD YOU'RE BLEEDING OUT.
DRIP
IT'S ONLY A MATTER OF TIME BEFORE YOU DIE.
LICK
WELL?

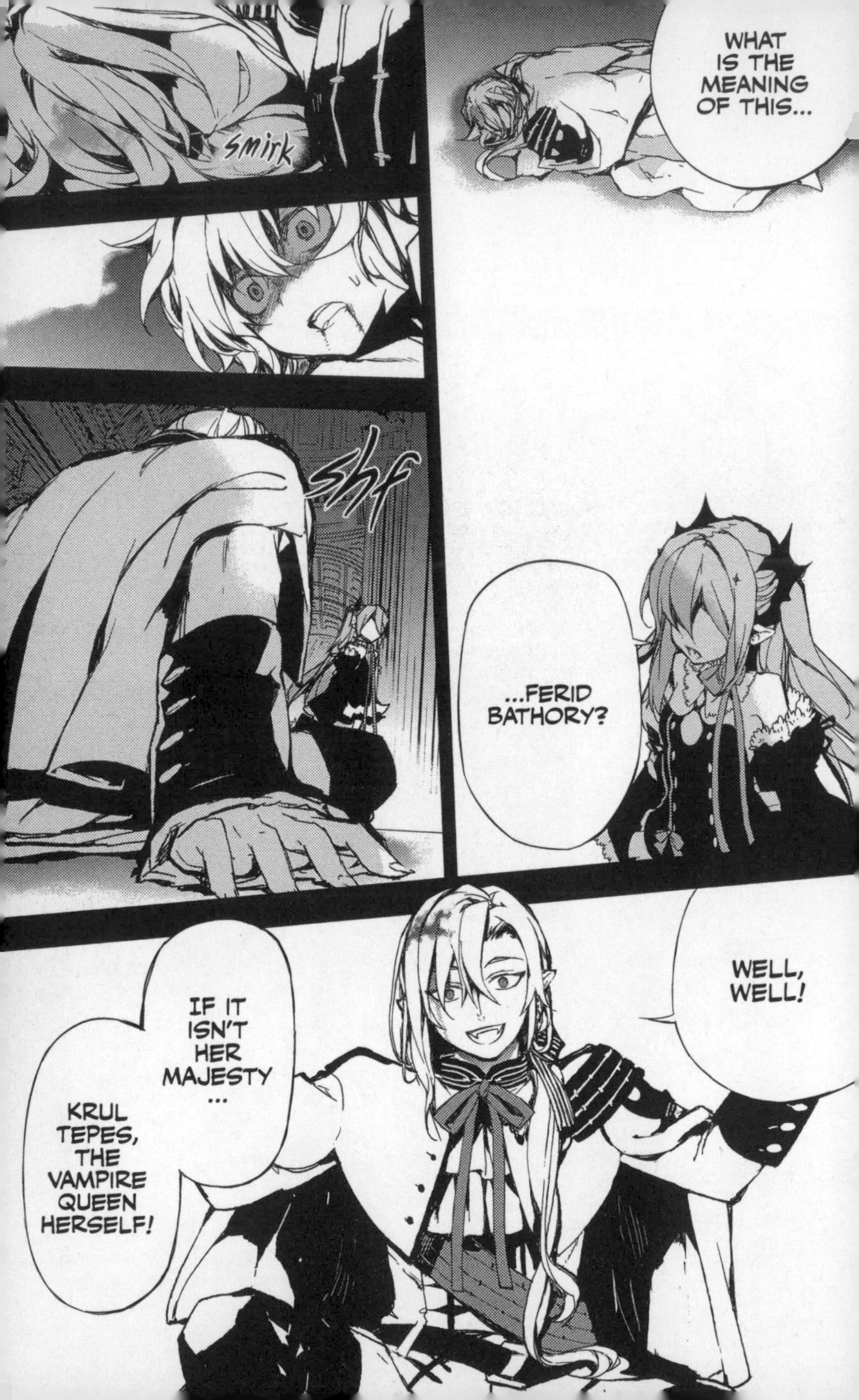
WHAT IS THE MEANING OF THIS...
...FERID BATHORY?
smirk
shf
WELL, WELL!
IF IT ISN'T HER MAJESTY ...
KRUL TEPES, THE VAMPIRE QUEEN HERSELF!

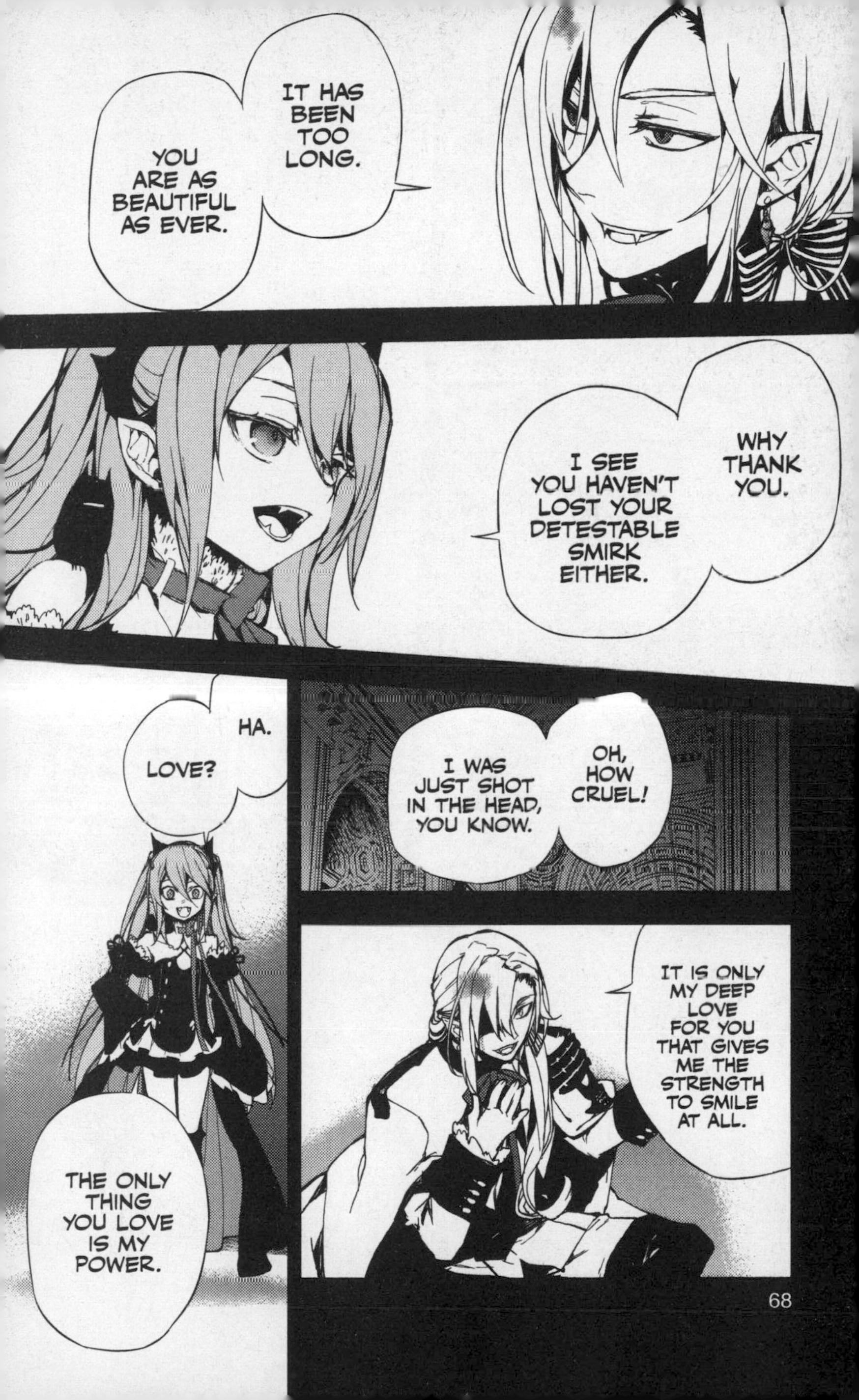
IT HAS BEEN TOO LONG.
YOU ARE AS BEAUTIFUL AS EVER.
WHY THANK YOU.
I SEE YOU HAVEN'T LOST YOUR DETESTABLE SMIRK EITHER.
OH, HOW CRUEL!
I WAS JUST SHOT IN THE HEAD, YOU KNOW.
IT IS ONLY MY DEEP LOVE FOR YOU THAT GIVES ME THE STRENGTH TO SMILE AT ALL.
HA.
LOVE?
THE ONLY THING YOU LOVE IS MY POWER.

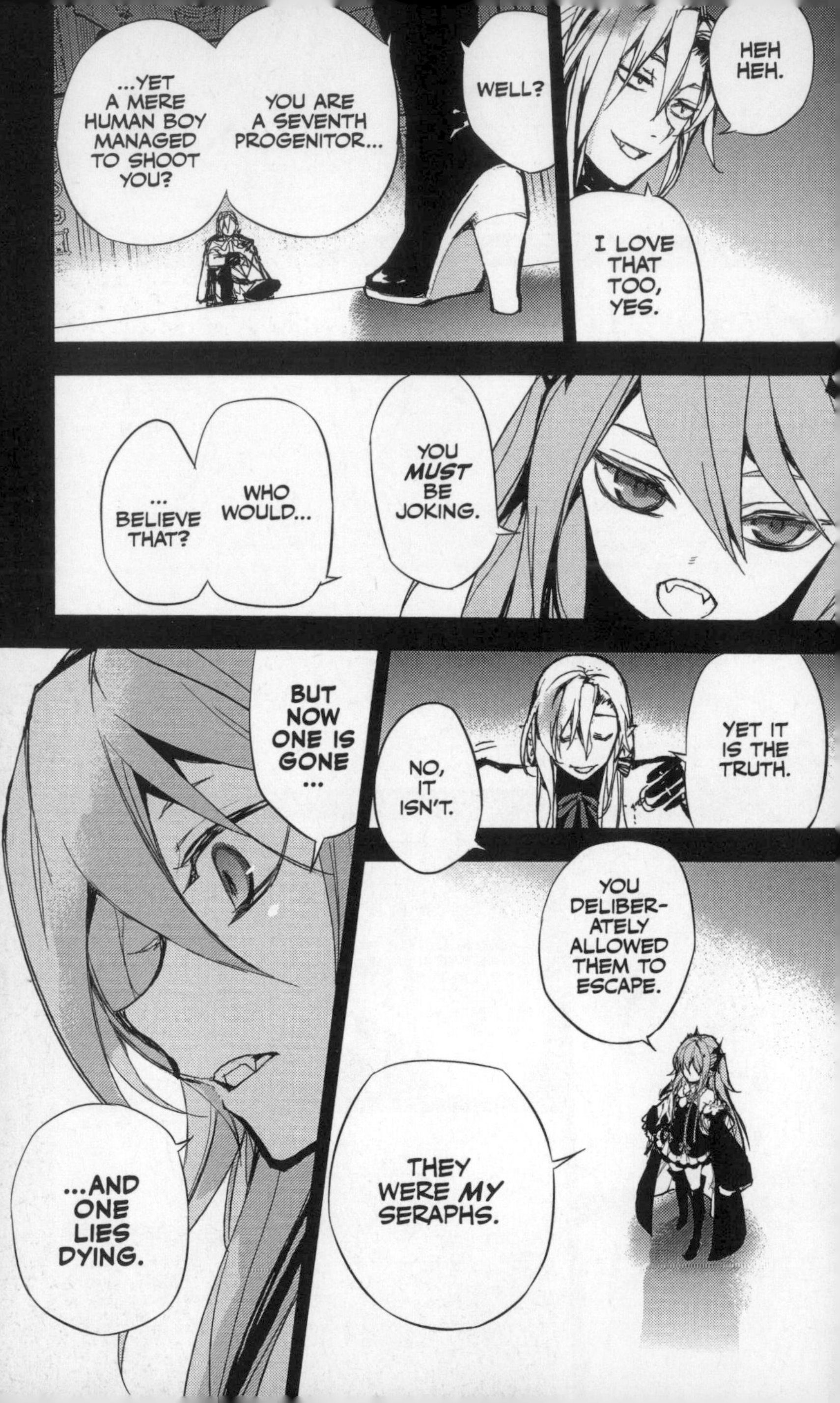
HEH HEH.
I LOVE THAT TOO, YES.
WELL?
YOU ARE A SEVENTH PROGENITOR...
...YET A MERE HUMAN BOY MANAGED TO SHOOT YOU?
YOU *MUST* BE JOKING.
WHO WOULD...
...BELIEVE THAT?
YET IT IS THE TRUTH.
NO, IT ISN'T.
YOU DELIBER-ATELY ALLOWED THEM TO ESCAPE.
THEY WERE *MY* SERAPHS.
BUT NOW ONE IS GONE...
...AND ONE LIES DYING.

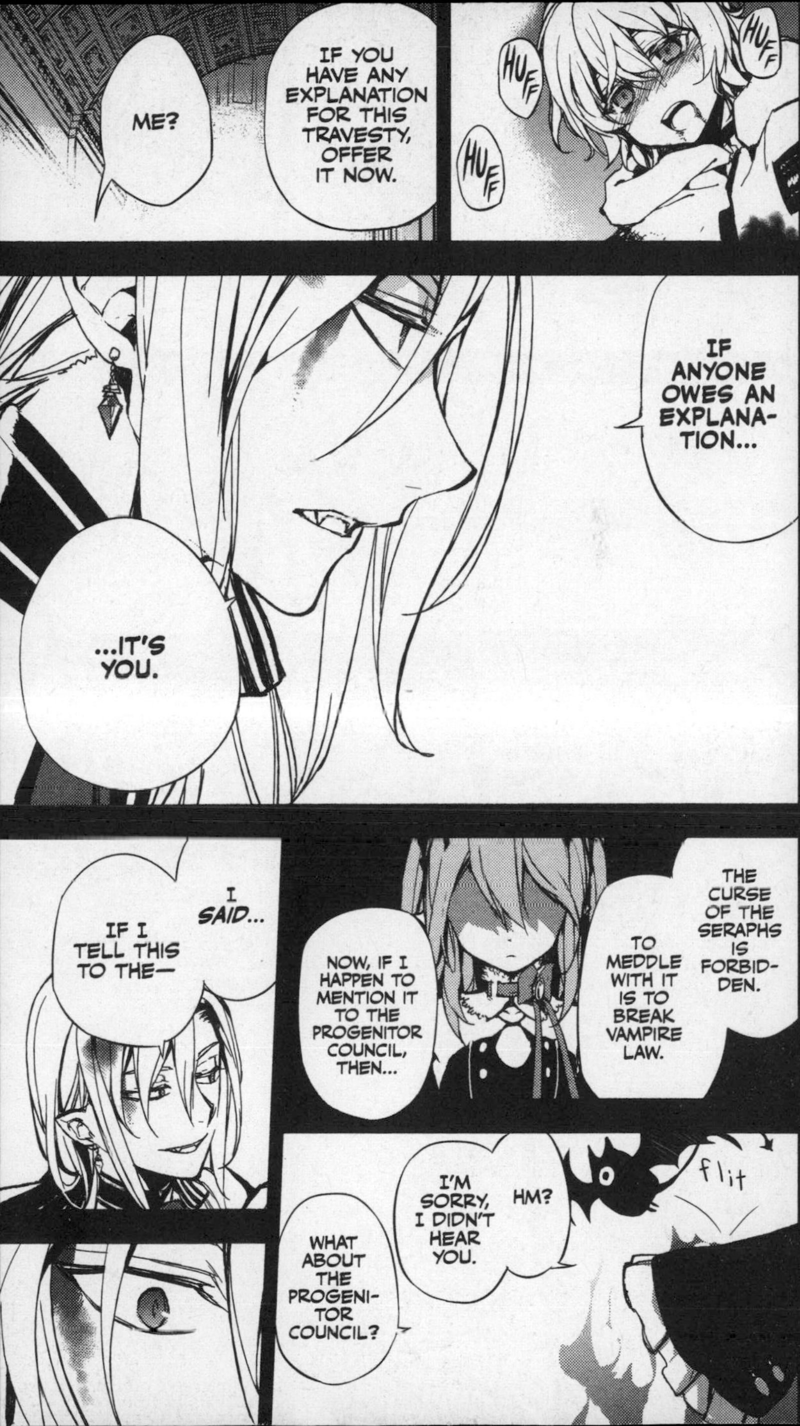
HUFF
HUFF
HUFF
IF YOU HAVE ANY EXPLANATION FOR THIS TRAVESTY, OFFER IT NOW.
ME?
IF ANYONE OWES AN EXPLANATION...
...IT'S YOU.
THE CURSE OF THE SERAPHS IS FORBIDDEN.
TO MEDDLE WITH IT IS TO BREAK VAMPIRE LAW.
NOW, IF I HAPPEN TO MENTION IT TO THE PROGENITOR COUNCIL, THEN...
flit
HM?
I'M SORRY, I DIDN'T HEAR YOU.
WHAT ABOUT THE PROGENITOR COUNCIL?
I SAID...
IF I TELL THIS TO THE—

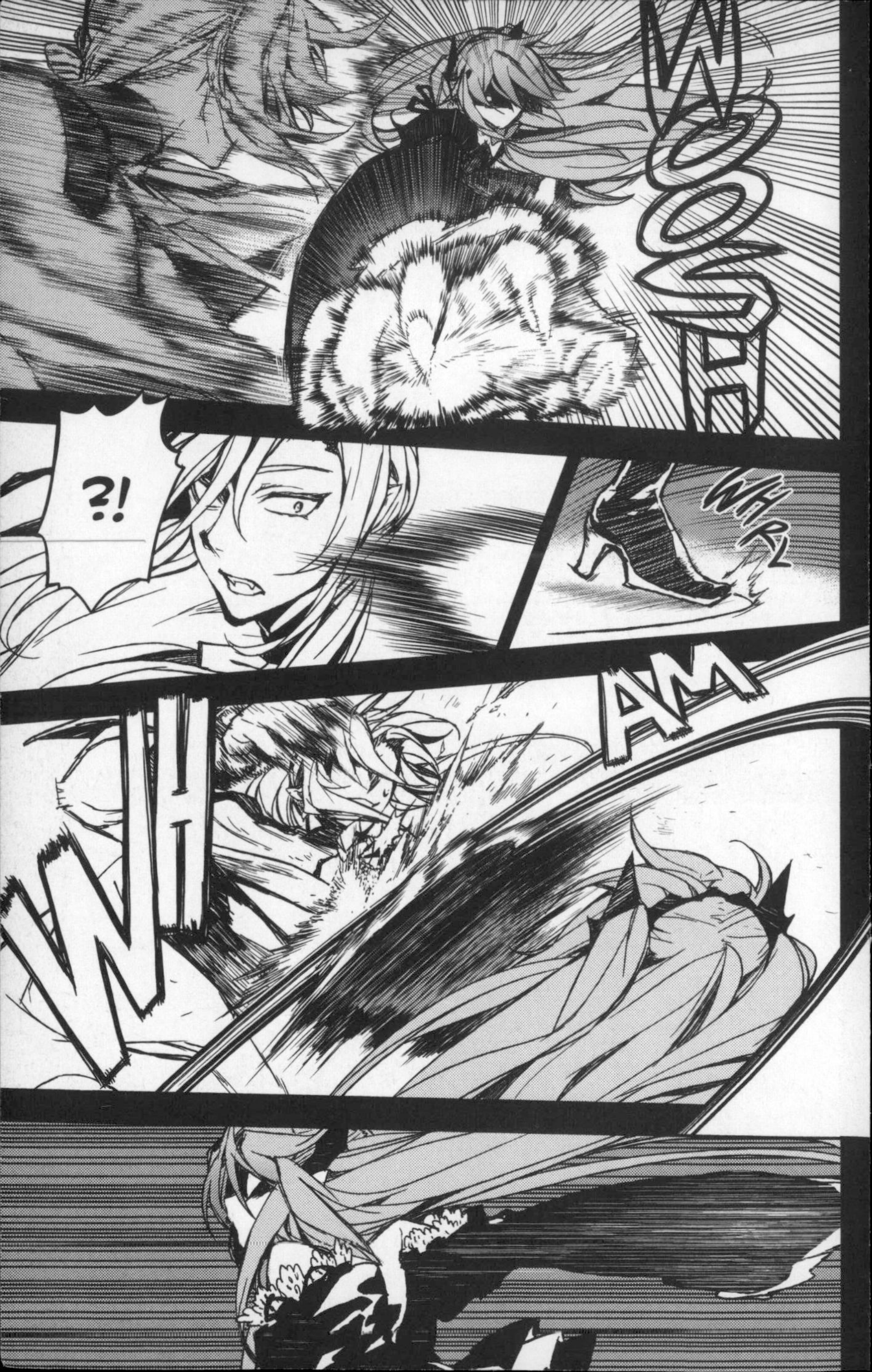
WOOSH
WHRL
?!
WHAM

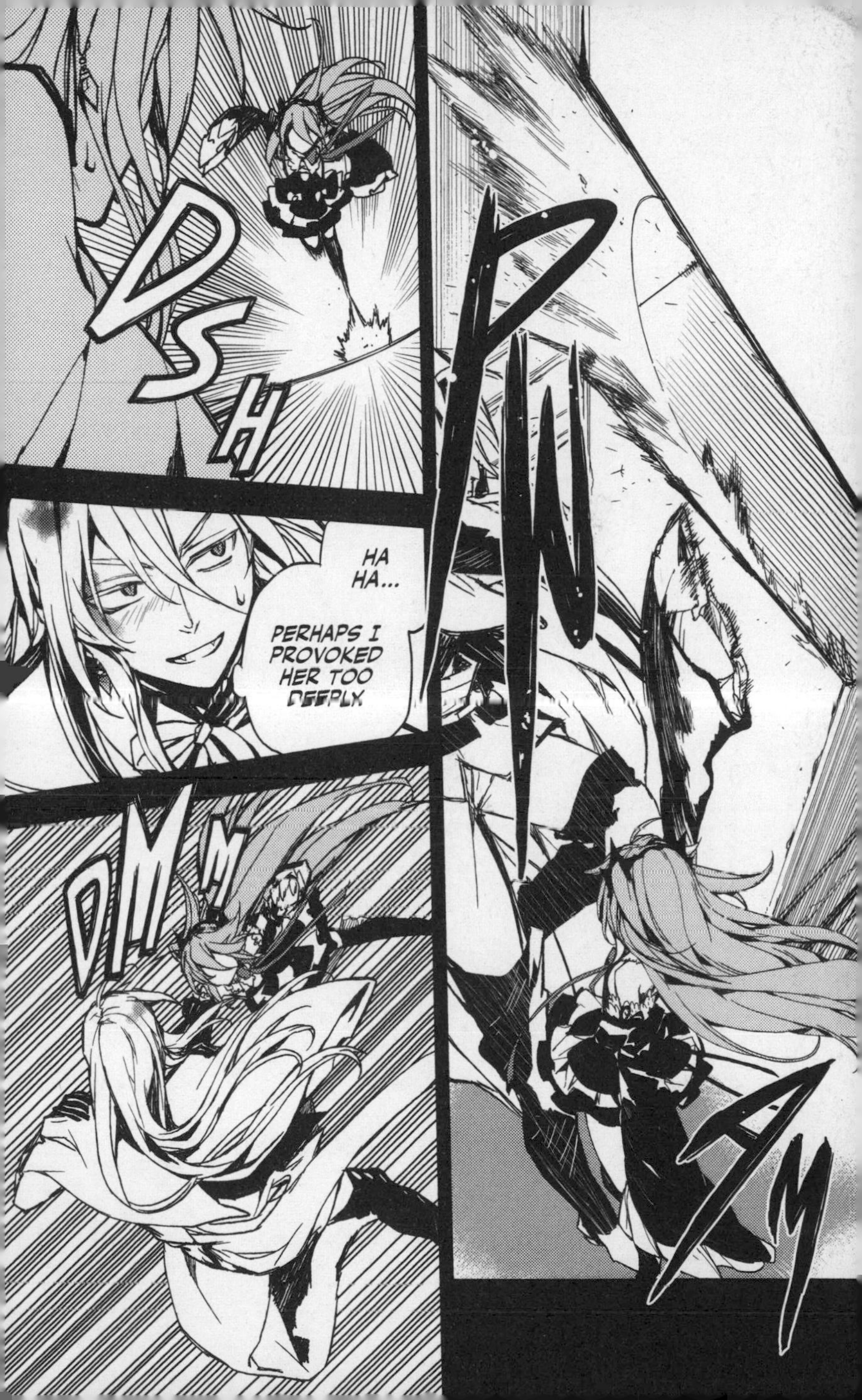
DSH
HA HA...
PERHAPS I PROVOKED HER TOO DEEPLY
DMMM

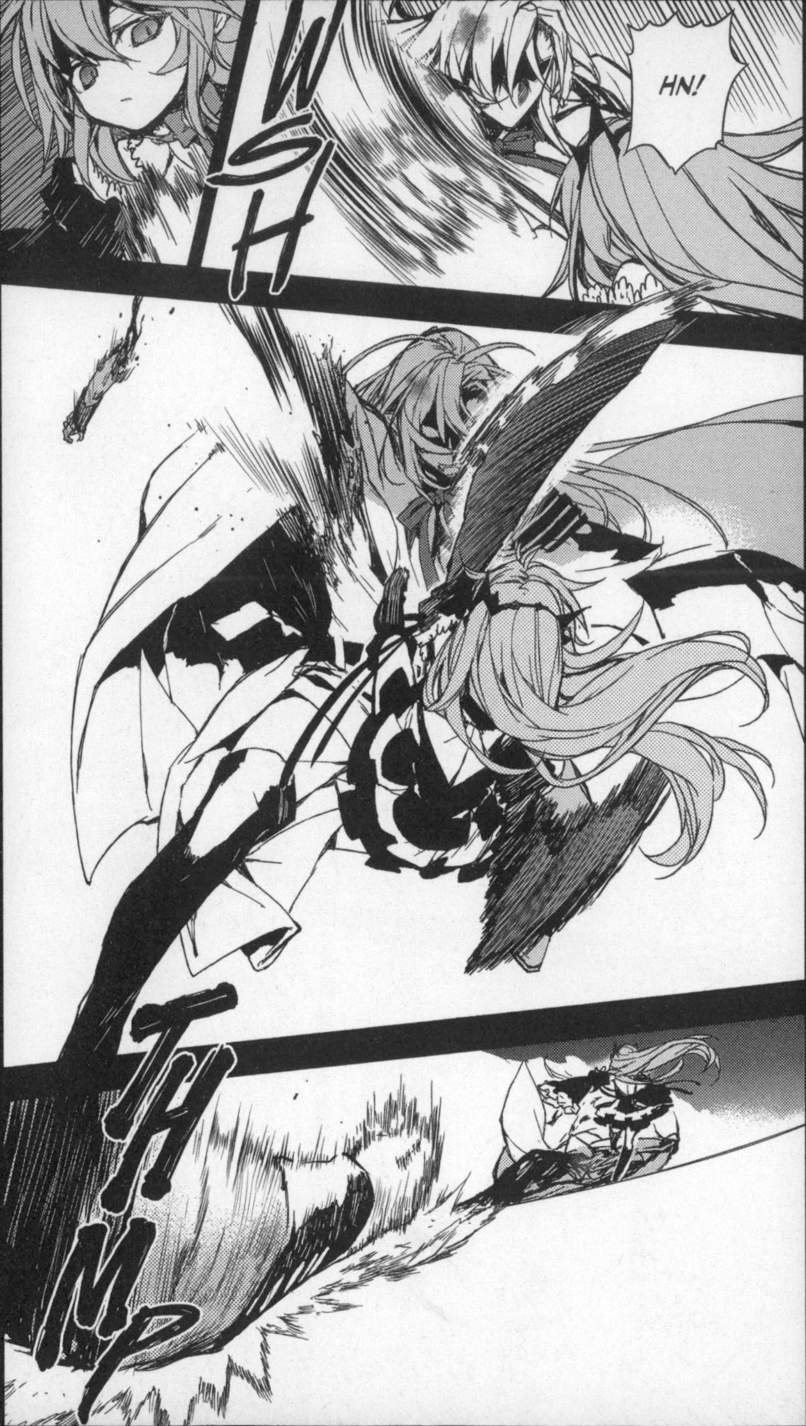
HN!
WSH
THMP

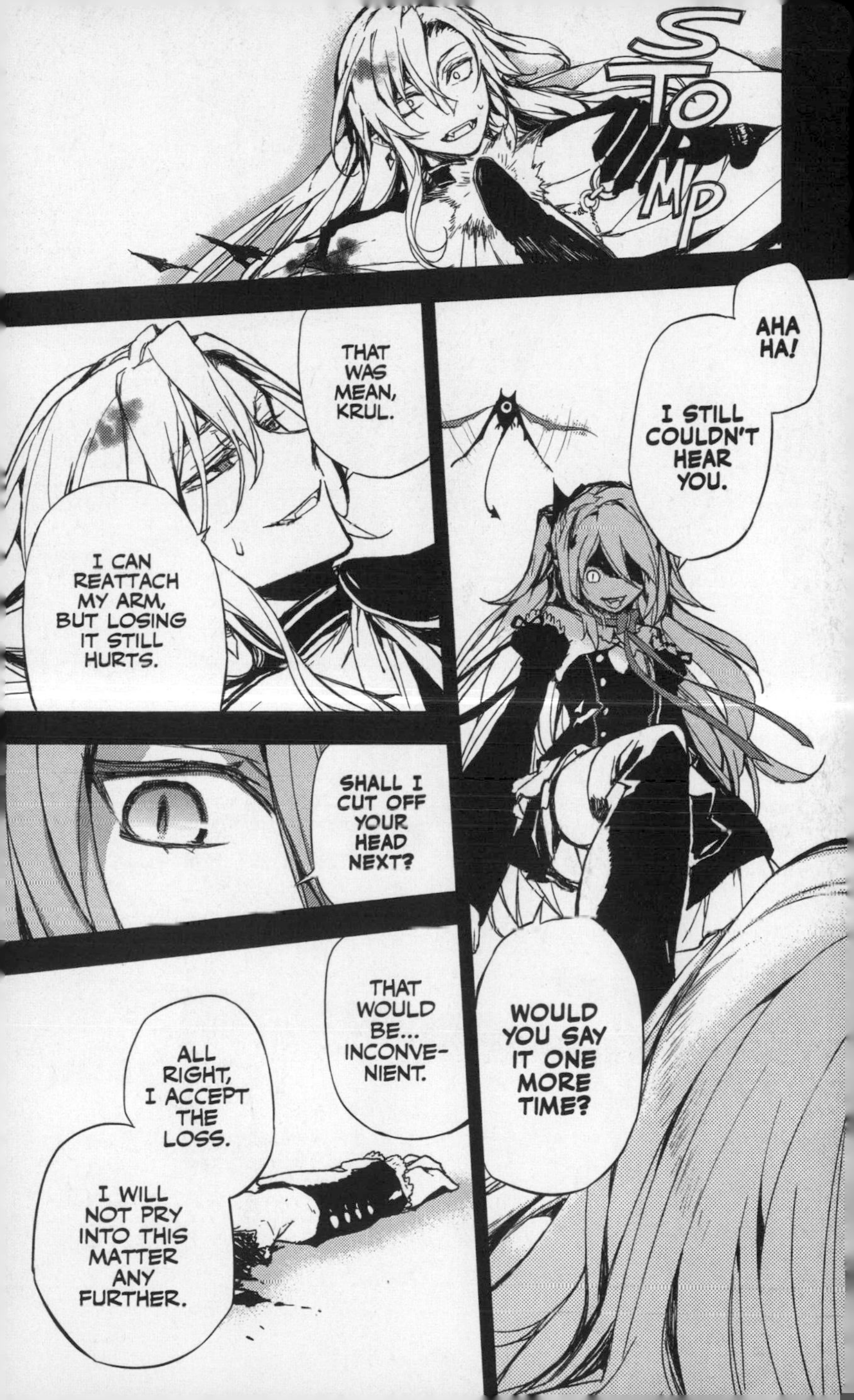
STOMP
AHA HA!
I STILL COULDN'T HEAR YOU.
THAT WAS MEAN, KRUL.
I CAN REATTACH MY ARM, BUT LOSING IT STILL HURTS.
SHALL I CUT OFF YOUR HEAD NEXT?
WOULD YOU SAY IT ONE MORE TIME?
THAT WOULD BE... INCONVE-NIENT.
ALL RIGHT, I ACCEPT THE LOSS.
I WILL NOT PRY INTO THIS MATTER ANY FURTHER.

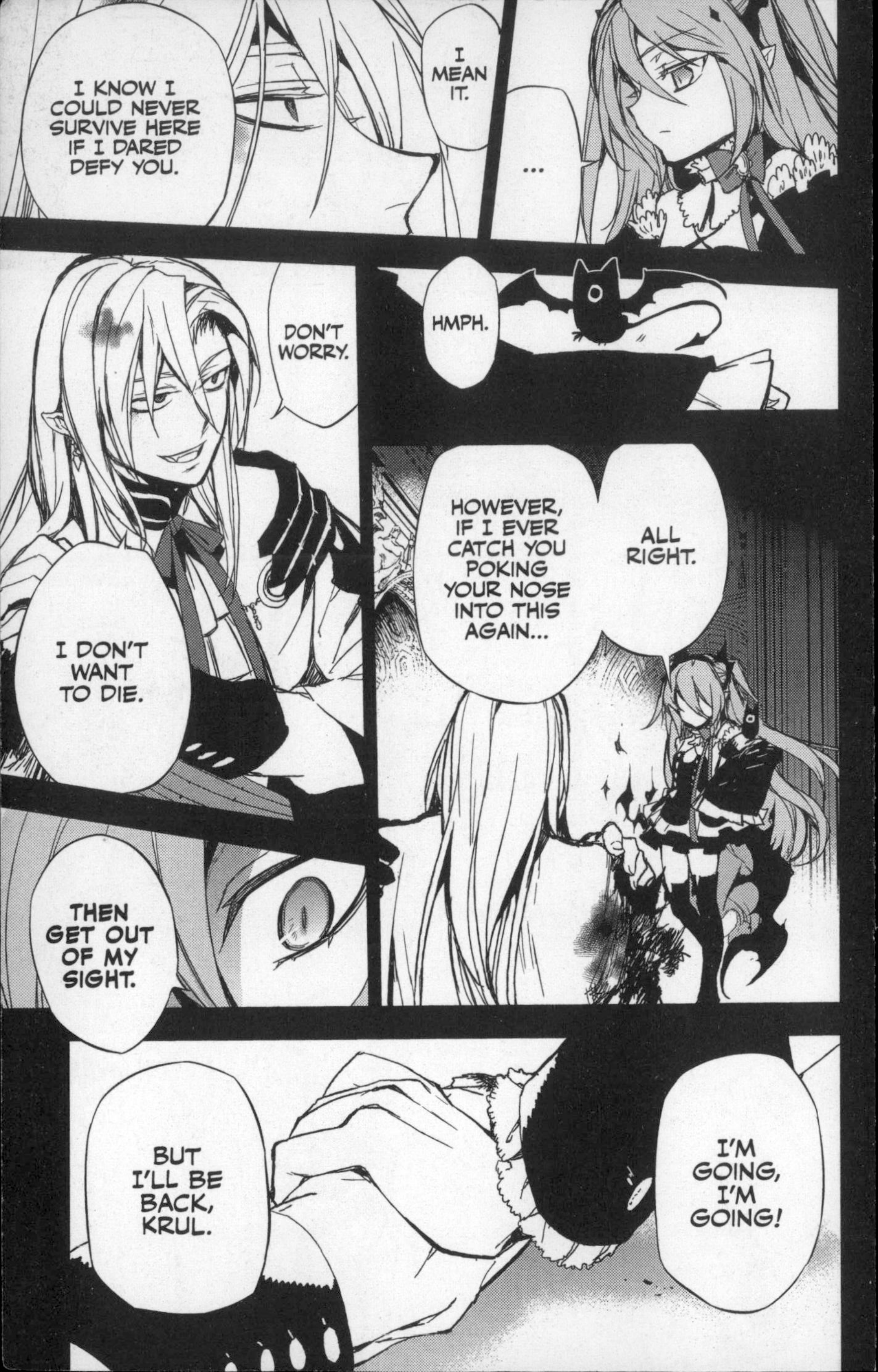
I MEAN IT.
...
I KNOW I COULD NEVER SURVIVE HERE IF I DARED DEFY YOU.
HMPH.
DON'T WORRY.
I DON'T WANT TO DIE.
ALL RIGHT.
HOWEVER, IF I EVER CATCH YOU POKING YOUR NOSE INTO THIS AGAIN...
THEN GET OUT OF MY SIGHT.
I'M GOING, I'M GOING!
BUT I'LL BE BACK, KRUL.

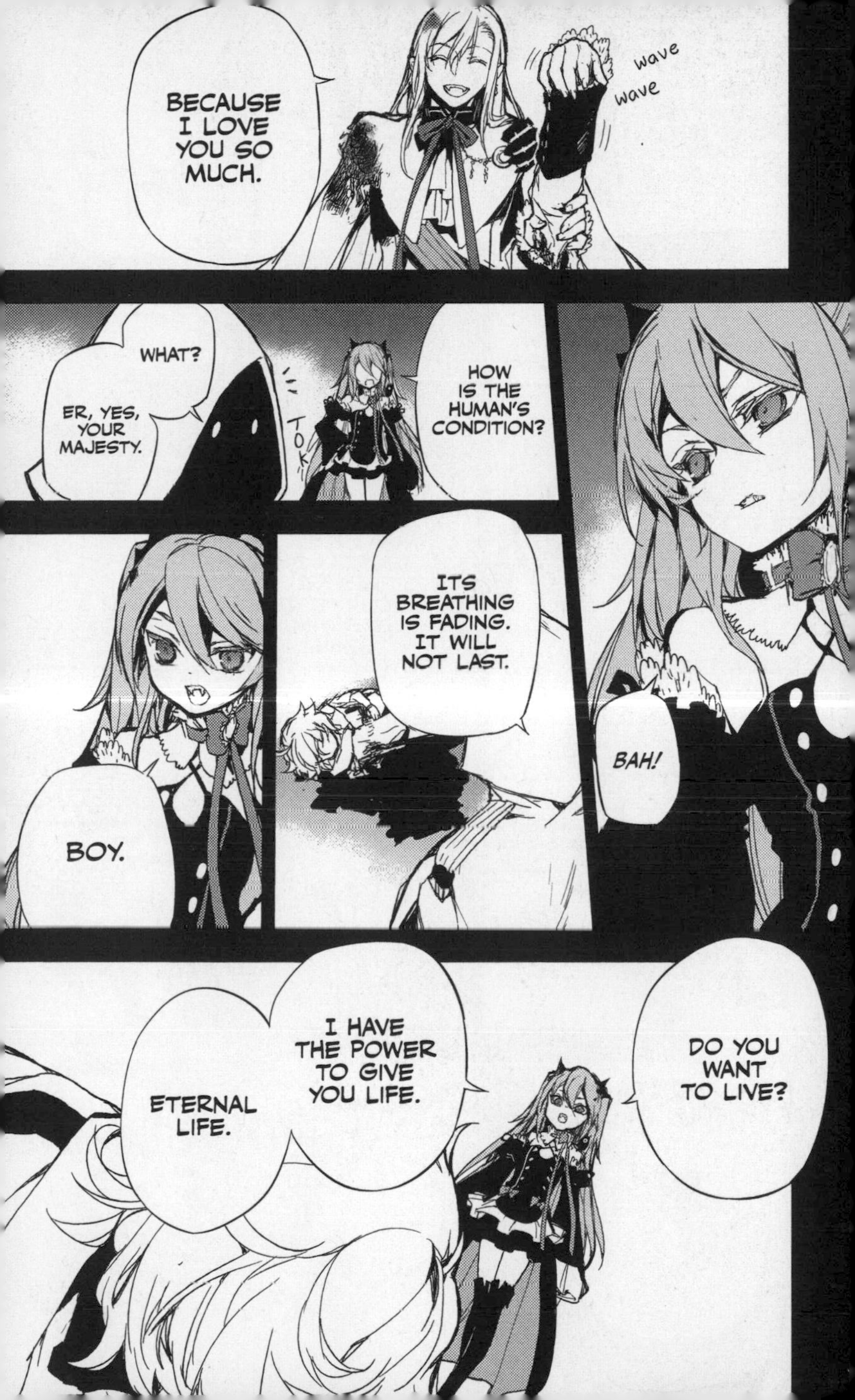
wave
wave
BECAUSE I LOVE YOU SO MUCH.
BAH!
HOW IS THE HUMAN'S CONDITION?
TOK
WHAT?
ER, YES, YOUR MAJESTY.
ITS BREATHING IS FADING. IT WILL NOT LAST.
BOY.
DO YOU WANT TO LIVE?
I HAVE THE POWER TO GIVE YOU LIFE.
ETERNAL LIFE.

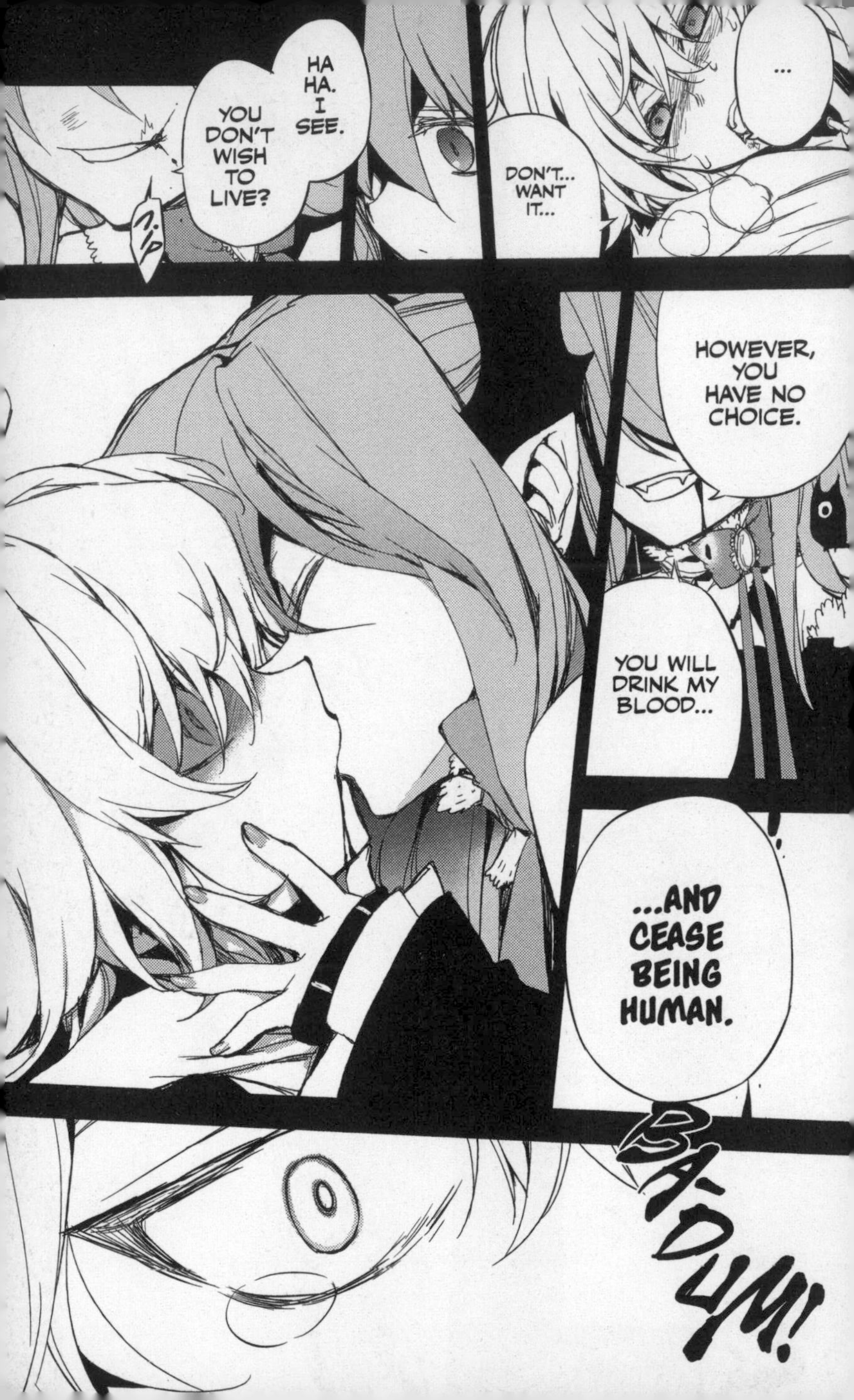
...
DON'T... WANT IT...
HA HA. I SEE.
YOU DON'T WISH TO LIVE?
HOWEVER, YOU HAVE NO CHOICE.
YOU WILL DRINK MY BLOOD...
...AND CEASE BEING HUMAN.
BA-DUM!

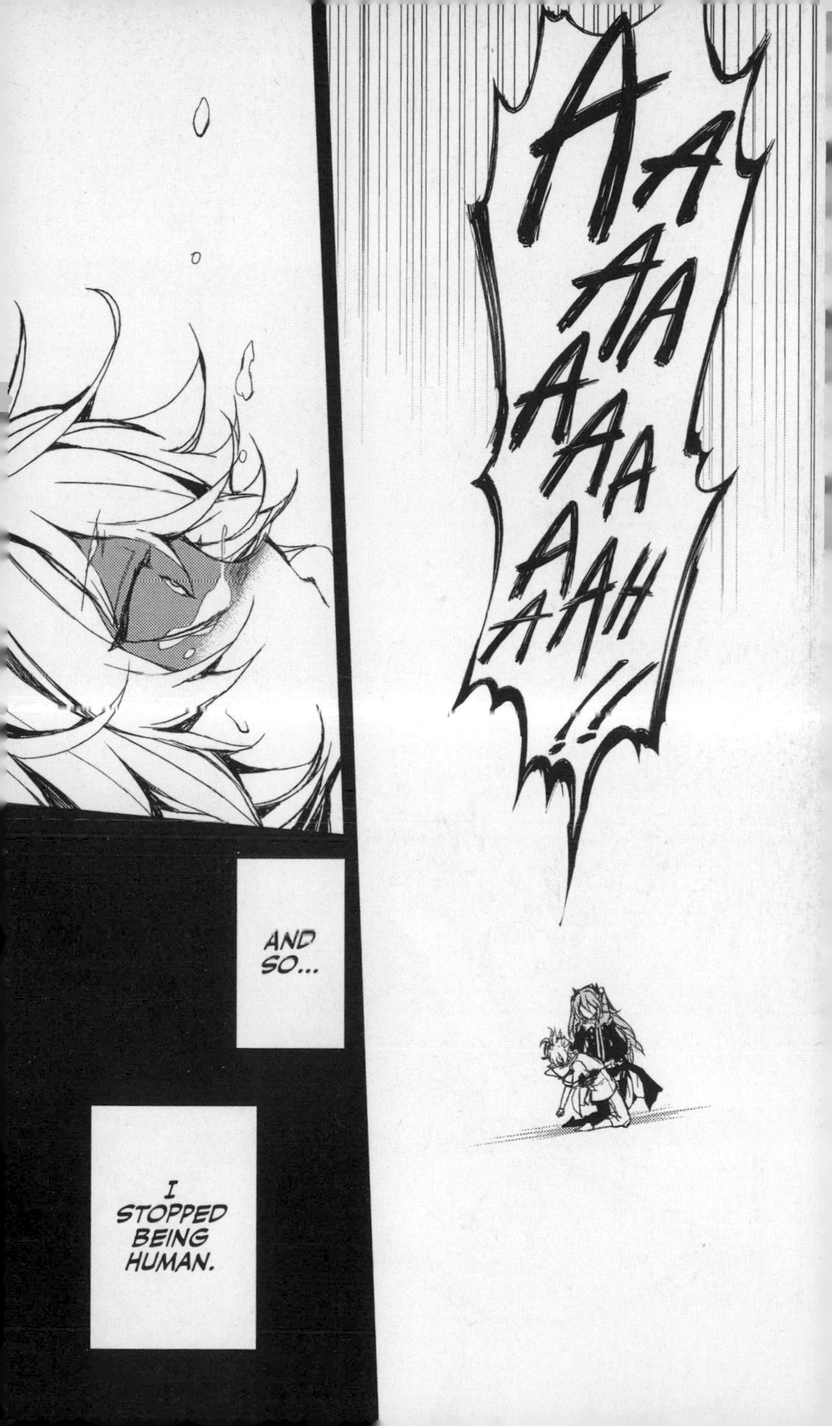
AAAAAAAAAAAAH!!!
AND SO...
I STOPPED BEING HUMAN.

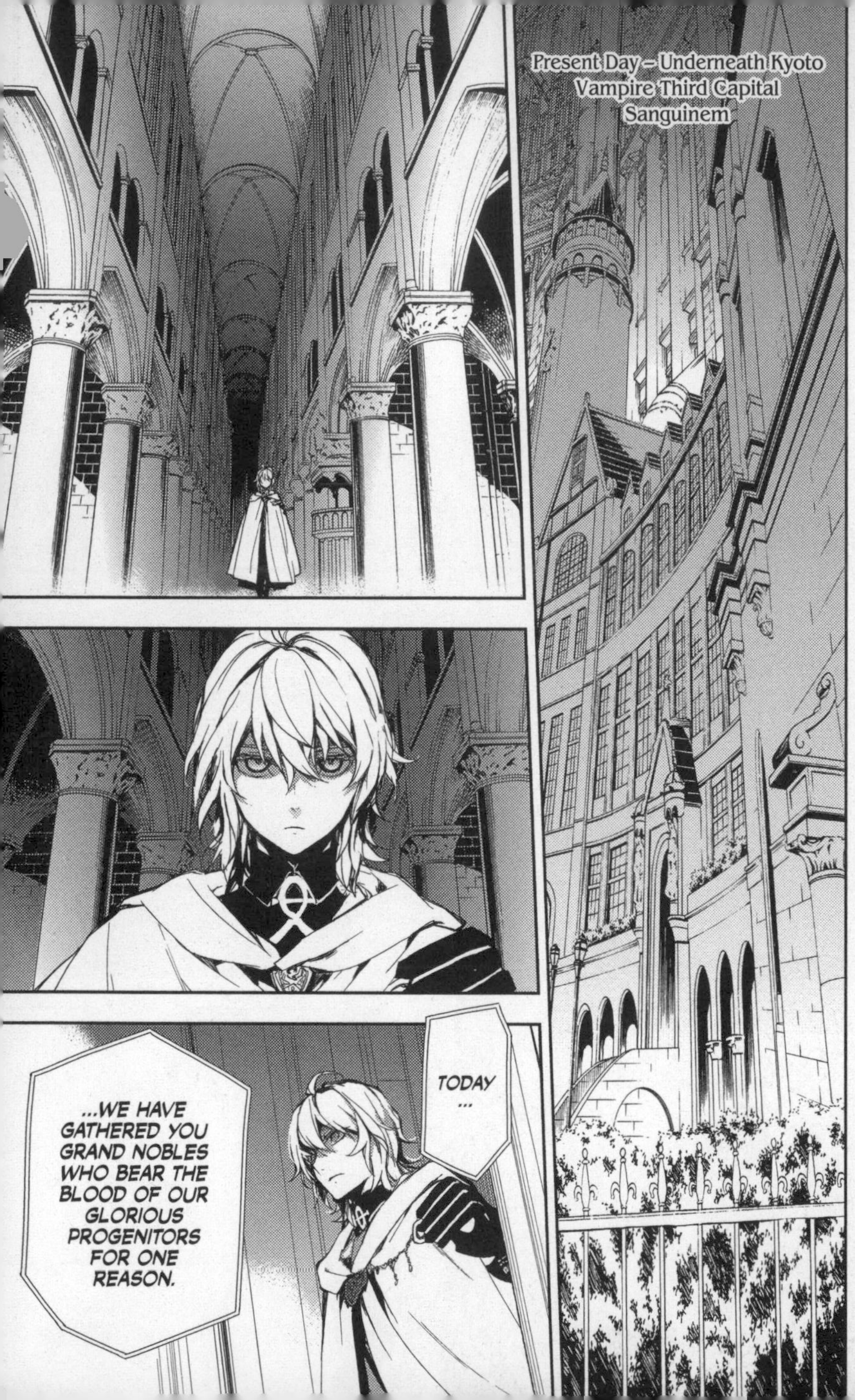
Present Day – Underneath Kyoto
Vampire Third Capital
Sanguinem
TODAY...
...WE HAVE GATHERED YOU GRAND NOBLES WHO BEAR THE BLOOD OF OUR GLORIOUS PROGENITORS FOR ONE REASON.

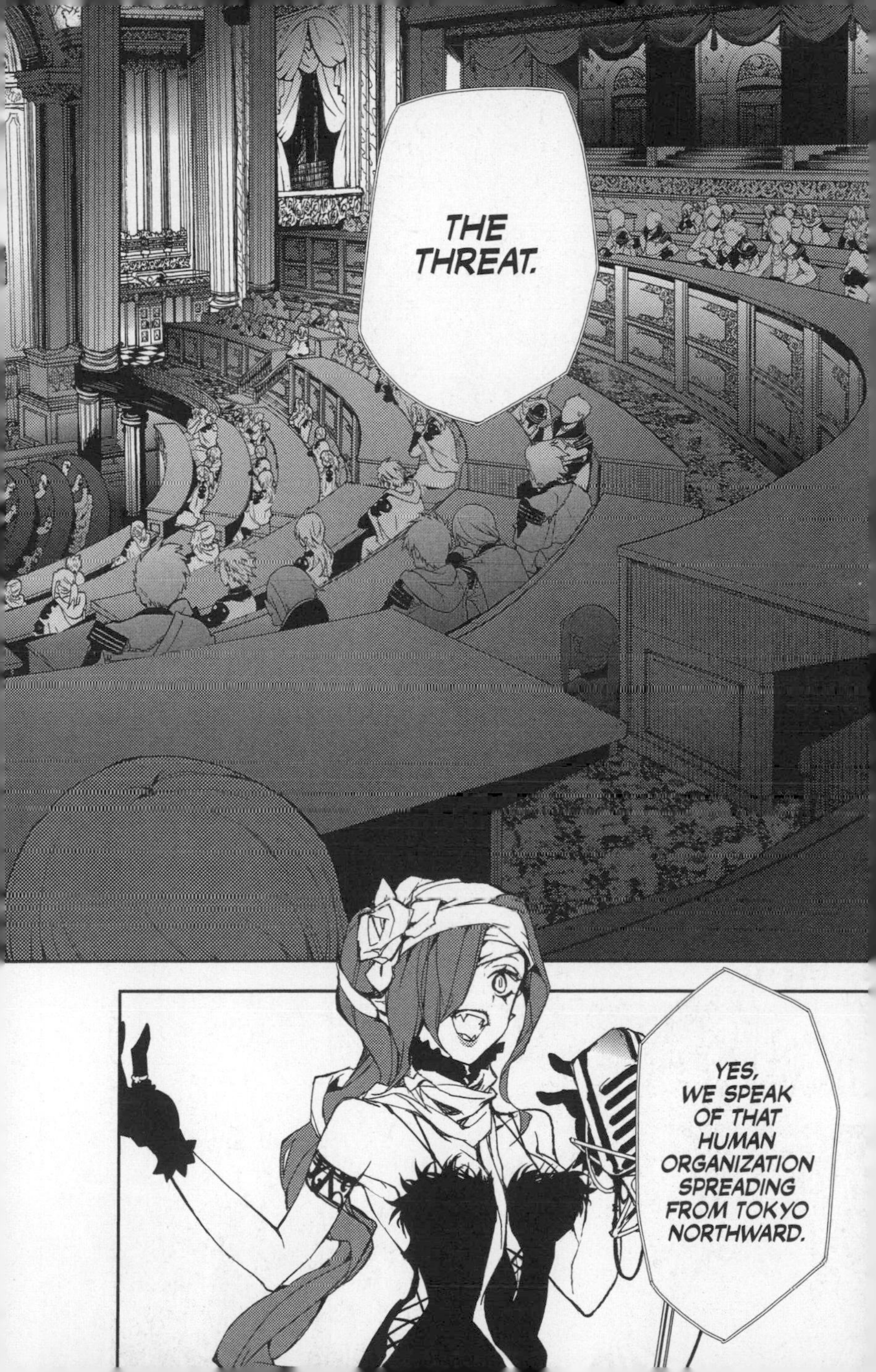
THE THREAT.
YES, WE SPEAK OF THAT HUMAN ORGANIZATION SPREADING FROM TOKYO NORTHWARD.

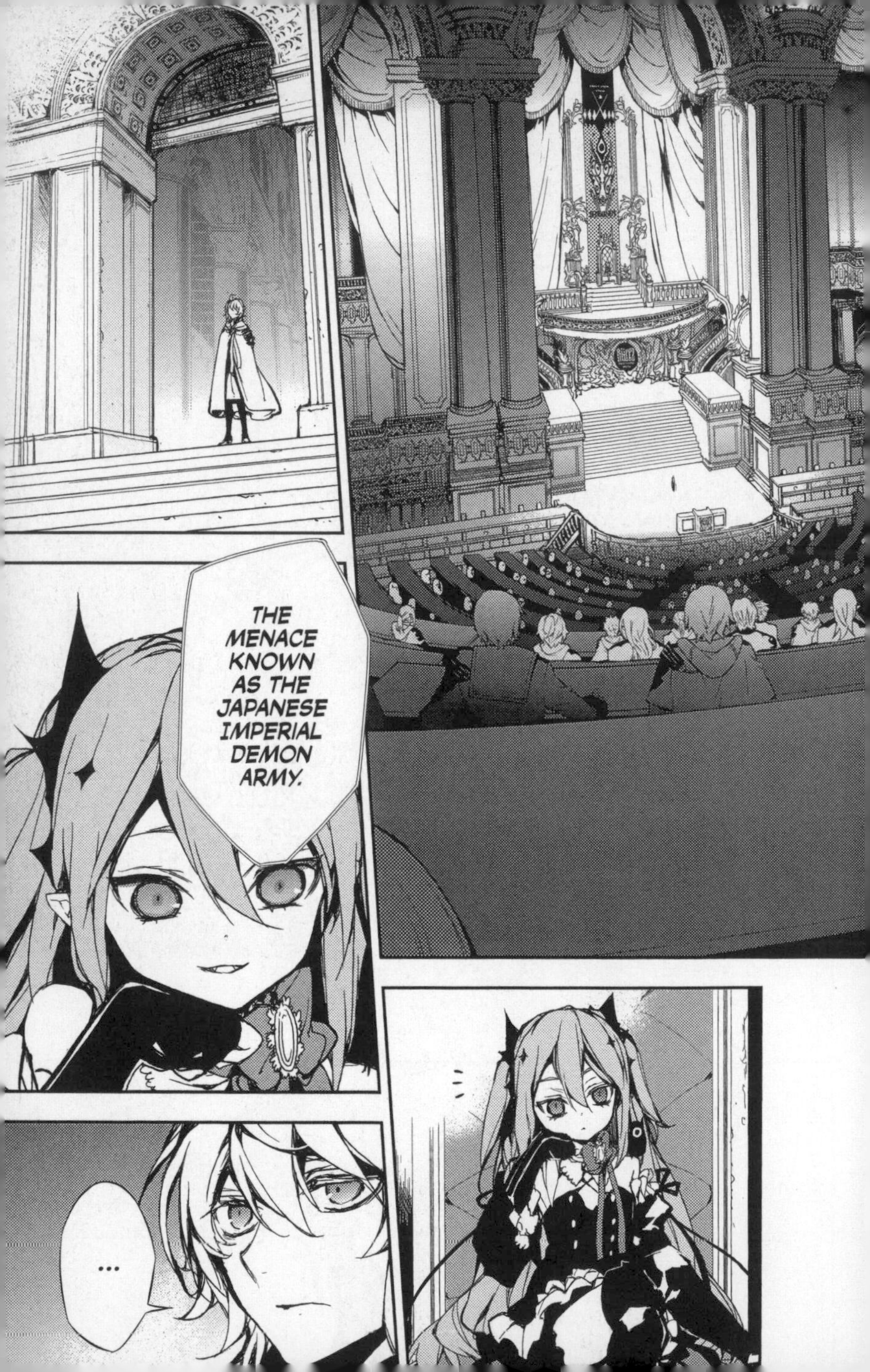
THE MENACE KNOWN AS THE JAPANESE IMPERIAL DEMON ARMY.
...

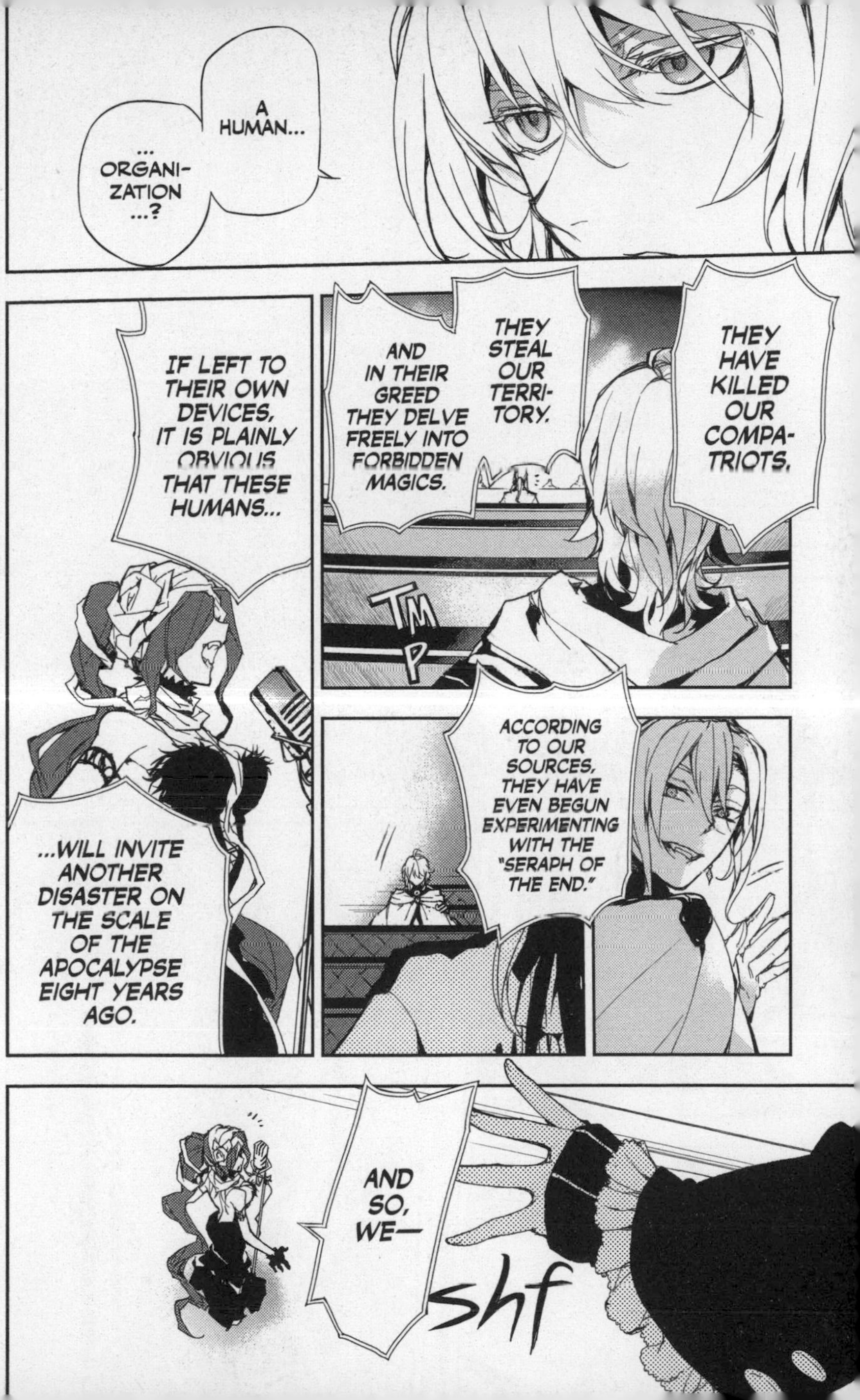
A HUMAN...
...ORGANIZATION...?
THEY HAVE KILLED OUR COMPATRIOTS.
THEY STEAL OUR TERRITORY.
AND IN THEIR GREED THEY DELVE FREELY INTO FORBIDDEN MAGICS.
TMP
ACCORDING TO OUR SOURCES, THEY HAVE EVEN BEGUN EXPERIMENTING WITH THE "SERAPH OF THE END."
IF LEFT TO THEIR OWN DEVICES, IT IS PLAINLY OBVIOUS THAT THESE HUMANS...
...WILL INVITE ANOTHER DISASTER ON THE SCALE OF THE APOCALYPSE EIGHT YEARS AGO.
AND SO, WE—
shf

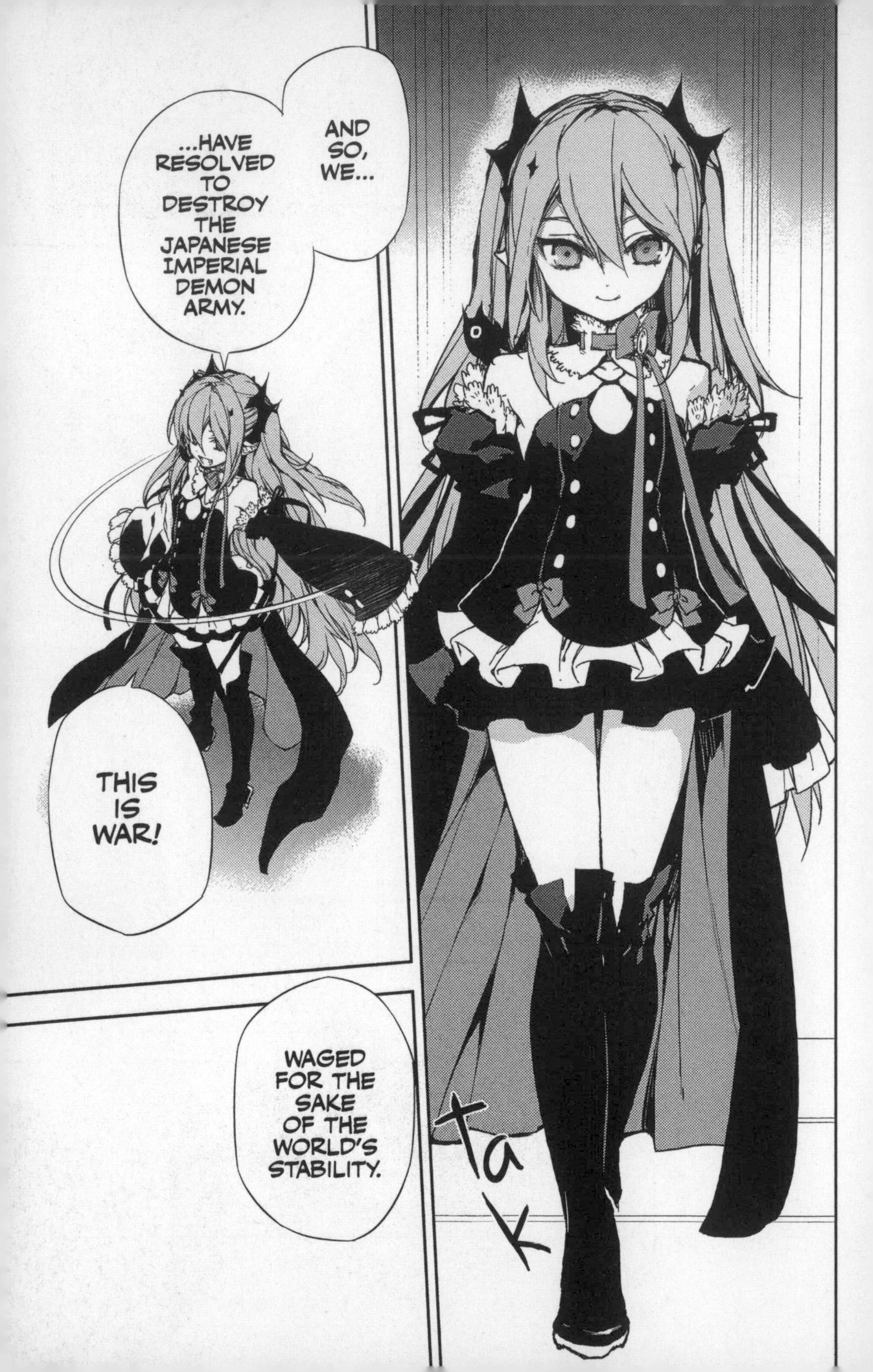
tak
AND SO, WE...
...HAVE RESOLVED TO DESTROY THE JAPANESE IMPERIAL DEMON ARMY.
THIS IS WAR!
WAGED FOR THE SAKE OF THE WORLD'S STABILITY.

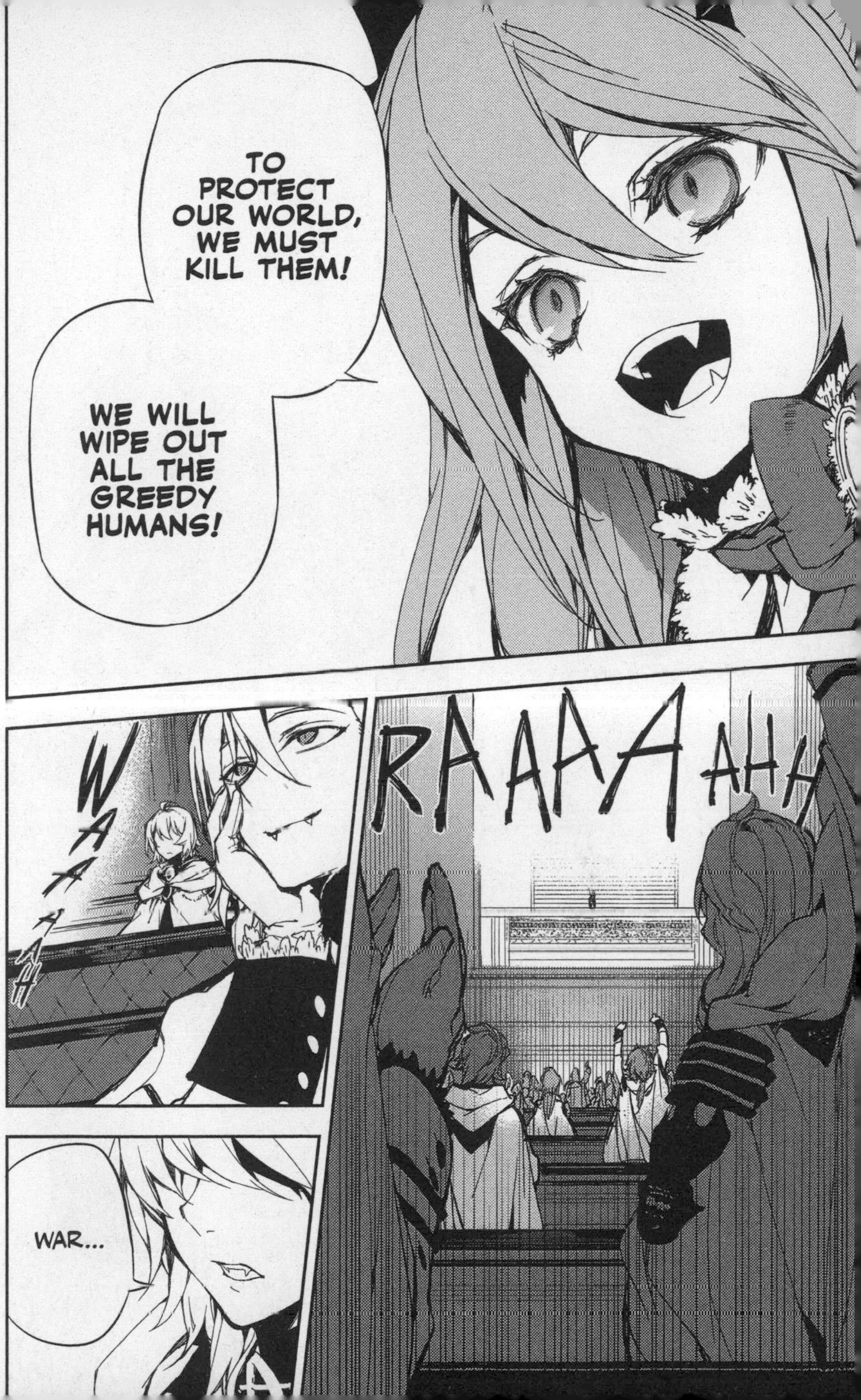
TO PROTECT OUR WORLD, WE MUST KILL THEM!
WE WILL WIPE OUT ALL THE GREEDY HUMANS!
RAAAAAHH
WAAAAH
WAR...

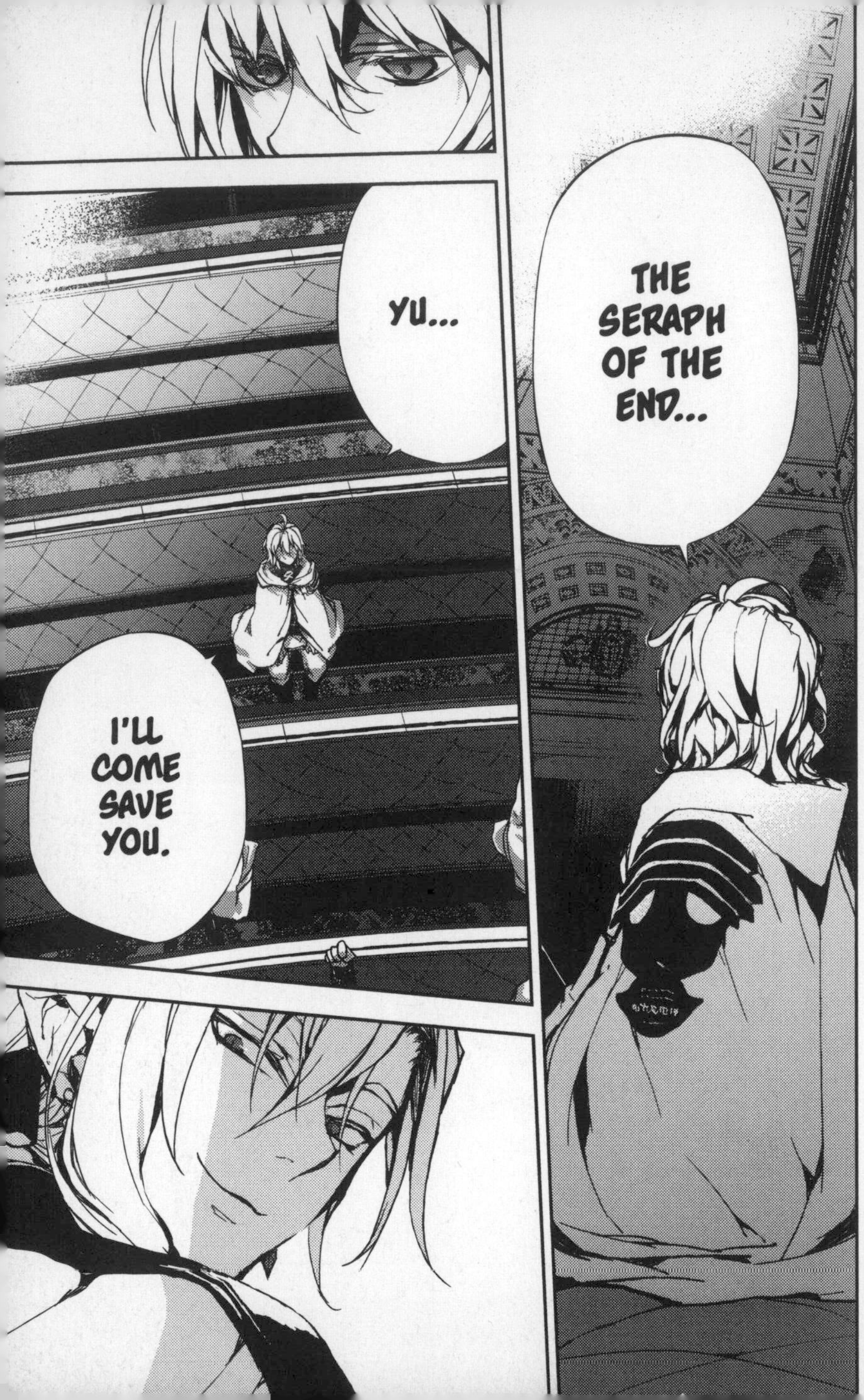
THE SERAPH OF THE END...
YU...
I'LL COME SAVE YOU.

Shibuya, Tokyo

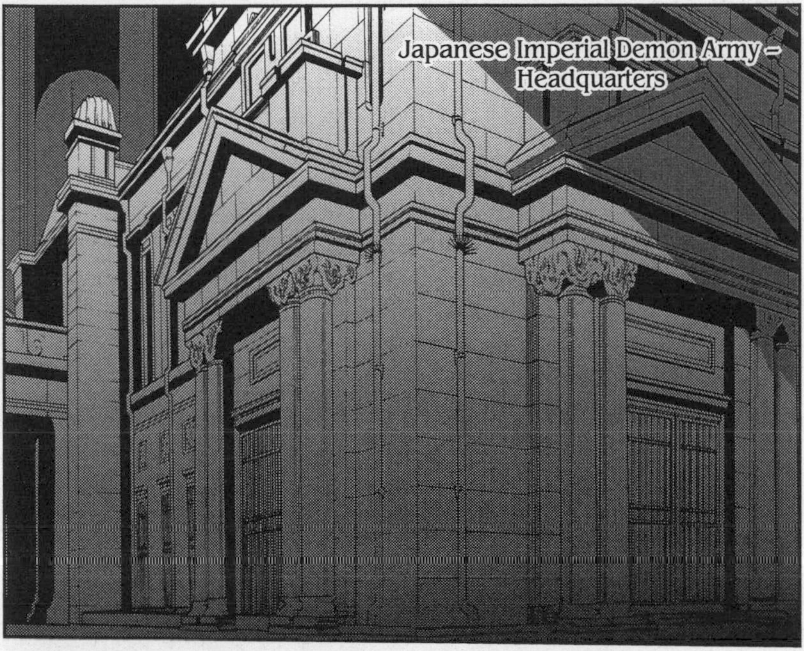
Japanese Imperial Demon Army –
Headquarters

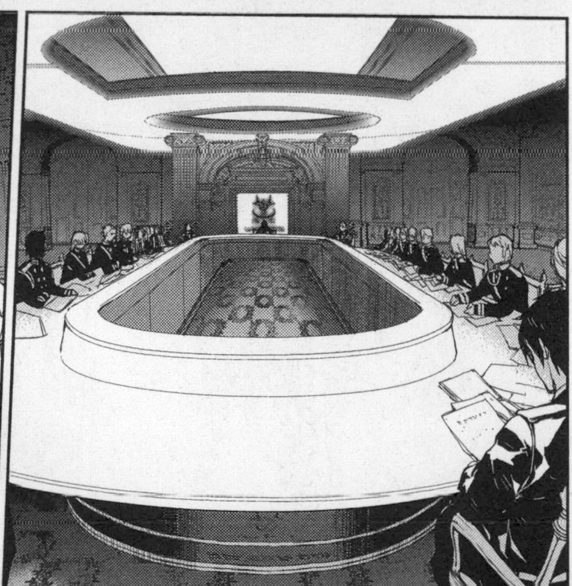

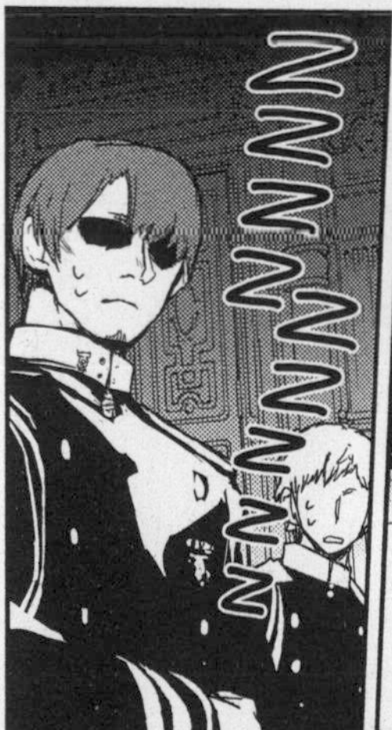

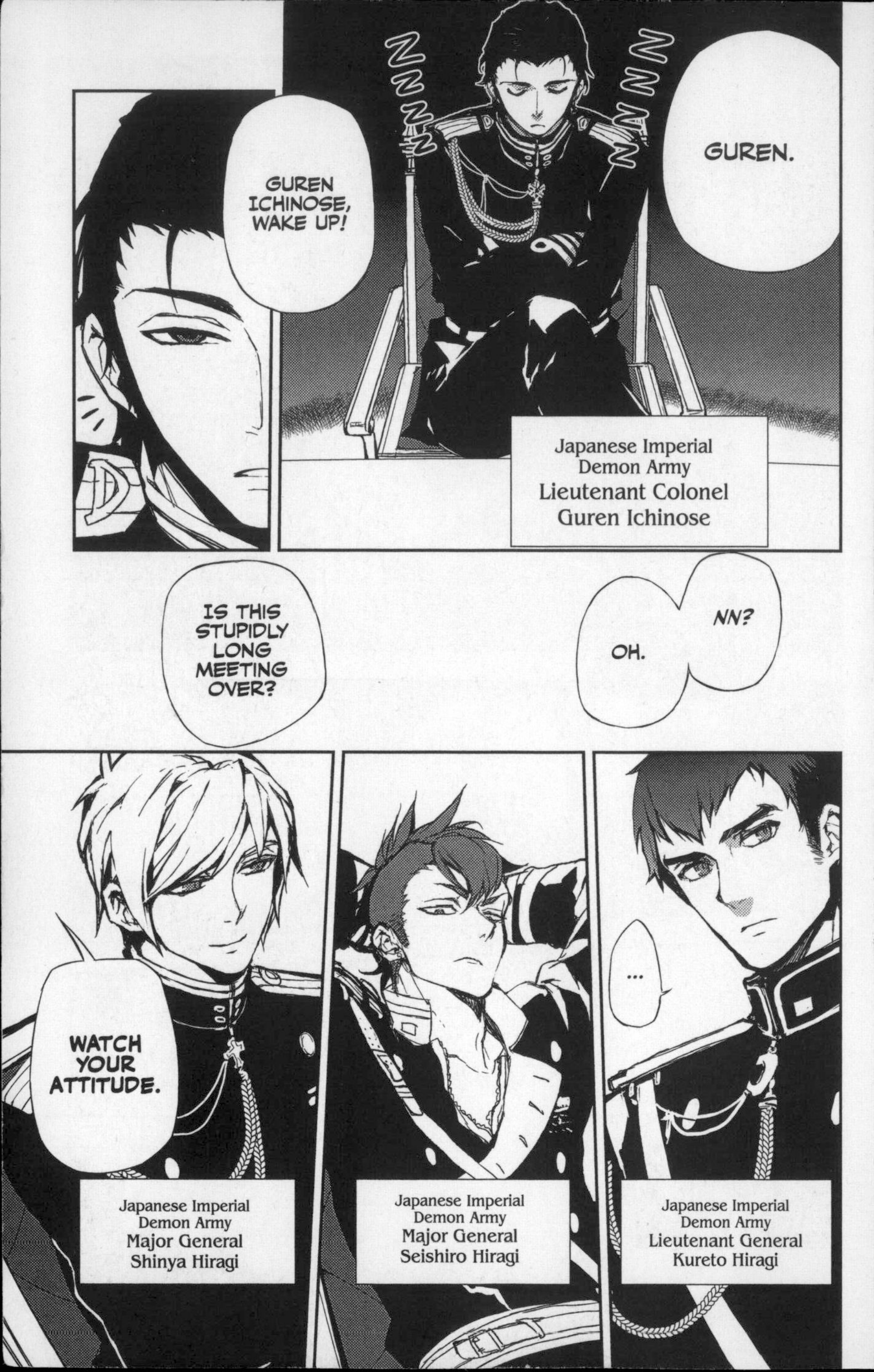
ZZZZ ZZZZ
GUREN.
Japanese Imperial Demon Army Lieutenant Colonel Guren Ichinose
GUREN ICHINOSE, WAKE UP!
NN?
OH.
IS THIS STUPIDLY LONG MEETING OVER?
...
Japanese Imperial Demon Army Lieutenant General Kureto Hiragi
Japanese Imperial Demon Army Major General Seishiro Hiragi
WATCH YOUR ATTITUDE.
Japanese Imperial Demon Army Major General Shinya Hiragi

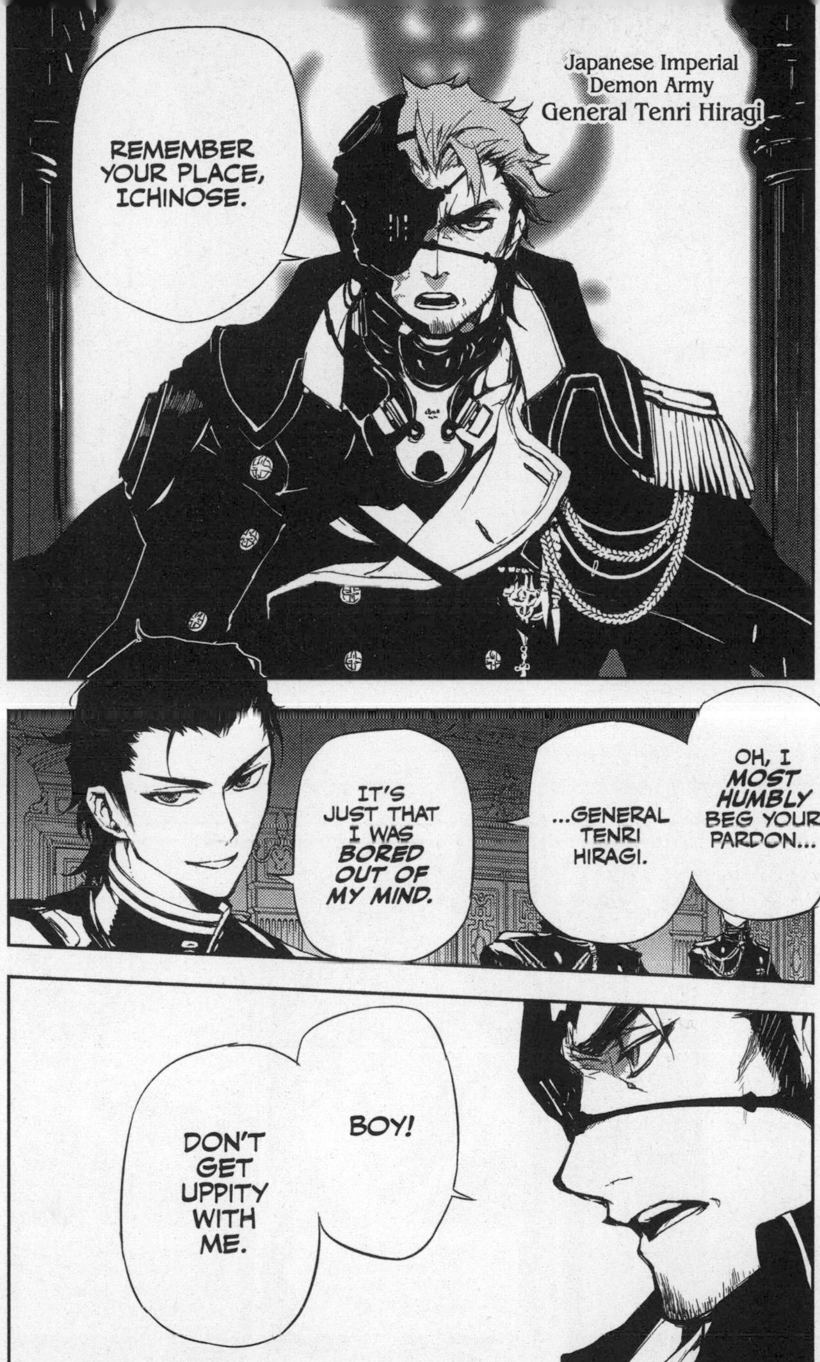
Japanese Imperial Demon Army General Tenri Hiragi
REMEMBER YOUR PLACE, ICHINOSE.
OH, I *MOST HUMBLY* BEG YOUR PARDON...
...GENERAL TENRI HIRAGI.
IT'S JUST THAT I WAS *BORED OUT OF MY MIND.*
BOY!
DON'T GET UPPITY WITH ME.

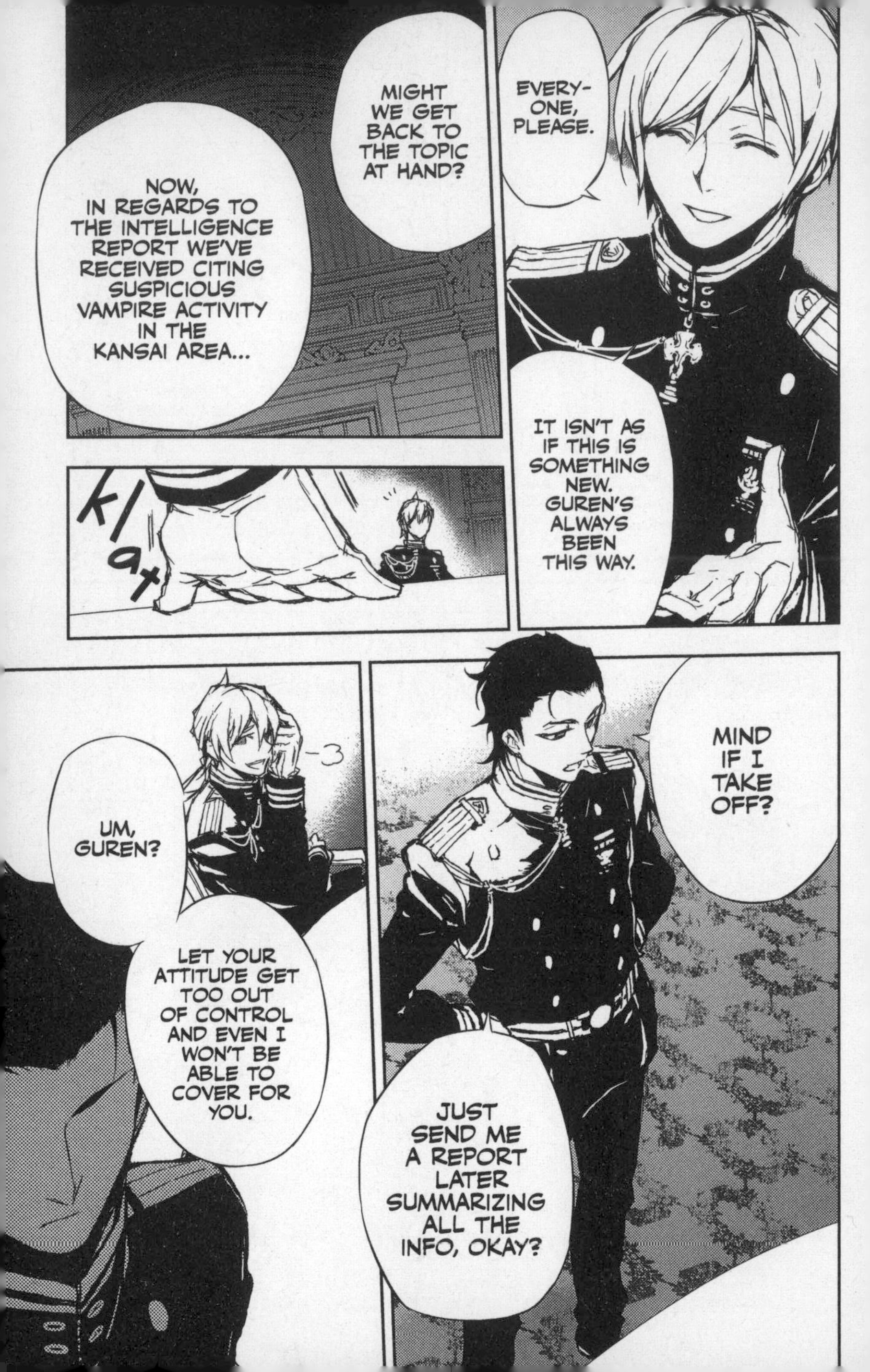
EVERY-ONE, PLEASE.
IT ISN'T AS IF THIS IS SOMETHING NEW. GUREN'S ALWAYS BEEN THIS WAY.
MIGHT WE GET BACK TO THE TOPIC AT HAND?
NOW, IN REGARDS TO THE INTELLIGENCE REPORT WE'VE RECEIVED CITING SUSPICIOUS VAMPIRE ACTIVITY IN THE KANSAI AREA...
klat
MIND IF I TAKE OFF?
JUST SEND ME A REPORT LATER SUMMARIZING ALL THE INFO, OKAY?
UM, GUREN?
LET YOUR ATTITUDE GET TOO OUT OF CONTROL AND EVEN I WON'T BE ABLE TO COVER FOR YOU.

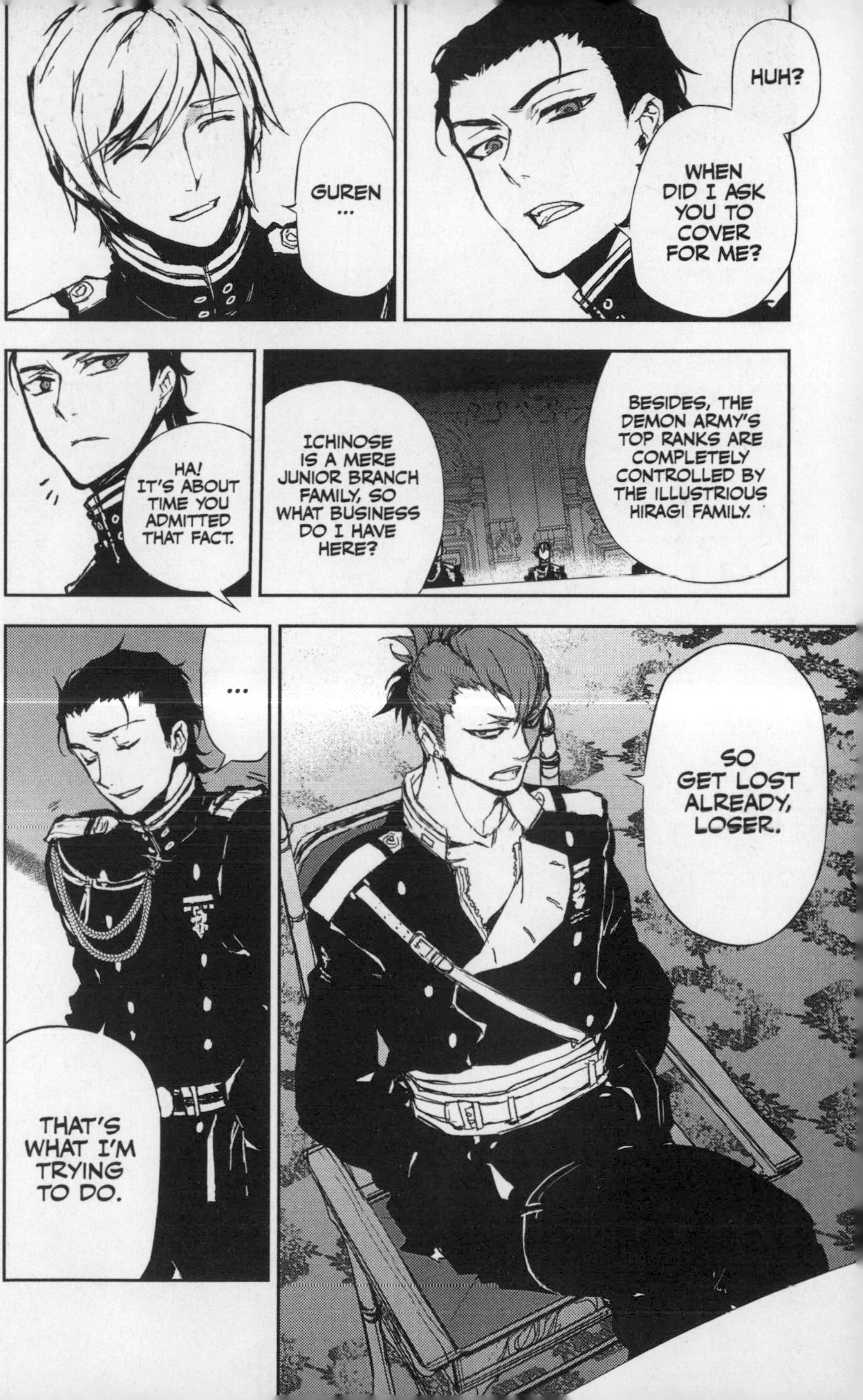
HUH?
WHEN DID I ASK YOU TO COVER FOR ME?
GUREN ...
BESIDES, THE DEMON ARMY'S TOP RANKS ARE COMPLETELY CONTROLLED BY THE ILLUSTRIOUS HIRAGI FAMILY.
ICHINOSE IS A MERE JUNIOR BRANCH FAMILY, SO WHAT BUSINESS DO I HAVE HERE?
HA! IT'S ABOUT TIME YOU ADMITTED THAT FACT.
SO GET LOST ALREADY, LOSER.
...
THAT'S WHAT I'M TRYING TO DO.

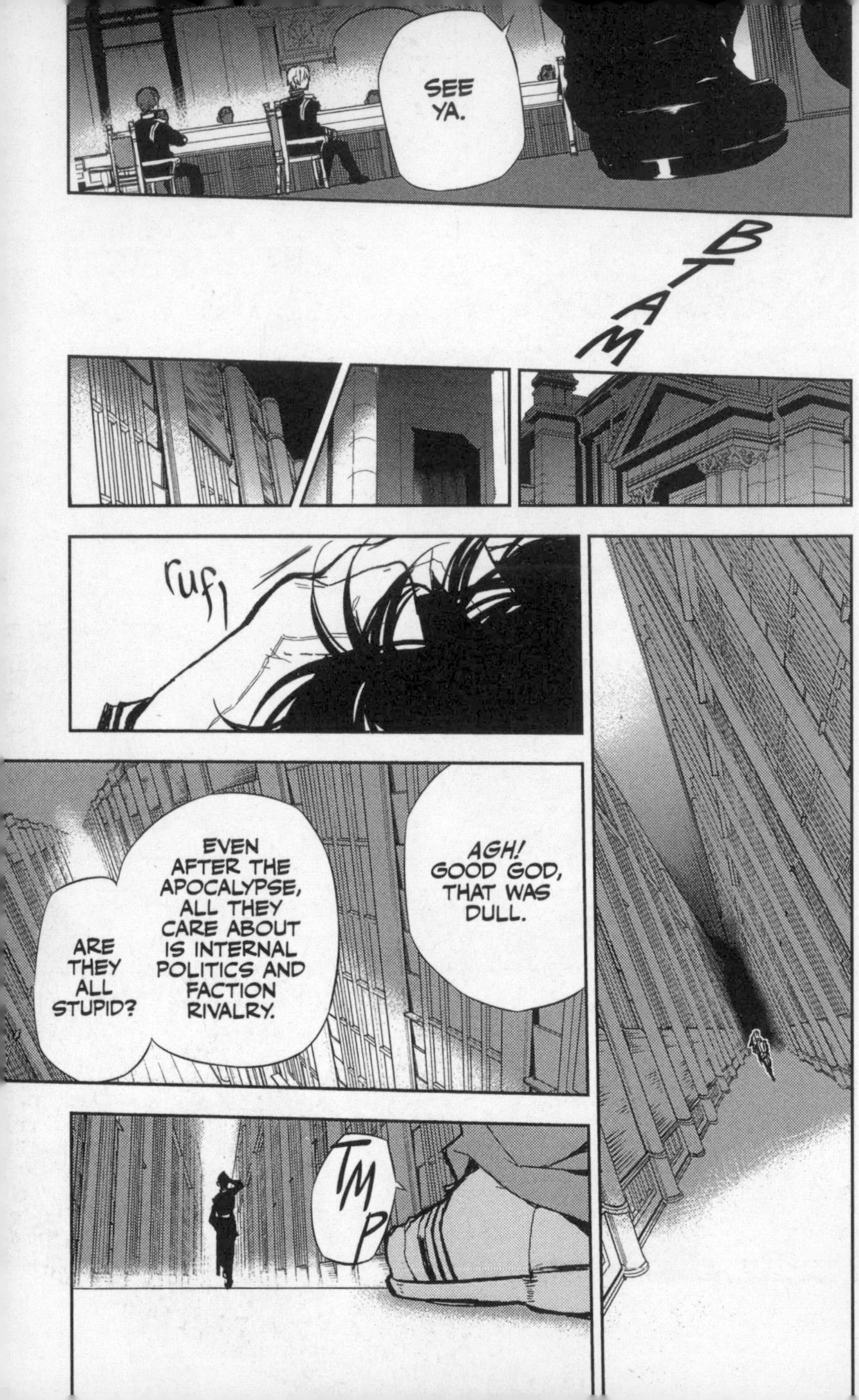
SEE YA.
BTAM
rufl
AGH! GOOD GOD, THAT WAS DULL.
EVEN AFTER THE APOCALYPSE, ALL THEY CARE ABOUT IS INTERNAL POLITICS AND FACTION RIVALRY.
ARE THEY ALL STUPID?
TMP

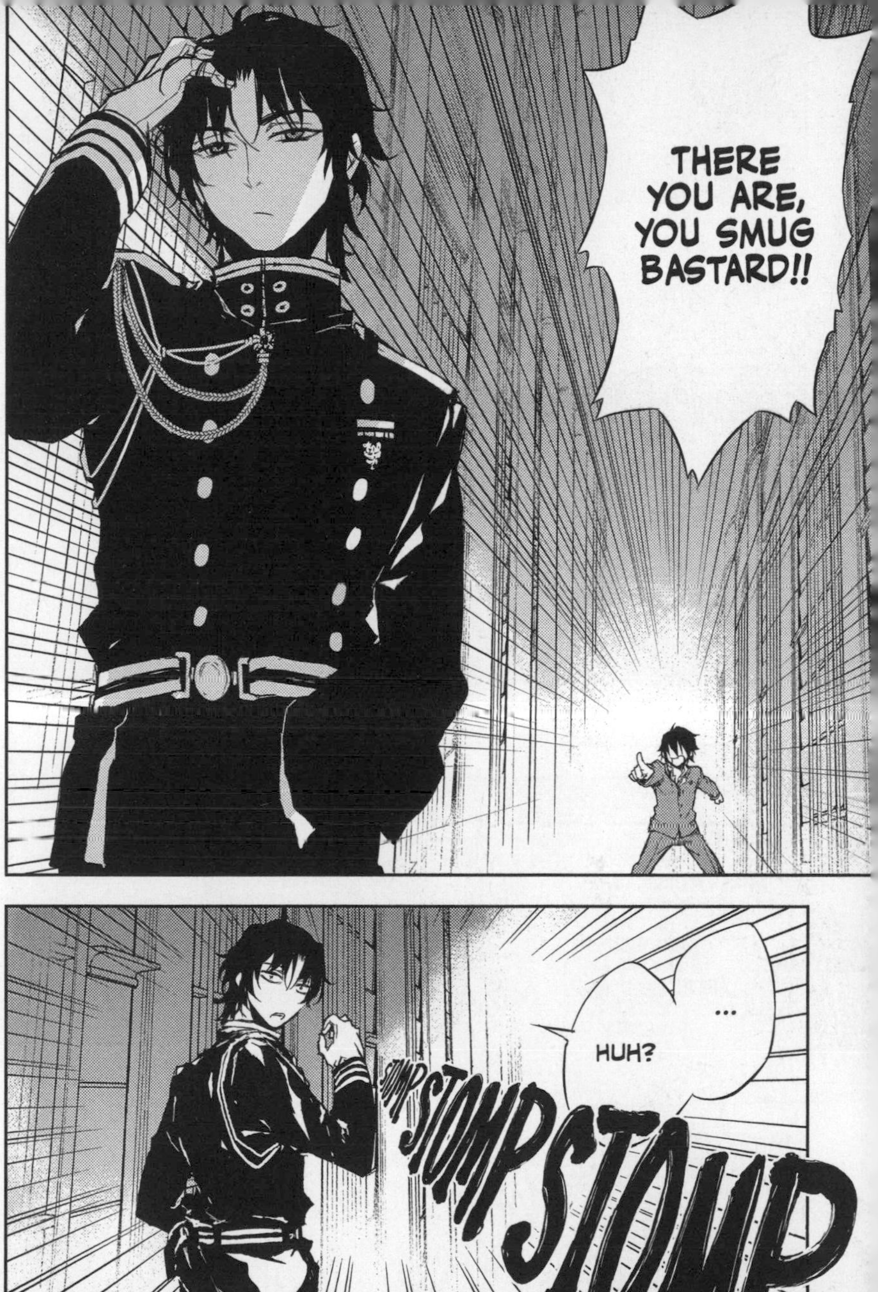
THERE YOU ARE, YOU SMUG BASTARD!!
...
HUH?
STOMP STOMP STOMP

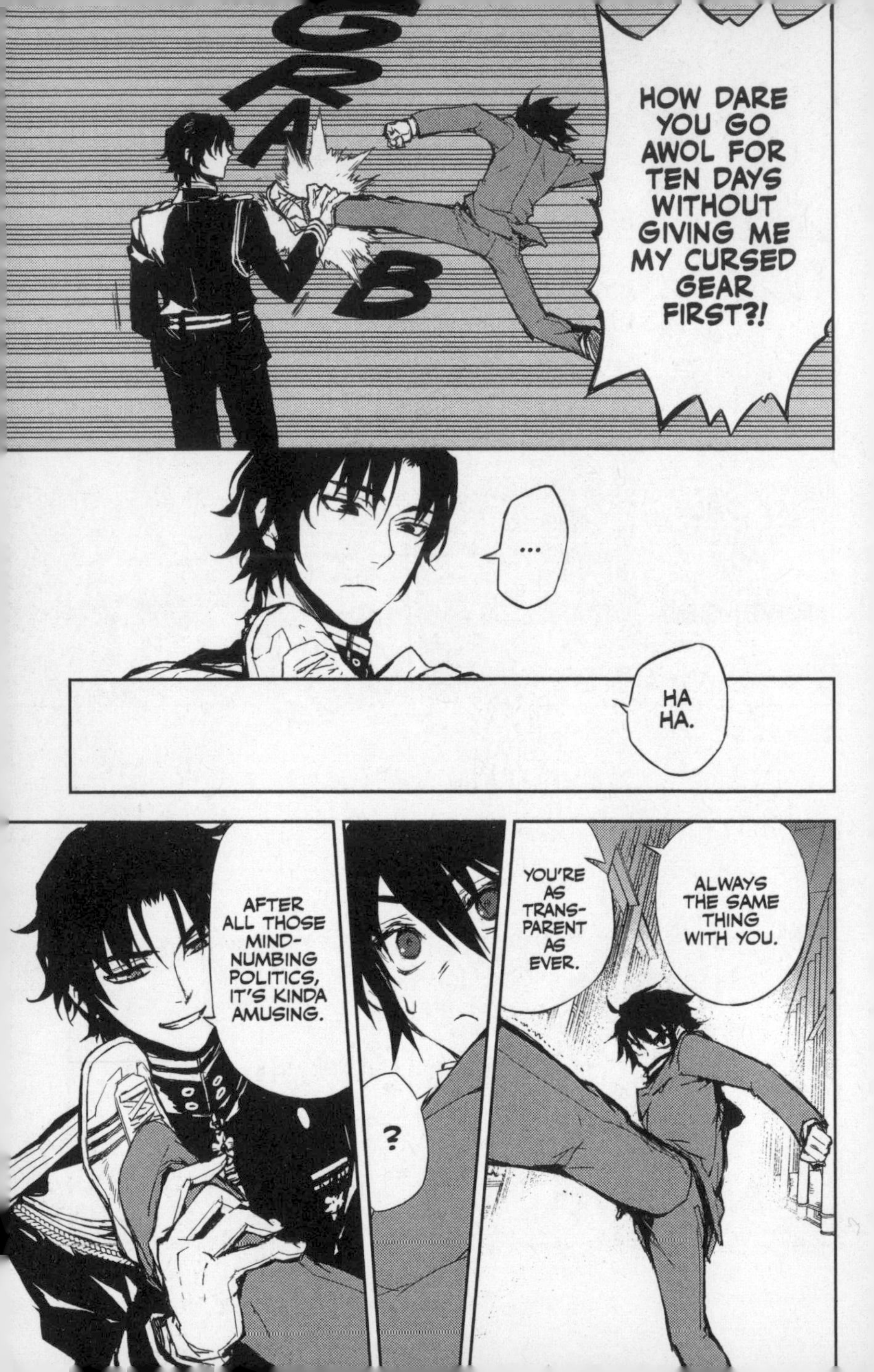
HOW DARE YOU GO AWOL FOR TEN DAYS WITHOUT GIVING ME MY CURSED GEAR FIRST?!
GRAB
...
HA HA.
ALWAYS THE SAME THING WITH YOU.
YOU'RE AS TRANS-PARENT AS EVER.
?
AFTER ALL THOSE MIND-NUMBING POLITICS, IT'S KINDA AMUSING.

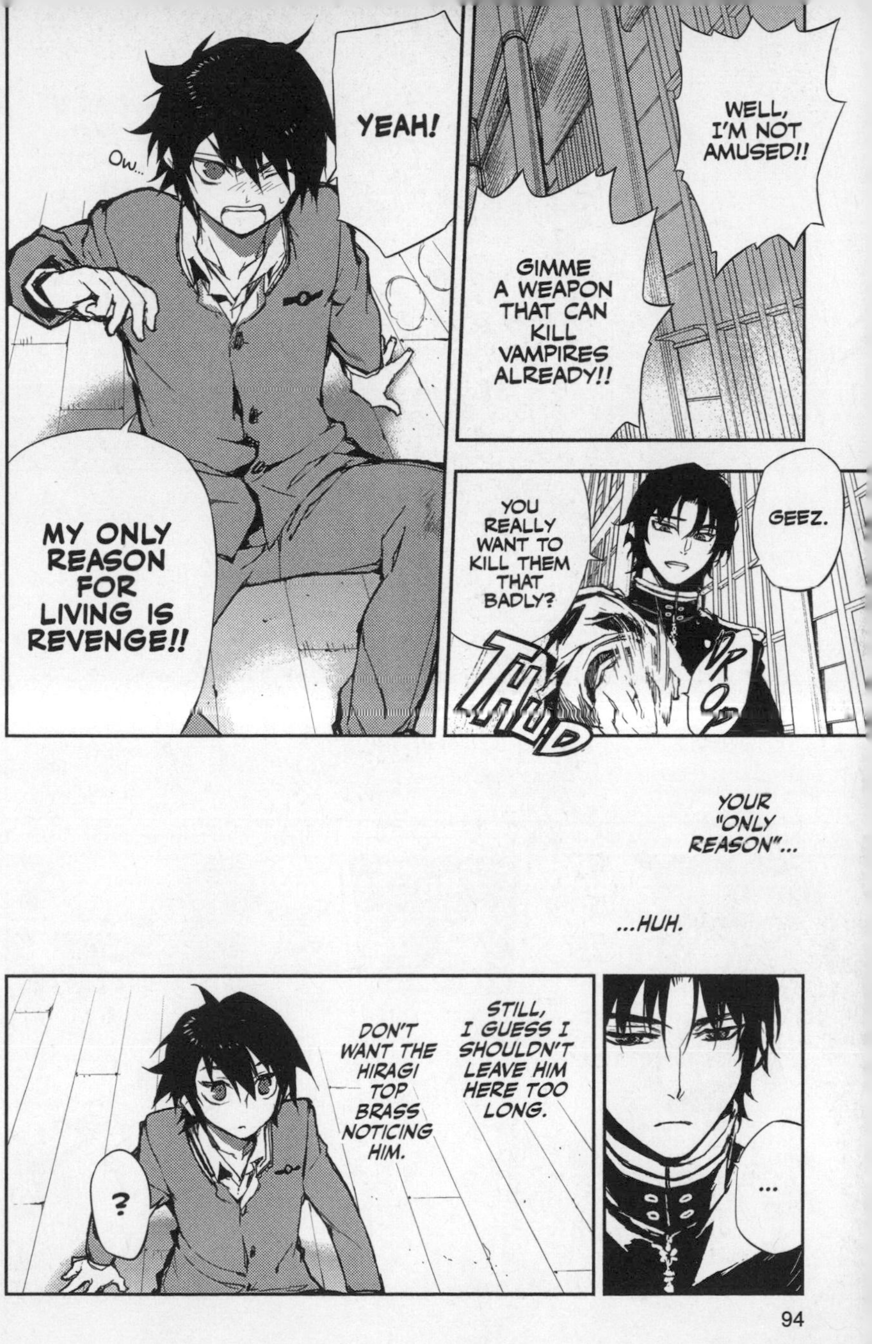
WELL, I'M NOT AMUSED!!
GIMME A WEAPON THAT CAN KILL VAMPIRES ALREADY!!
GEEZ.
YOU REALLY WANT TO KILL THEM THAT BADLY?
THUD
DROP
Ow...
YEAH!
MY ONLY REASON FOR LIVING IS REVENGE!!
YOUR "ONLY REASON"...
...HUH.
...
STILL, I GUESS I SHOULDN'T LEAVE HIM HERE TOO LONG.
DON'T WANT THE HIRAGI TOP BRASS NOTICING HIM.
?

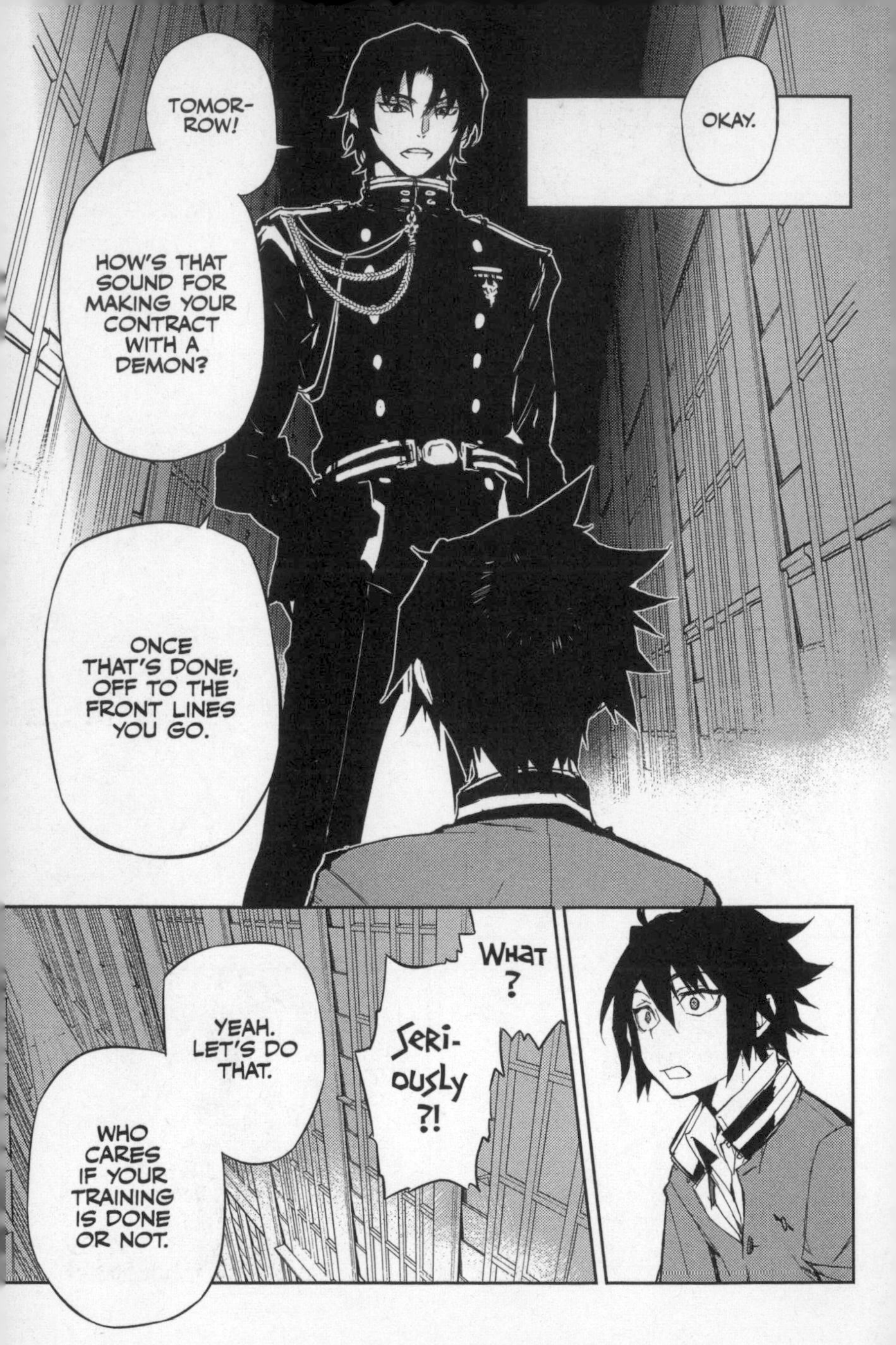
OKAY.
TOMORROW!
HOW'S THAT SOUND FOR MAKING YOUR CONTRACT WITH A DEMON?
ONCE THAT'S DONE, OFF TO THE FRONT LINES YOU GO.
WHAT?
SERIOUSLY?!
YEAH. LET'S DO THAT.
WHO CARES IF YOUR TRAINING IS DONE OR NOT.

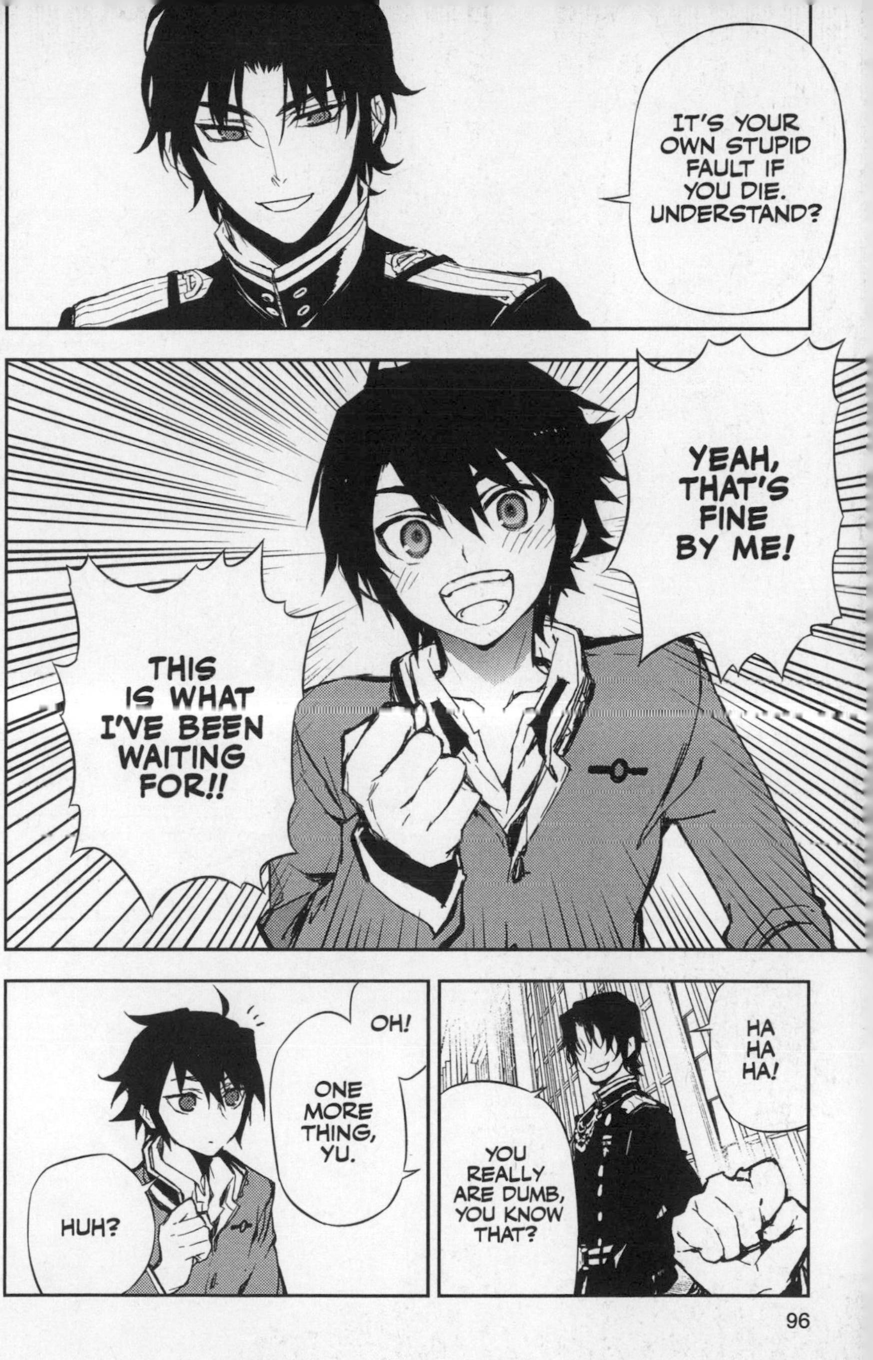
IT'S YOUR OWN STUPID FAULT IF YOU DIE. UNDERSTAND?
YEAH, THAT'S FINE BY ME!
THIS IS WHAT I'VE BEEN WAITING FOR!!
HA HA HA!
YOU REALLY ARE DUMB, YOU KNOW THAT?
OH!
ONE MORE THING, YU.
HUH?

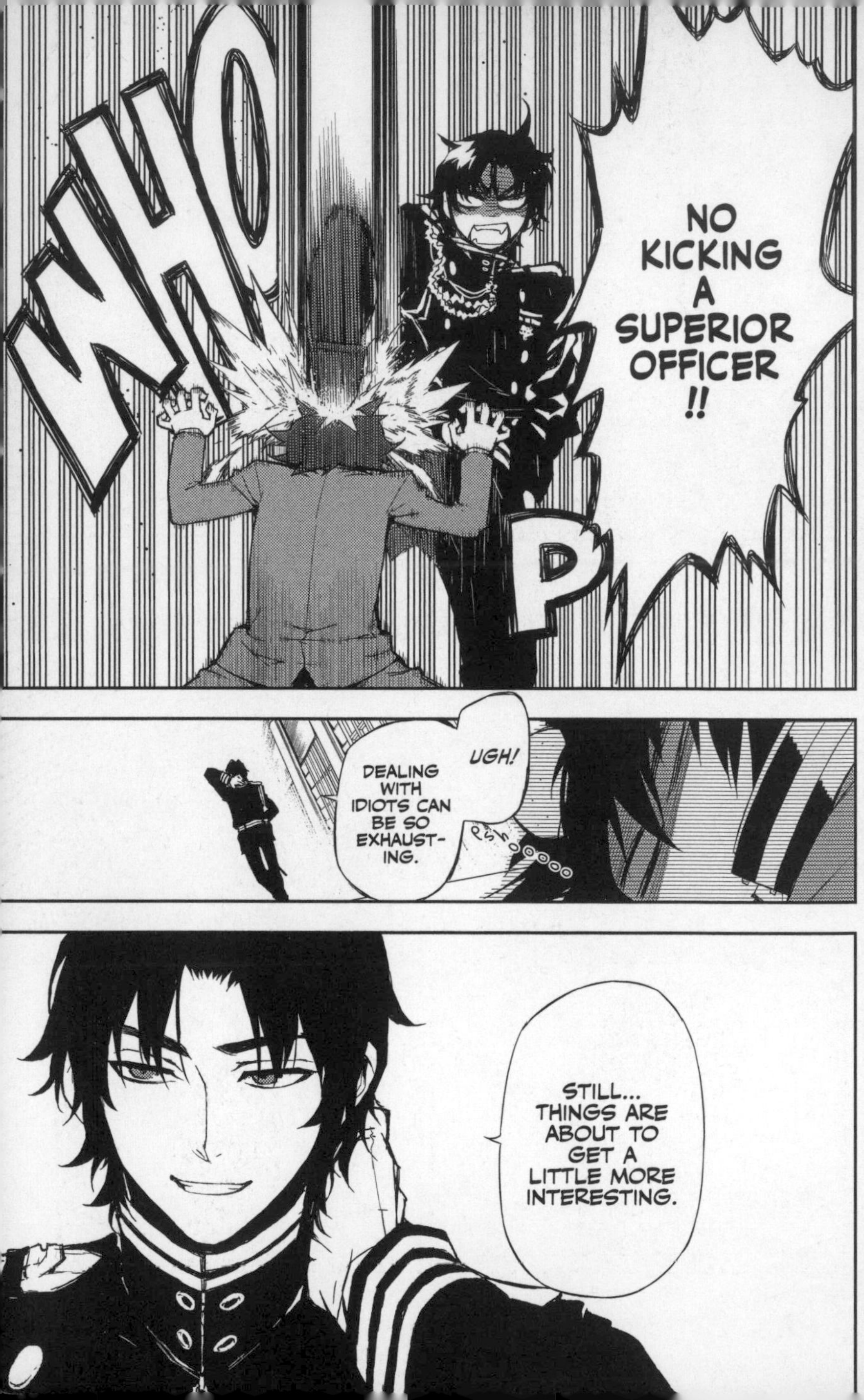
NO KICKING A SUPERIOR OFFICER !!
WHOP
UGH!
Pshooooo
DEALING WITH IDIOTS CAN BE SO EXHAUST-ING.
STILL... THINGS ARE ABOUT TO GET A LITTLE MORE INTERESTING.

Seraph of the End
VAMPIRE REIGN

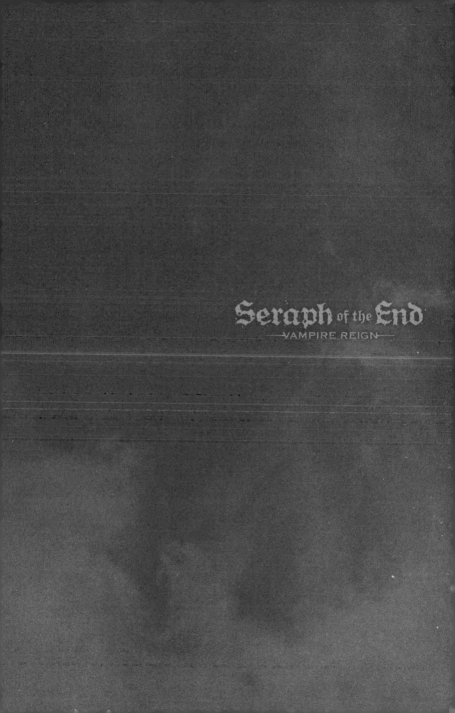

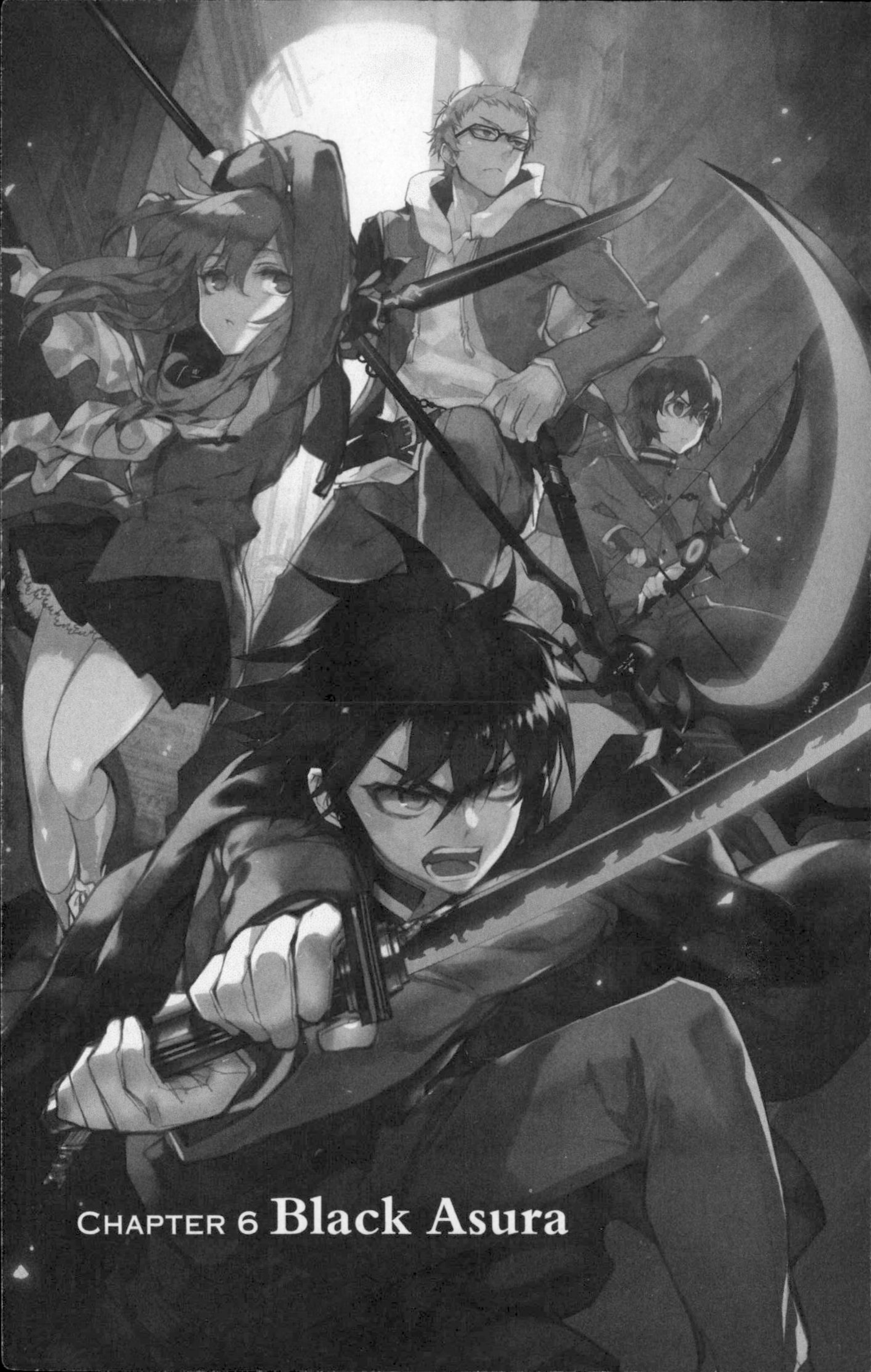

CHAPTER 6 Black Asura

Seraph of the End
VAMPIRE REIGN

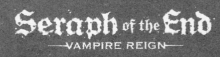

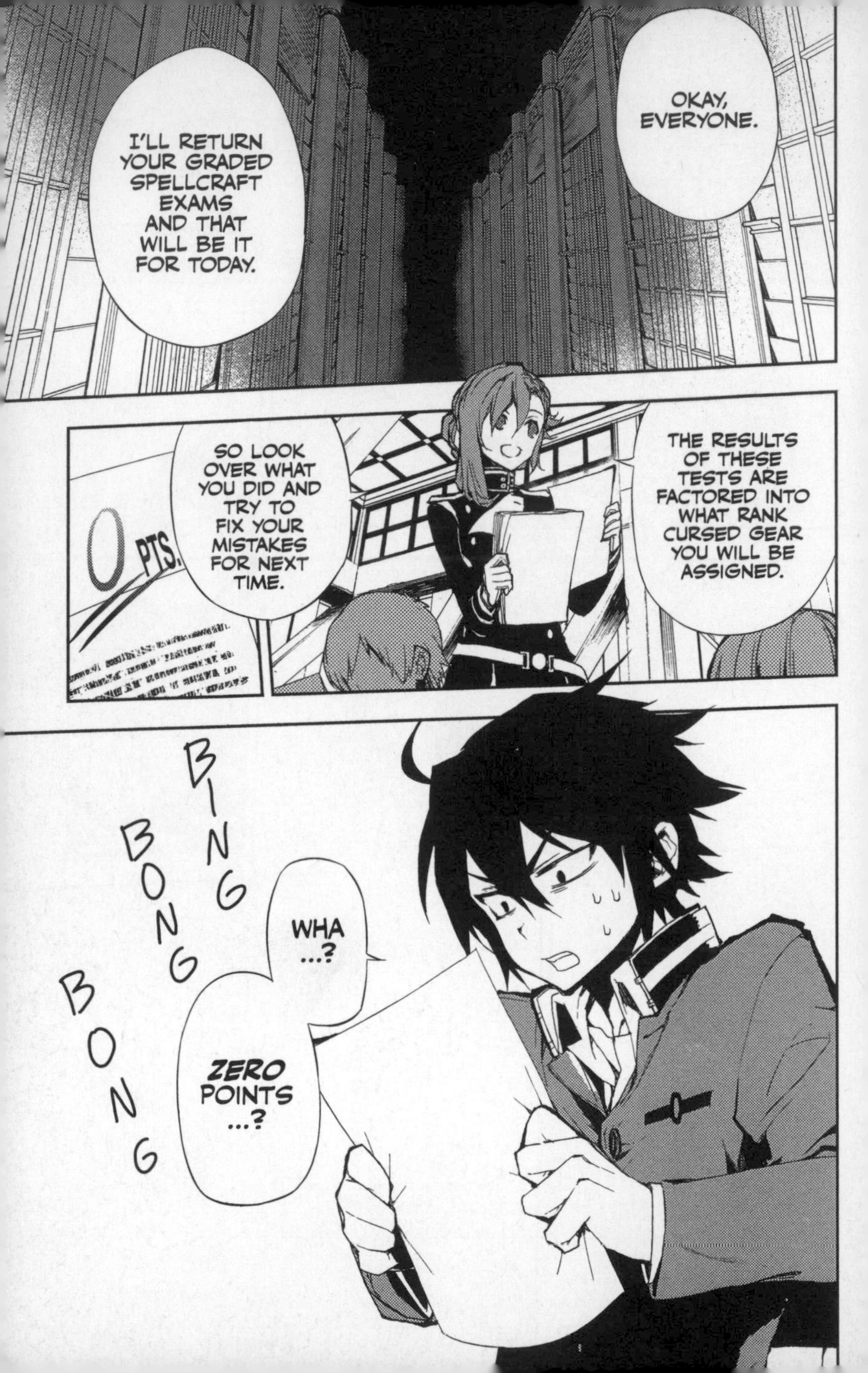
OKAY, EVERYONE.
I'LL RETURN YOUR GRADED SPELLCRAFT EXAMS AND THAT WILL BE IT FOR TODAY.
THE RESULTS OF THESE TESTS ARE FACTORED INTO WHAT RANK CURSED GEAR YOU WILL BE ASSIGNED.
SO LOOK OVER WHAT YOU DID AND TRY TO FIX YOUR MISTAKES FOR NEXT TIME.
0 PTS.
BING
BONG
BONG
WHA ...?
ZERO POINTS ...?

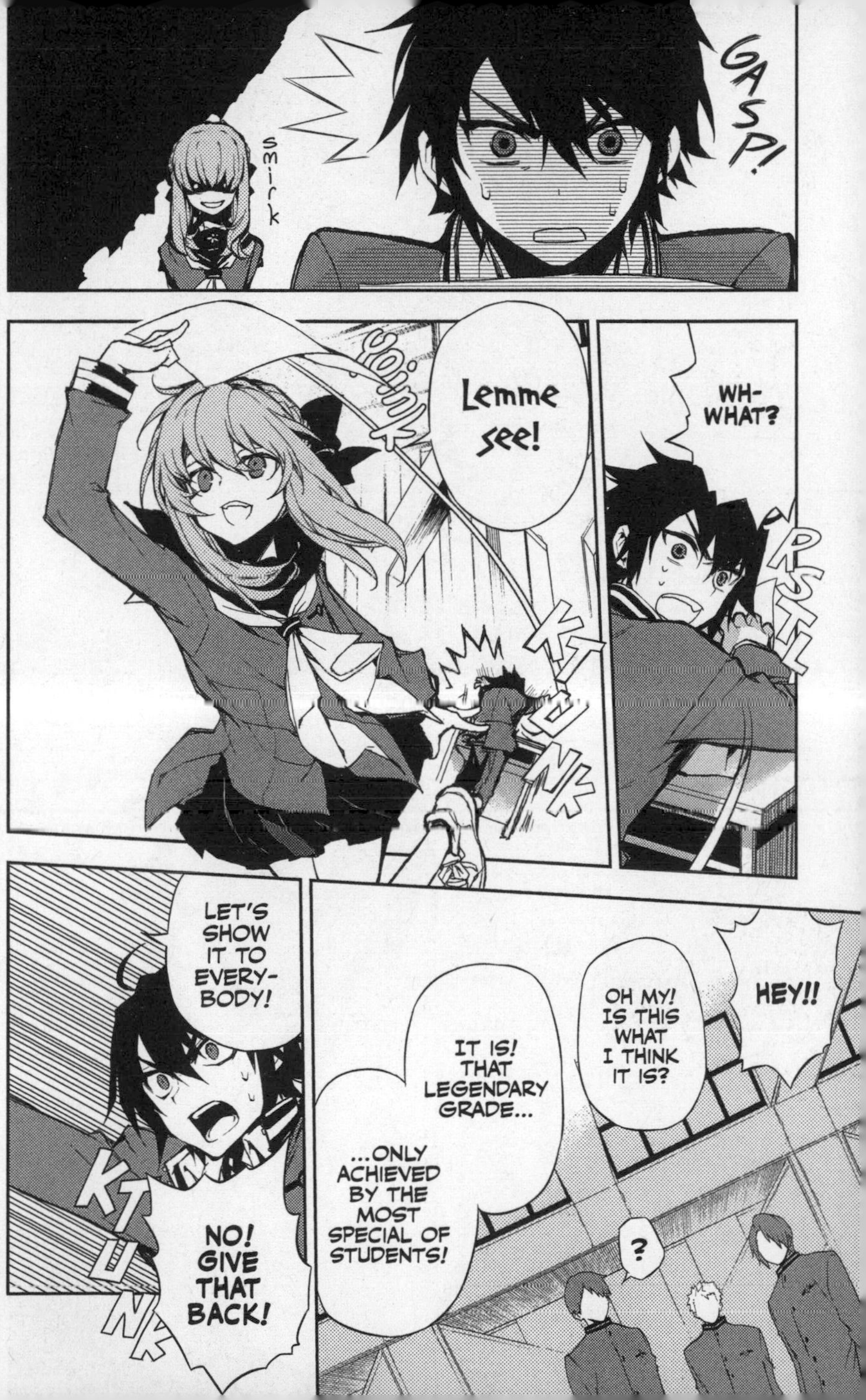
GASP!
smirk
WH- WHAT?
RSTL
Lemme see!
yoink
KTUNK
HEY!!
OH MY! IS THIS WHAT I THINK IT IS?
IT IS! THAT LEGENDARY GRADE...
...ONLY ACHIEVED BY THE MOST SPECIAL OF STUDENTS!
?
LET'S SHOW IT TO EVERY-BODY!
NO! GIVE THAT BACK!
KTUNK

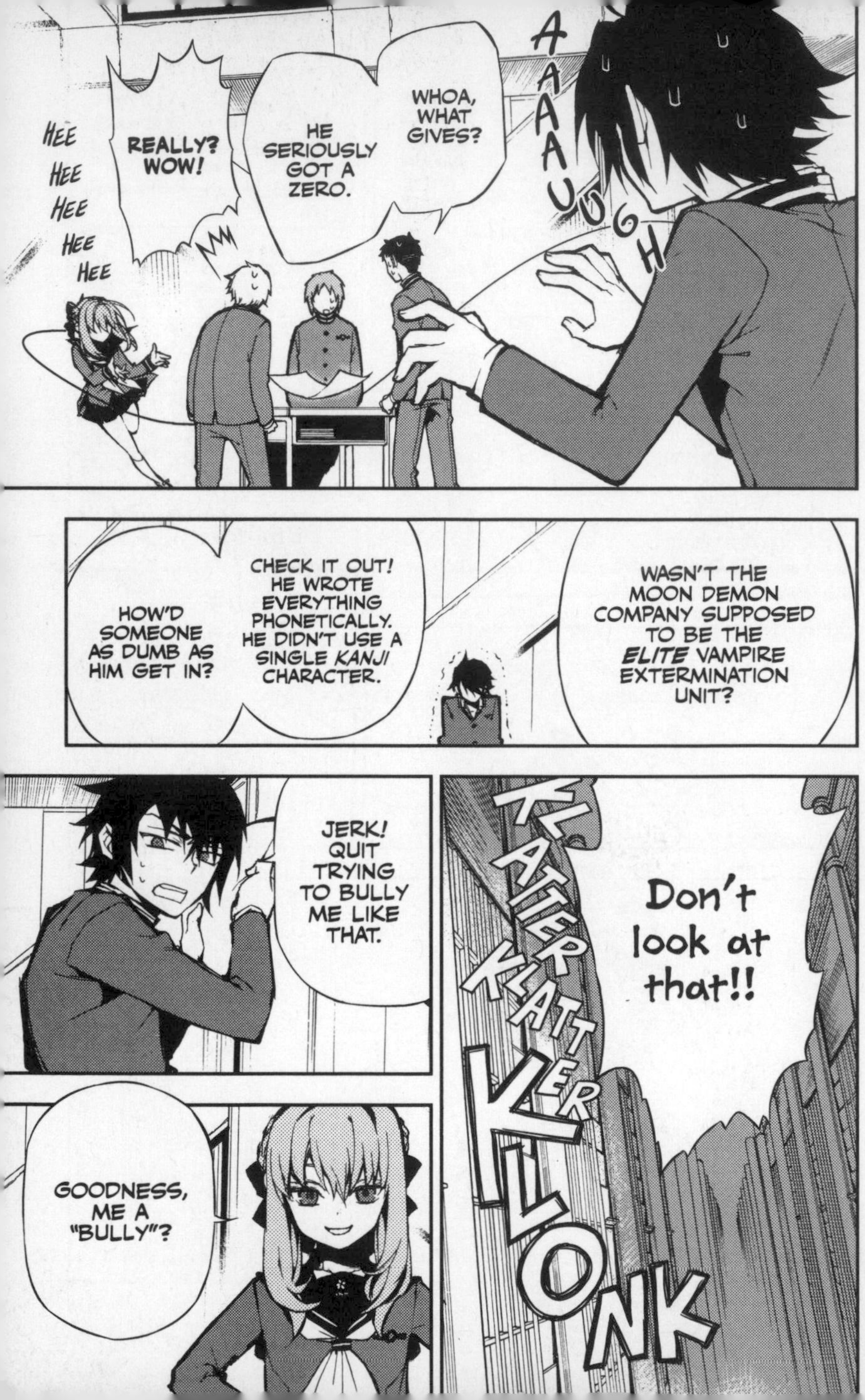
AAAAAUUGH
WHOA, WHAT GIVES?
HE SERIOUSLY GOT A ZERO.
REALLY? WOW!
HEE HEE HEE HEE HEE
WASN'T THE MOON DEMON COMPANY SUPPOSED TO BE THE *ELITE* VAMPIRE EXTERMINATION UNIT?
CHECK IT OUT! HE WROTE EVERYTHING PHONETICALLY. HE DIDN'T USE A SINGLE *KANJI* CHARACTER.
HOW'D SOMEONE AS DUMB AS HIM GET IN?
Don't look at that!!
KLATTER KLATTER KLONK
JERK! QUIT TRYING TO BULLY ME LIKE THAT.
GOODNESS, ME A "BULLY"?

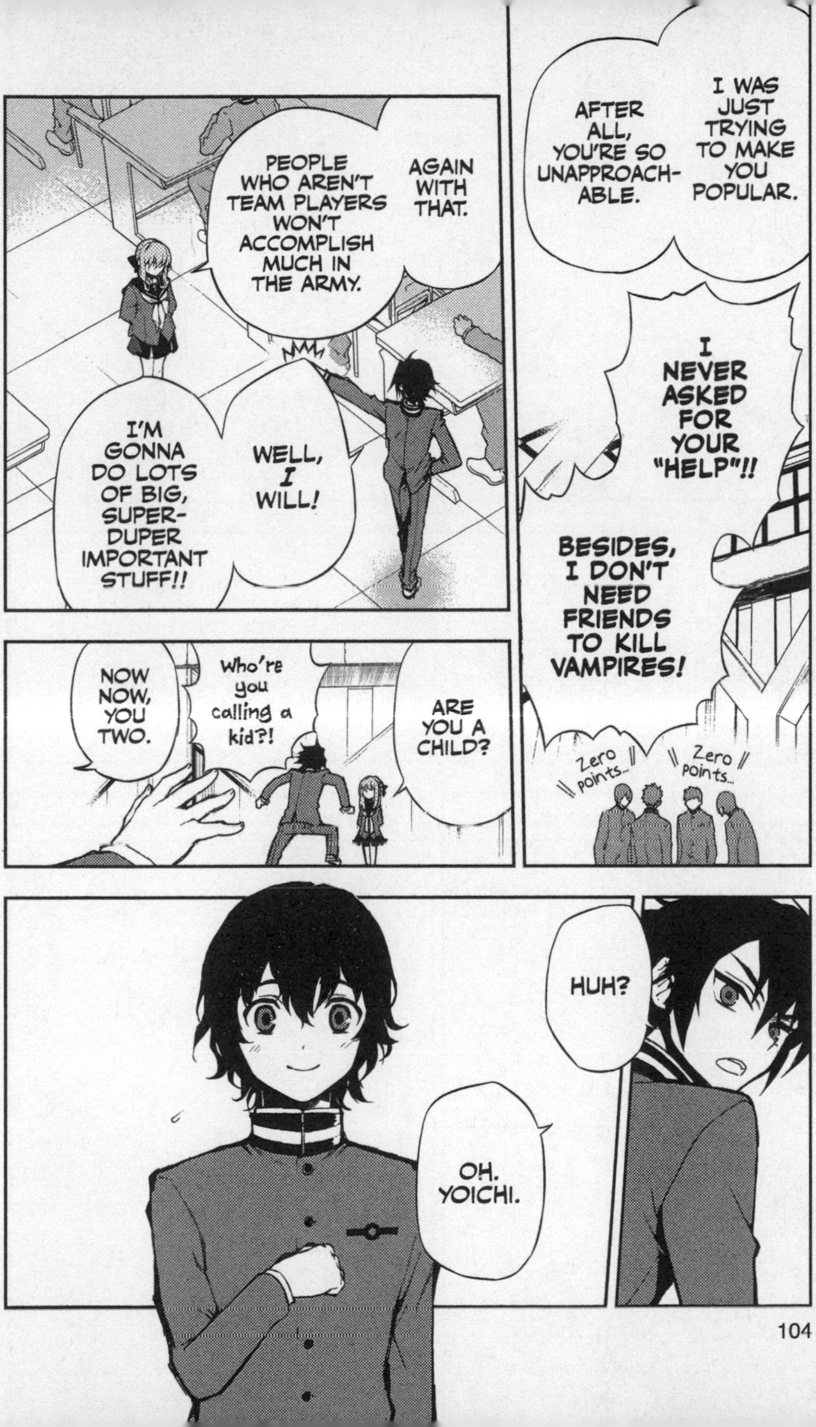
I WAS JUST TRYING TO MAKE YOU POPULAR.
AFTER ALL, YOU'RE SO UNAPPROACH-ABLE.
I NEVER ASKED FOR YOUR "HELP"!!
BESIDES, I DON'T NEED FRIENDS TO KILL VAMPIRES!
Zero points...
Zero points...
AGAIN WITH THAT.
PEOPLE WHO AREN'T TEAM PLAYERS WON'T ACCOMPLISH MUCH IN THE ARMY.
WELL, *I* WILL!
I'M GONNA DO LOTS OF BIG, SUPER-DUPER IMPORTANT STUFF!!
ARE YOU A CHILD?
Who're you calling a kid?!
NOW NOW, YOU TWO.
HUH?
OH. YOICHI.

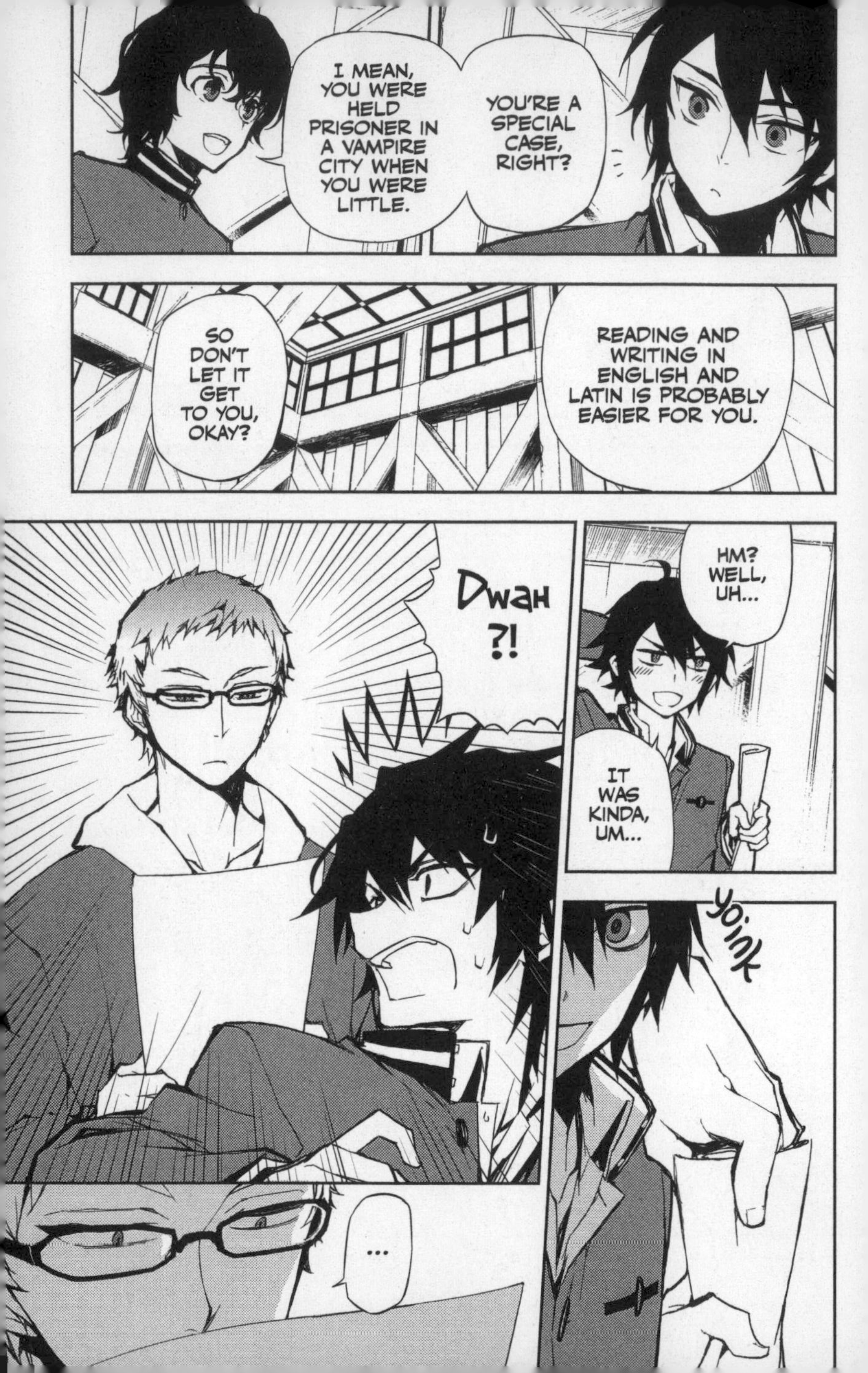
YOU'RE A SPECIAL CASE, RIGHT?
I MEAN, YOU WERE HELD PRISONER IN A VAMPIRE CITY WHEN YOU WERE LITTLE.
READING AND WRITING IN ENGLISH AND LATIN IS PROBABLY EASIER FOR YOU.
SO DON'T LET IT GET TO YOU, OKAY?
HM? WELL, UH...
IT WAS KINDA, UM...
yoink
Dwah ?!
...

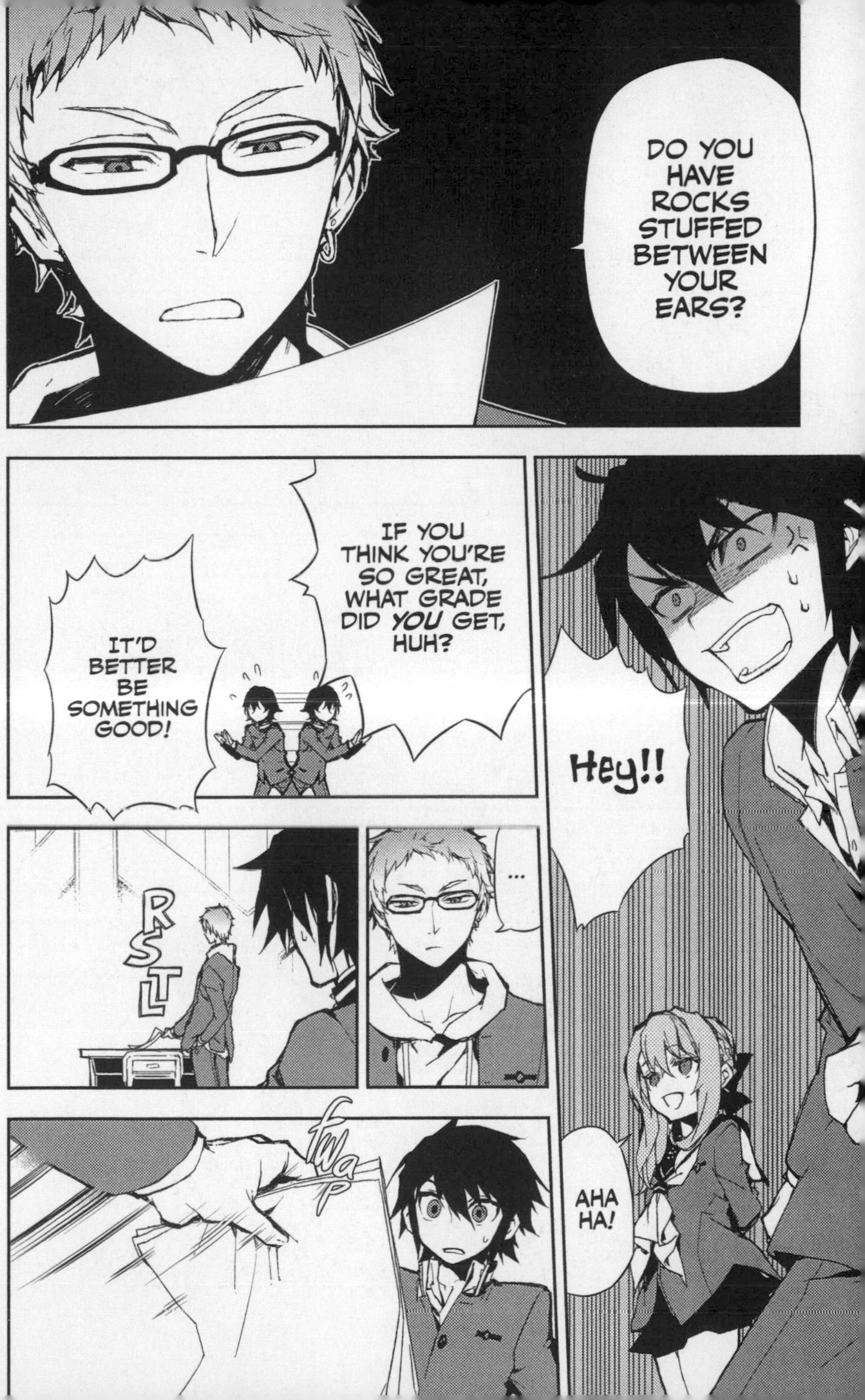

DO YOU HAVE ROCKS STUFFED BETWEEN YOUR EARS?
Hey!!
AHA HA!
IF YOU THINK YOU'RE SO GREAT, WHAT GRADE DID *YOU* GET, HUH?
IT'D BETTER BE SOMETHING GOOD!
...
RSTL
fwap

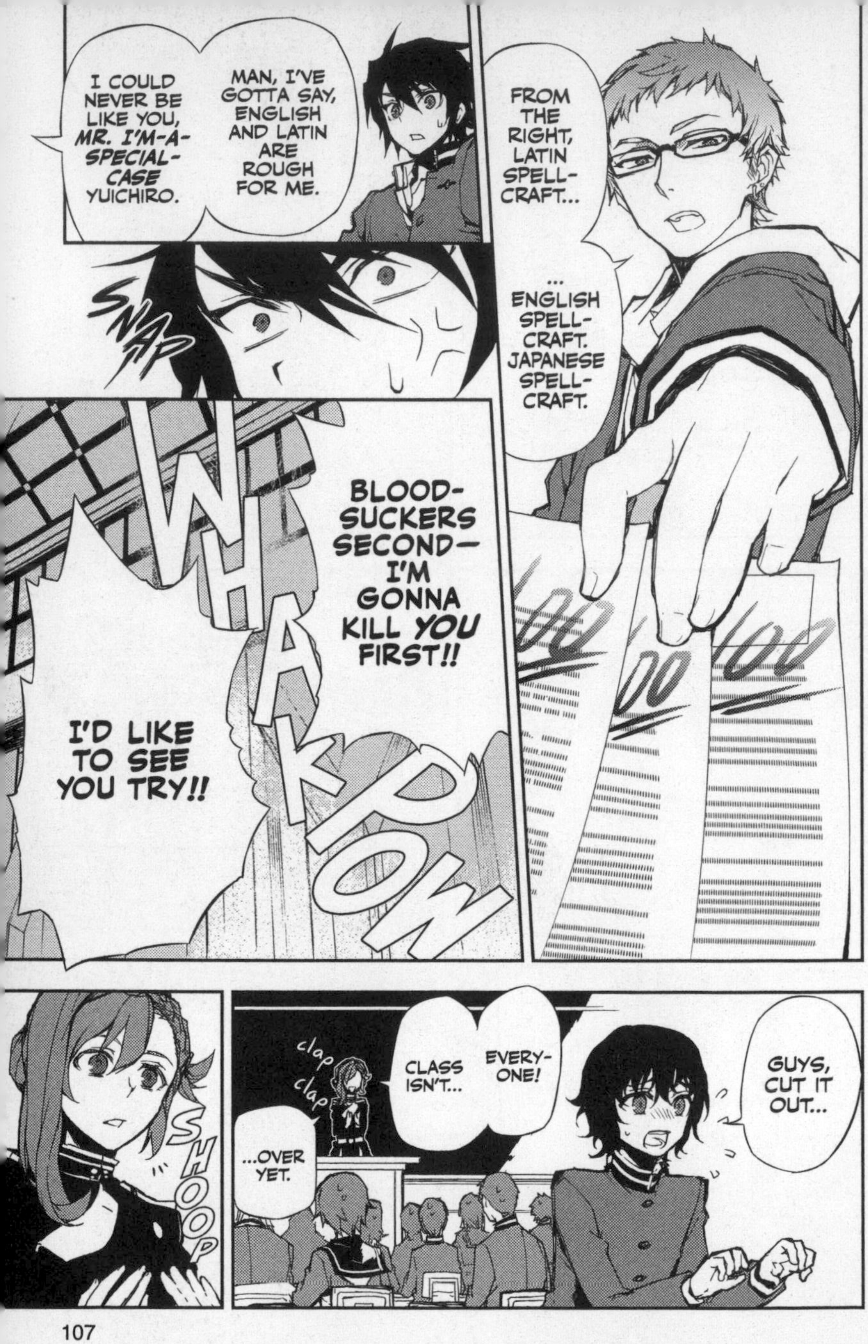
FROM THE RIGHT, LATIN SPELL-CRAFT...
...ENGLISH SPELL-CRAFT. JAPANESE SPELL-CRAFT.
100 100 100
MAN, I'VE GOTTA SAY, ENGLISH AND LATIN ARE ROUGH FOR ME.
I COULD NEVER BE LIKE YOU, *MR. I'M-A-SPECIAL-CASE* YUICHIRO.
SNAP
WHAK
POW
BLOOD-SUCKERS SECOND—I'M GONNA KILL *YOU* FIRST!!
I'D LIKE TO SEE YOU TRY!!
GUYS, CUT IT OUT...
EVERY-ONE!
CLASS ISN'T...
clap clap
...OVER YET.
SHOOOP

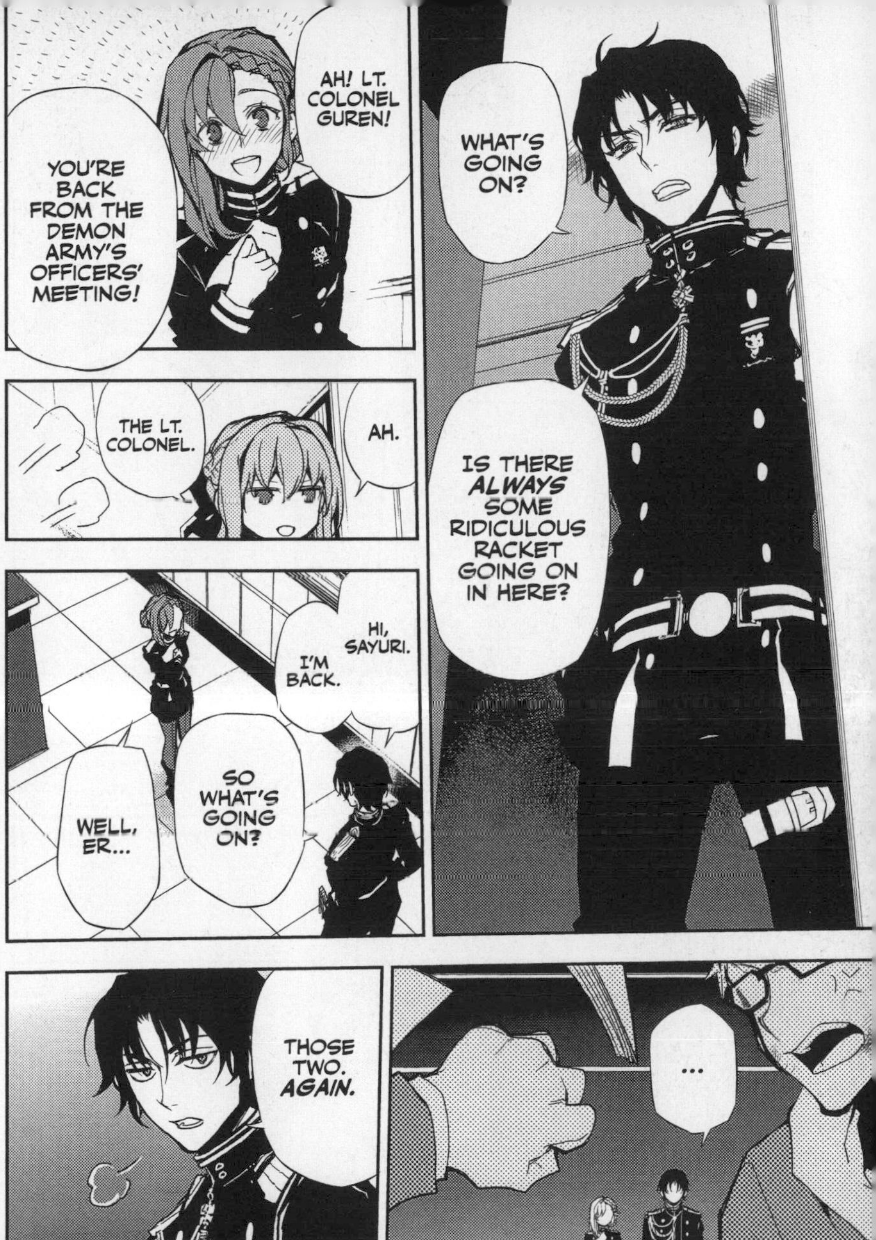
WHAT'S GOING ON?
IS THERE *ALWAYS* SOME RIDICULOUS RACKET GOING ON IN HERE?
AH! LT. COLONEL GUREN!
YOU'RE BACK FROM THE DEMON ARMY'S OFFICERS' MEETING!
AH.
THE LT. COLONEL.
HI, SAYURI.
I'M BACK.
SO WHAT'S GOING ON?
WELL, ER...
...
THOSE TWO. *AGAIN.*

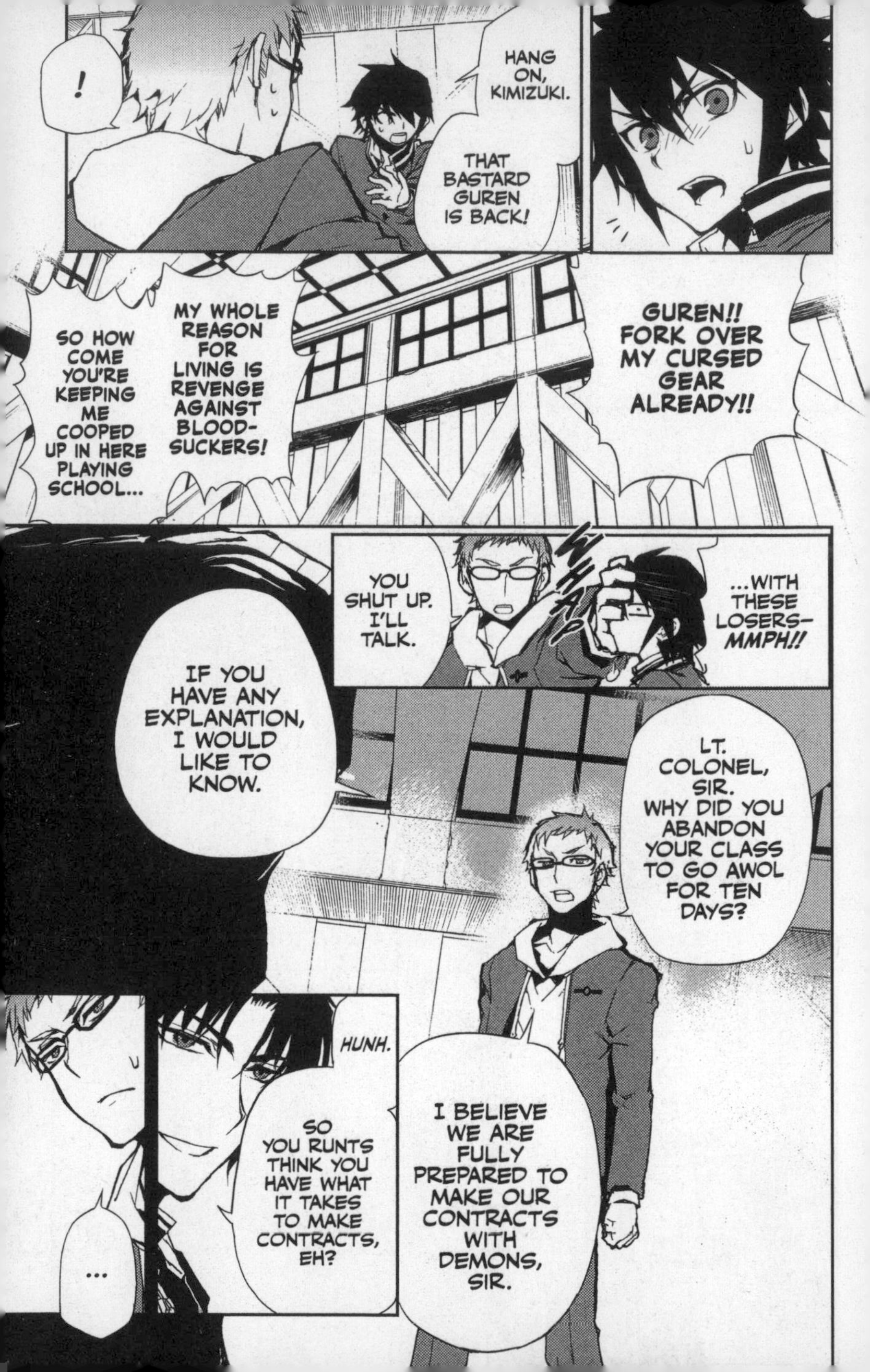
HANG ON, KIMIZUKI.
THAT BASTARD GUREN IS BACK!
!
GUREN!! FORK OVER MY CURSED GEAR ALREADY!!
MY WHOLE REASON FOR LIVING IS REVENGE AGAINST BLOOD-SUCKERS!
SO HOW COME YOU'RE KEEPING ME COOPED UP IN HERE PLAYING SCHOOL...
...WITH THESE LOSERS—MMPH!!
WHAP
YOU SHUT UP. I'LL TALK.
LT. COLONEL, SIR. WHY DID YOU ABANDON YOUR CLASS TO GO AWOL FOR TEN DAYS?
IF YOU HAVE ANY EXPLANATION, I WOULD LIKE TO KNOW.
I BELIEVE WE ARE FULLY PREPARED TO MAKE OUR CONTRACTS WITH DEMONS, SIR.
HUNH.
SO YOU RUNTS THINK YOU HAVE WHAT IT TAKES TO MAKE CONTRACTS, EH?
...

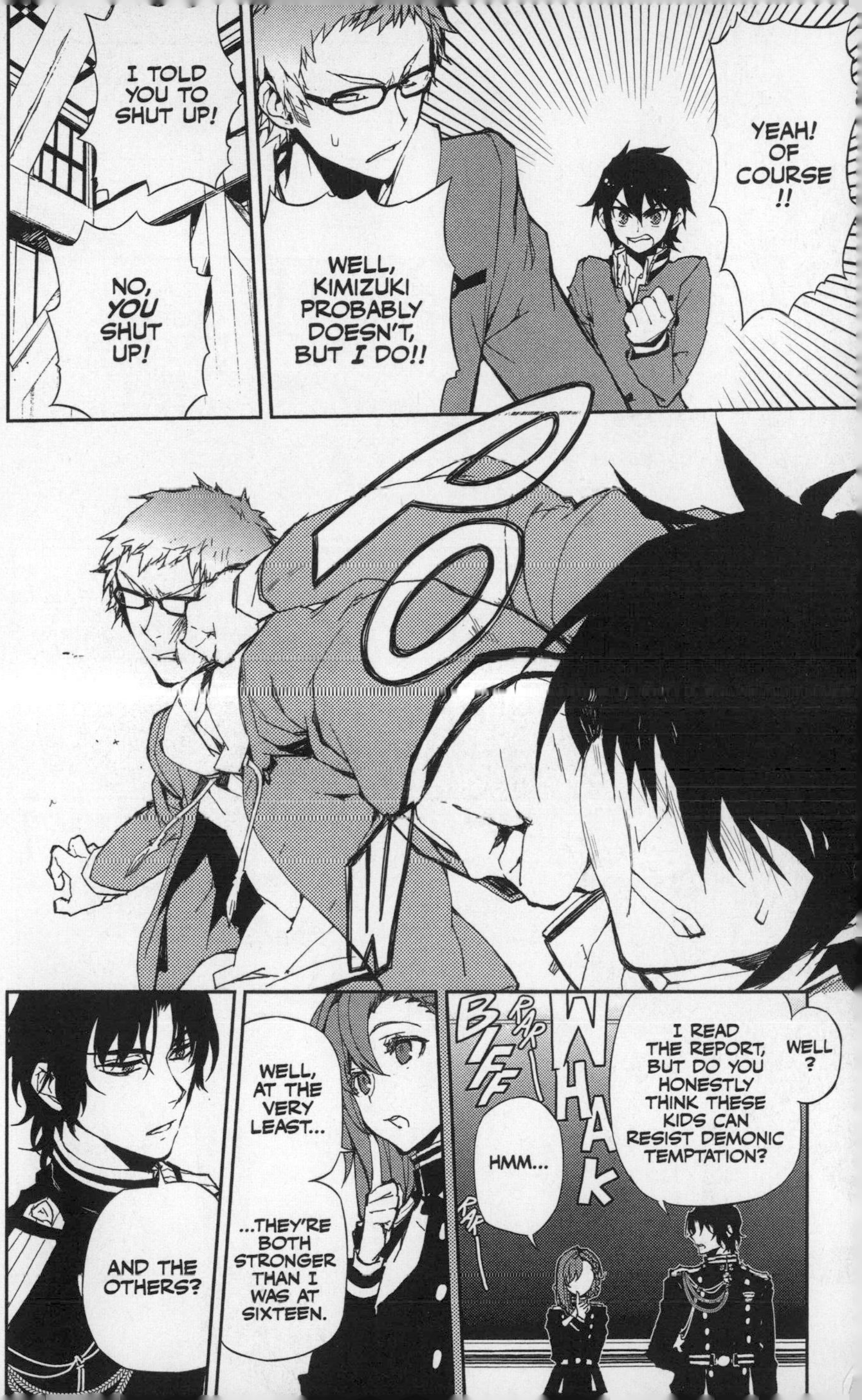
YEAH! OF COURSE !!
WELL, KIMIZUKI PROBABLY DOESN'T, BUT I DO!!
I TOLD YOU TO SHUT UP!
NO, YOU SHUT UP!
WELL ?
I READ THE REPORT, BUT DO YOU HONESTLY THINK THESE KIDS CAN RESIST DEMONIC TEMPTATION?
WHAK
BIFF
RAR
HMM...
RAR
WELL, AT THE VERY LEAST...
...THEY'RE BOTH STRONGER THAN I WAS AT SIXTEEN.
AND THE OTHERS?

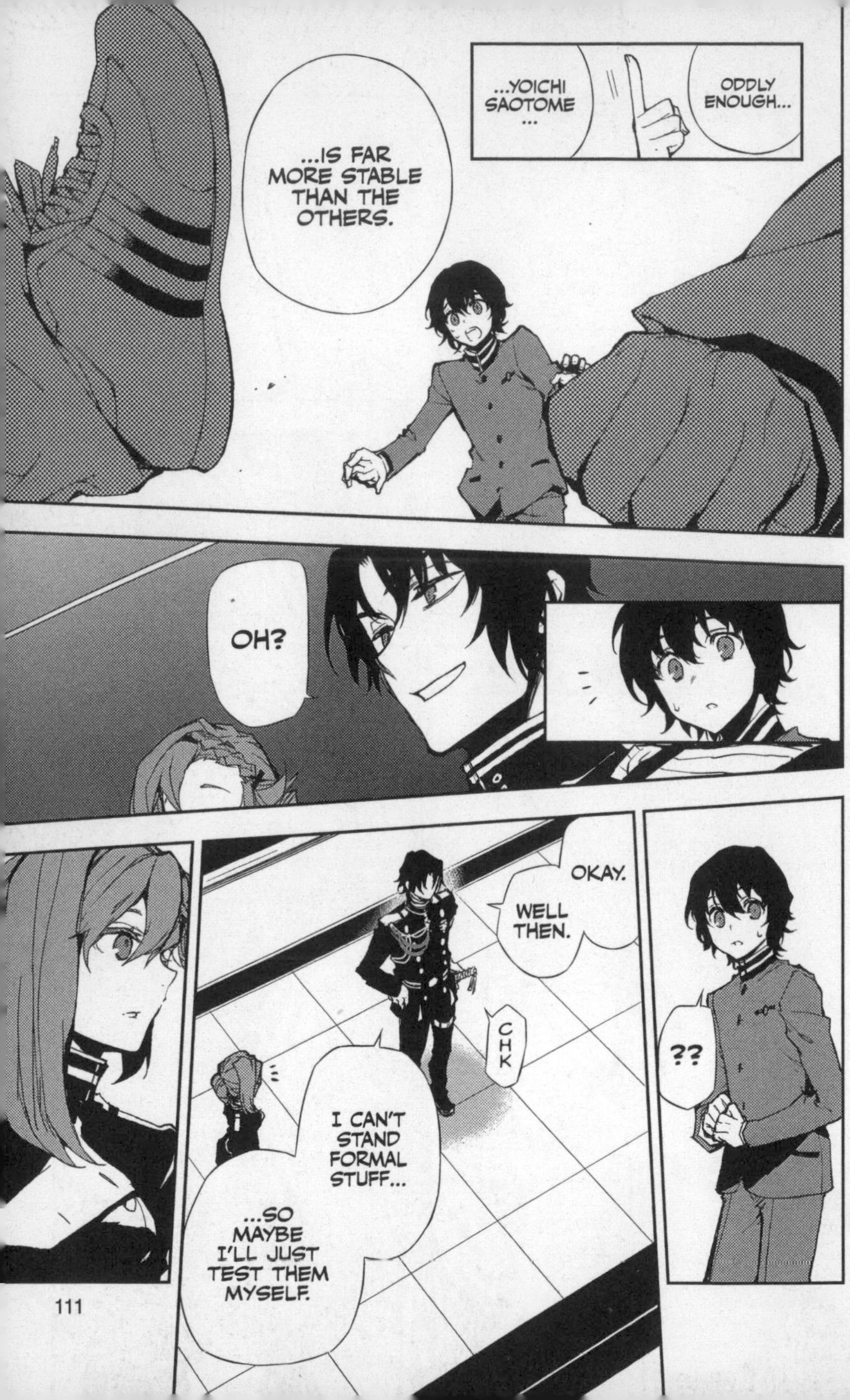
ODDLY ENOUGH...
...YOICHI SAOTOME ...
...IS FAR MORE STABLE THAN THE OTHERS.
OH?
??
OKAY.
WELL THEN.
CHK
I CAN'T STAND FORMAL STUFF...
...SO MAYBE I'LL JUST TEST THEM MYSELF.

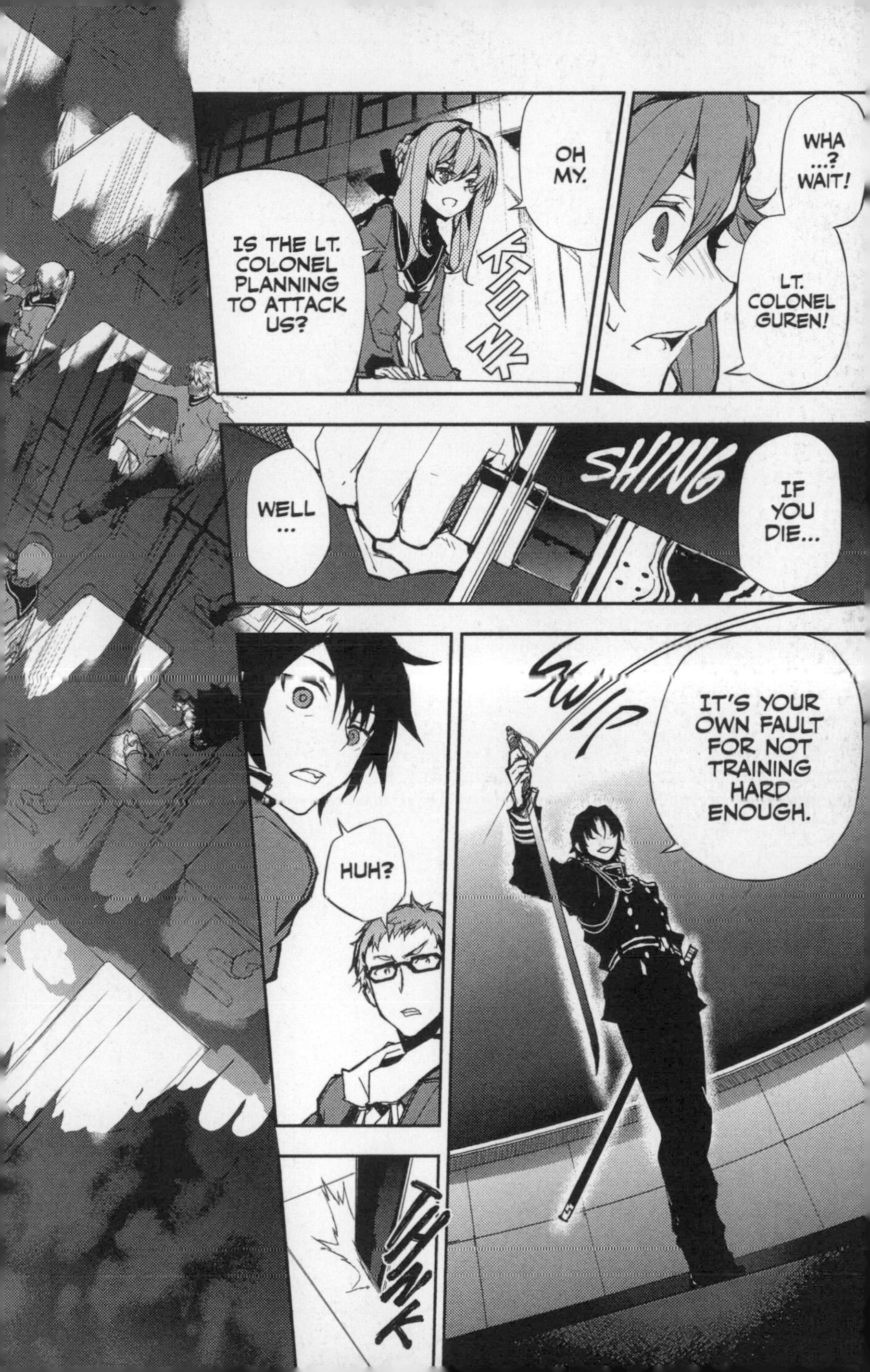
WHA ...? WAIT!
LT. COLONEL GUREN!
OH MY.
KTUNK
IS THE LT. COLONEL PLANNING TO ATTACK US?
SHING
IF YOU DIE...
WELL ...
SWIP
IT'S YOUR OWN FAULT FOR NOT TRAINING HARD ENOUGH.
HUH?
THWNK

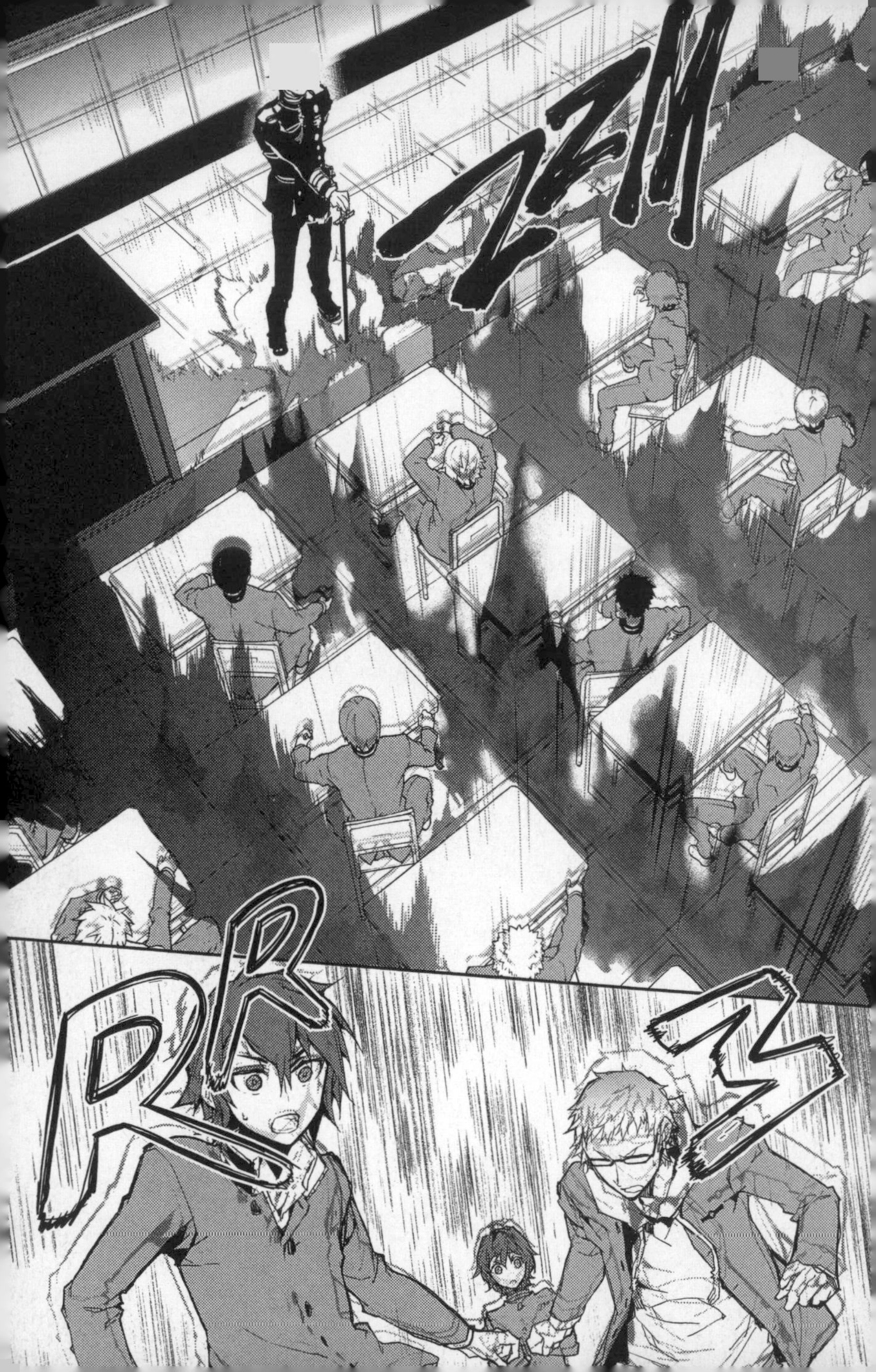

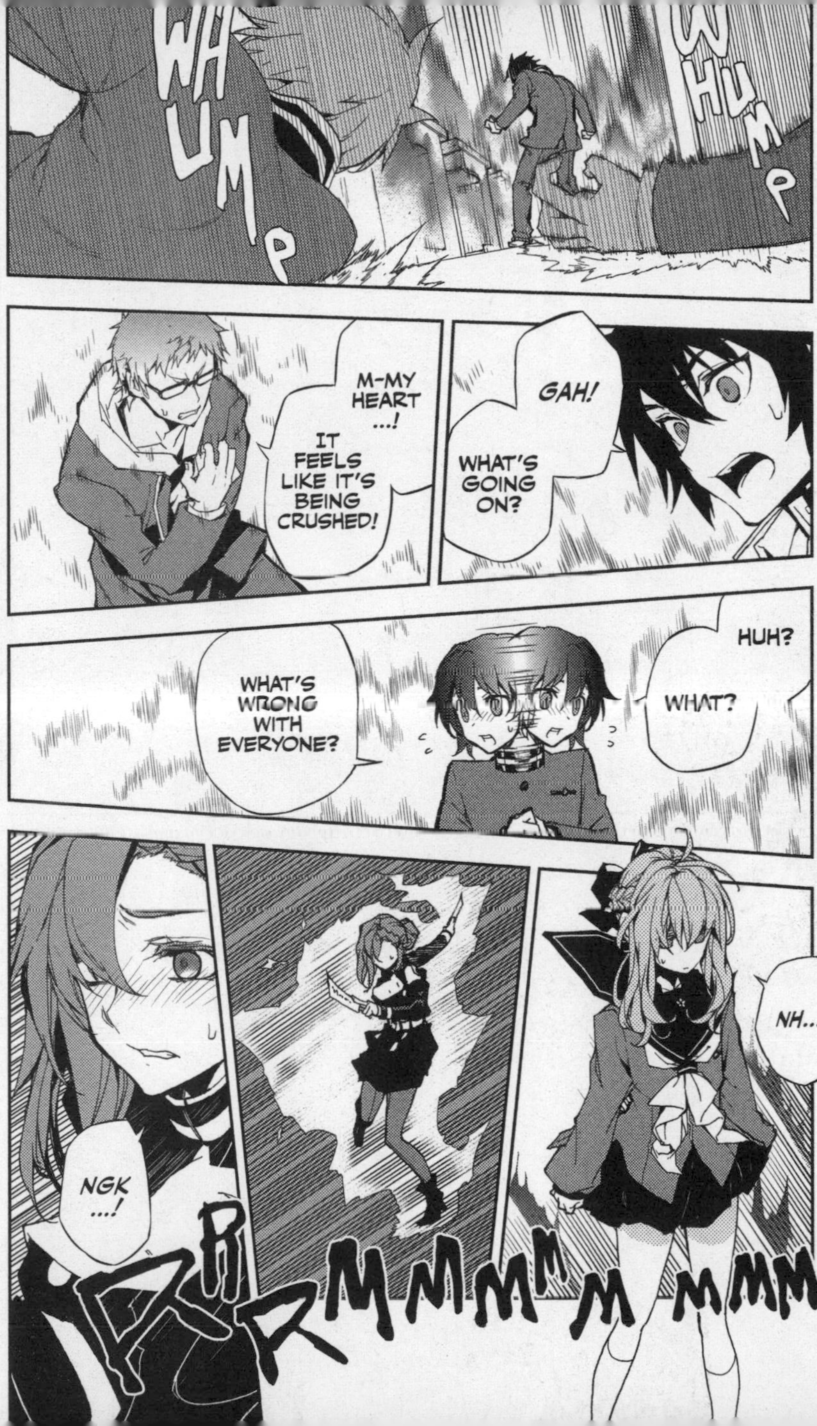
WHUMP
WHUMP
GAH!
WHAT'S GOING ON?
M-MY HEART ...!
IT FEELS LIKE IT'S BEING CRUSHED!
HUH?
WHAT?
WHAT'S WRONG WITH EVERYONE?
NH...
NGK ...!
RRMMMMM MMMMM

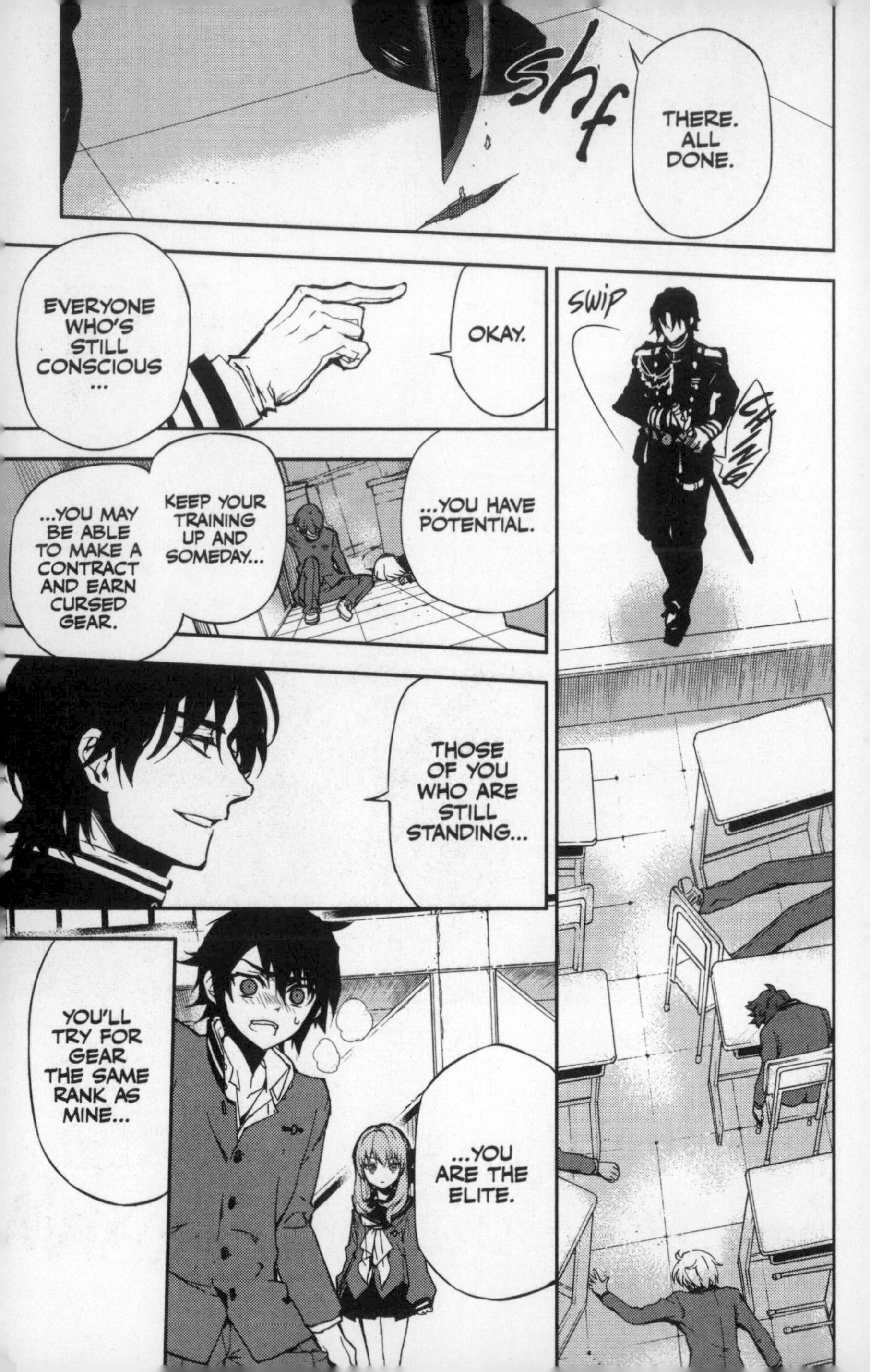
shf
THERE. ALL DONE.
SWIP
CHING
OKAY.
EVERYONE WHO'S STILL CONSCIOUS ...
...YOU HAVE POTENTIAL.
KEEP YOUR TRAINING UP AND SOMEDAY...
...YOU MAY BE ABLE TO MAKE A CONTRACT AND EARN CURSED GEAR.
THOSE OF YOU WHO ARE STILL STANDING...
...YOU ARE THE ELITE.
YOU'LL TRY FOR GEAR THE SAME RANK AS MINE...

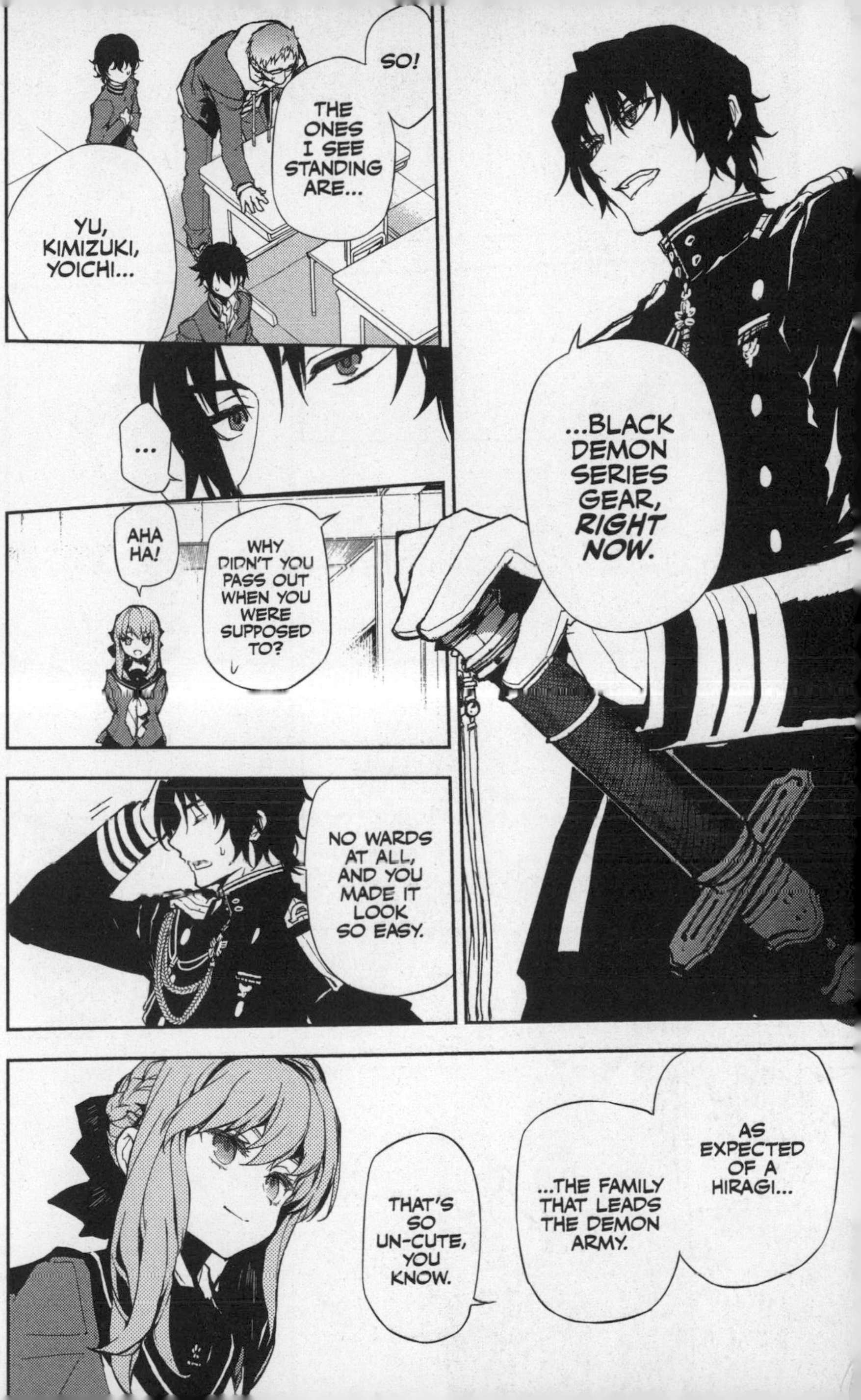
...BLACK DEMON SERIES GEAR, *RIGHT NOW.*
SO!
THE ONES I SEE STANDING ARE...
YU, KIMIZUKI, YOICHI...
...
AHA HA!
WHY DIDN'T YOU PASS OUT WHEN YOU WERE SUPPOSED TO?
NO WARDS AT ALL, AND YOU MADE IT LOOK SO EASY.
AS EXPECTED OF A HIRAGI...
...THE FAMILY THAT LEADS THE DEMON ARMY.
THAT'S SO UN-CUTE, YOU KNOW.

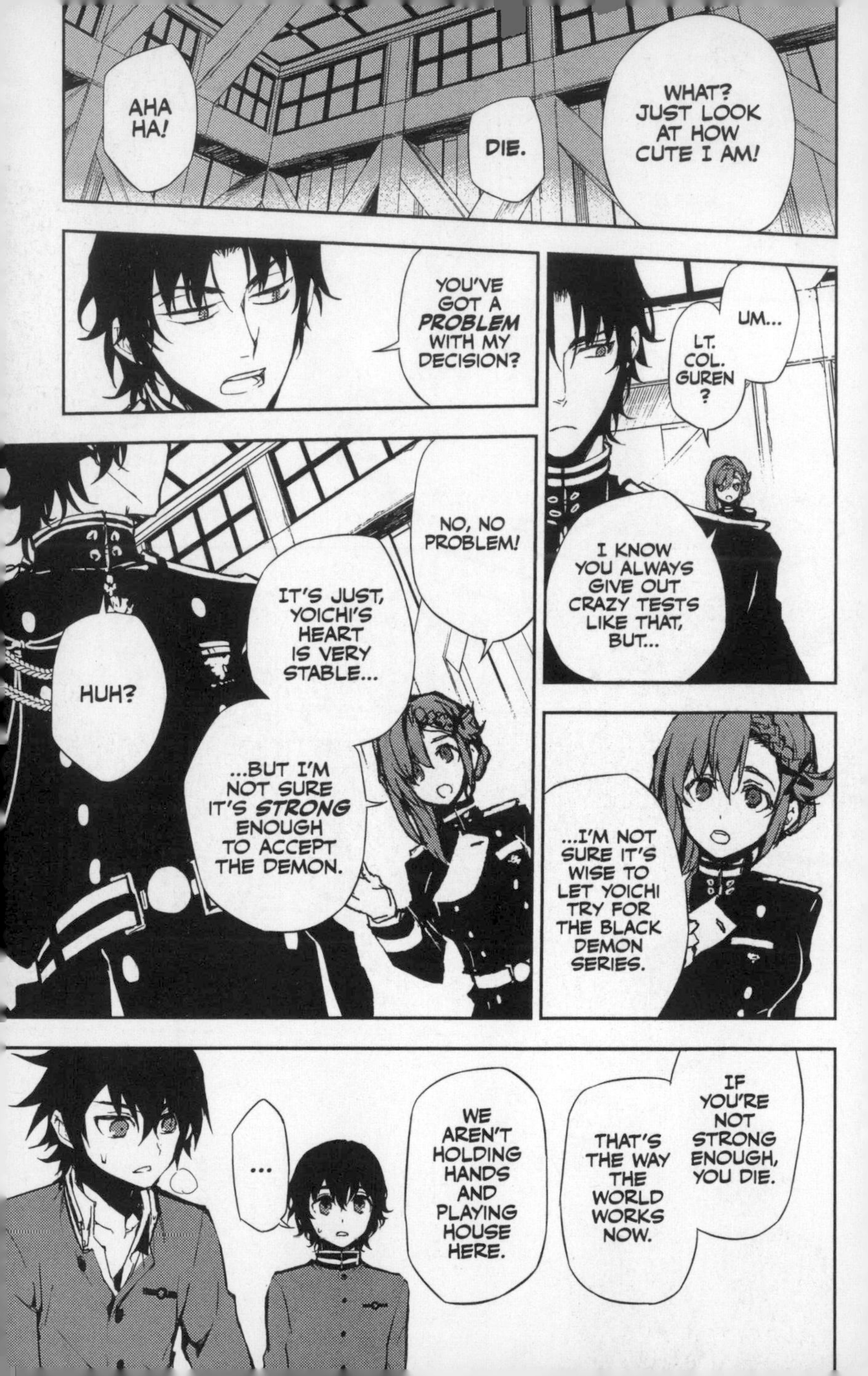
WHAT? JUST LOOK AT HOW CUTE I AM!
DIE.
AHA HA!
UM...
LT. COL. GUREN?
I KNOW YOU ALWAYS GIVE OUT CRAZY TESTS LIKE THAT, BUT...
...I'M NOT SURE IT'S WISE TO LET YOICHI TRY FOR THE BLACK DEMON SERIES.
YOU'VE GOT A PROBLEM WITH MY DECISION?
NO, NO PROBLEM!
IT'S JUST, YOICHI'S HEART IS VERY STABLE...
HUH?
...BUT I'M NOT SURE IT'S STRONG ENOUGH TO ACCEPT THE DEMON.
IF YOU'RE NOT STRONG ENOUGH, YOU DIE.
THAT'S THE WAY THE WORLD WORKS NOW.
WE AREN'T HOLDING HANDS AND PLAYING HOUSE HERE.
...

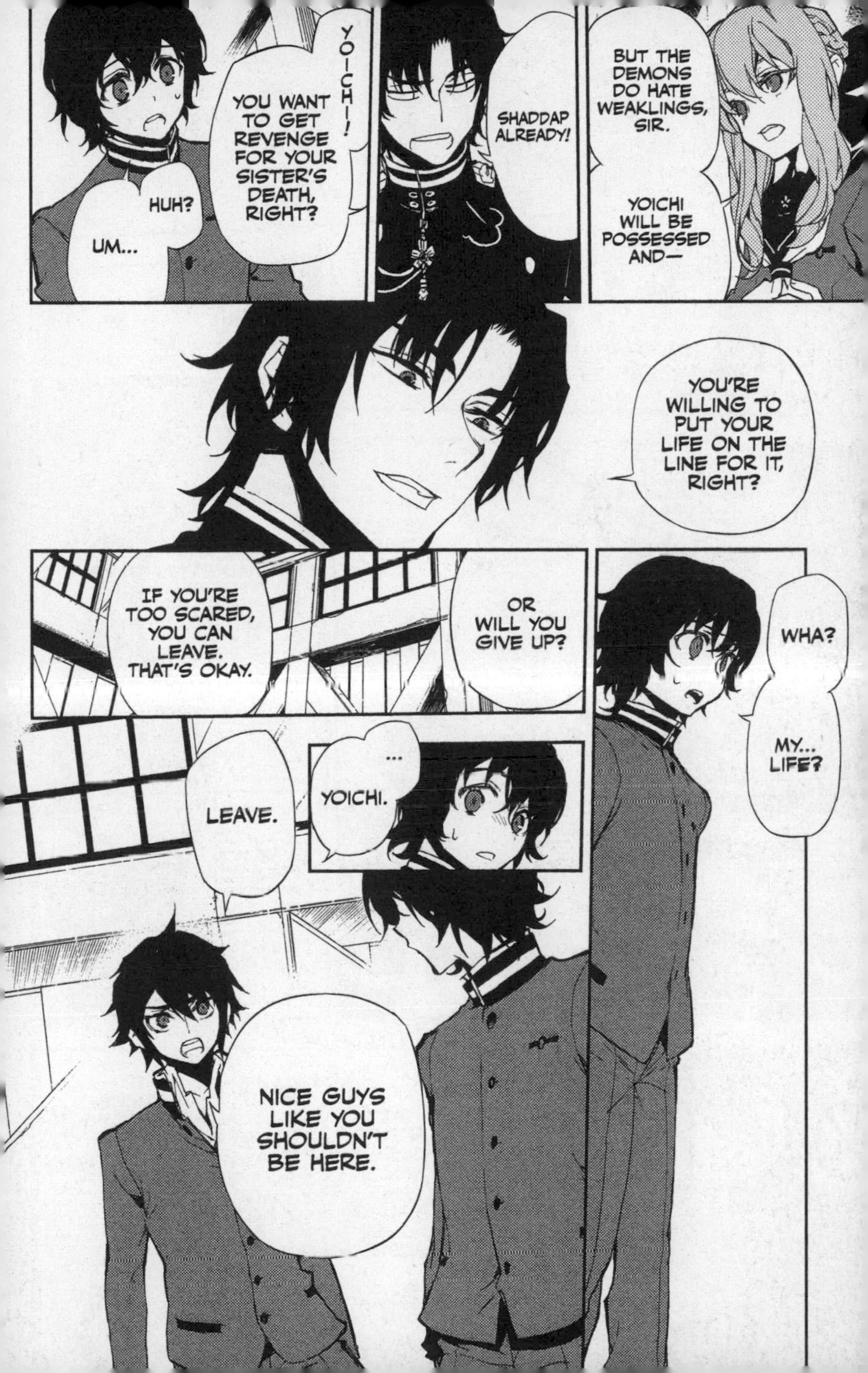
BUT THE DEMONS DO HATE WEAKLINGS, SIR.
YOICHI WILL BE POSSESSED AND—
SHADDAP ALREADY!
YOICHI!
YOU WANT TO GET REVENGE FOR YOUR SISTER'S DEATH, RIGHT?
HUH?
UM...
YOU'RE WILLING TO PUT YOUR LIFE ON THE LINE FOR IT, RIGHT?
WHA?
MY... LIFE?
OR WILL YOU GIVE UP?
IF YOU'RE TOO SCARED, YOU CAN LEAVE. THAT'S OKAY.
...
YOICHI.
LEAVE.
NICE GUYS LIKE YOU SHOULDN'T BE HERE.

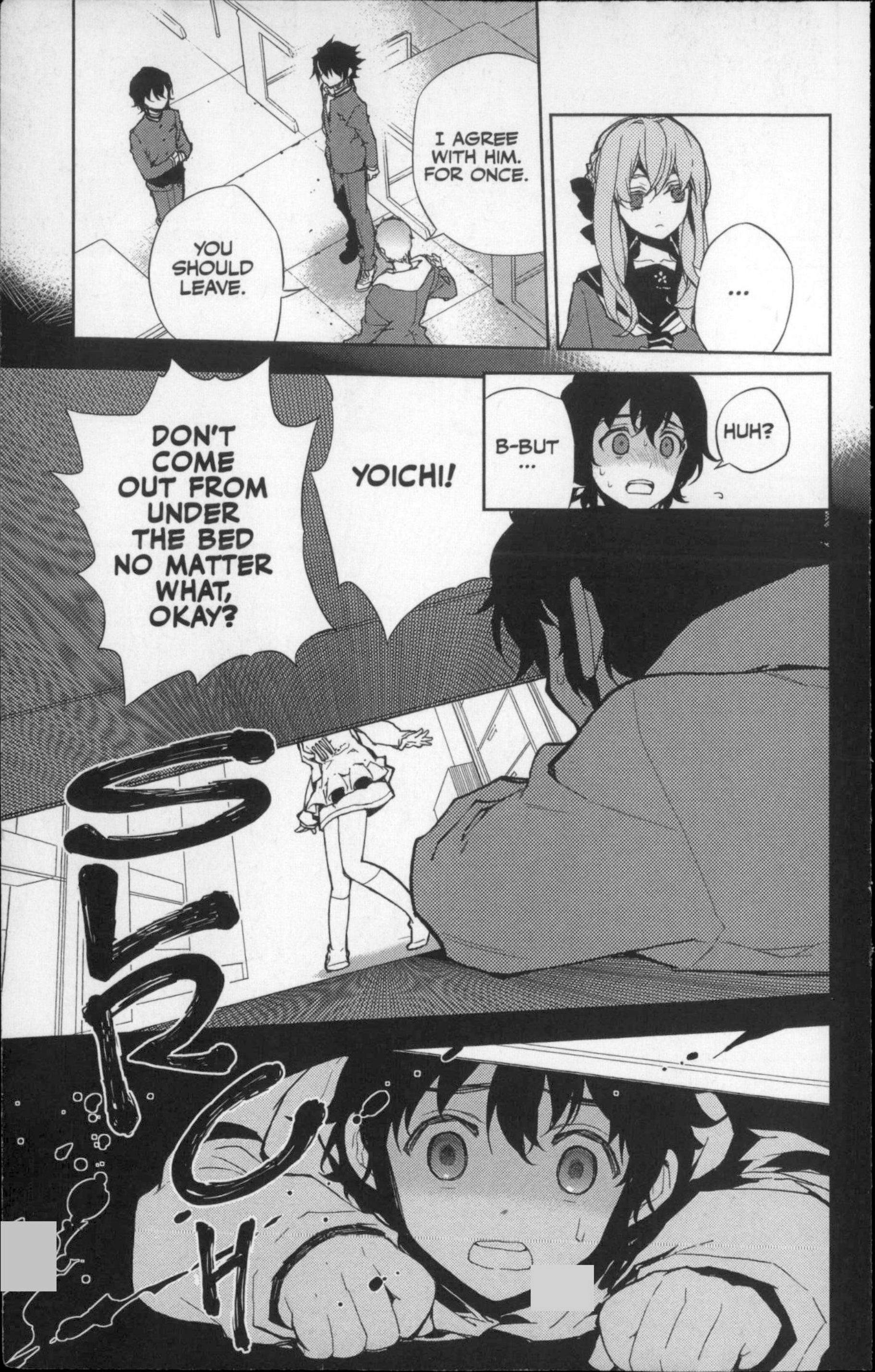
...
I AGREE WITH HIM. FOR ONCE.
YOU SHOULD LEAVE.
HUH?
B-BUT ...
YOICHI!
DON'T COME OUT FROM UNDER THE BED NO MATTER WHAT, OKAY?

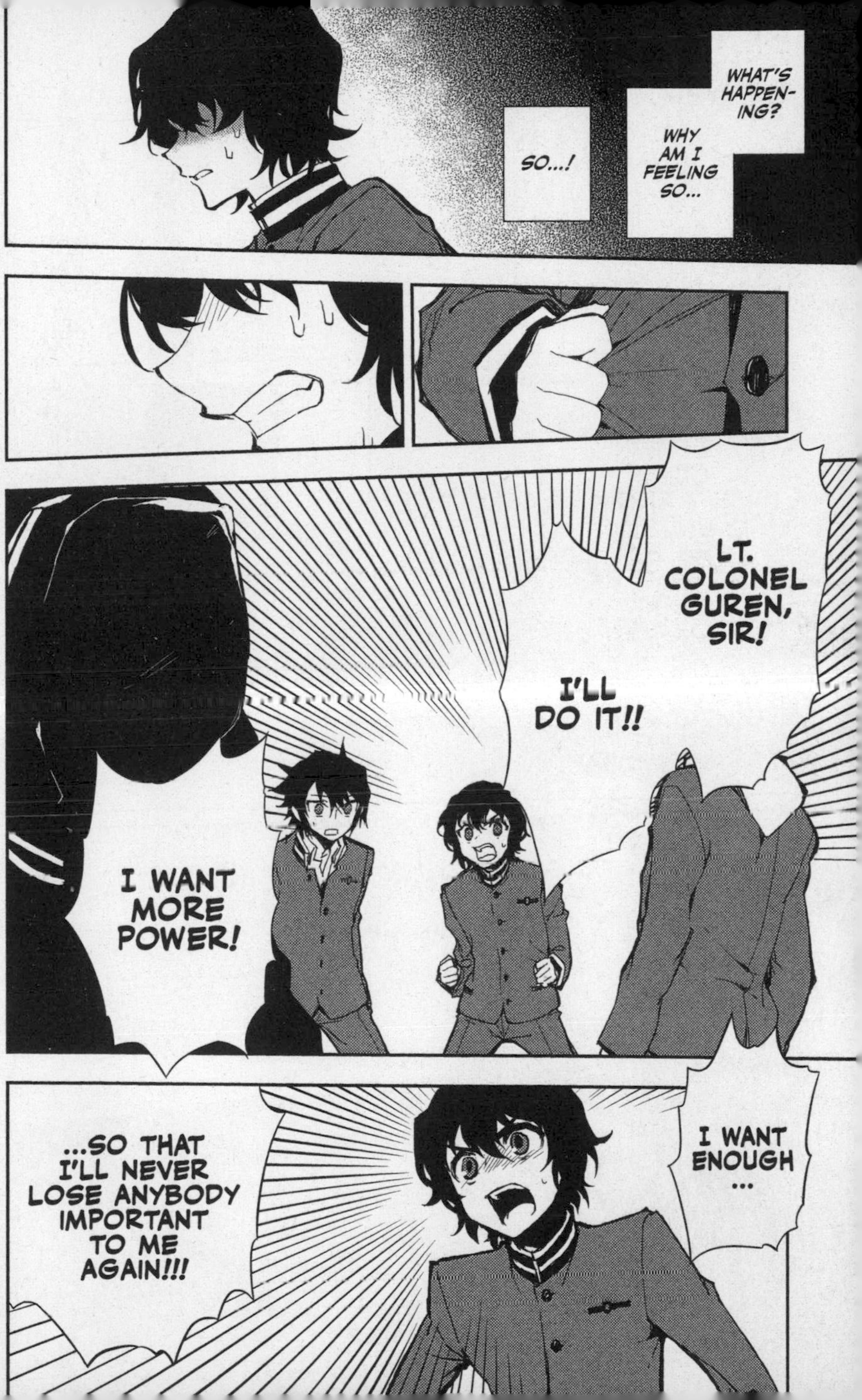
WHAT'S HAPPEN-ING?
WHY AM I FEELING SO...
SO...!
LT. COLONEL GUREN, SIR!
I'LL DO IT!!
I WANT MORE POWER!
I WANT ENOUGH...
...SO THAT I'LL NEVER LOSE ANYBODY IMPORTANT TO ME AGAIN!!!

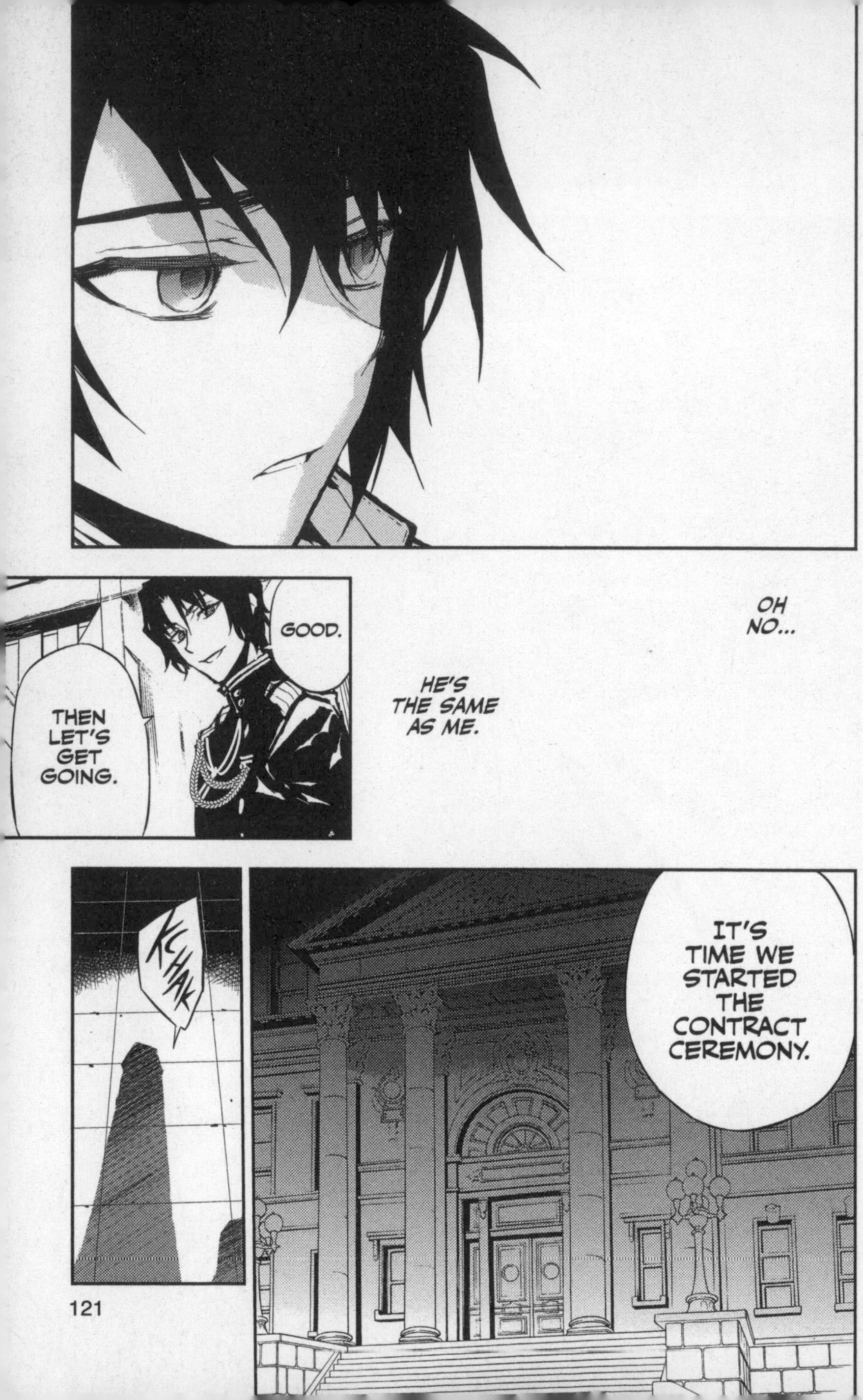
OH NO...
HE'S THE SAME AS ME.
GOOD.
THEN LET'S GET GOING.
IT'S TIME WE STARTED THE CONTRACT CEREMONY.
KCHAK

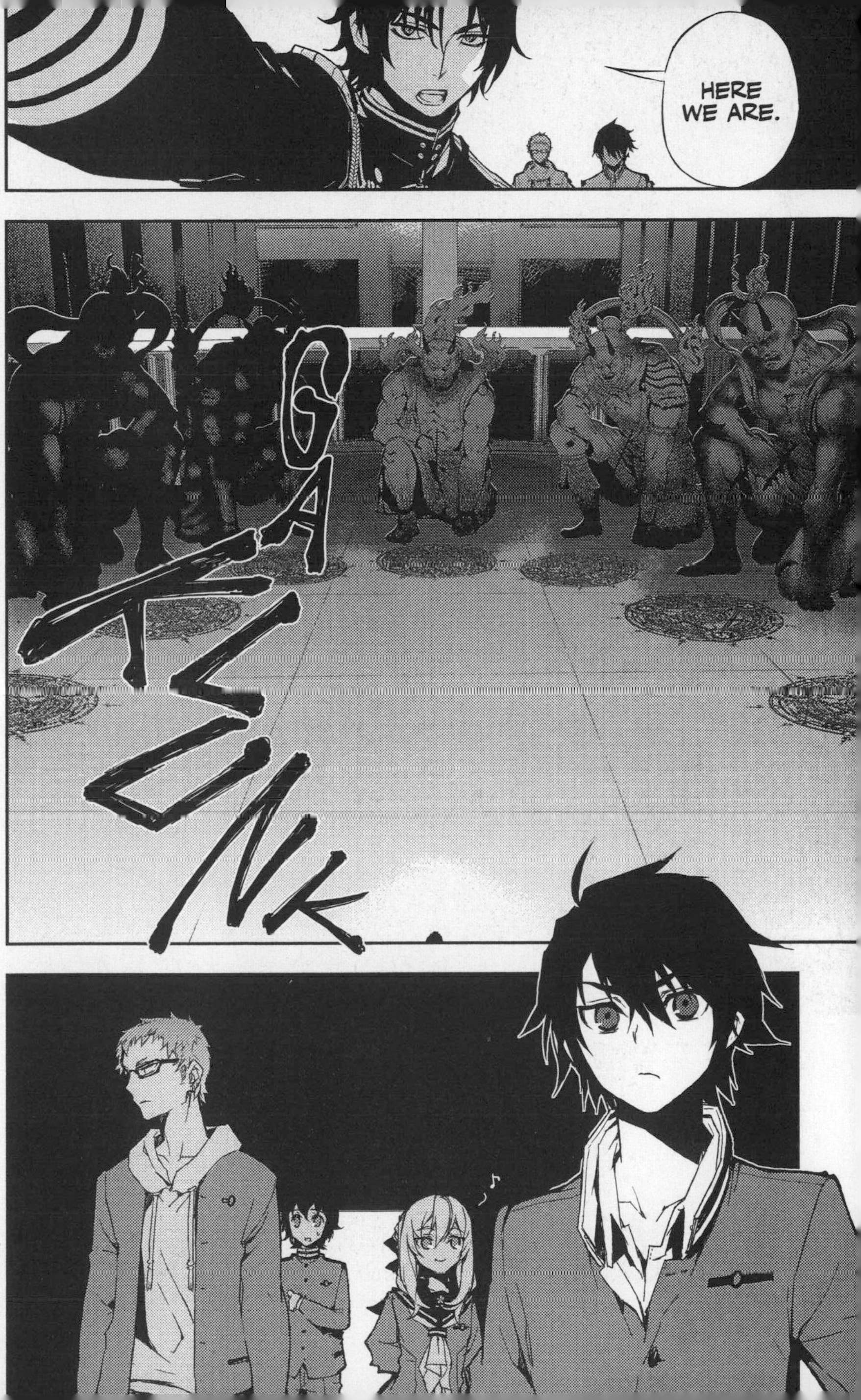
HERE WE ARE.
GATINK

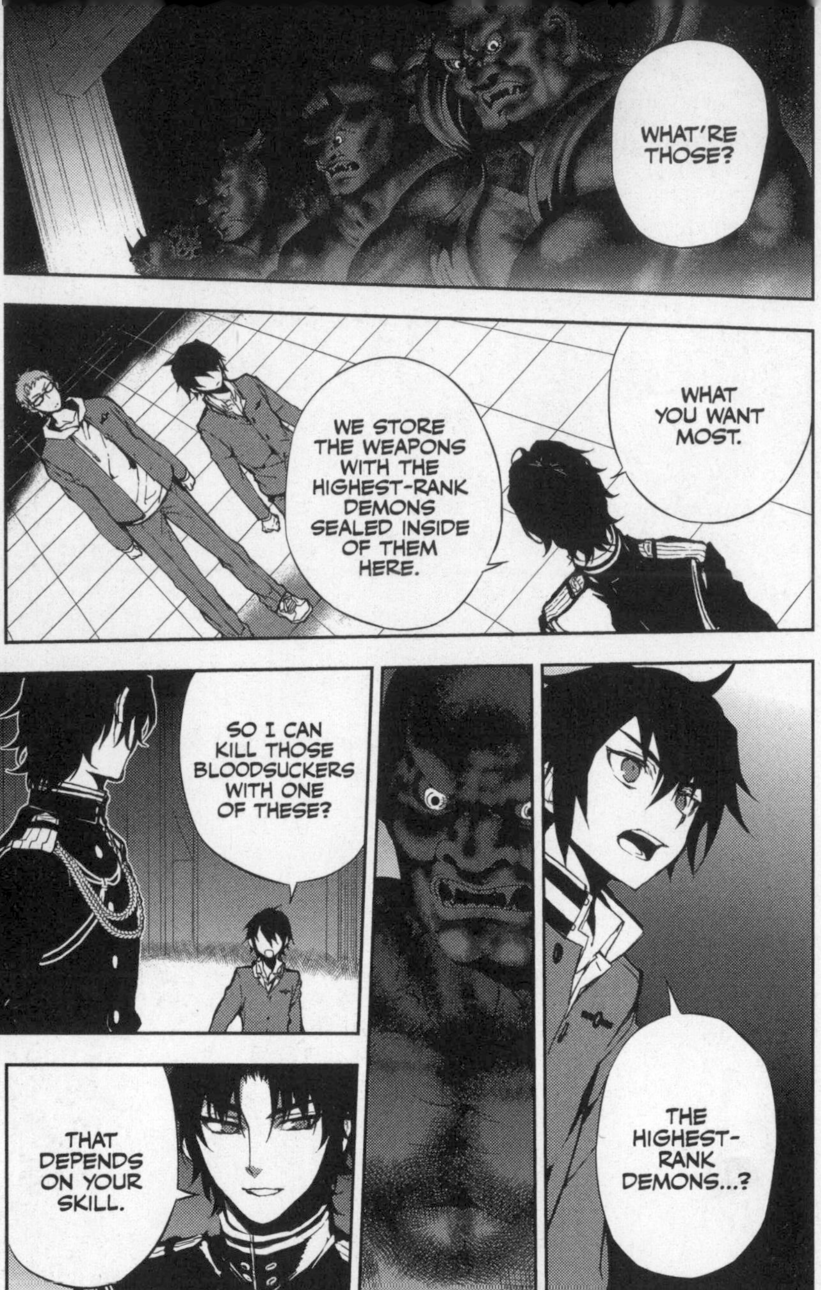
WHAT'RE THOSE?
WHAT YOU WANT MOST.
WE STORE THE WEAPONS WITH THE HIGHEST-RANK DEMONS SEALED INSIDE OF THEM HERE.
THE HIGHEST-RANK DEMONS...?
SO I CAN KILL THOSE BLOODSUCKERS WITH ONE OF THESE?
THAT DEPENDS ON YOUR SKILL.

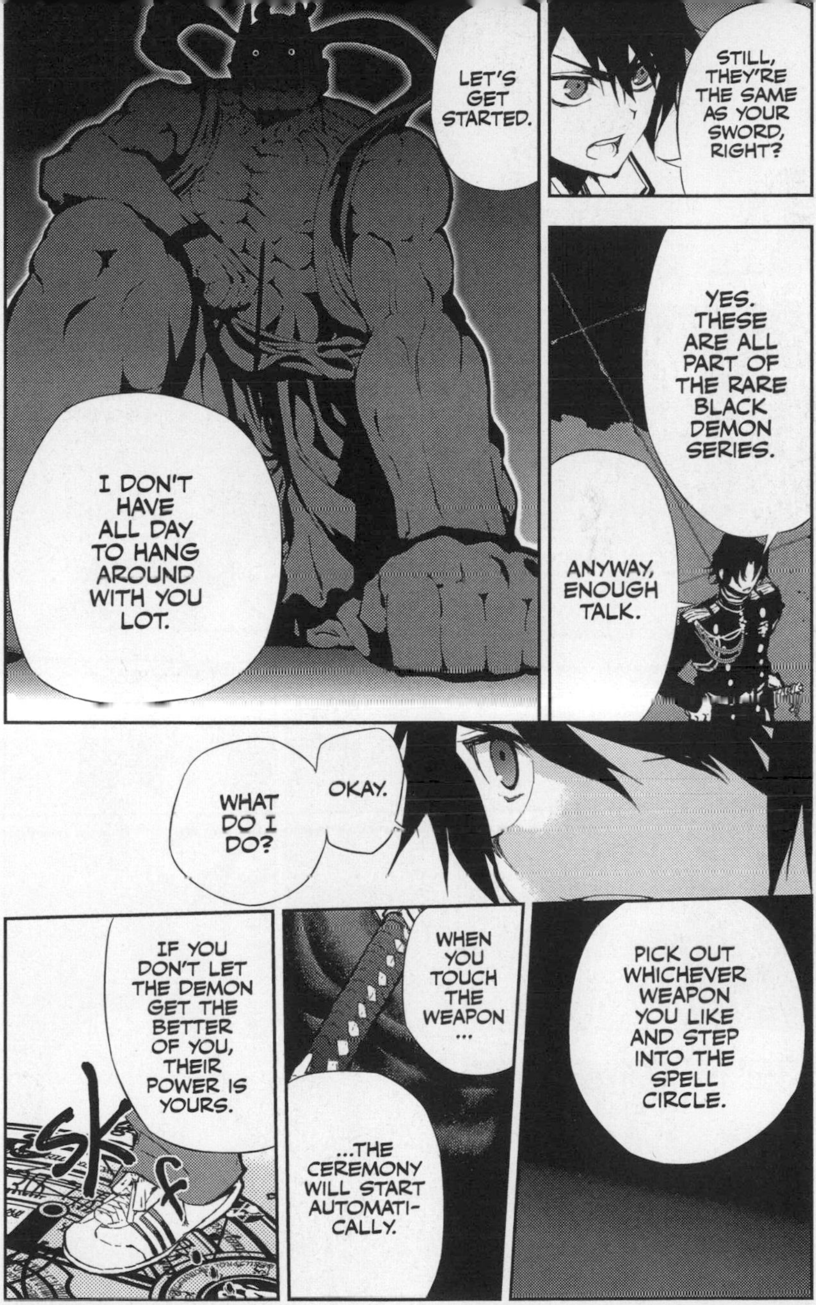
STILL, THEY'RE THE SAME AS YOUR SWORD, RIGHT?
YES. THESE ARE ALL PART OF THE RARE BLACK DEMON SERIES.
ANYWAY, ENOUGH TALK.
LET'S GET STARTED.
I DON'T HAVE ALL DAY TO HANG AROUND WITH YOU LOT.
OKAY.
WHAT DO I DO?
PICK OUT WHICHEVER WEAPON YOU LIKE AND STEP INTO THE SPELL CIRCLE.
WHEN YOU TOUCH THE WEAPON...
...THE CEREMONY WILL START AUTOMATI-CALLY.
IF YOU DON'T LET THE DEMON GET THE BETTER OF YOU, THEIR POWER IS YOURS.

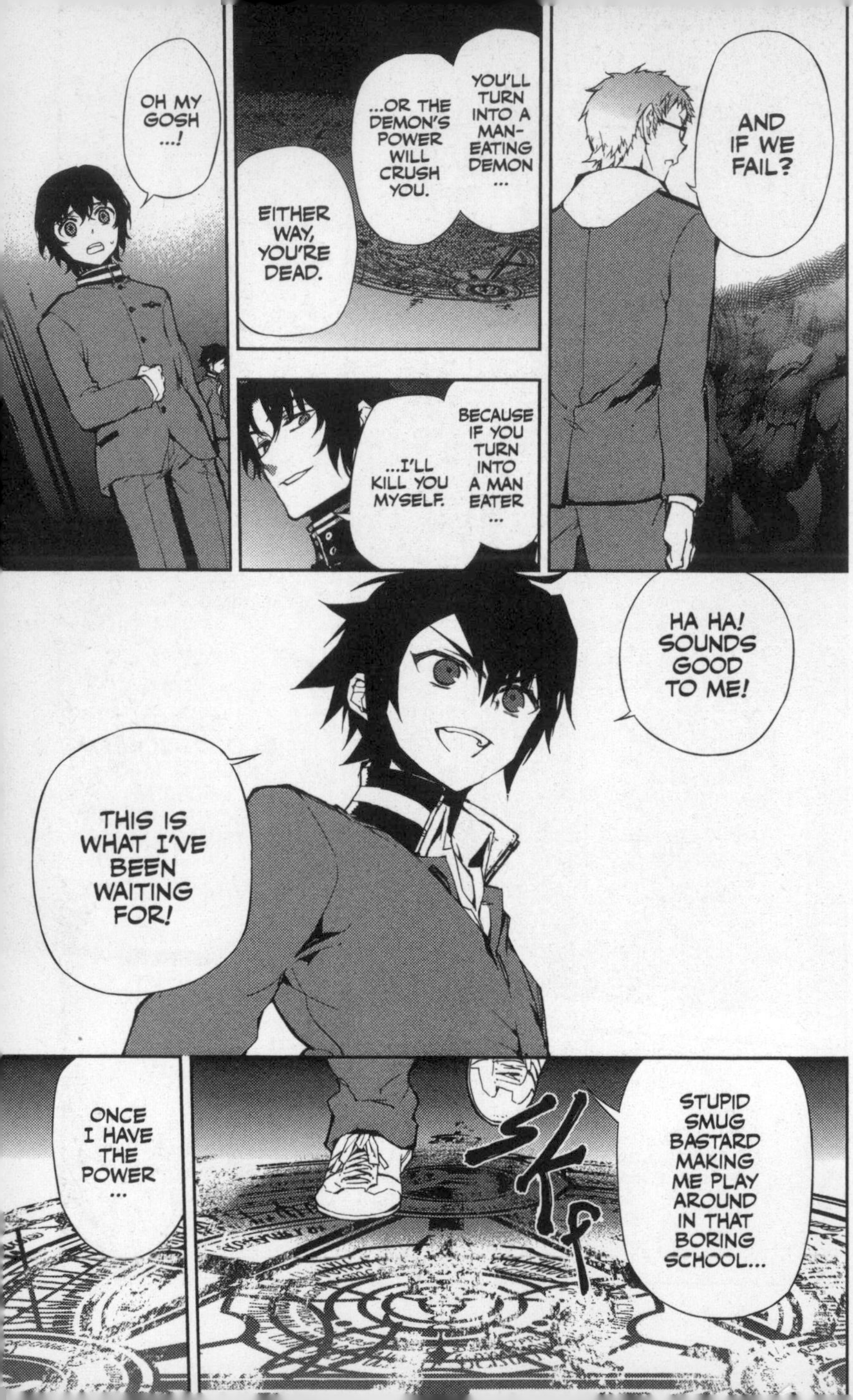
AND IF WE FAIL?
YOU'LL TURN INTO A MAN-EATING DEMON...
...OR THE DEMON'S POWER WILL CRUSH YOU.
EITHER WAY, YOU'RE DEAD.
BECAUSE IF YOU TURN INTO A MAN EATER...
...I'LL KILL YOU MYSELF.
OH MY GOSH ...!
HA HA! SOUNDS GOOD TO ME!
THIS IS WHAT I'VE BEEN WAITING FOR!
STUPID SMUG BASTARD MAKING ME PLAY AROUND IN THAT BORING SCHOOL...
SKF
ONCE I HAVE THE POWER...

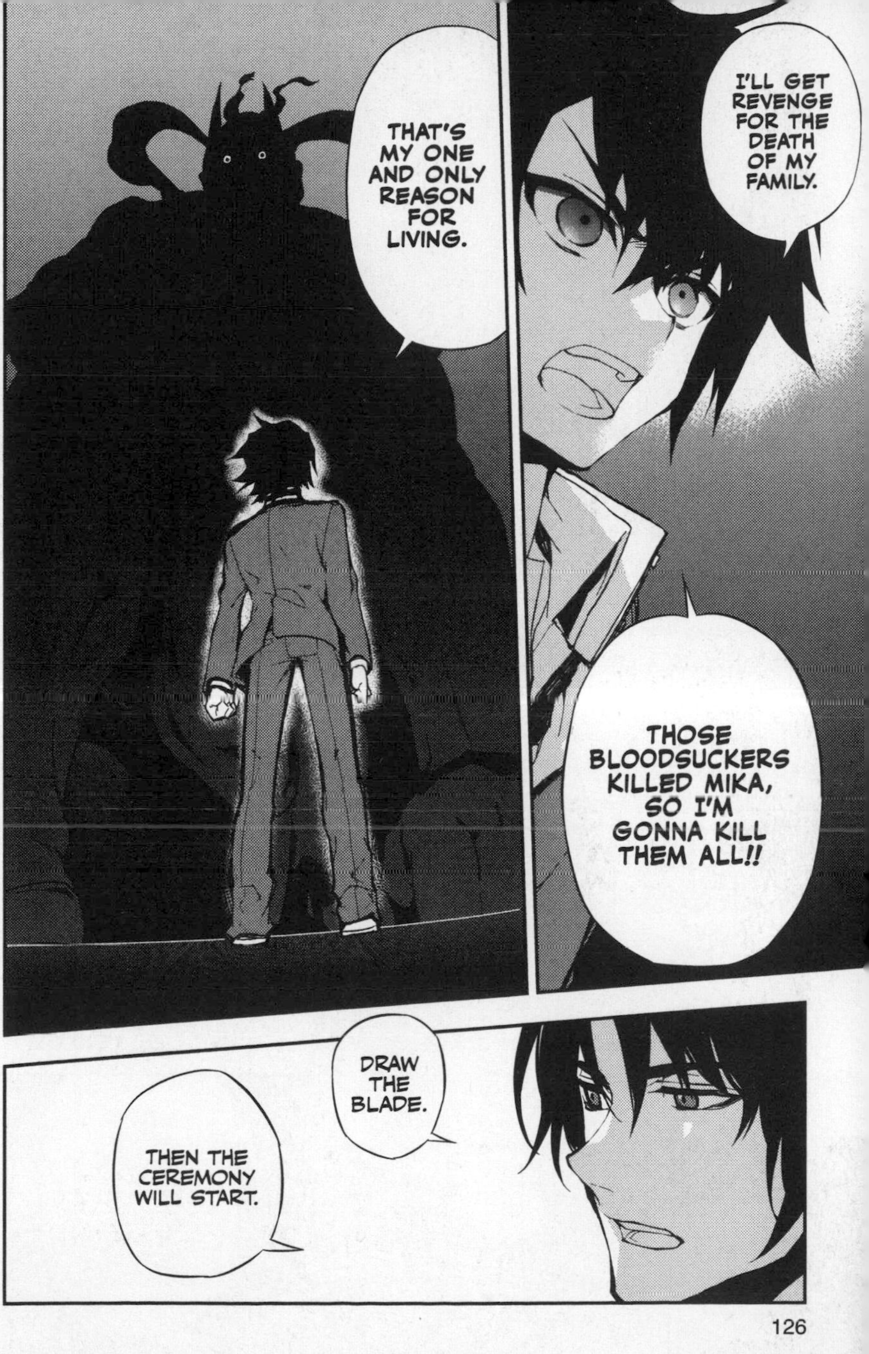
I'LL GET REVENGE FOR THE DEATH OF MY FAMILY.
THOSE BLOODSUCKERS KILLED MIKA, SO I'M GONNA KILL THEM ALL!!
THAT'S MY ONE AND ONLY REASON FOR LIVING.
DRAW THE BLADE.
THEN THE CEREMONY WILL START.

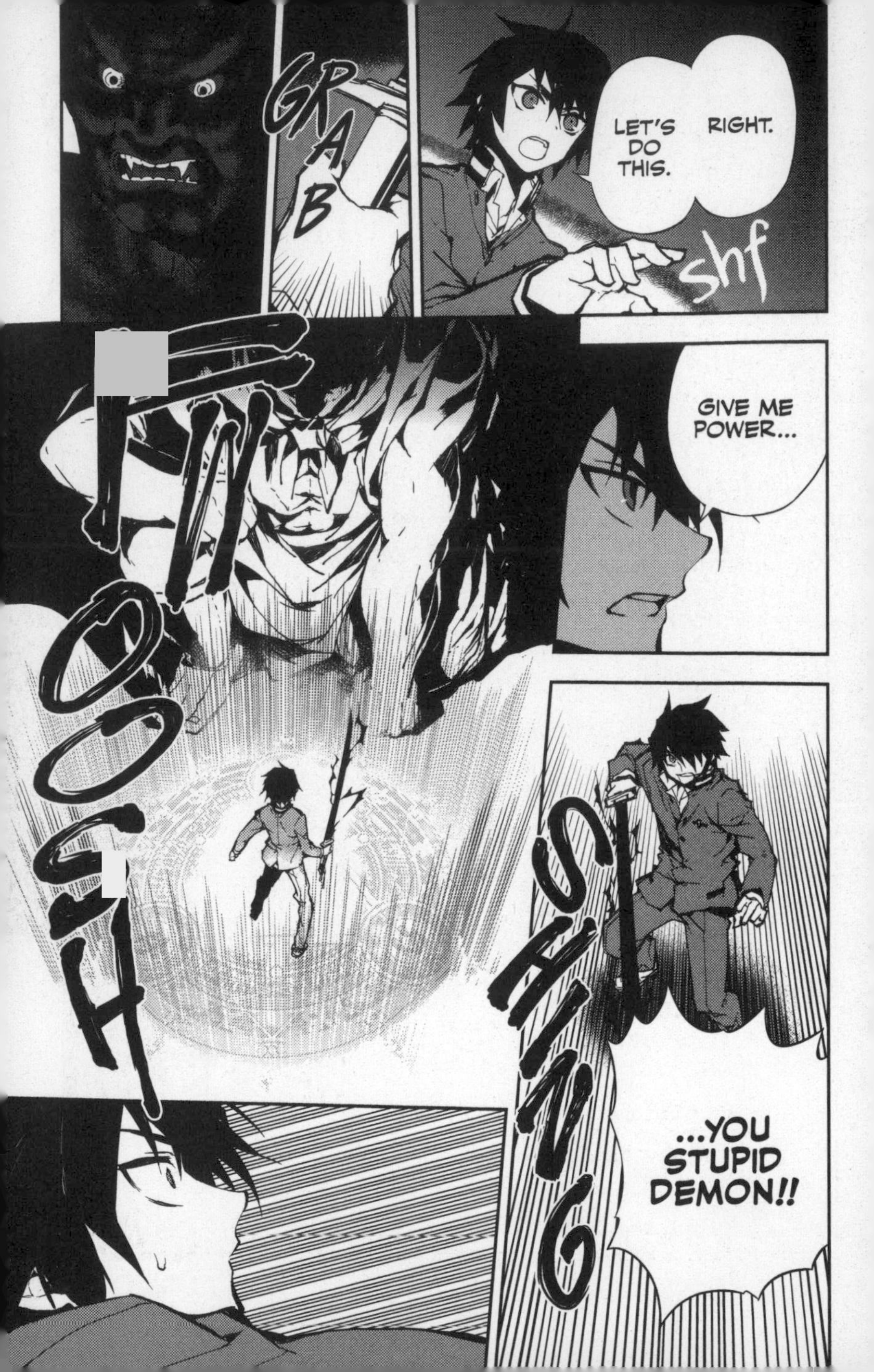
RIGHT.
LET'S DO THIS.
shf
GRAB
GIVE ME POWER...
FWOOSH
SHING
...YOU STUPID DEMON!!

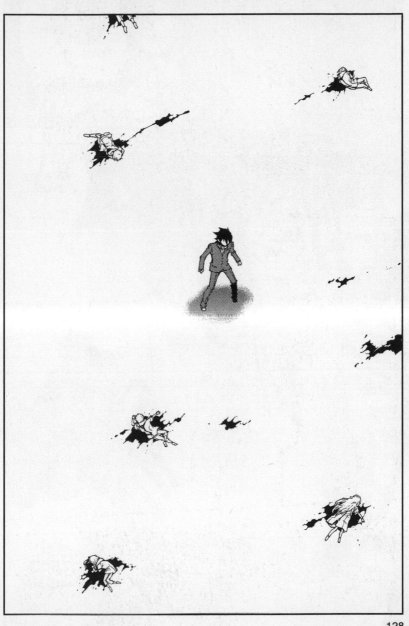

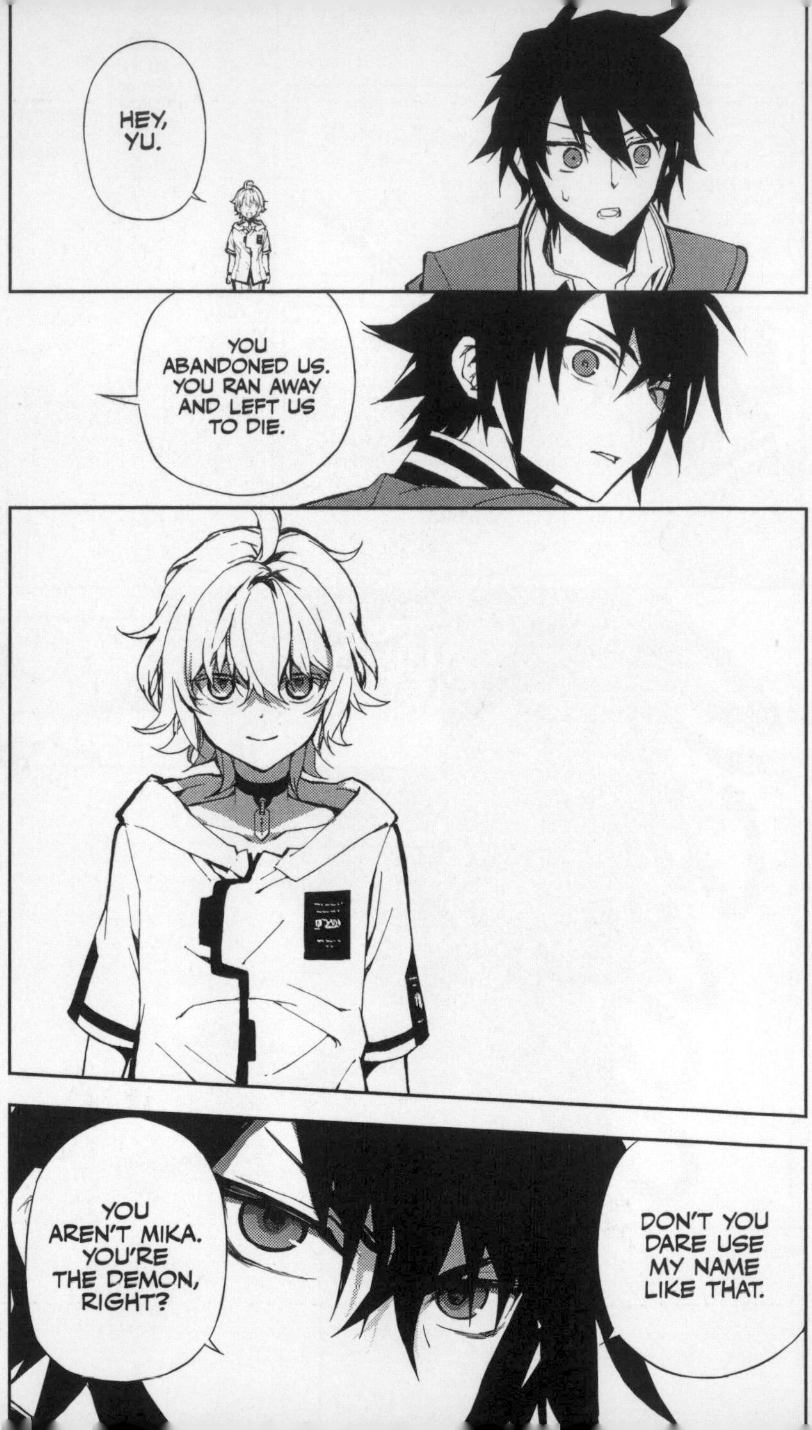
HEY, YU.
YOU ABANDONED US. YOU RAN AWAY AND LEFT US TO DIE.
DON'T YOU DARE USE MY NAME LIKE THAT.
YOU AREN'T MIKA. YOU'RE THE DEMON, RIGHT?

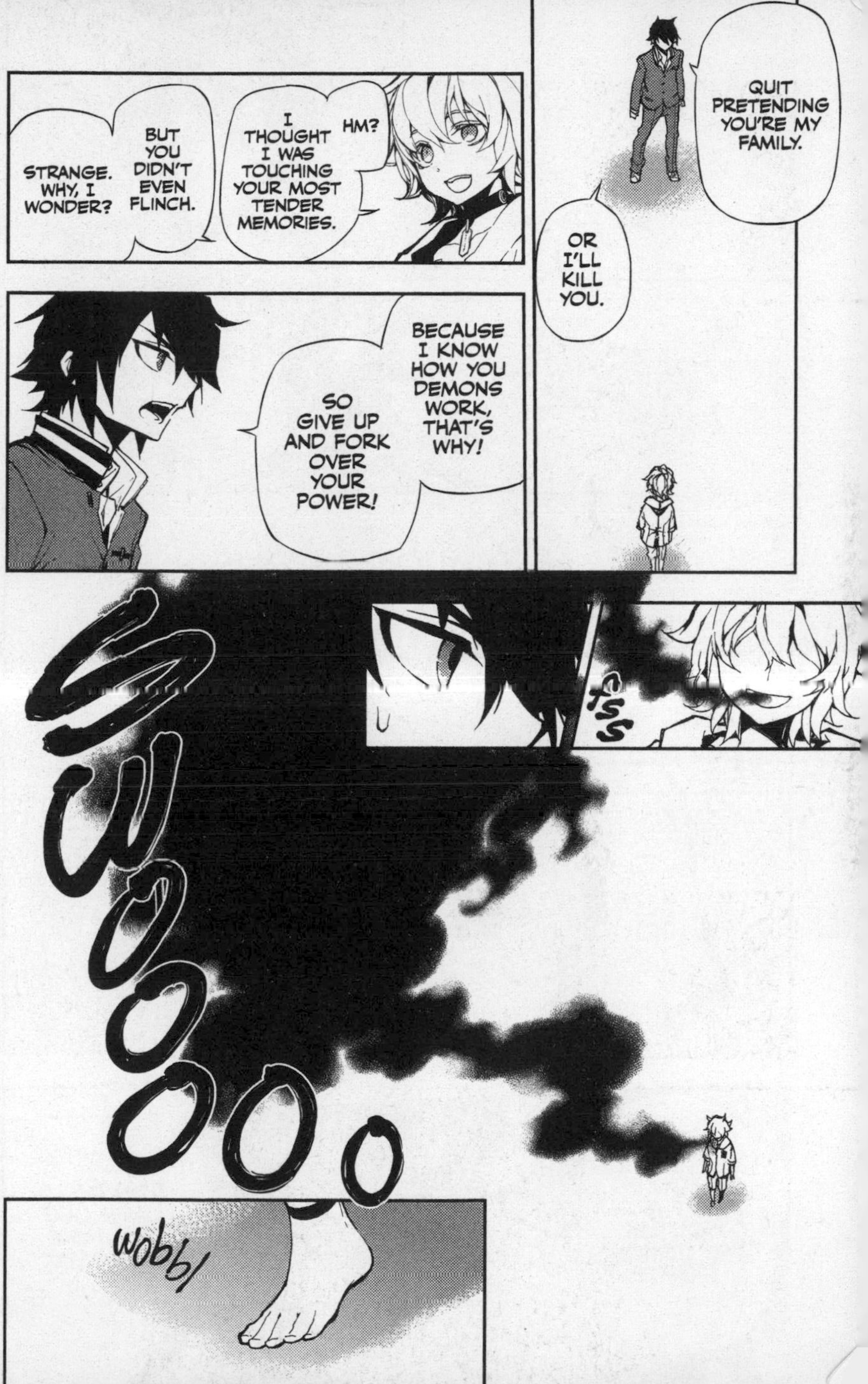
QUIT PRETENDING YOU'RE MY FAMILY.
OR I'LL KILL YOU.
HM?
I THOUGHT I WAS TOUCHING YOUR MOST TENDER MEMORIES.
BUT YOU DIDN'T EVEN FLINCH.
STRANGE. WHY, I WONDER?
BECAUSE I KNOW HOW YOU DEMONS WORK, THAT'S WHY!
SO GIVE UP AND FORK OVER YOUR POWER!
fss
SWOOOOOO
wobbl

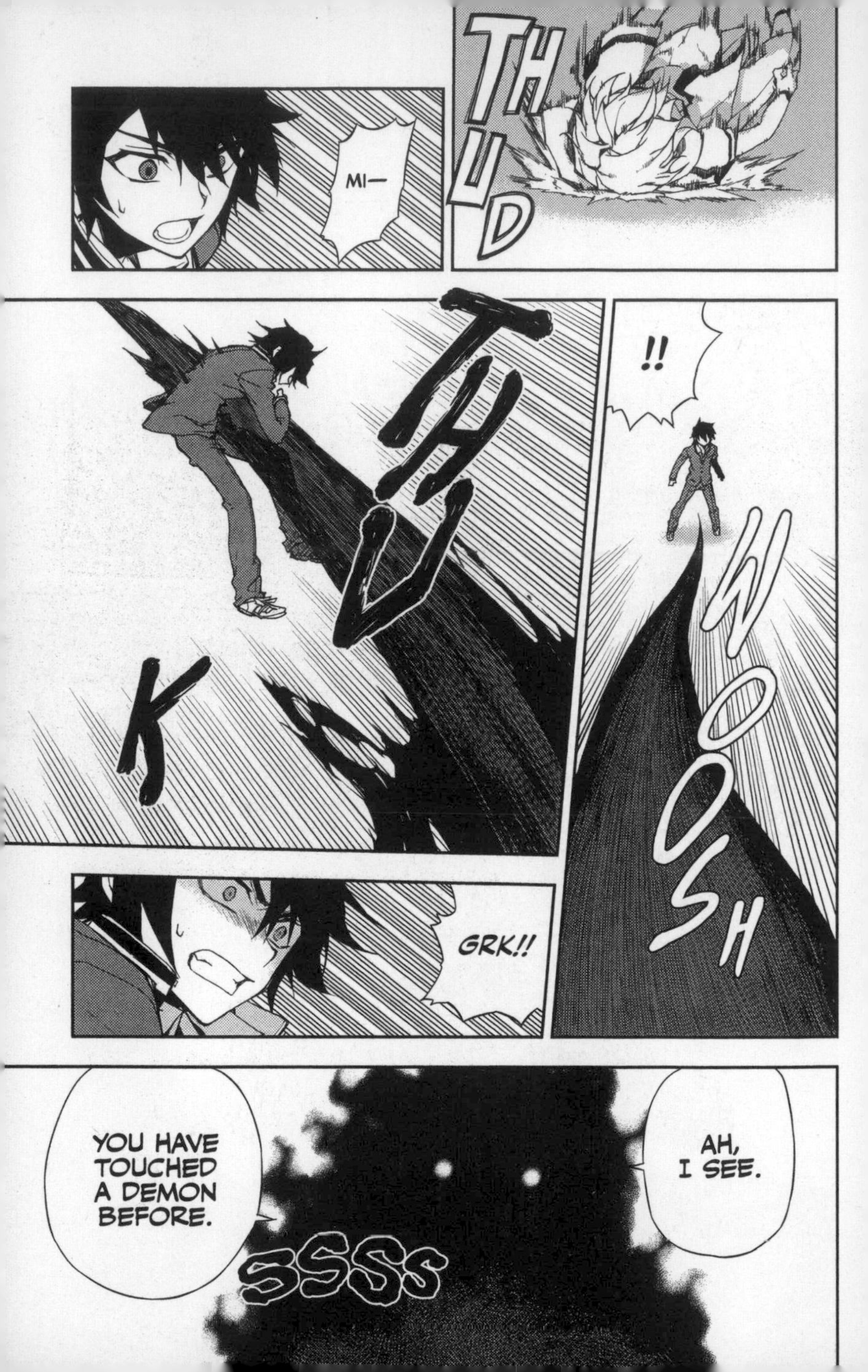
THUD
MI—
!!
WHOOSH
THUNK
GRK!!
AH, I SEE.
YOU HAVE TOUCHED A DEMON BEFORE.
SSSS

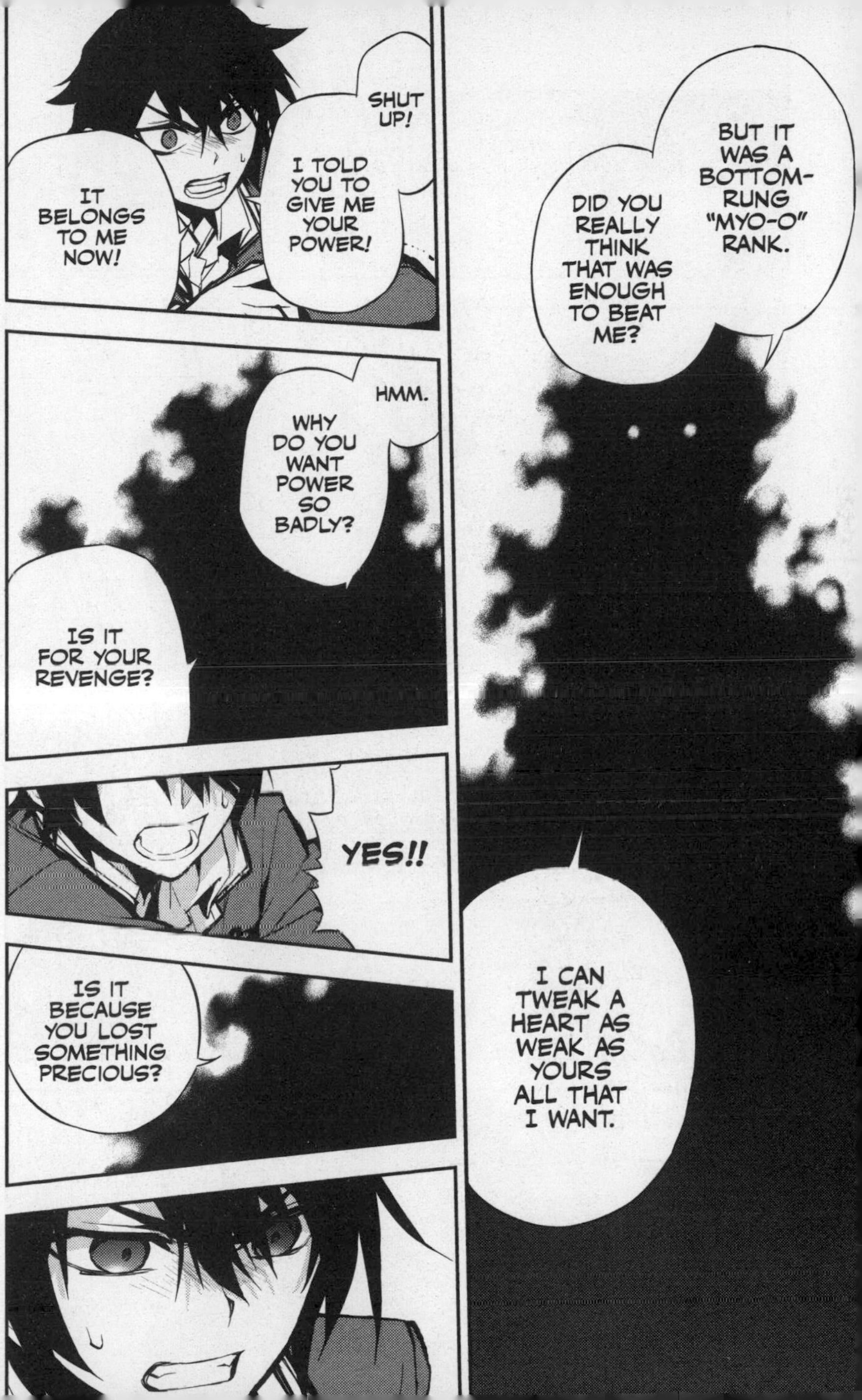
BUT IT WAS A BOTTOM-RUNG "MYO-O" RANK.
DID YOU REALLY THINK THAT WAS ENOUGH TO BEAT ME?
I CAN TWEAK A HEART AS WEAK AS YOURS ALL THAT I WANT.
SHUT UP!
I TOLD YOU TO GIVE ME YOUR POWER!
IT BELONGS TO ME NOW!
HMM.
WHY DO YOU WANT POWER SO BADLY?
IS IT FOR YOUR REVENGE?
YES!!
IS IT BECAUSE YOU LOST SOMETHING PRECIOUS?

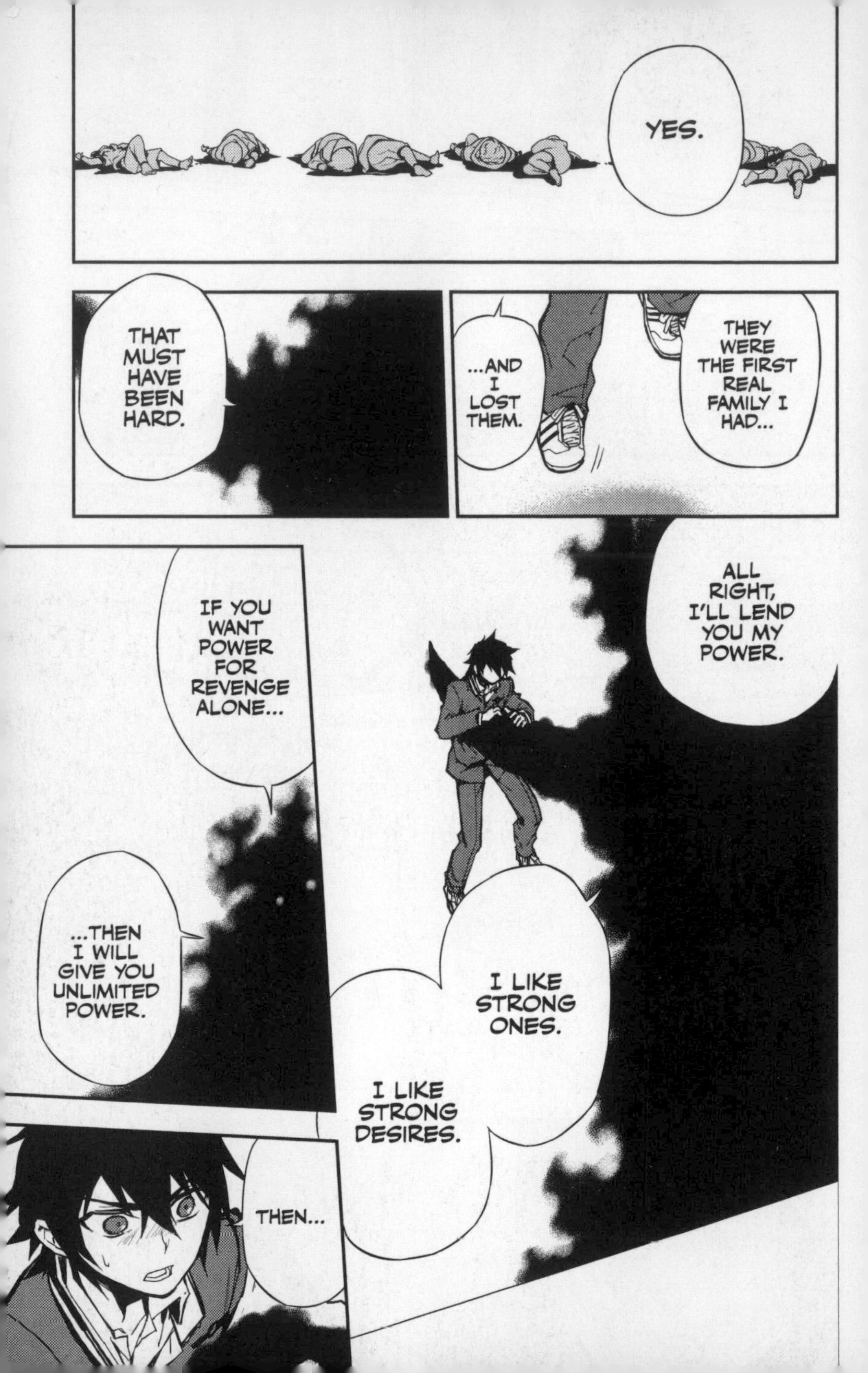
YES.
THEY WERE THE FIRST REAL FAMILY I HAD...
...AND I LOST THEM.
THAT MUST HAVE BEEN HARD.
ALL RIGHT, I'LL LEND YOU MY POWER.
I LIKE STRONG ONES.
I LIKE STRONG DESIRES.
IF YOU WANT POWER FOR REVENGE ALONE...
...THEN I WILL GIVE YOU UNLIMITED POWER.
THEN...

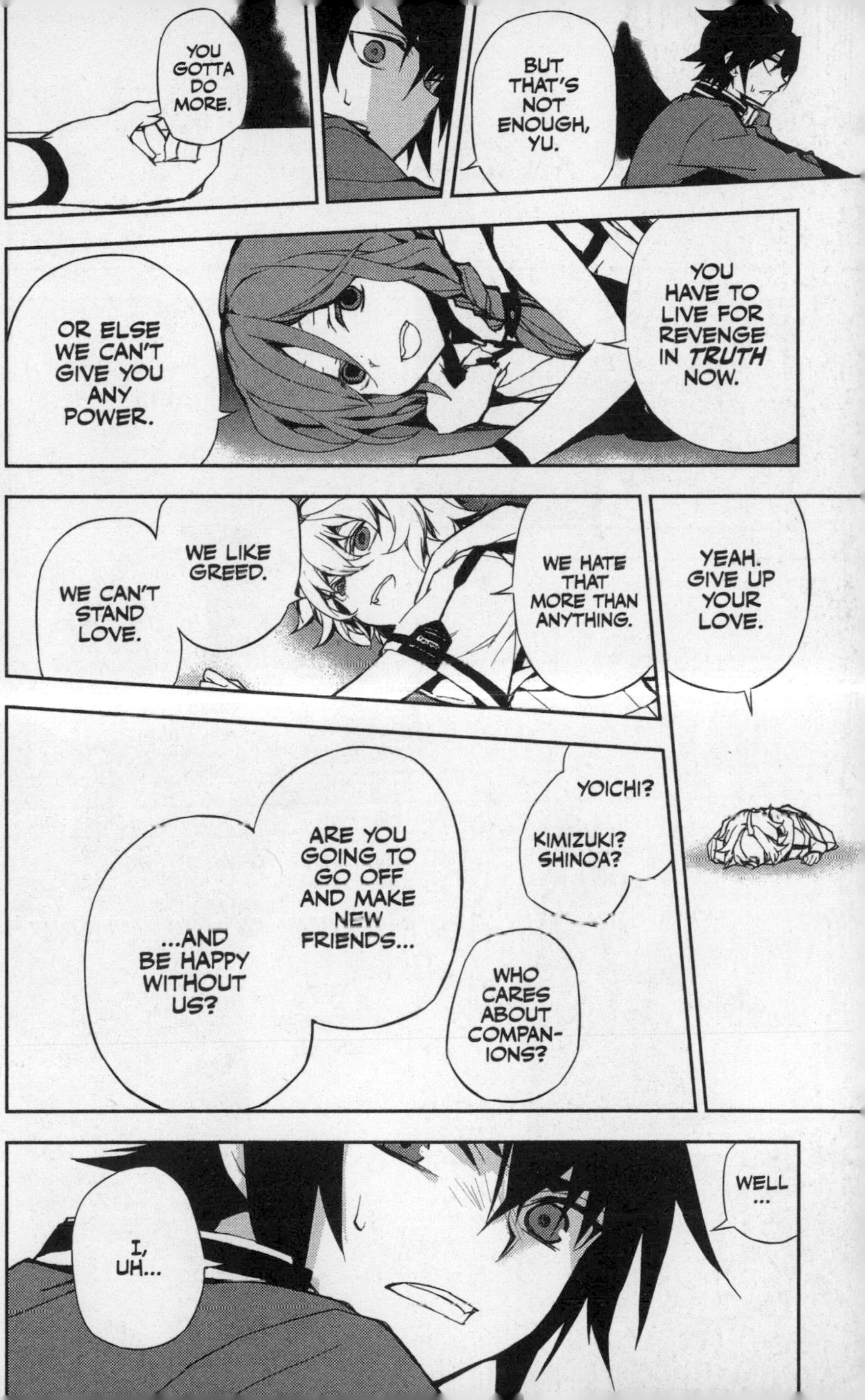
BUT THAT'S NOT ENOUGH, YU.
YOU GOTTA DO MORE.
YOU HAVE TO LIVE FOR REVENGE IN *TRUTH* NOW.
OR ELSE WE CAN'T GIVE YOU ANY POWER.
YEAH. GIVE UP YOUR LOVE.
WE HATE THAT MORE THAN ANYTHING.
WE LIKE GREED.
WE CAN'T STAND LOVE.
YOICHI?
KIMIZUKI? SHINOA?
WHO CARES ABOUT COMPANIONS?
ARE YOU GOING TO GO OFF AND MAKE NEW FRIENDS...
...AND BE HAPPY WITHOUT US?
WELL...
I, UH...

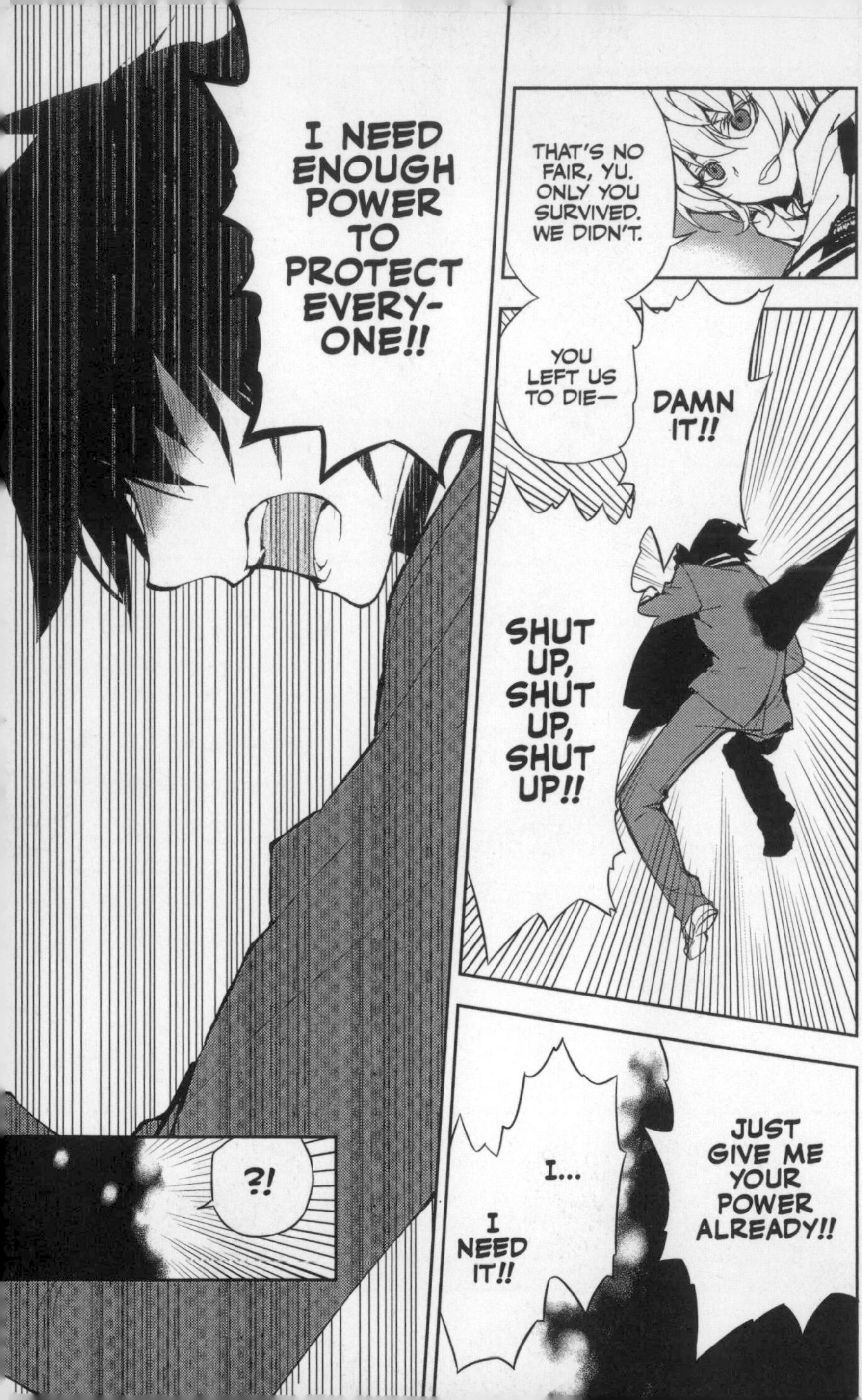
THAT'S NO FAIR, YU. ONLY YOU SURVIVED. WE DIDN'T.
YOU LEFT US TO DIE—
DAMN IT!!
SHUT UP, SHUT UP, SHUT UP!!
JUST GIVE ME YOUR POWER ALREADY!!
I...
I NEED IT!!
I NEED ENOUGH POWER TO PROTECT EVERY-ONE!!
?!

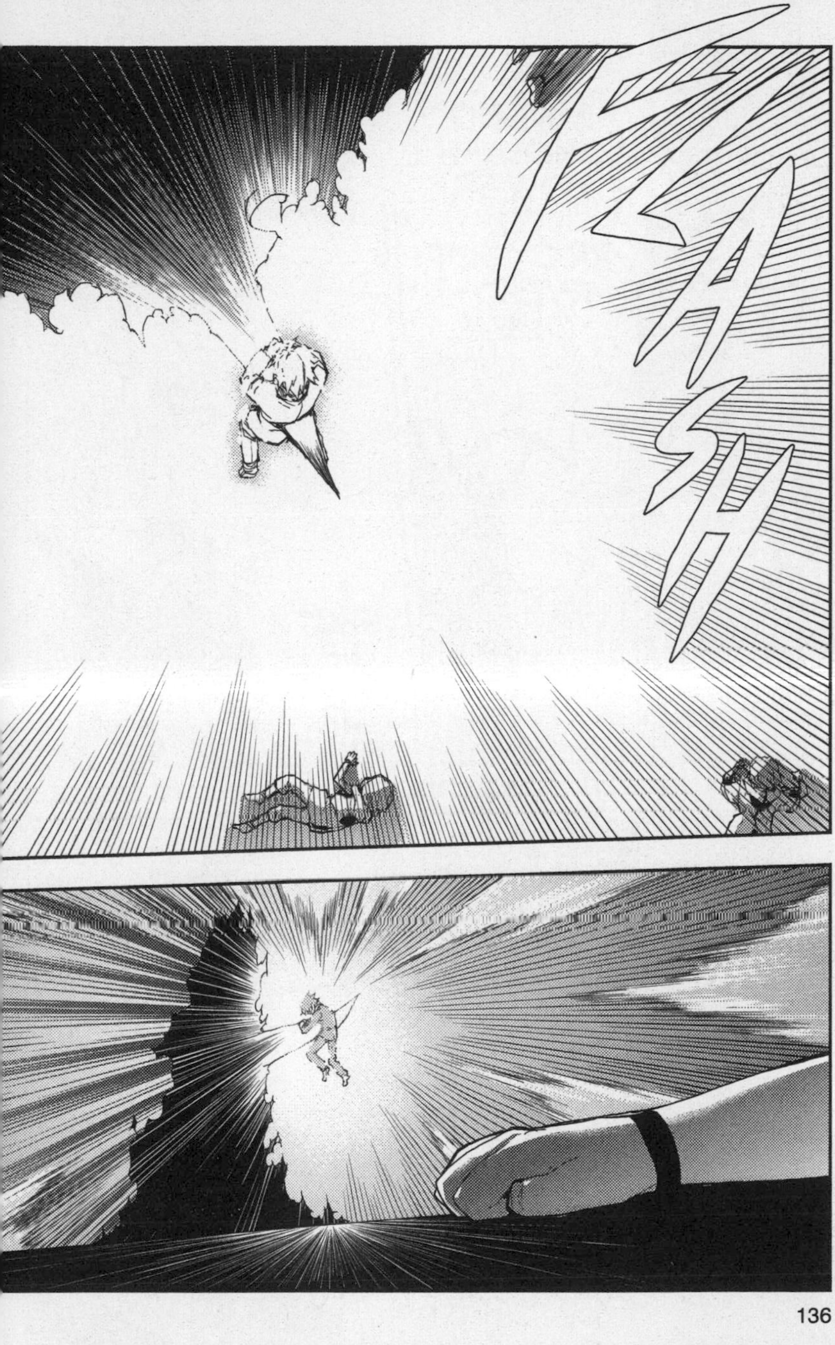
FLASH

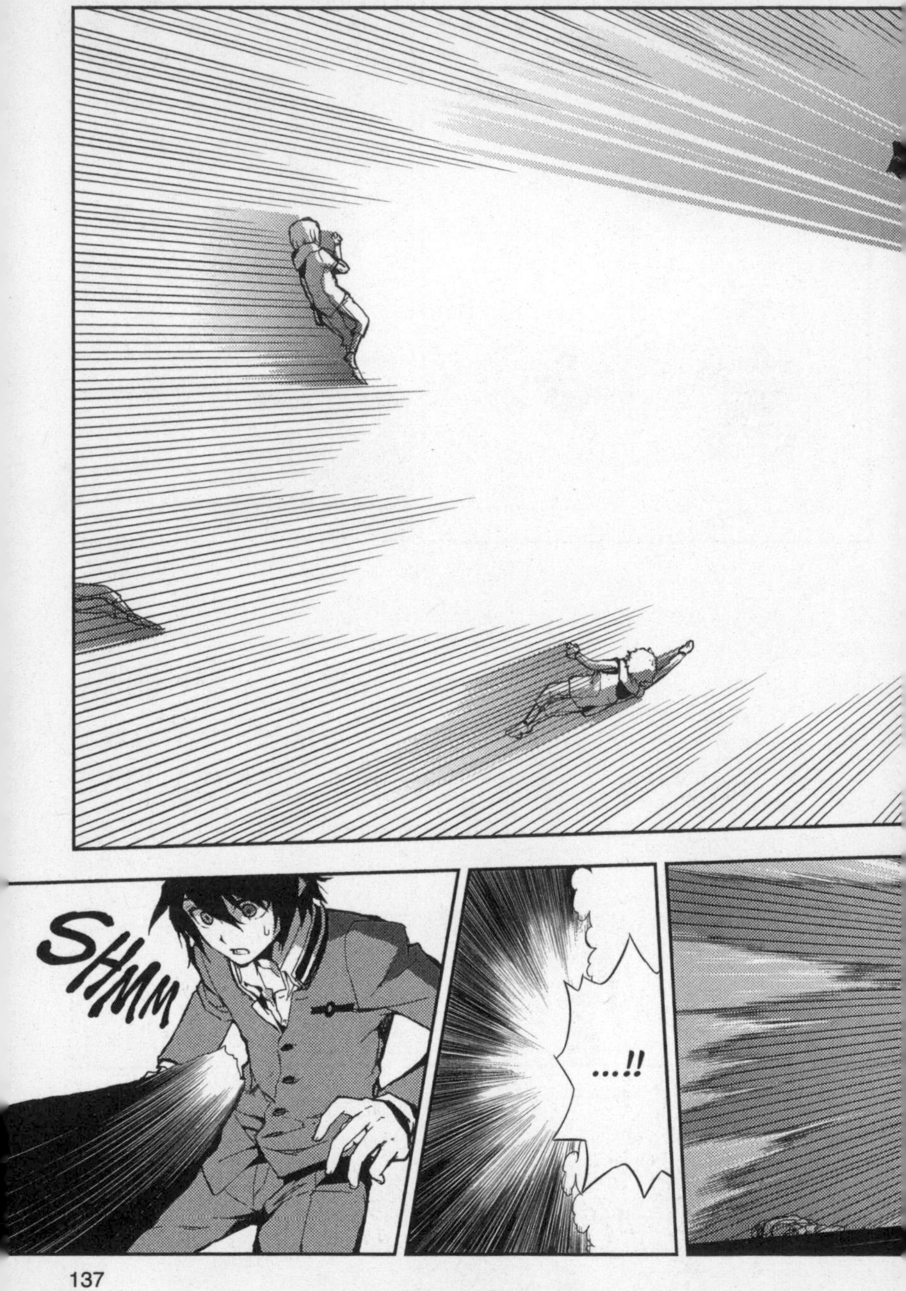
...!!
SHMM

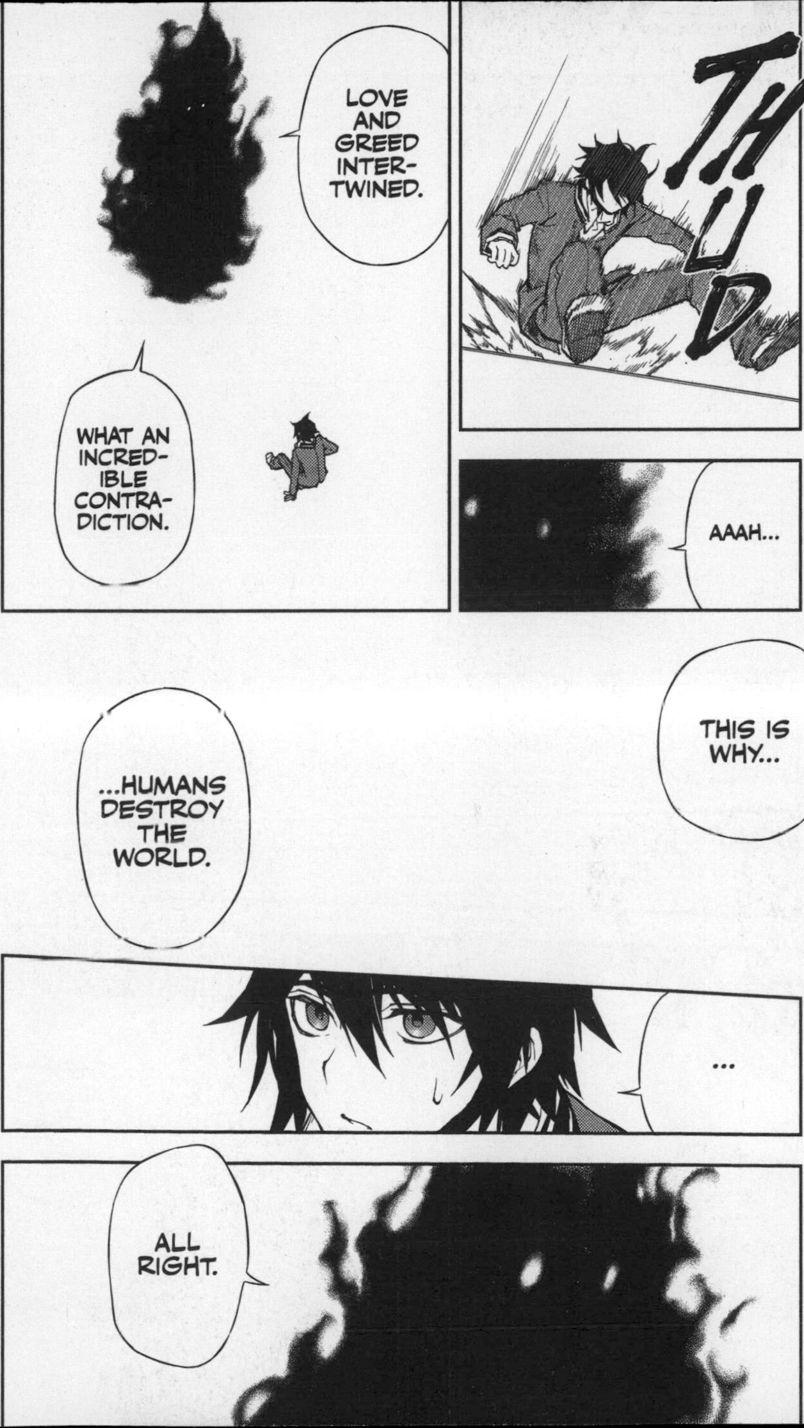
THUD
AAAH...
LOVE AND GREED INTER-TWINED.
WHAT AN INCRED-IBLE CONTRA-DICTION.
THIS IS WHY...
...HUMANS DESTROY THE WORLD.
...
ALL RIGHT.

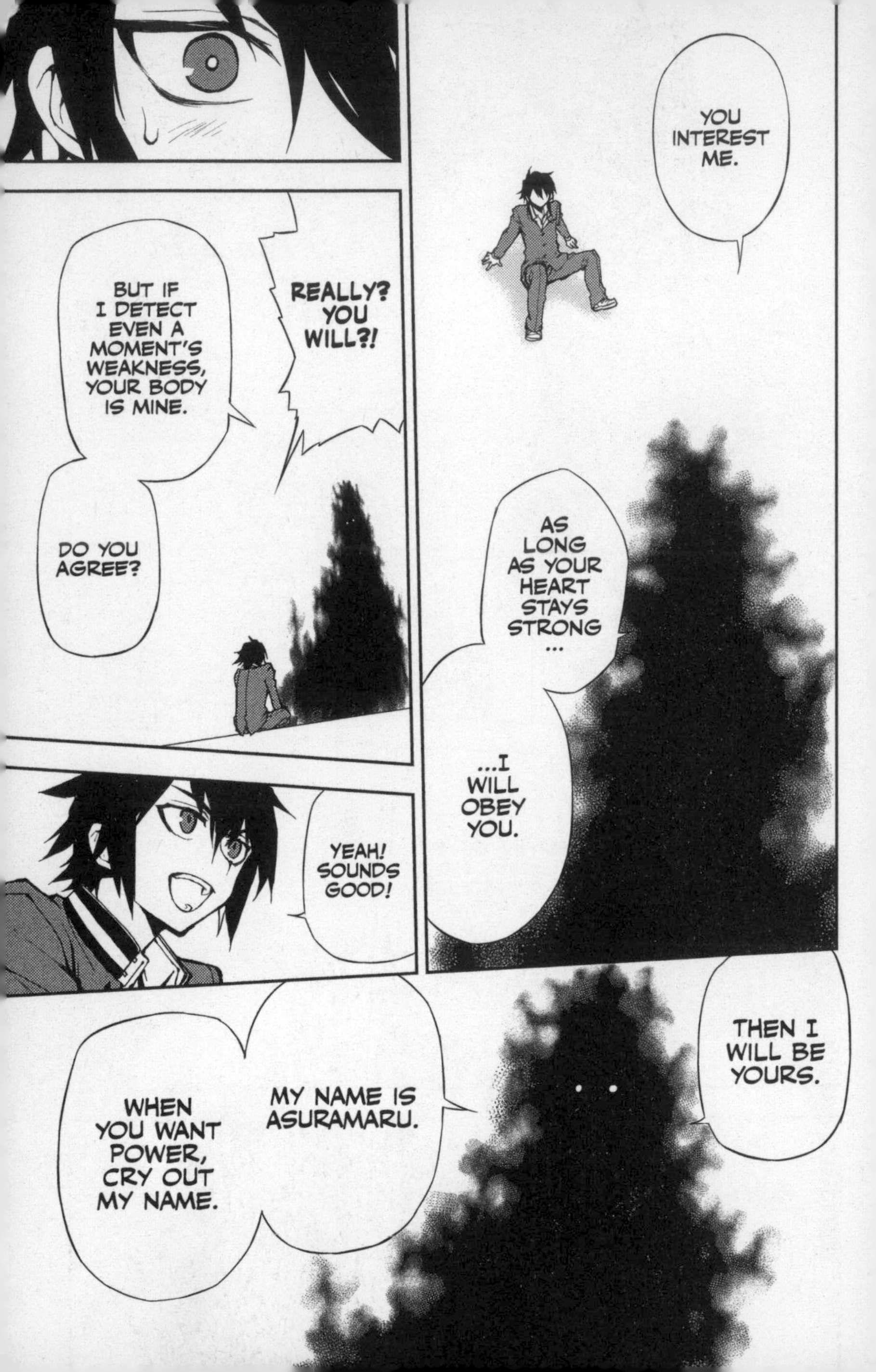
YOU INTEREST ME.
AS LONG AS YOUR HEART STAYS STRONG...
...I WILL OBEY YOU.
REALLY? YOU WILL?!
BUT IF I DETECT EVEN A MOMENT'S WEAKNESS, YOUR BODY IS MINE.
DO YOU AGREE?
YEAH! SOUNDS GOOD!
THEN I WILL BE YOURS.
MY NAME IS ASURAMARU.
WHEN YOU WANT POWER, CRY OUT MY NAME.

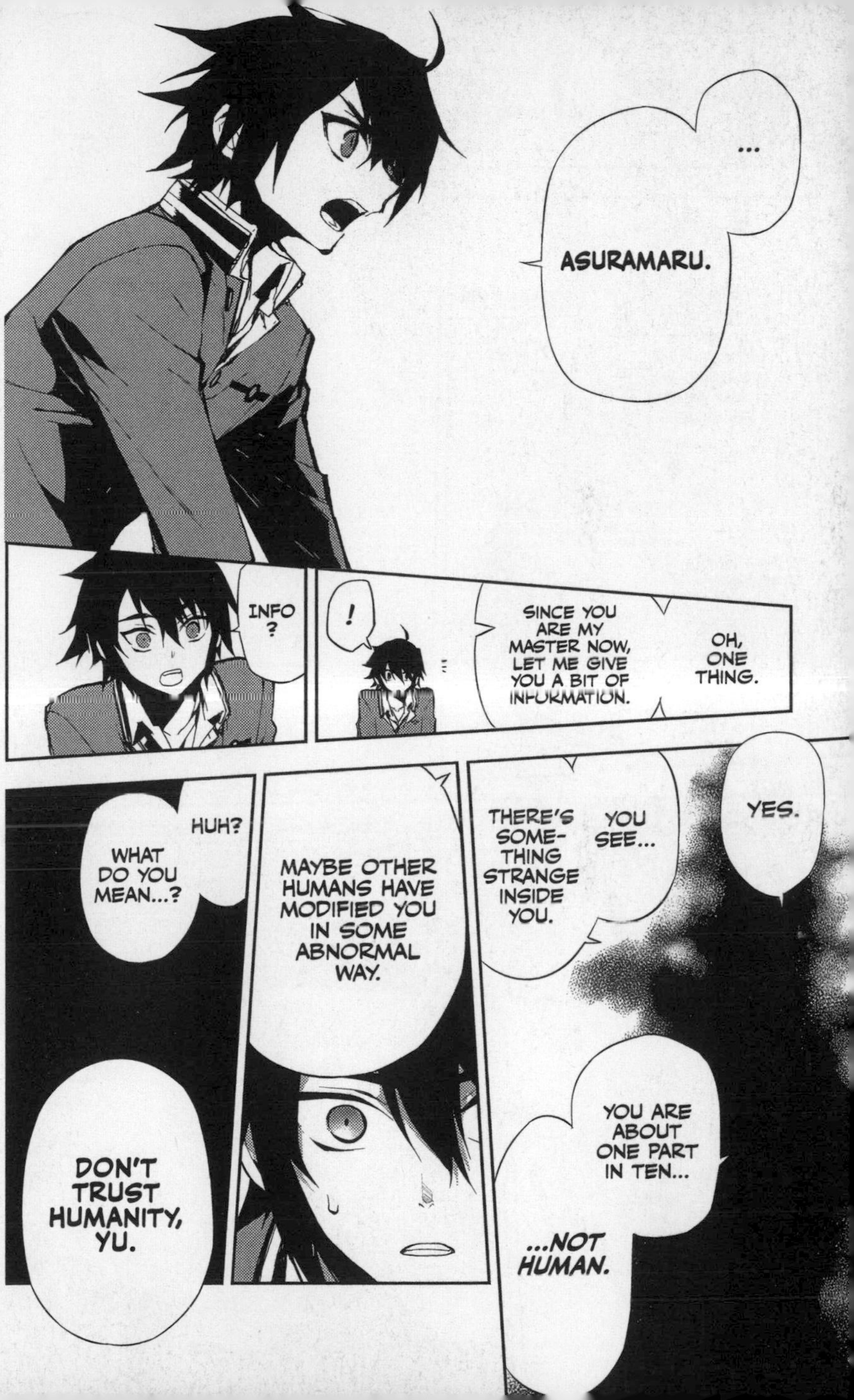
...
ASURAMARU.
OH, ONE THING.
SINCE YOU ARE MY MASTER NOW, LET ME GIVE YOU A BIT OF INFORMATION.
!
INFO?
YES.
YOU SEE...
THERE'S SOME-THING STRANGE INSIDE YOU.
YOU ARE ABOUT ONE PART IN TEN...
...NOT HUMAN.
MAYBE OTHER HUMANS HAVE MODIFIED YOU IN SOME ABNORMAL WAY.
HUH?
WHAT DO YOU MEAN...?
DON'T TRUST HUMANITY, YU.

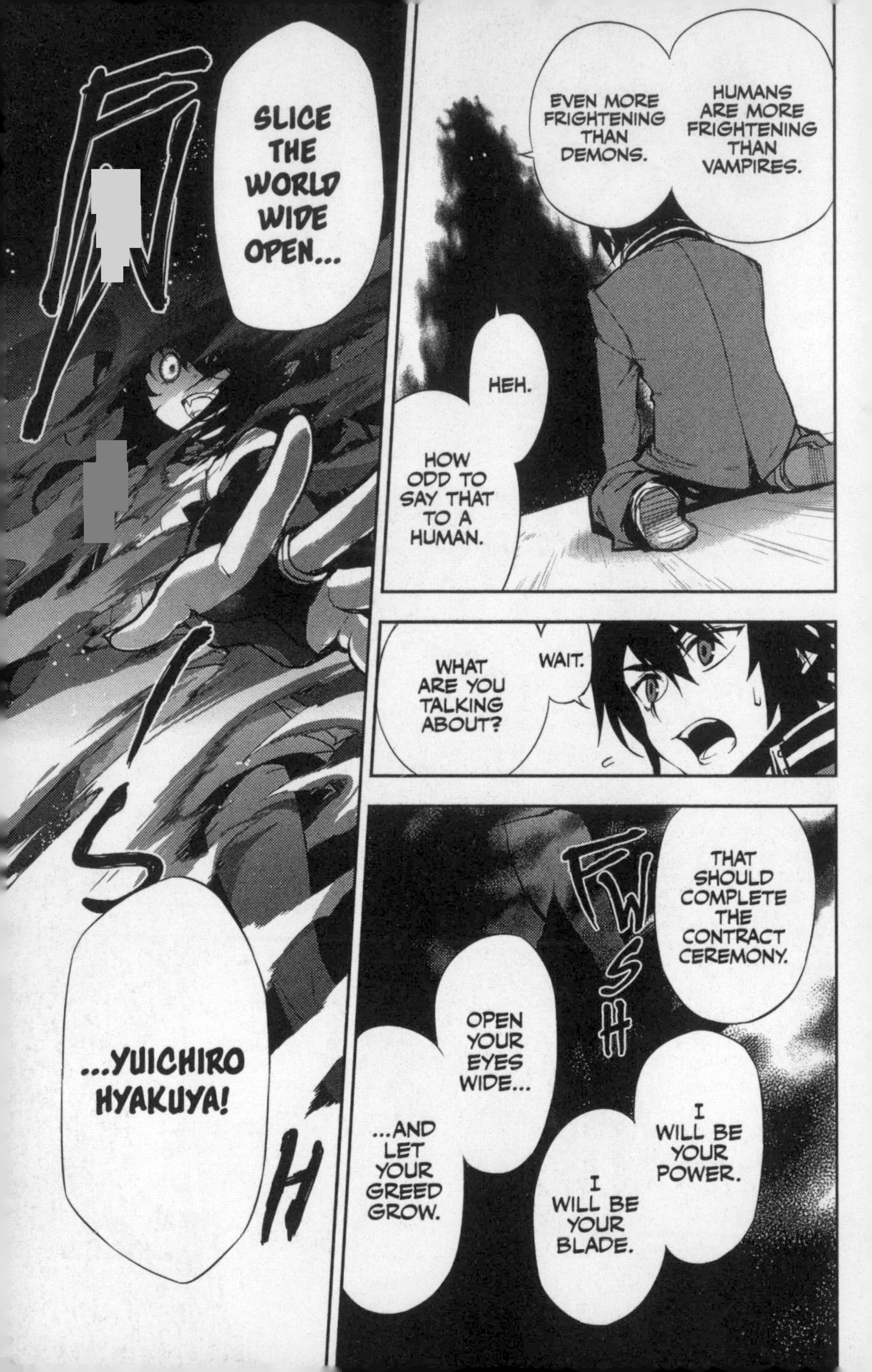
HUMANS ARE MORE FRIGHTENING THAN VAMPIRES.
EVEN MORE FRIGHTENING THAN DEMONS.
HEH.
HOW ODD TO SAY THAT TO A HUMAN.
WAIT.
WHAT ARE YOU TALKING ABOUT?
THAT SHOULD COMPLETE THE CONTRACT CEREMONY.
FWSH
OPEN YOUR EYES WIDE...
I WILL BE YOUR POWER.
I WILL BE YOUR BLADE.
...AND LET YOUR GREED GROW.
SLICE THE WORLD WIDE OPEN...
...YUICHIRO HYAKUYA!

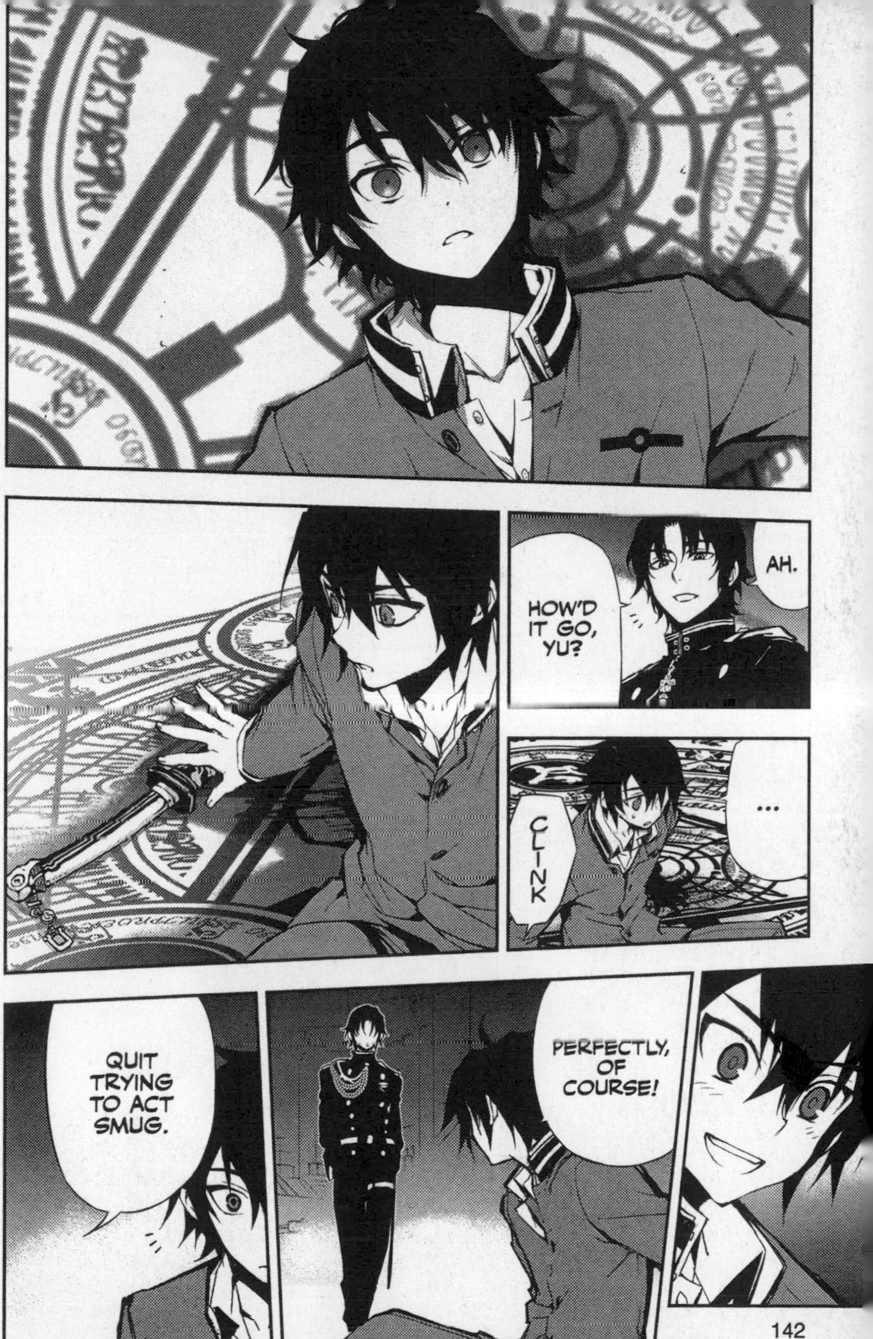
AH.
HOW'D IT GO, YU?
...
CLINK
PERFECTLY, OF COURSE!
QUIT TRYING TO ACT SMUG.

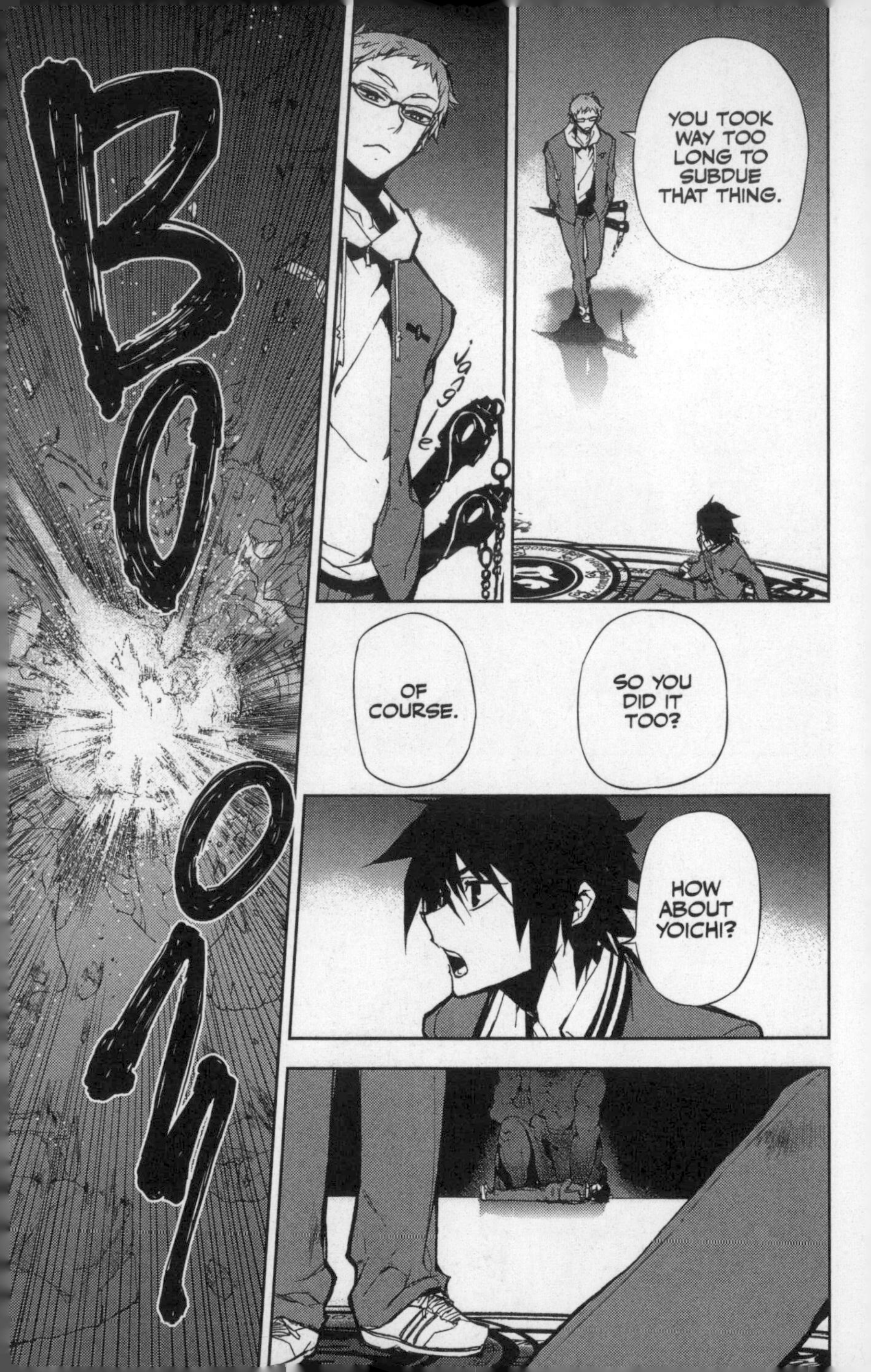
YOU TOOK WAY TOO LONG TO SUBDUE THAT THING.
jangle
SO YOU DID IT TOO?
OF COURSE.
HOW ABOUT YOICHI?
BOOM

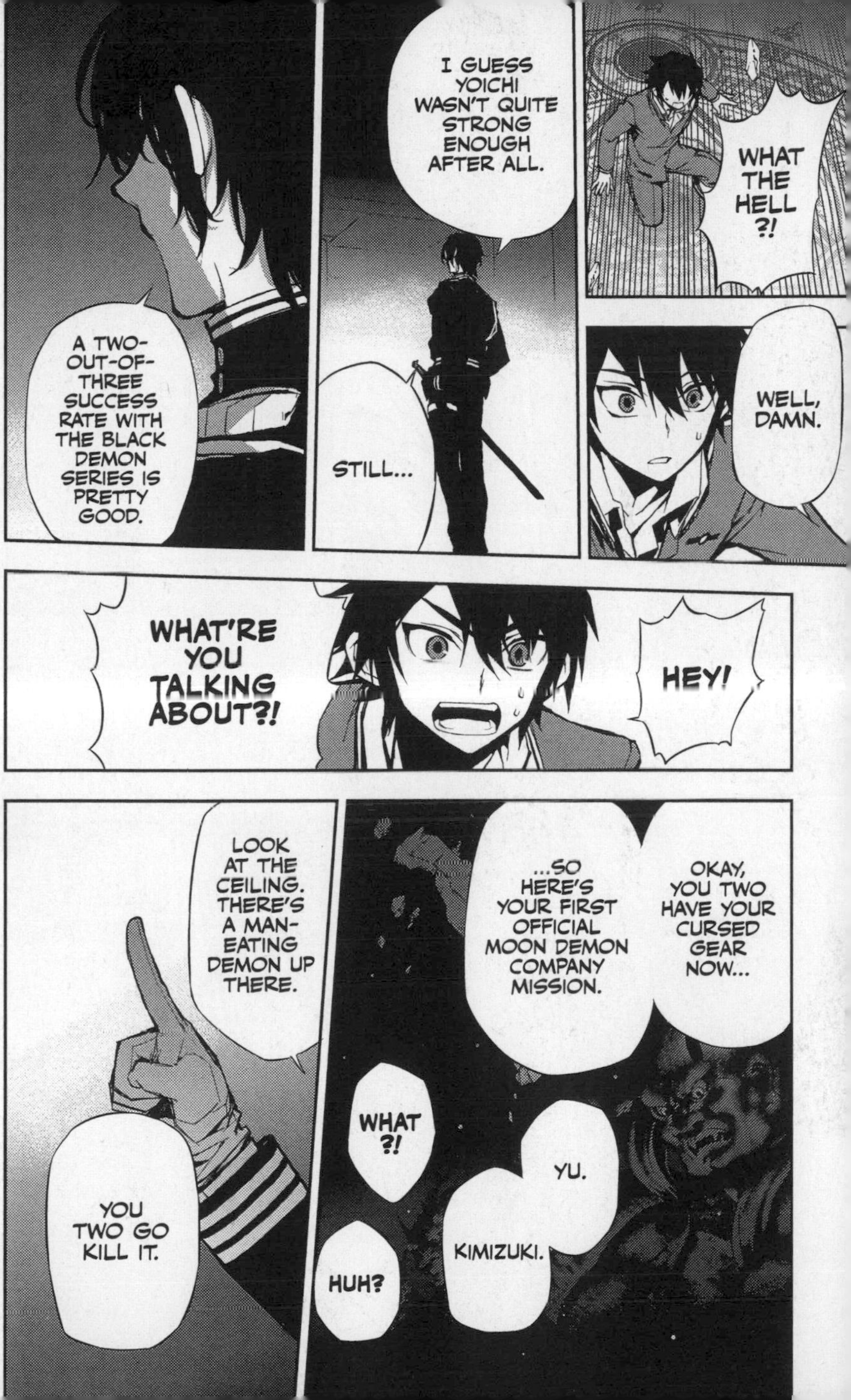
WHAT THE HELL ?!
WELL, DAMN.
I GUESS YOICHI WASN'T QUITE STRONG ENOUGH AFTER ALL.
STILL...
A TWO-OUT-OF-THREE SUCCESS RATE WITH THE BLACK DEMON SERIES IS PRETTY GOOD.
HEY!
WHAT'RE YOU TALKING ABOUT?!
OKAY, YOU TWO HAVE YOUR CURSED GEAR NOW...
...SO HERE'S YOUR FIRST OFFICIAL MOON DEMON COMPANY MISSION.
YU.
KIMIZUKI.
WHAT ?!
HUH?
LOOK AT THE CEILING. THERE'S A MAN-EATING DEMON UP THERE.
YOU TWO GO KILL IT.

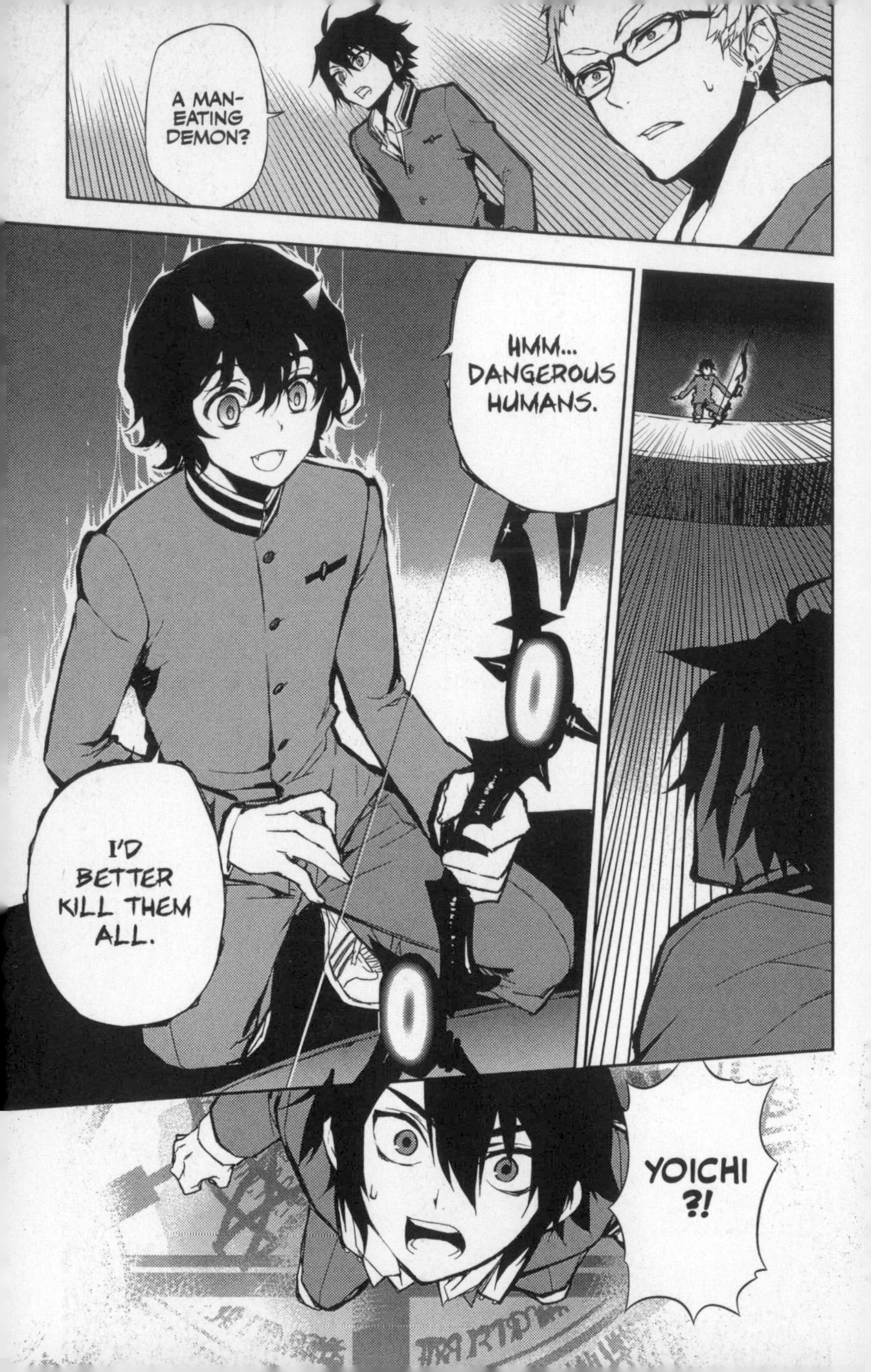
A MAN-EATING DEMON?
HMM... DANGEROUS HUMANS.
I'D BETTER KILL THEM ALL.
YOICHI?!

Seraph of the End
VAMPIRE REIGN

CHAPTER 7
New Family

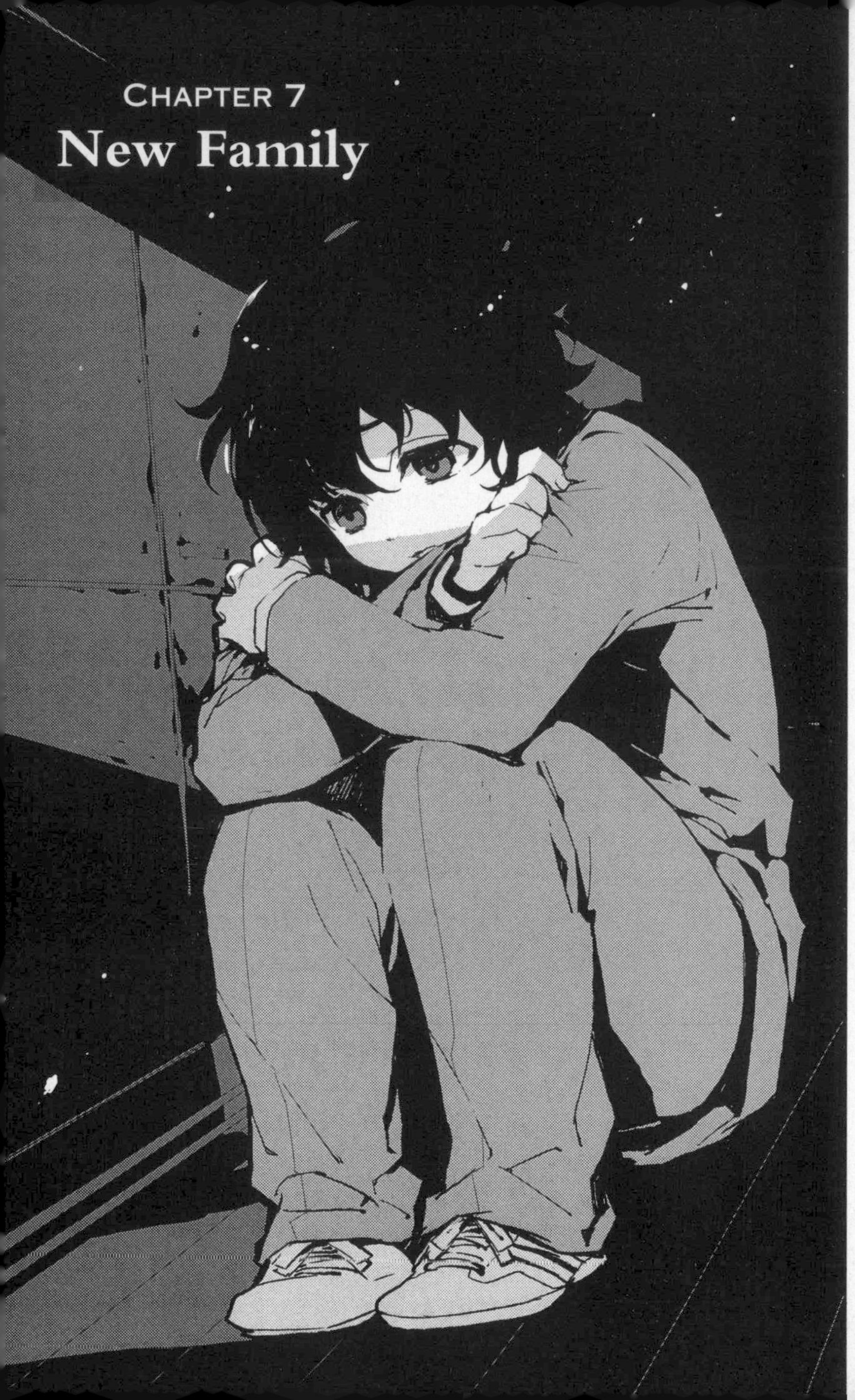

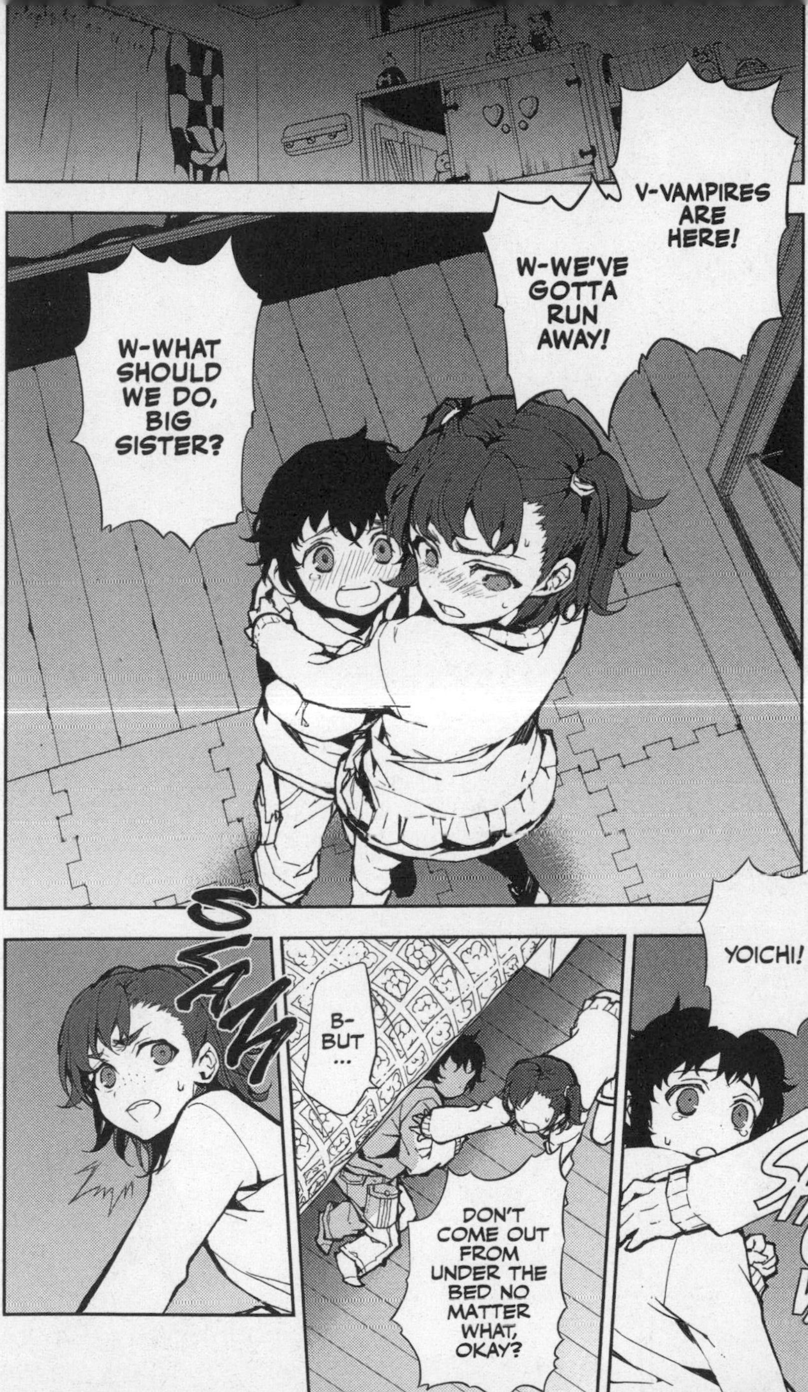
V-VAMPIRES ARE HERE!
W-WE'VE GOTTA RUN AWAY!
W-WHAT SHOULD WE DO, BIG SISTER?
YOICHI!
SHOVE
B-BUT ...
DON'T COME OUT FROM UNDER THE BED NO MATTER WHAT, OKAY?
SLAM

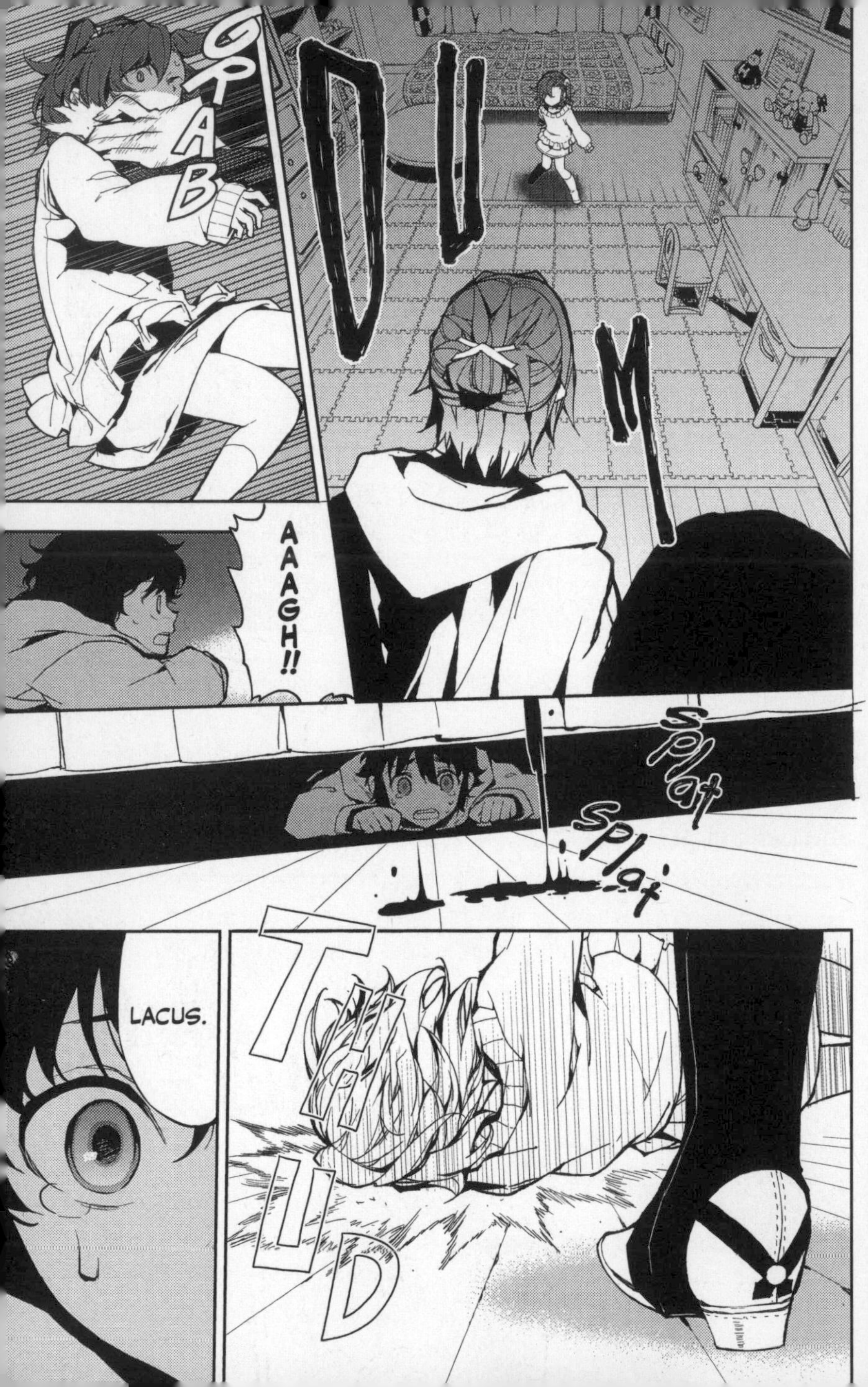
DUM
GRAB
AAAGH!!
splat
splat
THUD
LACUS.

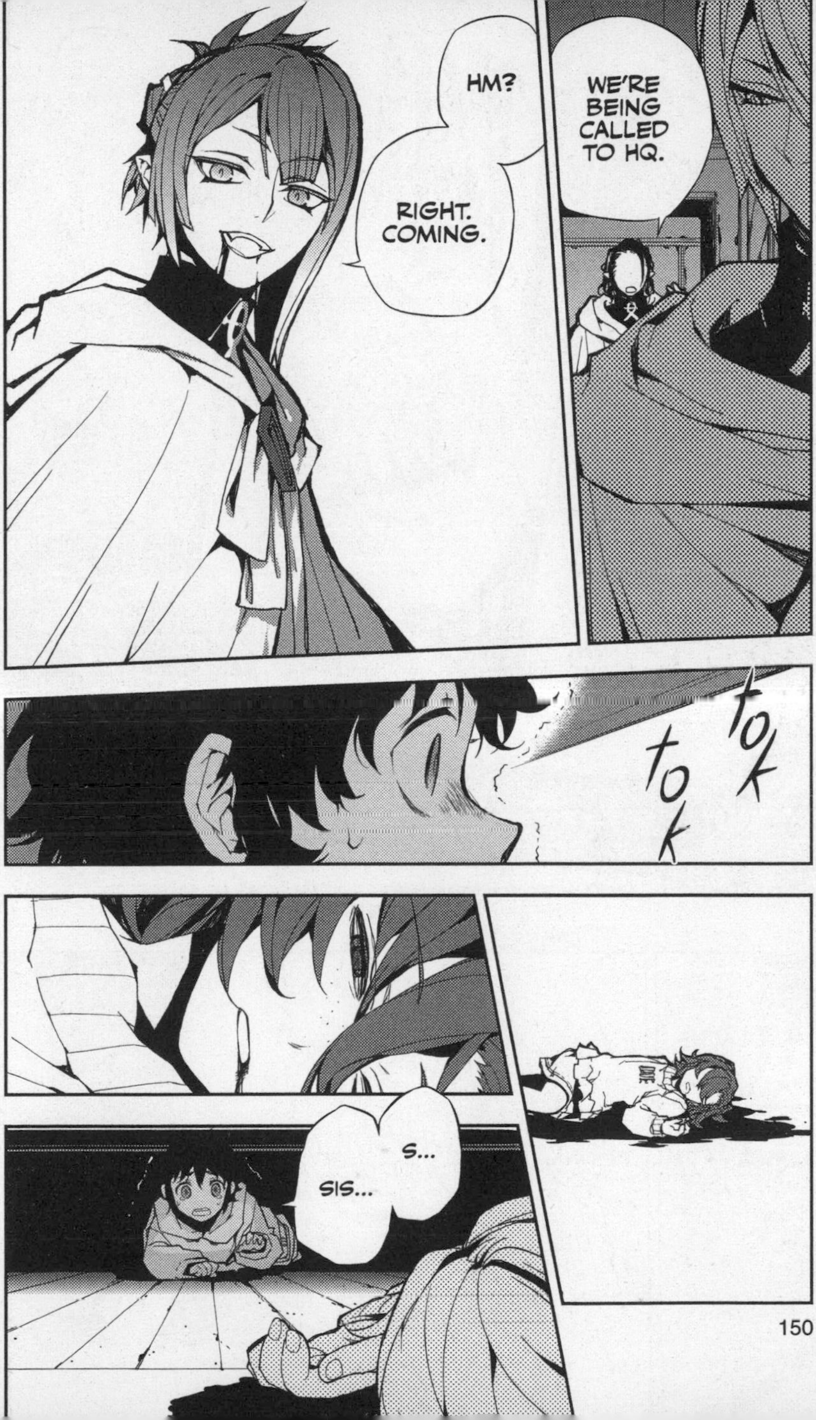
WE'RE BEING CALLED TO HQ.
HM?
RIGHT. COMING.
tok tok
S...
SIS...

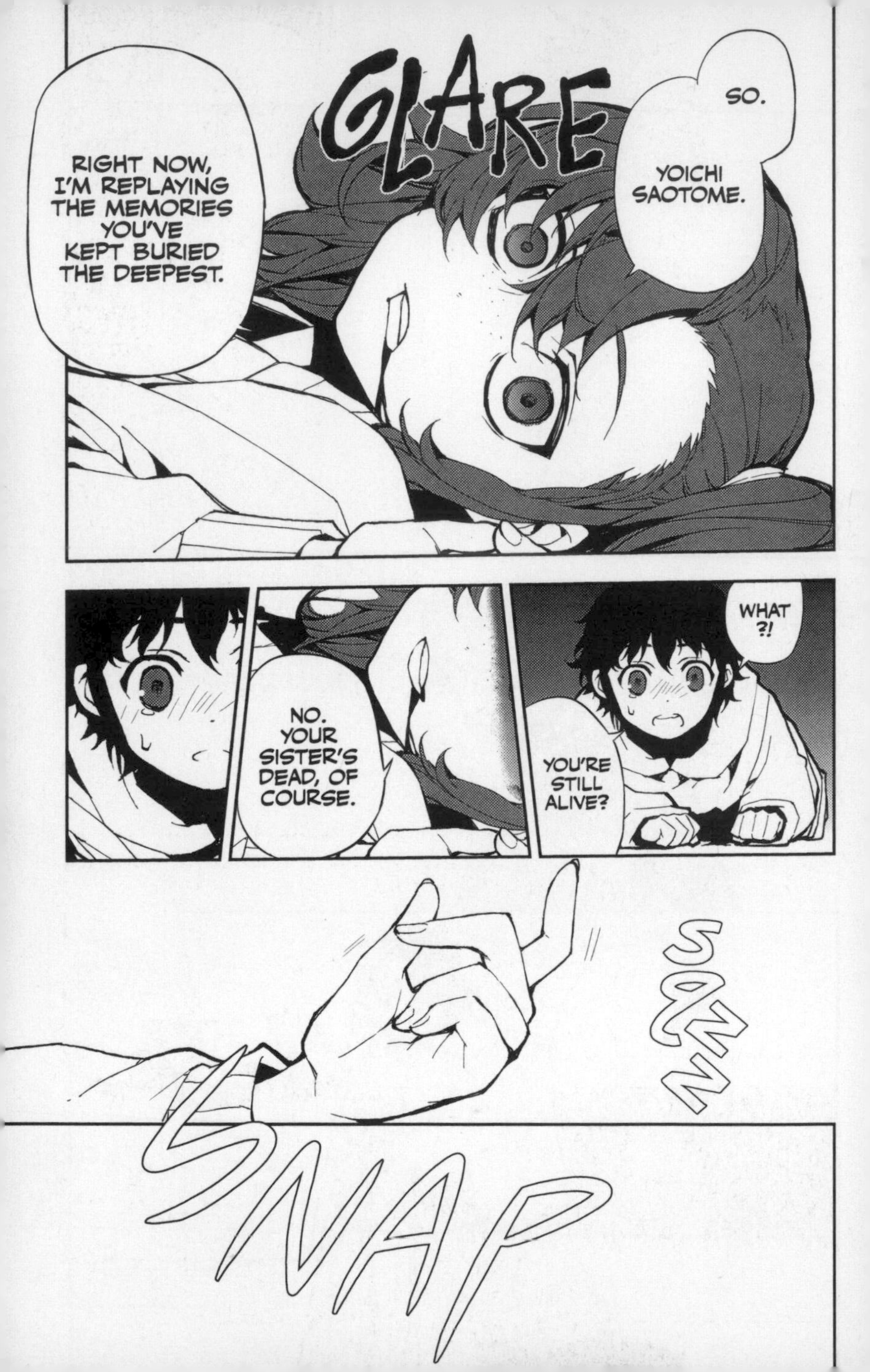
SO.
YOICHI SAOTOME.
GLARE
RIGHT NOW, I'M REPLAYING THE MEMORIES YOU'VE KEPT BURIED THE DEEPEST.
WHAT?!
YOU'RE STILL ALIVE?
NO. YOUR SISTER'S DEAD, OF COURSE.
SNAP
SNAP

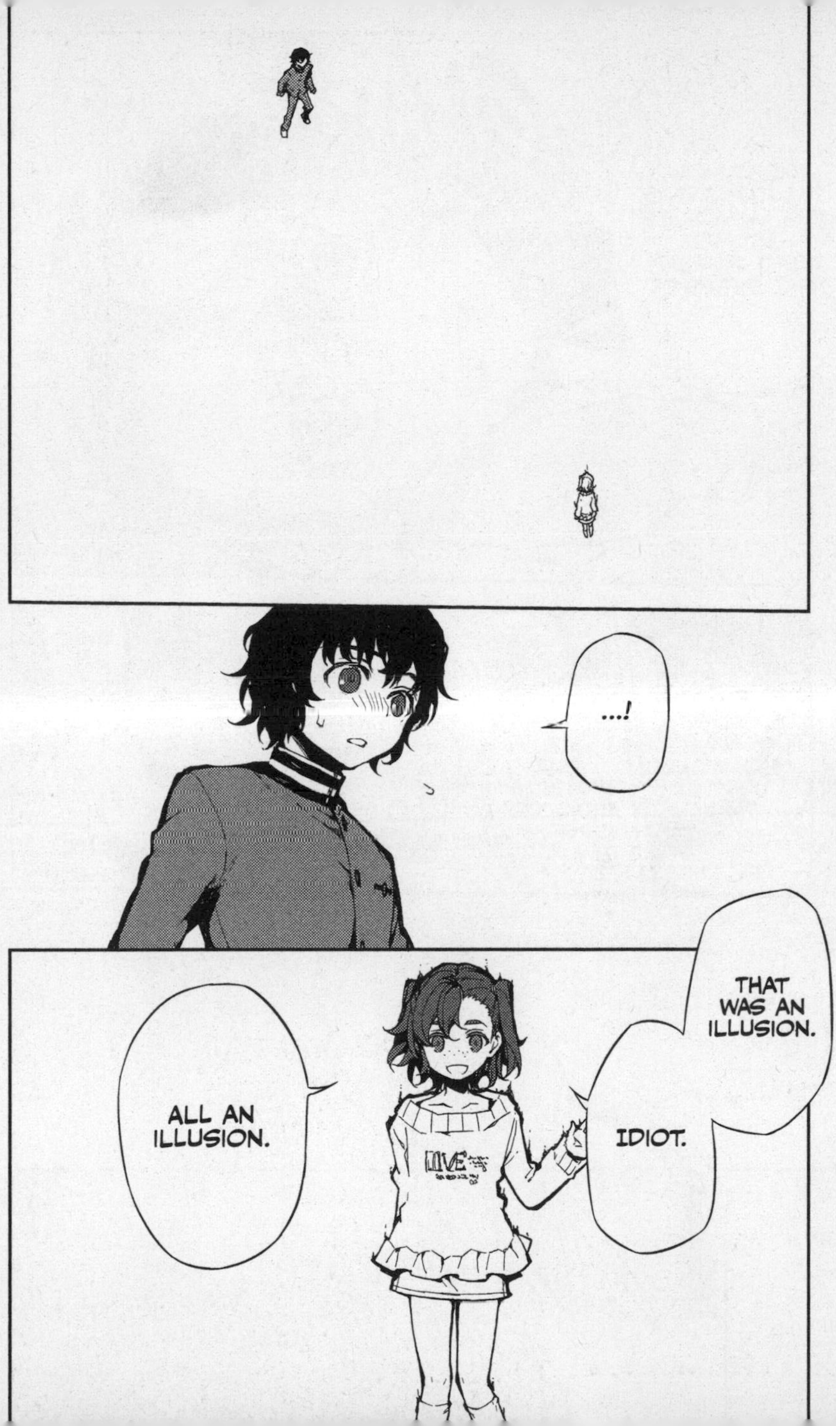
...!
THAT WAS AN ILLUSION.
IDIOT.
ALL AN ILLUSION.

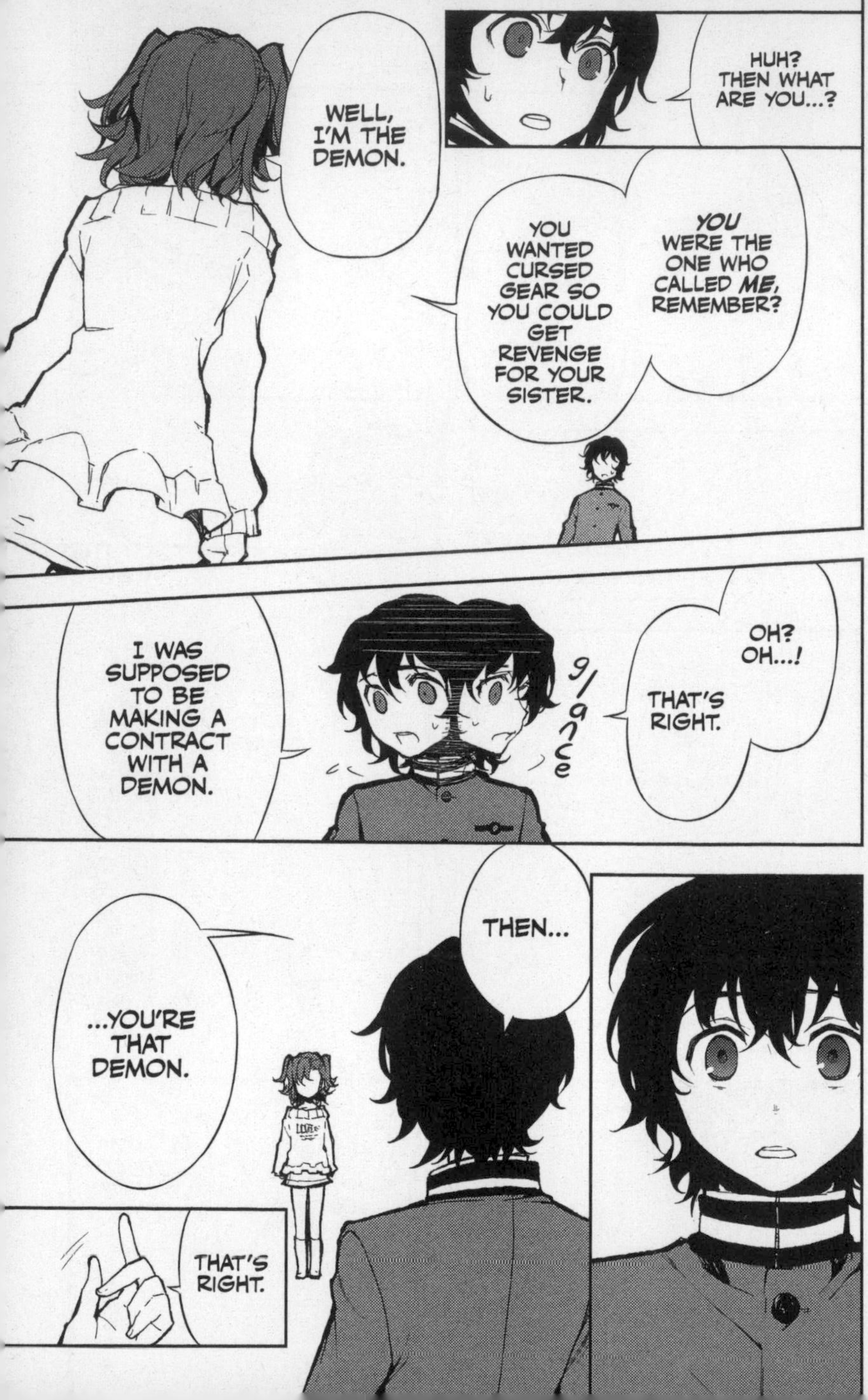
HUH? THEN WHAT ARE YOU...?
WELL, I'M THE DEMON.
YOU WERE THE ONE WHO CALLED *ME*, REMEMBER?
YOU WANTED CURSED GEAR SO YOU COULD GET REVENGE FOR YOUR SISTER.
OH? OH...!
THAT'S RIGHT.
glance
I WAS SUPPOSED TO BE MAKING A CONTRACT WITH A DEMON.
THEN...
...YOU'RE THAT DEMON.
THAT'S RIGHT.

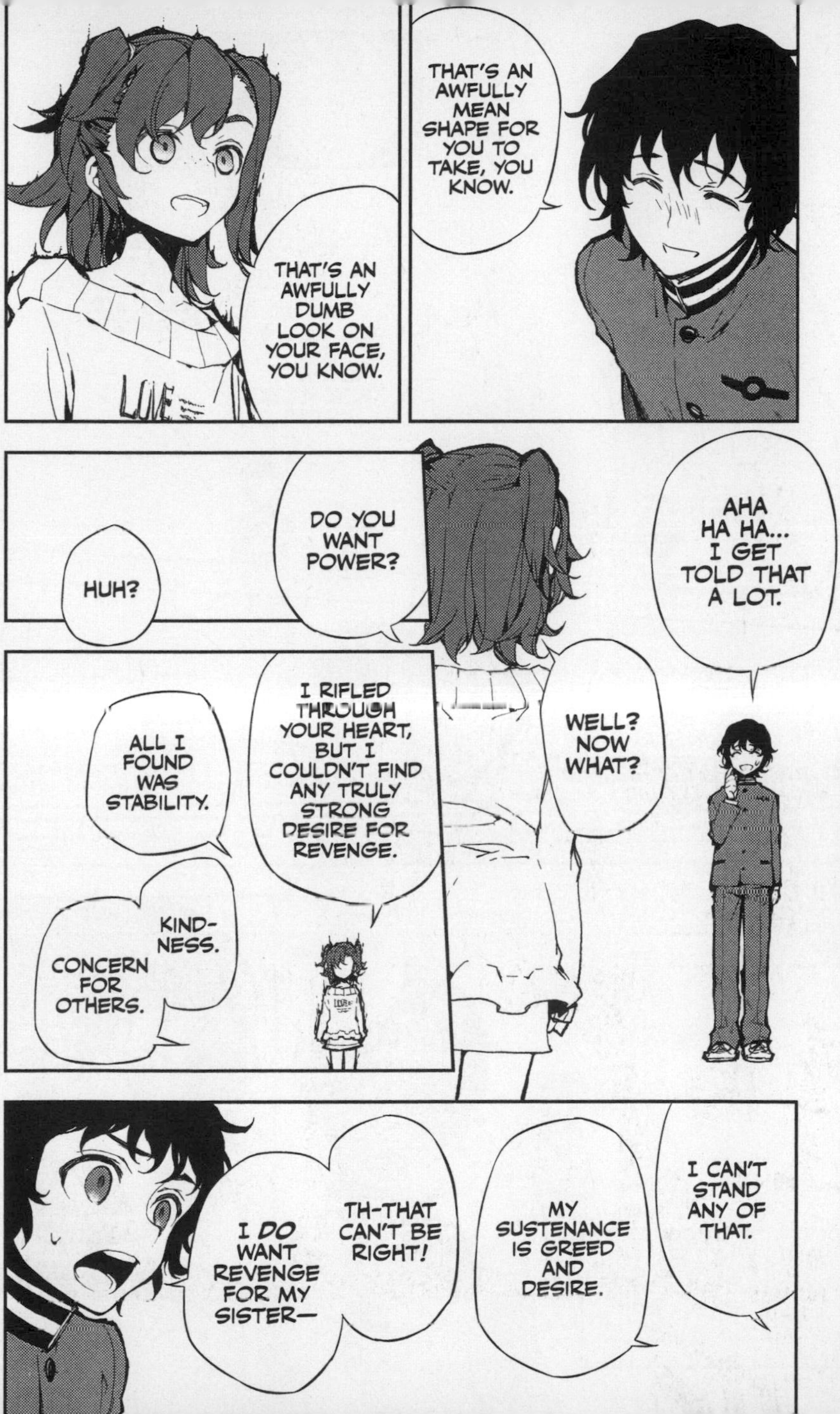
THAT'S AN AWFULLY MEAN SHAPE FOR YOU TO TAKE, YOU KNOW.
THAT'S AN AWFULLY DUMB LOOK ON YOUR FACE, YOU KNOW.
AHA HA HA... I GET TOLD THAT A LOT.
DO YOU WANT POWER?
HUH?
WELL? NOW WHAT?
I RIFLED THROUGH YOUR HEART, BUT I COULDN'T FIND ANY TRULY STRONG DESIRE FOR REVENGE.
ALL I FOUND WAS STABILITY.
KIND-NESS.
CONCERN FOR OTHERS.
I CAN'T STAND ANY OF THAT.
MY SUSTENANCE IS GREED AND DESIRE.
TH-THAT CAN'T BE RIGHT!
I *DO* WANT REVENGE FOR MY SISTER—

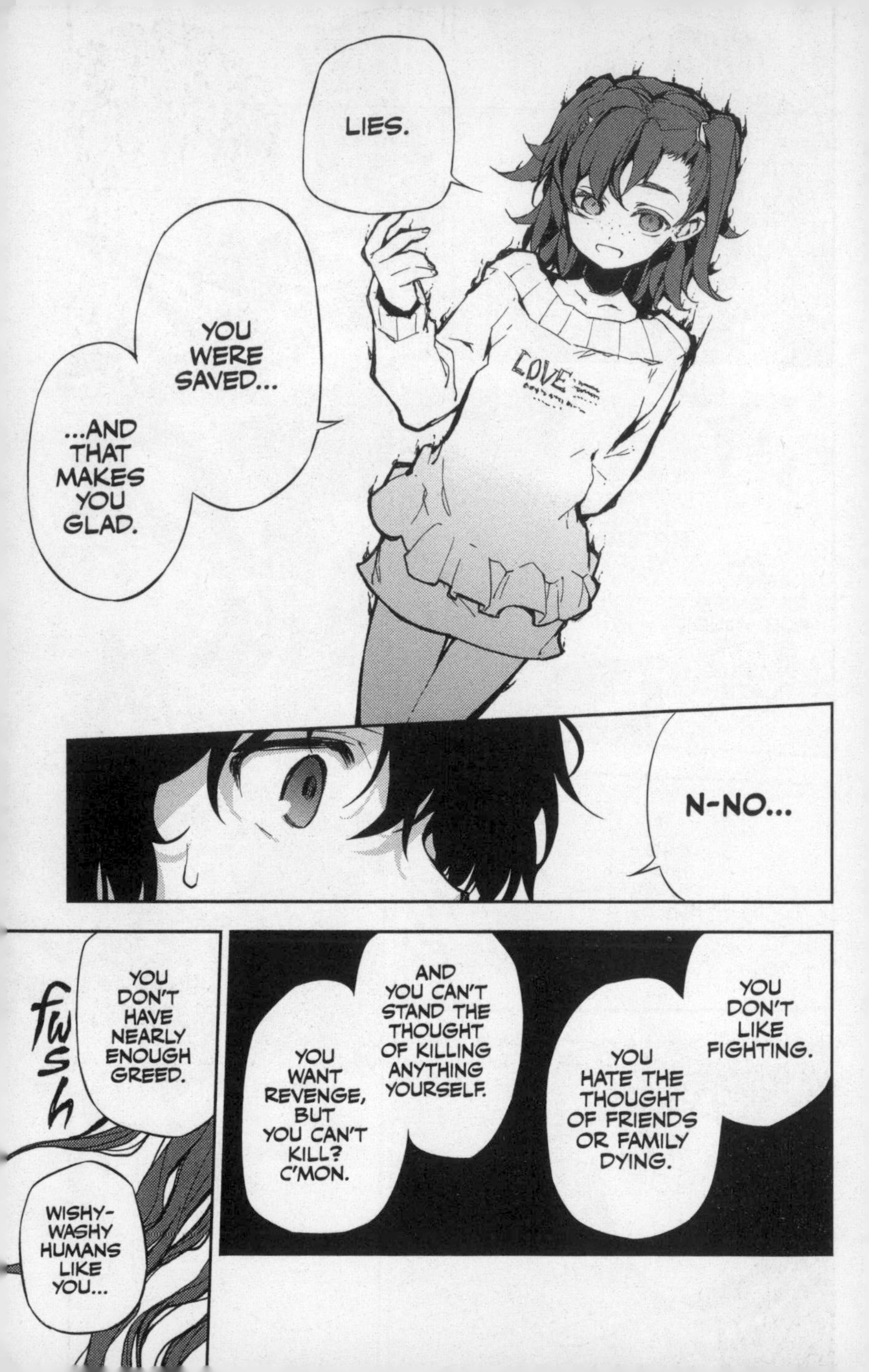
LIES.
YOU WERE SAVED... ...AND THAT MAKES YOU GLAD.
N-NO...
YOU DON'T LIKE FIGHTING.
YOU HATE THE THOUGHT OF FRIENDS OR FAMILY DYING.
AND YOU CAN'T STAND THE THOUGHT OF KILLING ANYTHING YOURSELF.
YOU WANT REVENGE, BUT YOU CAN'T KILL? C'MON.
YOU DON'T HAVE NEARLY ENOUGH GREED.
fwsh
WISHY-WASHY HUMANS LIKE YOU...

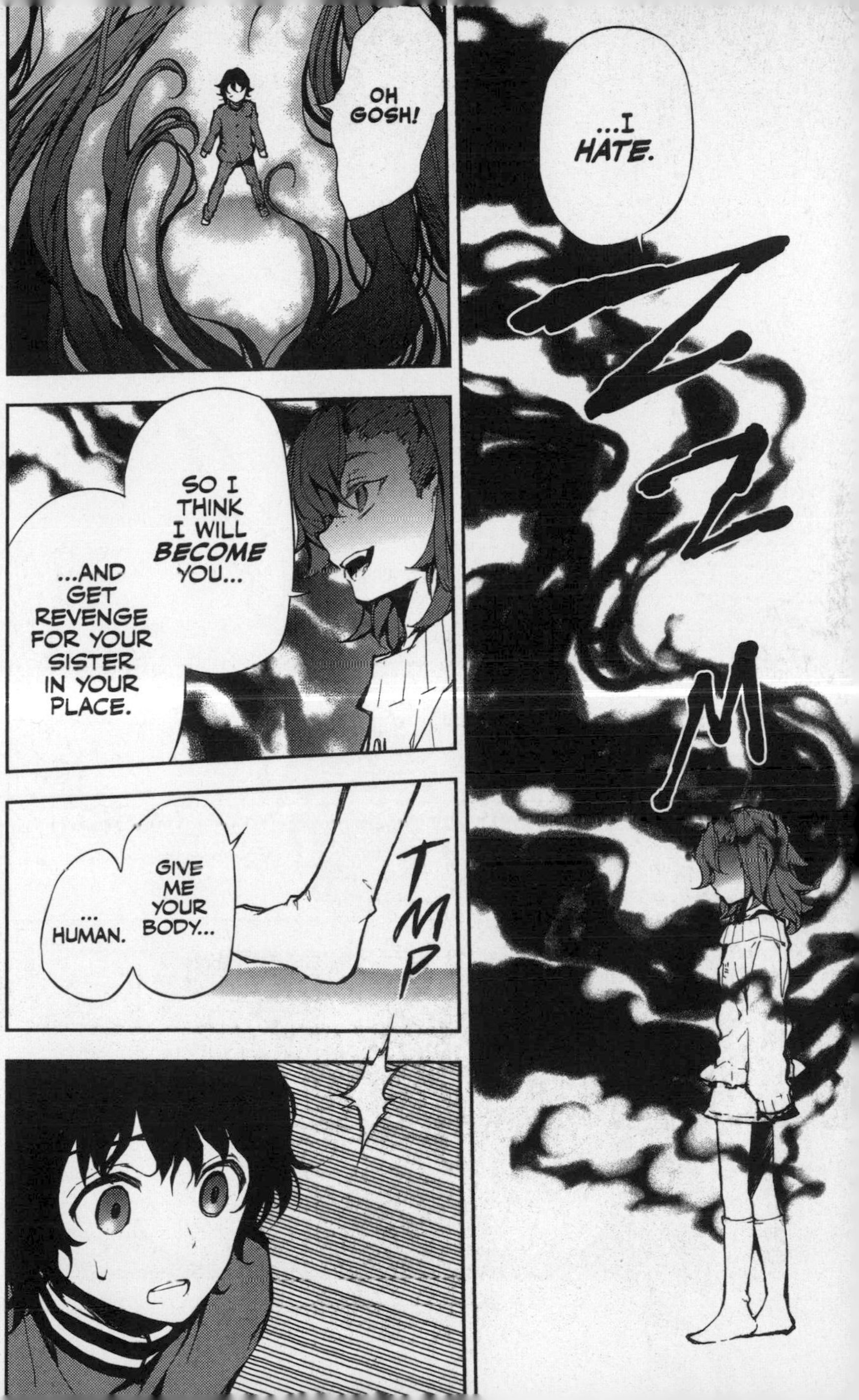
...I *HATE.*
OH GOSH!
SO I THINK I WILL *BECOME* YOU...
...AND GET REVENGE FOR YOUR SISTER IN YOUR PLACE.
GIVE ME YOUR BODY...
... HUMAN.
TMP

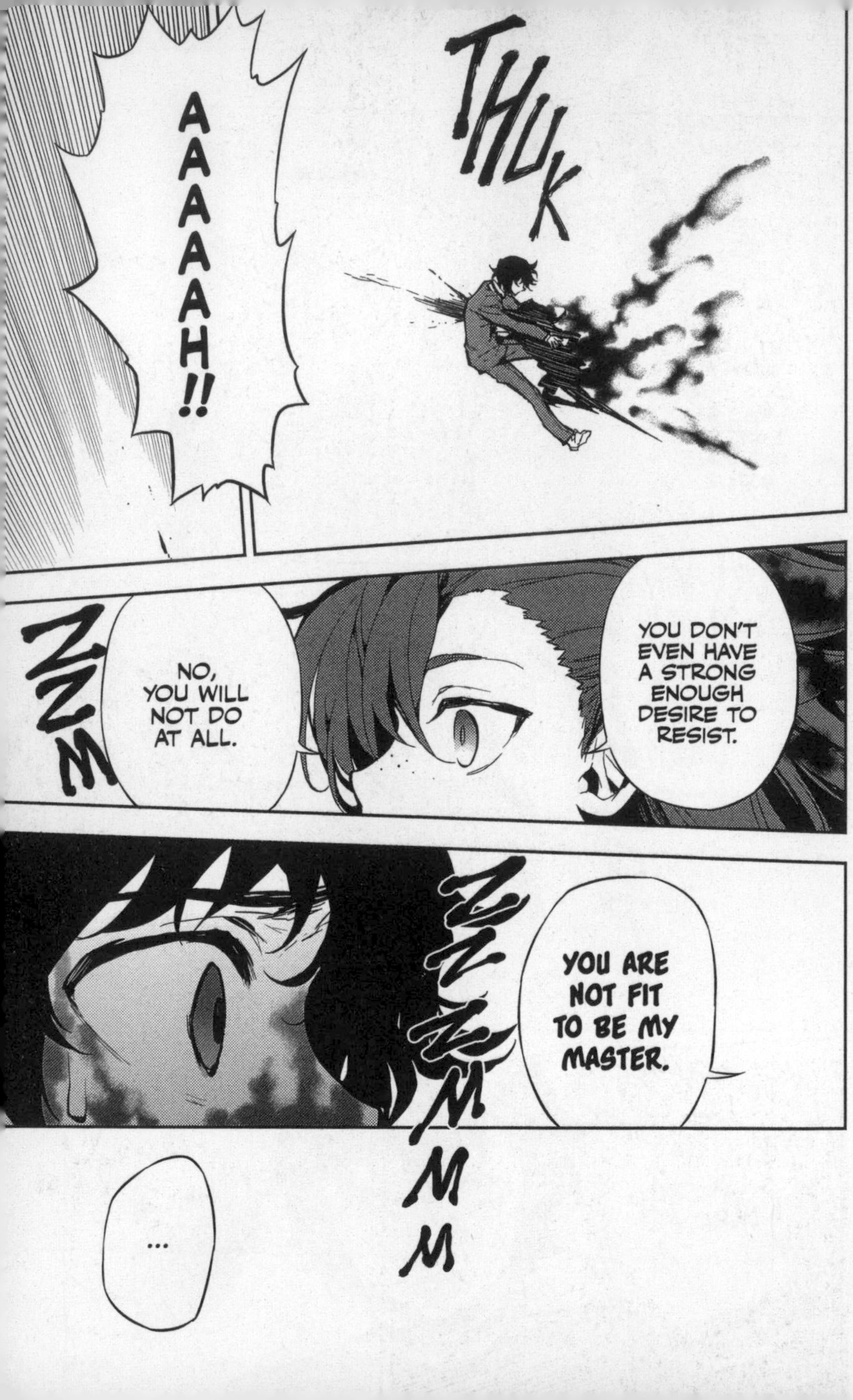
THUK
AAAAAH!!
YOU DON'T EVEN HAVE A STRONG ENOUGH DESIRE TO RESIST.
NO, YOU WILL NOT DO AT ALL.
YOU ARE NOT FIT TO BE MY MASTER.
...

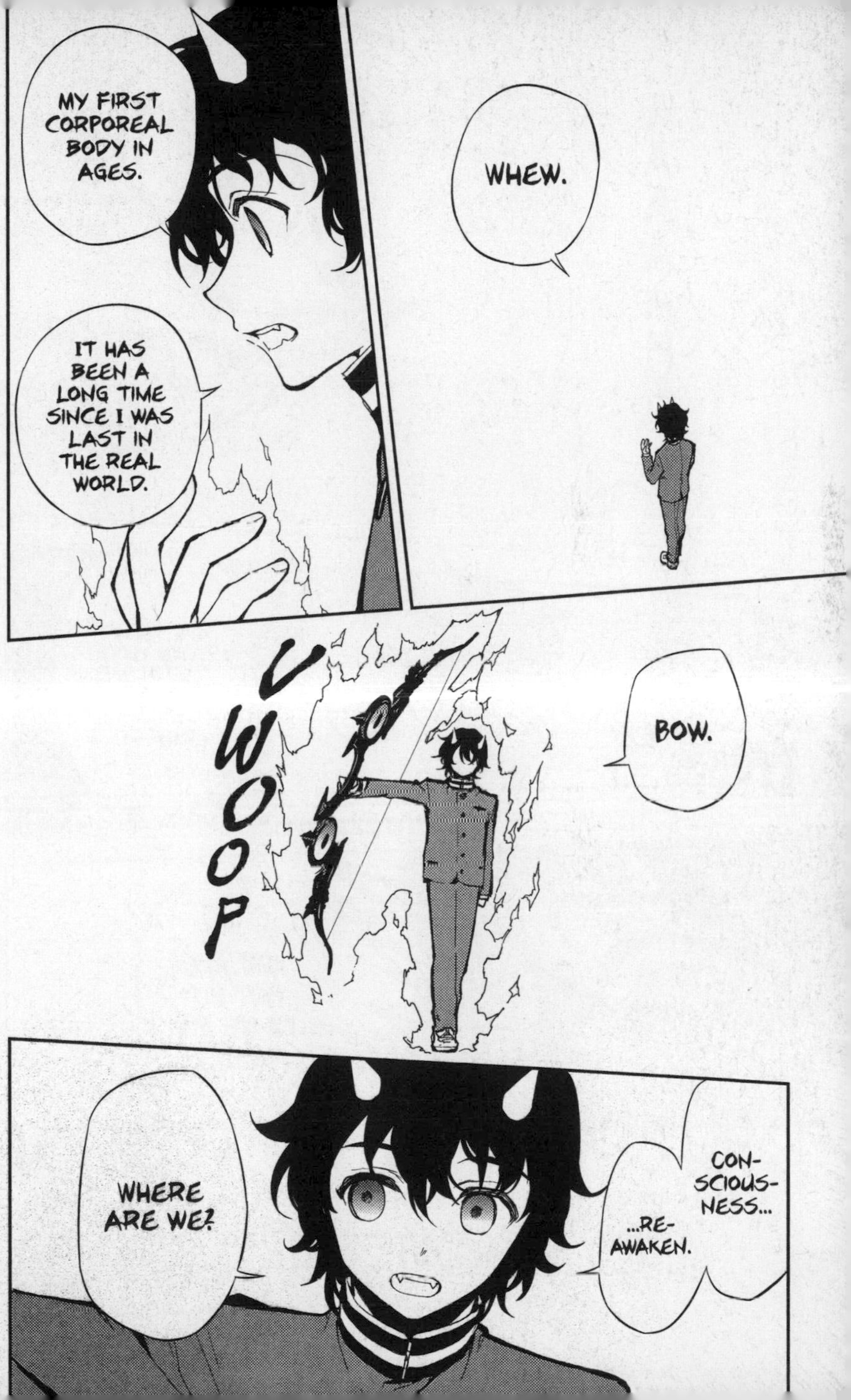
WHEW.
MY FIRST CORPOREAL BODY IN AGES.
IT HAS BEEN A LONG TIME SINCE I WAS LAST IN THE REAL WORLD.
BOW.
VWOOP
CON-SCIOUS-NESS...
...RE-AWAKEN.
WHERE ARE WE?

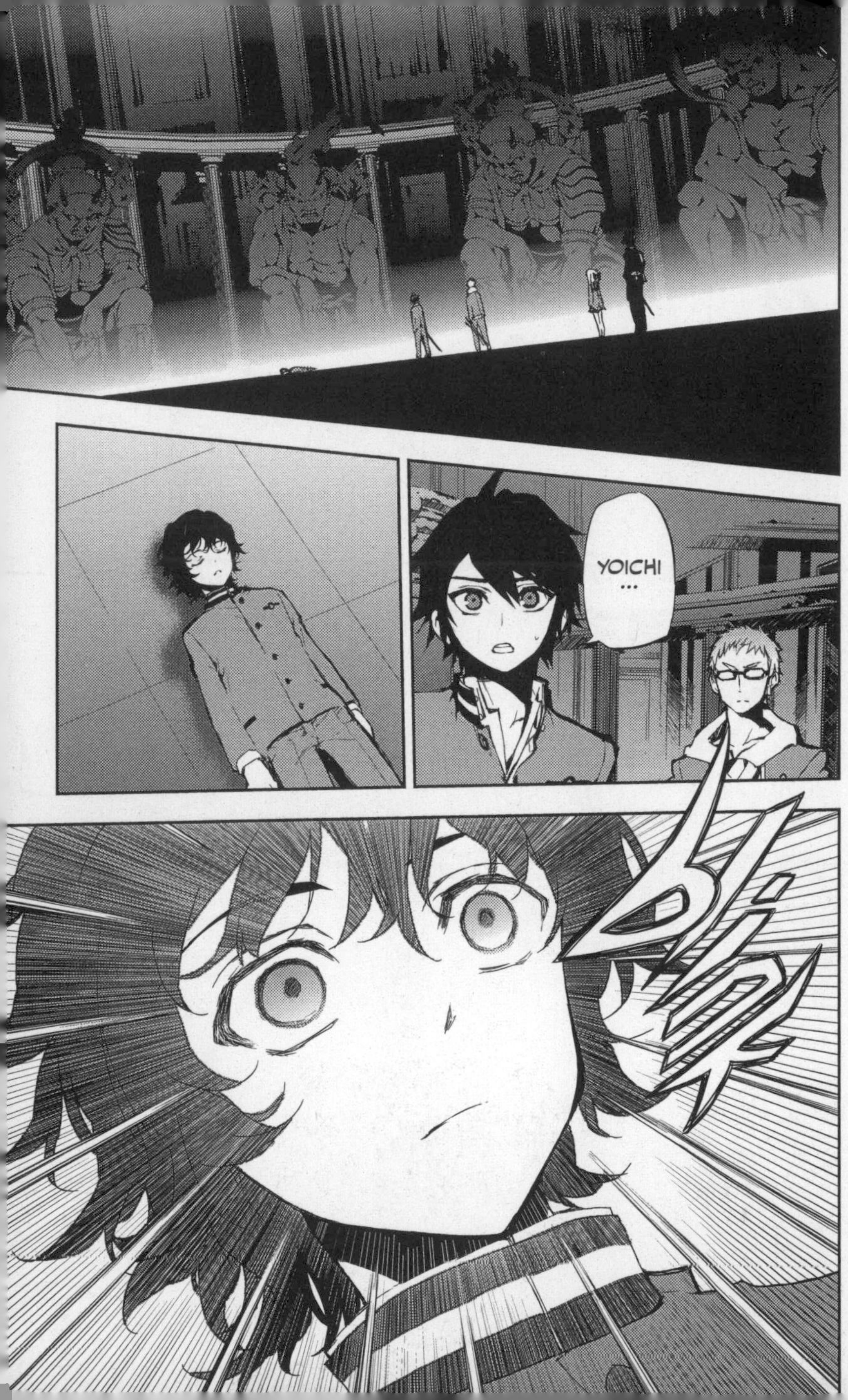
YOICHI
...

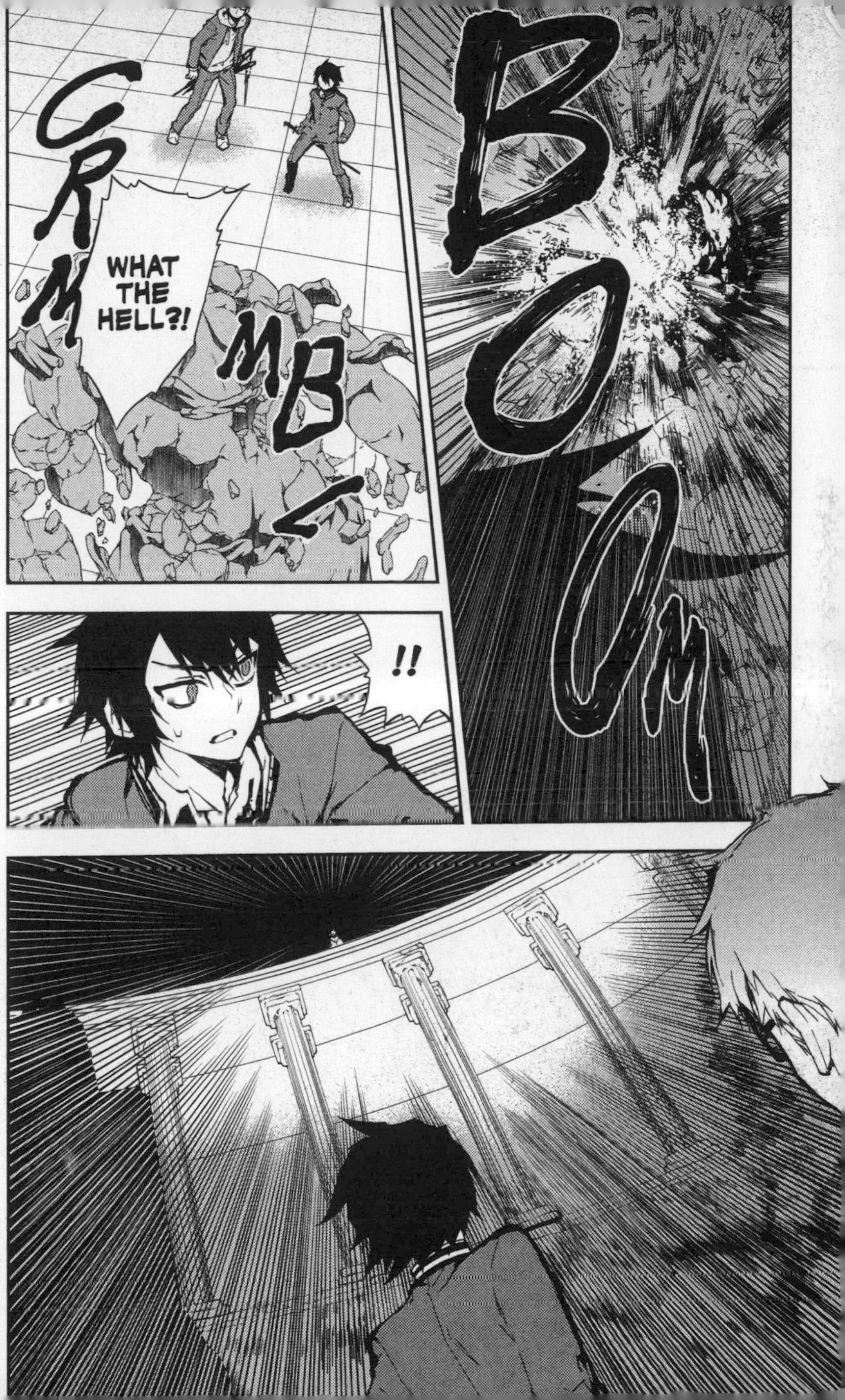
BOOM
CRMMBL
WHAT THE HELL?!
!!

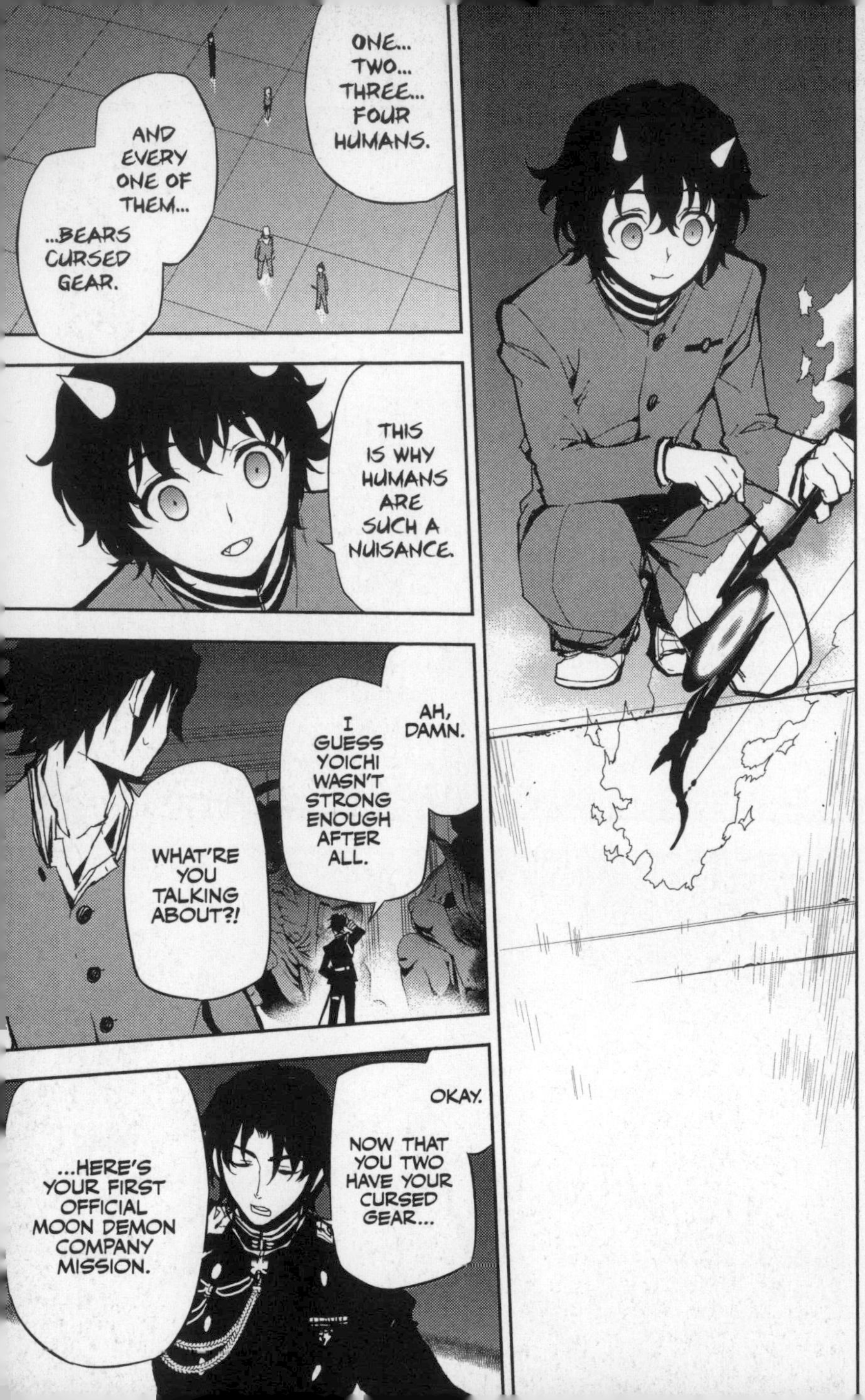
ONE... TWO... THREE... FOUR HUMANS.
AND EVERY ONE OF THEM... ...BEARS CURSED GEAR.
THIS IS WHY HUMANS ARE SUCH A NUISANCE.
AH, DAMN.
I GUESS YOICHI WASN'T STRONG ENOUGH AFTER ALL.
WHAT'RE YOU TALKING ABOUT?!
OKAY.
NOW THAT YOU TWO HAVE YOUR CURSED GEAR...
...HERE'S YOUR FIRST OFFICIAL MOON DEMON COMPANY MISSION.

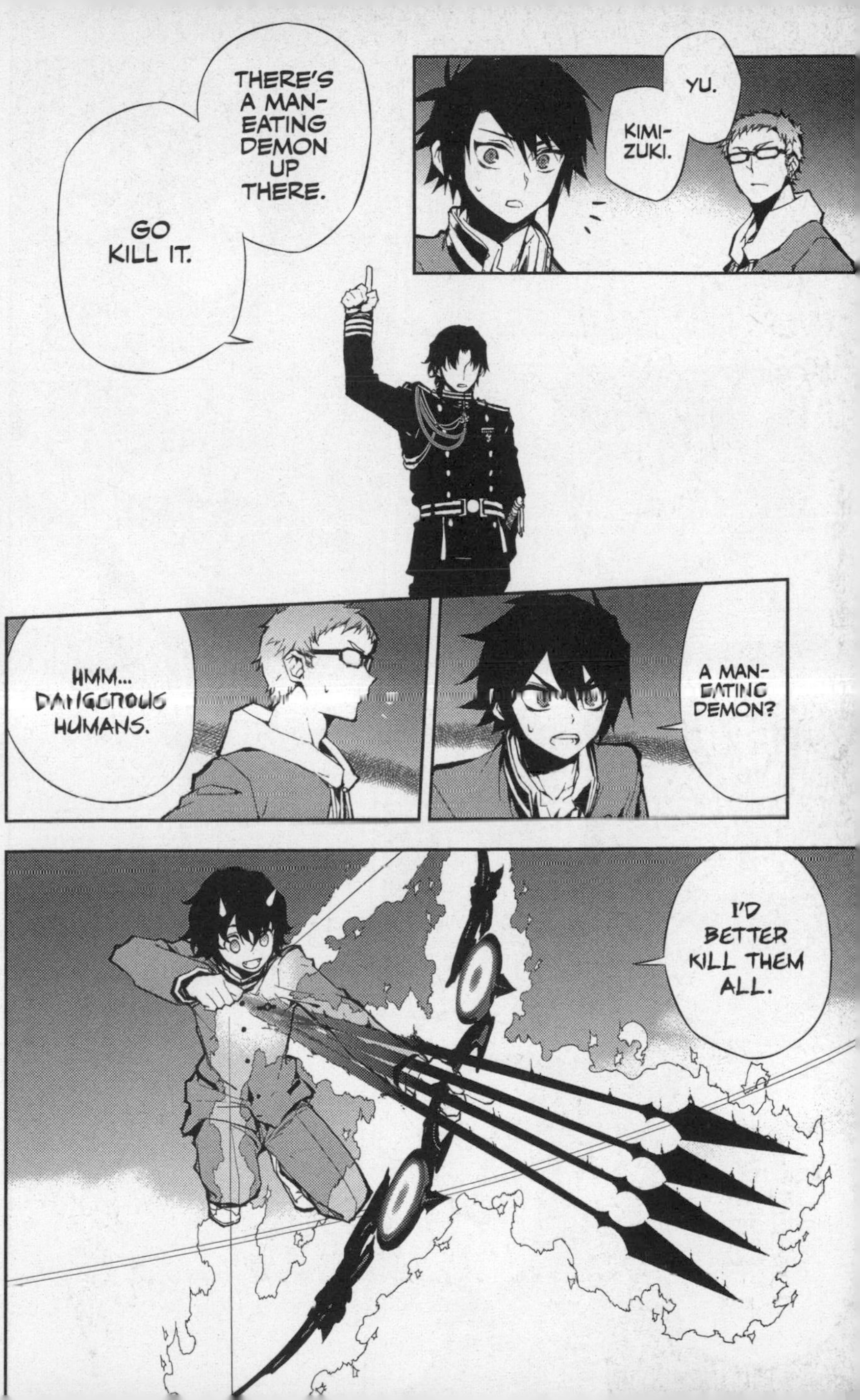
YU.
KIMI-ZUKI.
THERE'S A MAN-EATING DEMON UP THERE.
GO KILL IT.
A MAN-EATING DEMON?
HMM... DANGEROUS HUMANS.
I'D BETTER KILL THEM ALL.

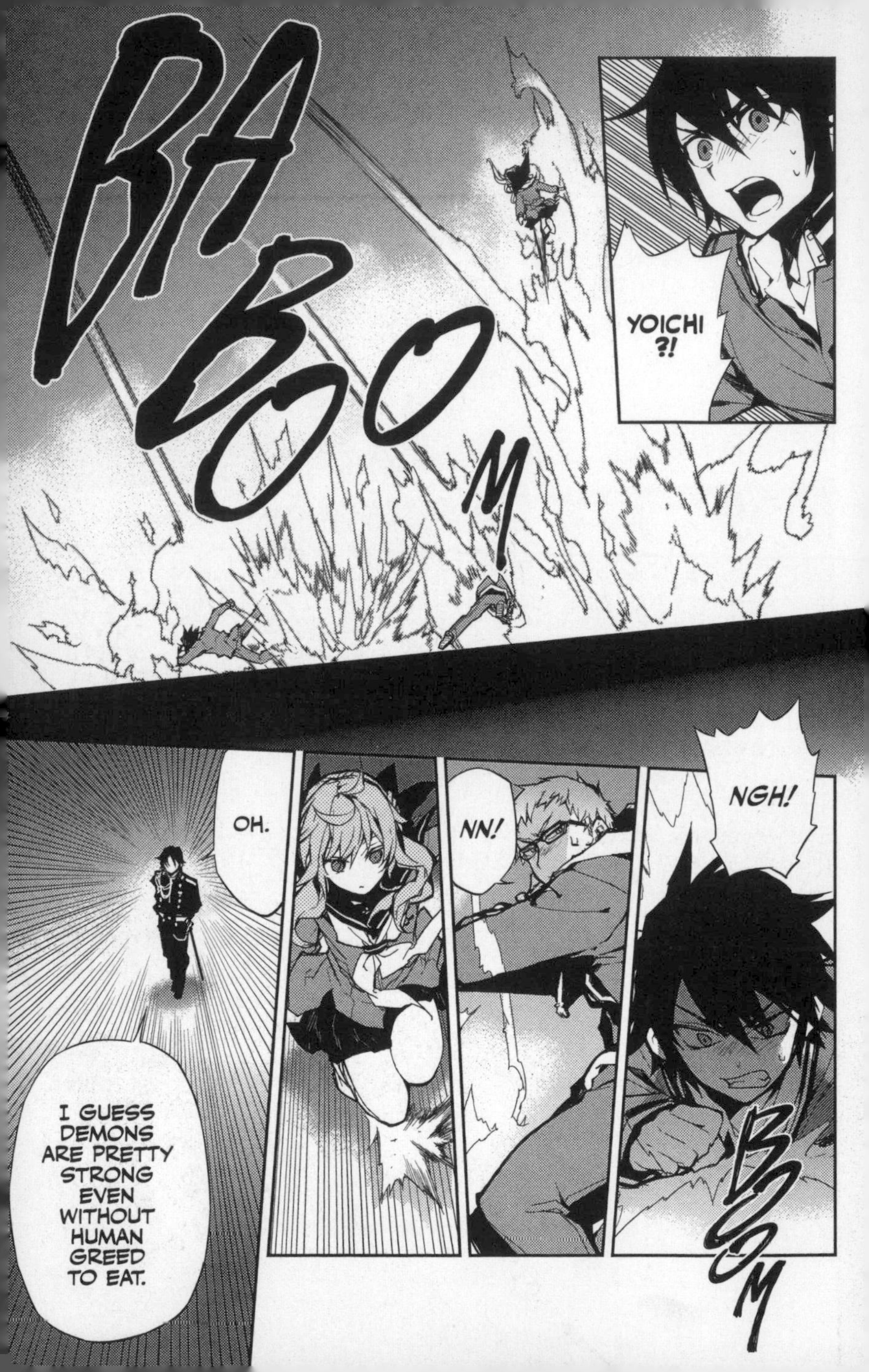
YOICHI ?!
BABOOOM
NGH!
BOOM
NN!
OH.
I GUESS DEMONS ARE PRETTY STRONG EVEN WITHOUT HUMAN GREED TO EAT.

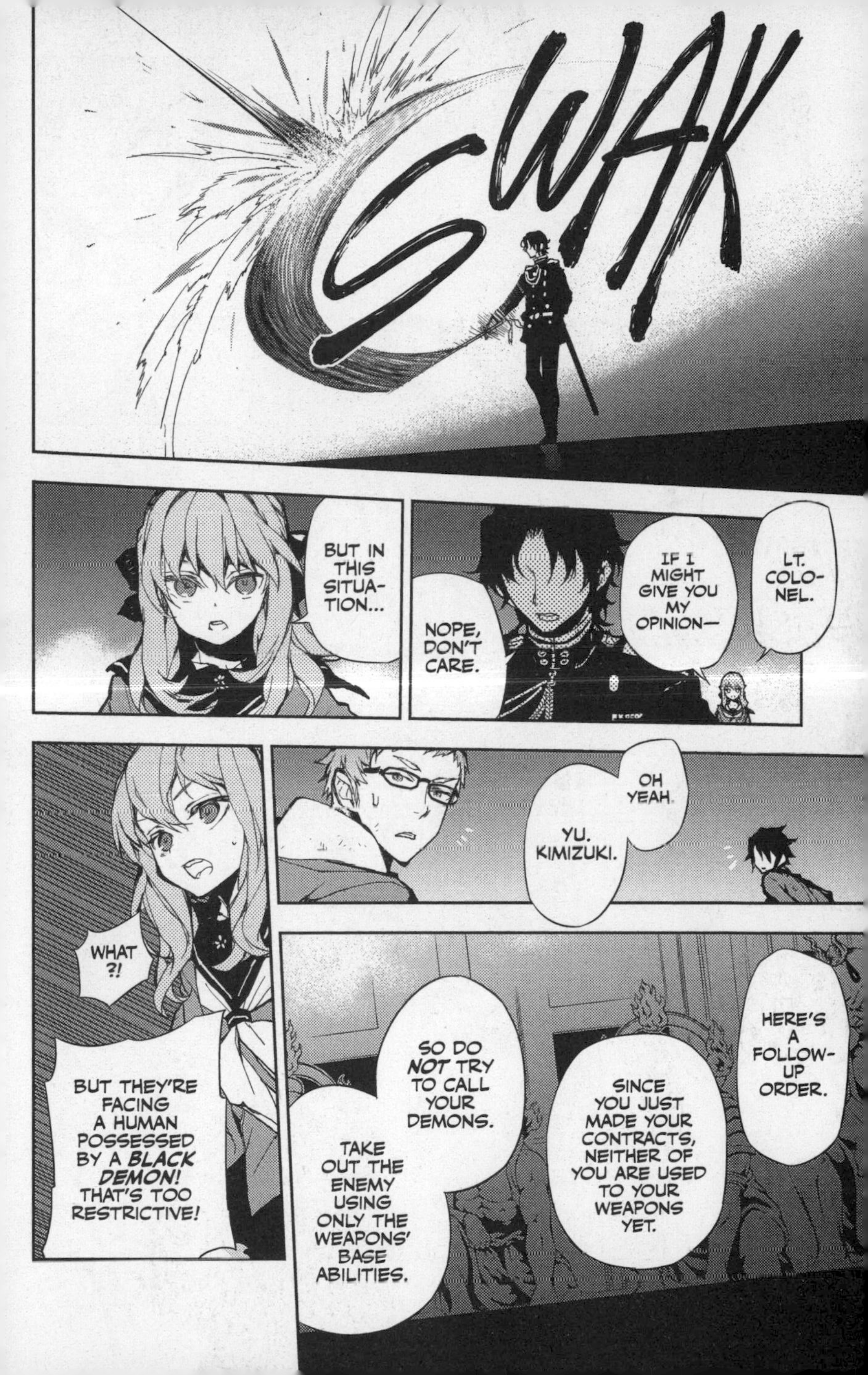
LT. COLONEL.
IF I MIGHT GIVE YOU MY OPINION—
NOPE, DON'T CARE.
BUT IN THIS SITUATION...
OH YEAH.
YU. KIMIZUKI.
HERE'S A FOLLOW-UP ORDER.
SINCE YOU JUST MADE YOUR CONTRACTS, NEITHER OF YOU ARE USED TO YOUR WEAPONS YET.
SO DO *NOT* TRY TO CALL YOUR DEMONS.
TAKE OUT THE ENEMY USING ONLY THE WEAPONS' BASE ABILITIES.
WHAT ?!
BUT THEY'RE FACING A HUMAN POSSESSED BY A ***BLACK DEMON***! THAT'S TOO RESTRICTIVE!

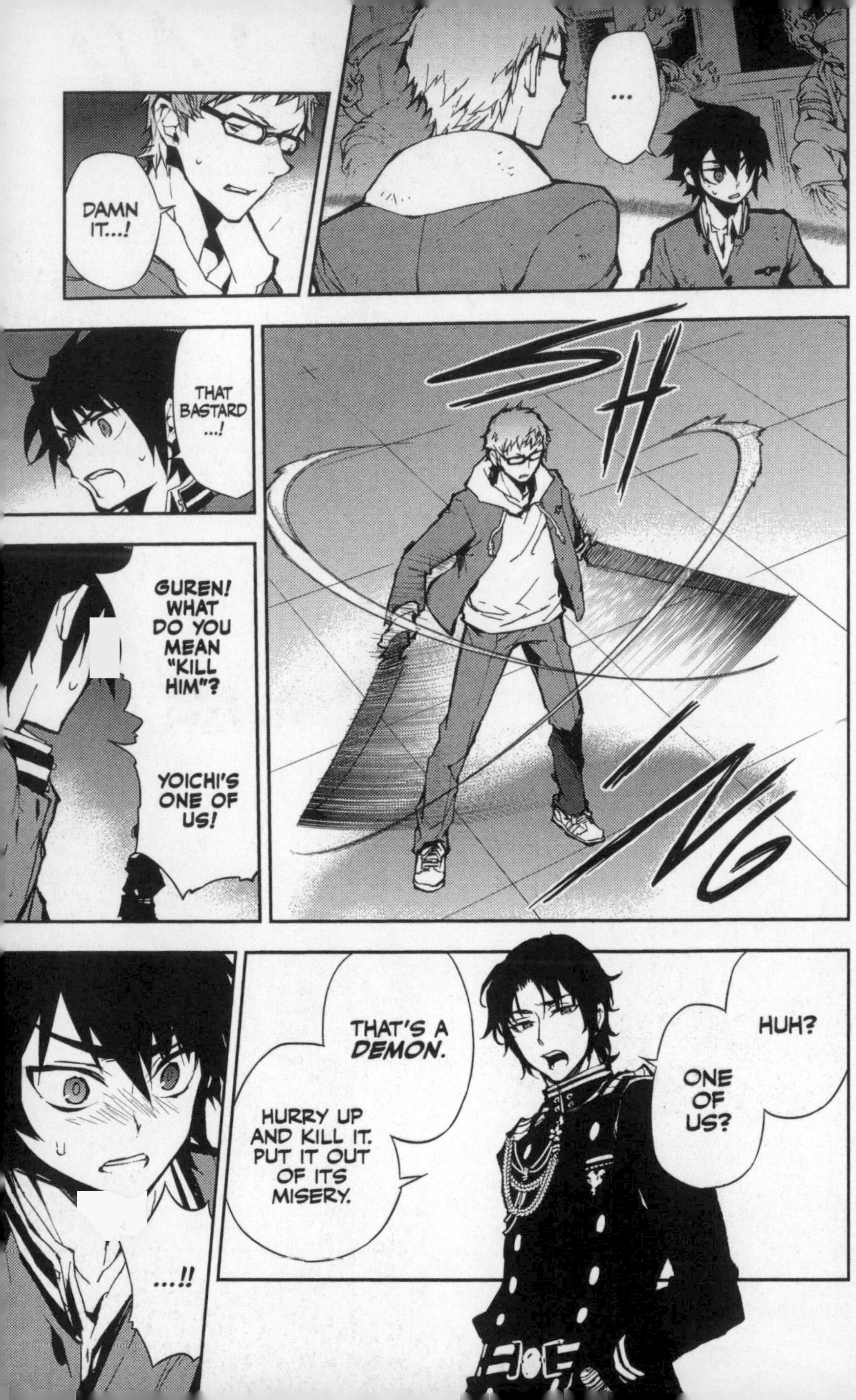
...
DAMN IT...!
SHING
THAT BASTARD ...!
GUREN! WHAT DO YOU MEAN "KILL HIM"?
YOICHI'S ONE OF US!
HUH?
ONE OF US?
THAT'S A *DEMON*.
HURRY UP AND KILL IT. PUT IT OUT OF ITS MISERY.
...!!

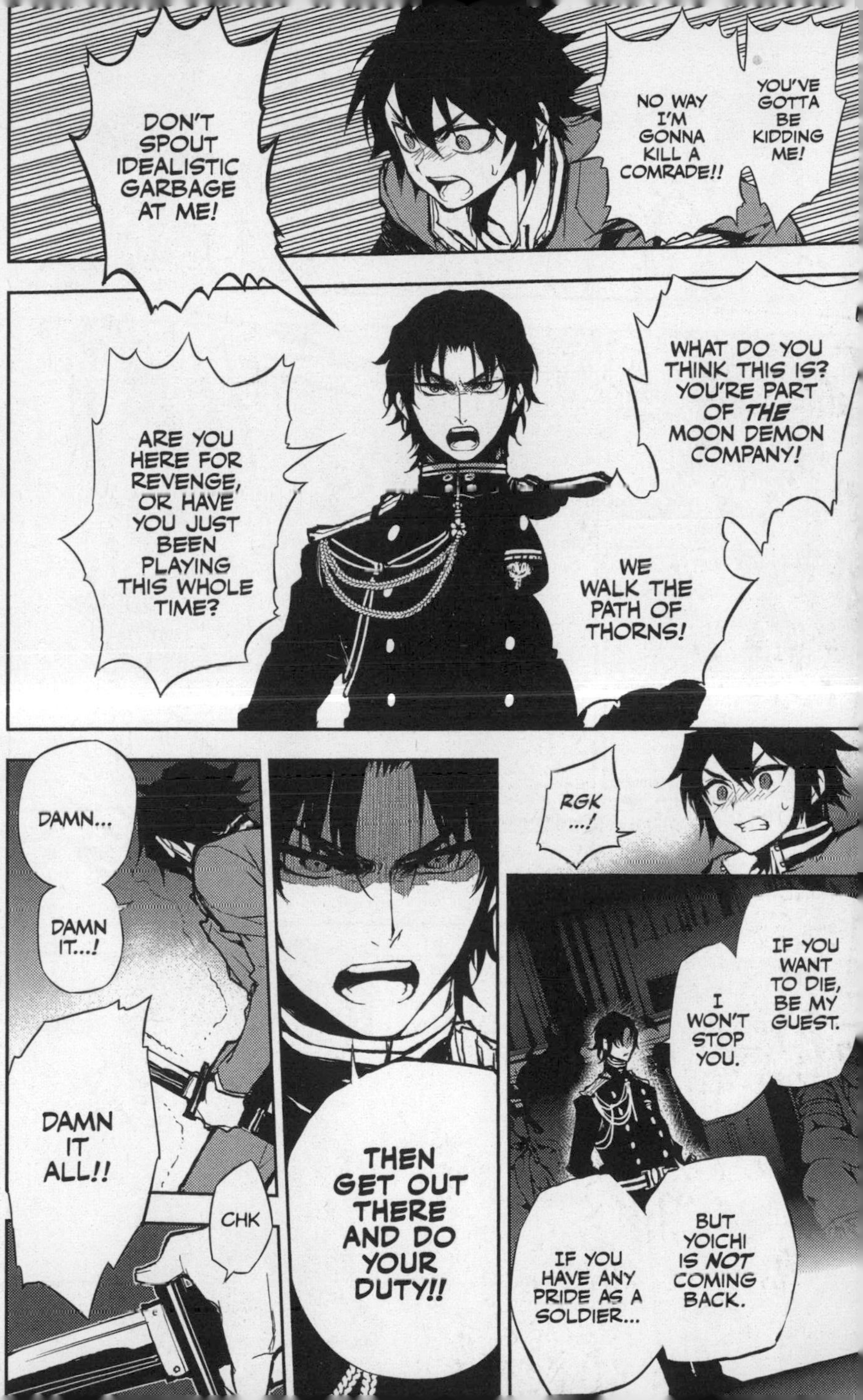
YOU'VE GOTTA BE KIDDING ME!
NO WAY I'M GONNA KILL A COMRADE!!
DON'T SPOUT IDEALISTIC GARBAGE AT ME!
WHAT DO YOU THINK THIS IS? YOU'RE PART OF *THE* MOON DEMON COMPANY!
WE WALK THE PATH OF THORNS!
ARE YOU HERE FOR REVENGE, OR HAVE YOU JUST BEEN PLAYING THIS WHOLE TIME?
RGK ...!
IF YOU WANT TO DIE, BE MY GUEST.
I WON'T STOP YOU.
BUT YOICHI IS *NOT* COMING BACK.
IF YOU HAVE ANY PRIDE AS A SOLDIER...
THEN GET OUT THERE AND DO YOUR DUTY!!
DAMN...
DAMN IT...!
DAMN IT ALL!!
CHK

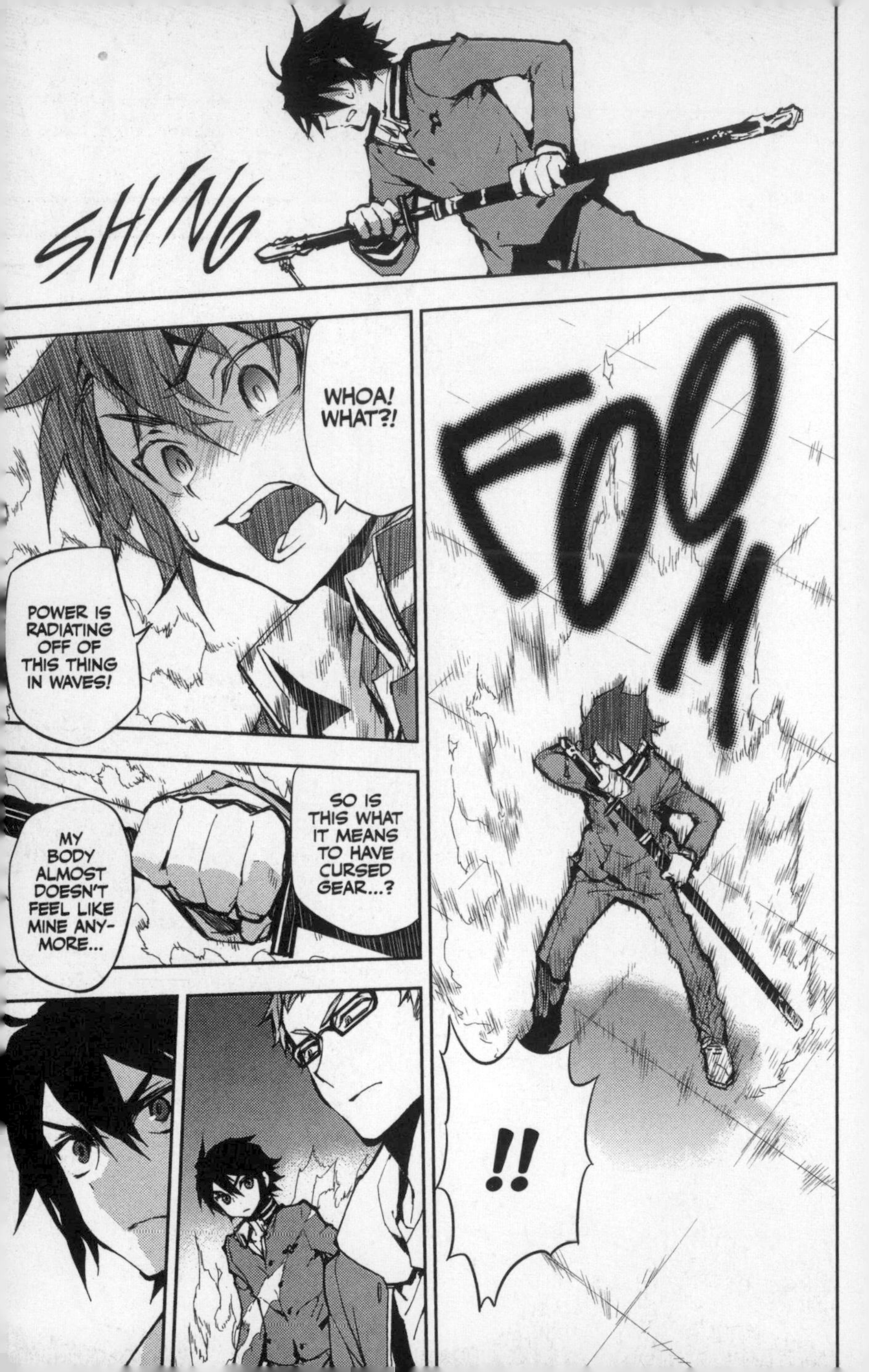
SHING
FOOM
!!
WHOA! WHAT?!
POWER IS RADIATING OFF OF THIS THING IN WAVES!
SO IS THIS WHAT IT MEANS TO HAVE CURSED GEAR...?
MY BODY ALMOST DOESN'T FEEL LIKE MINE ANY-MORE...

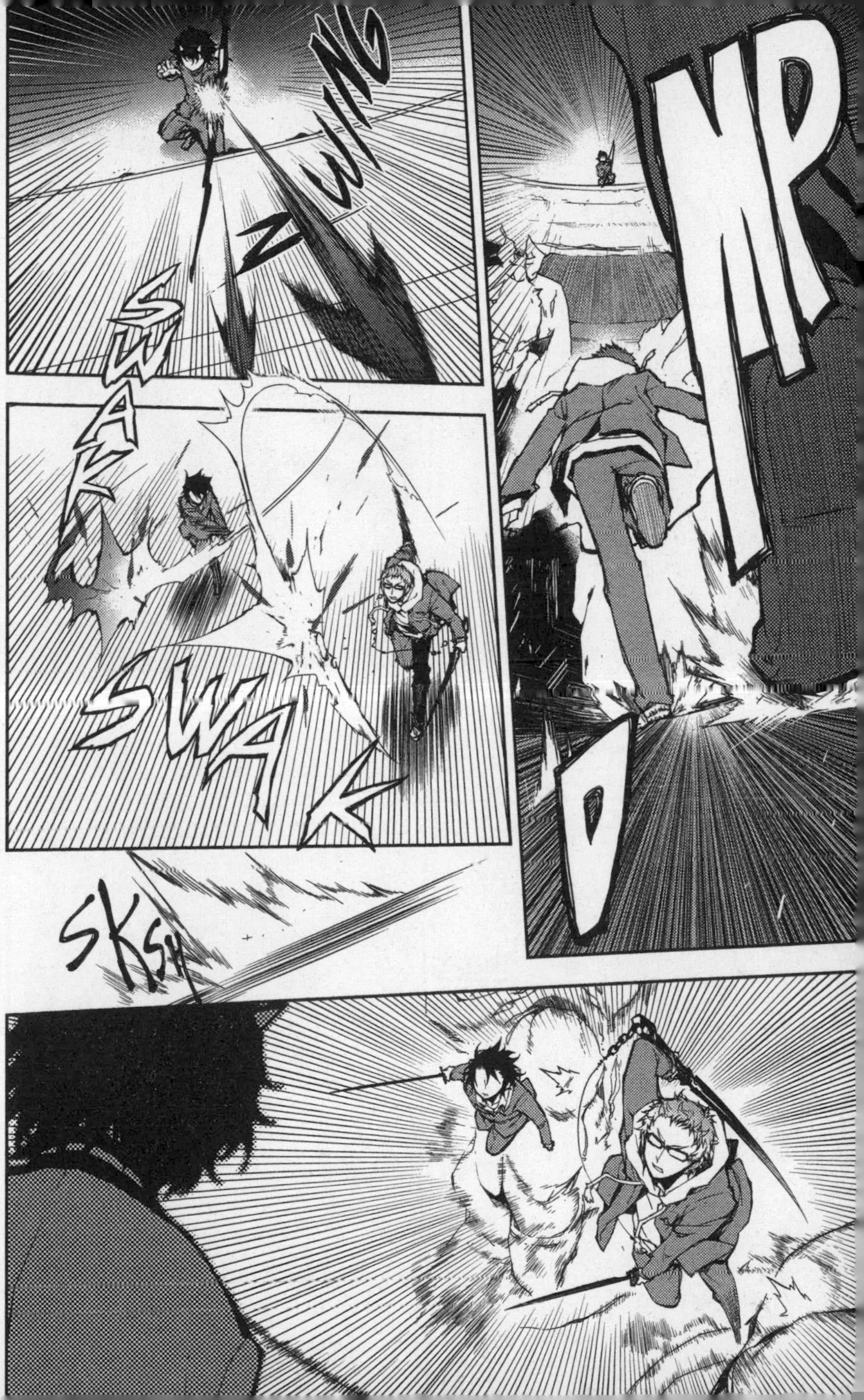
ZWING
SWAK
SWAK
SKSH

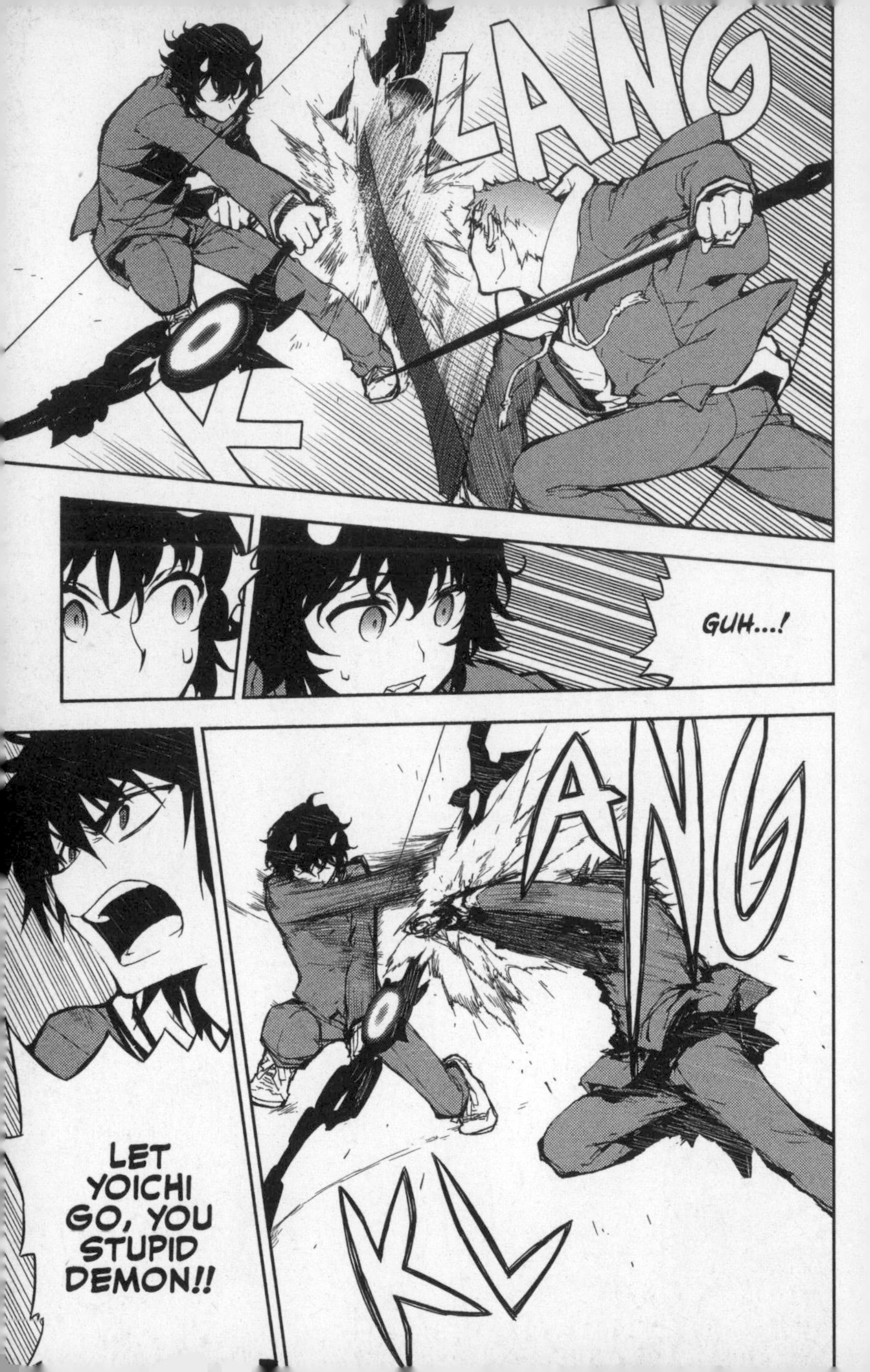
LANG
GUH...!
ANG
LET YOICHI GO, YOU STUPID DEMON!!

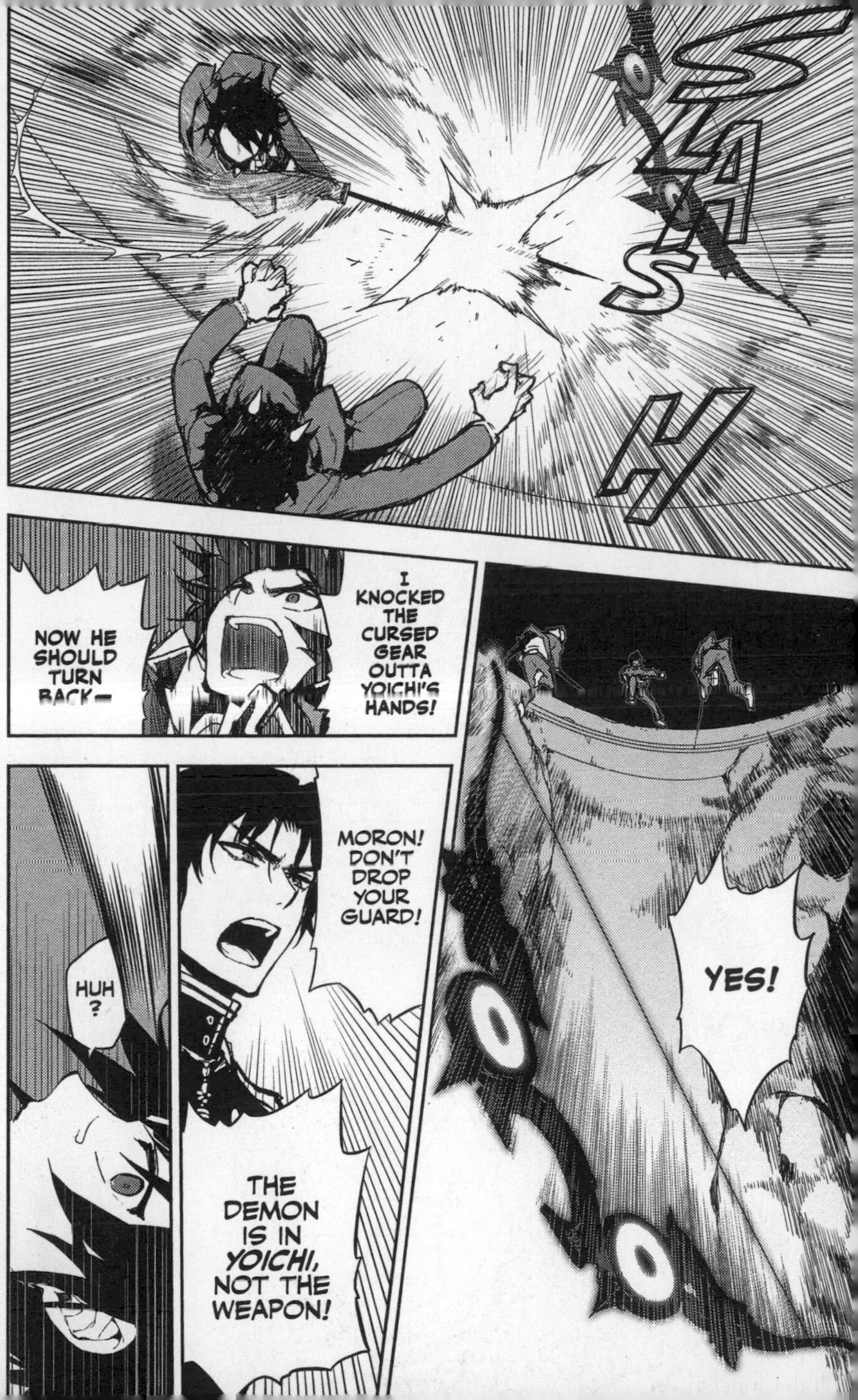
SLASH
YES!
I KNOCKED THE CURSED GEAR OUTTA YOICHI'S HANDS!
NOW HE SHOULD TURN BACK—
MORON! DON'T DROP YOUR GUARD!
THE DEMON IS IN *YOICHI*, NOT THE WEAPON!
HUH?

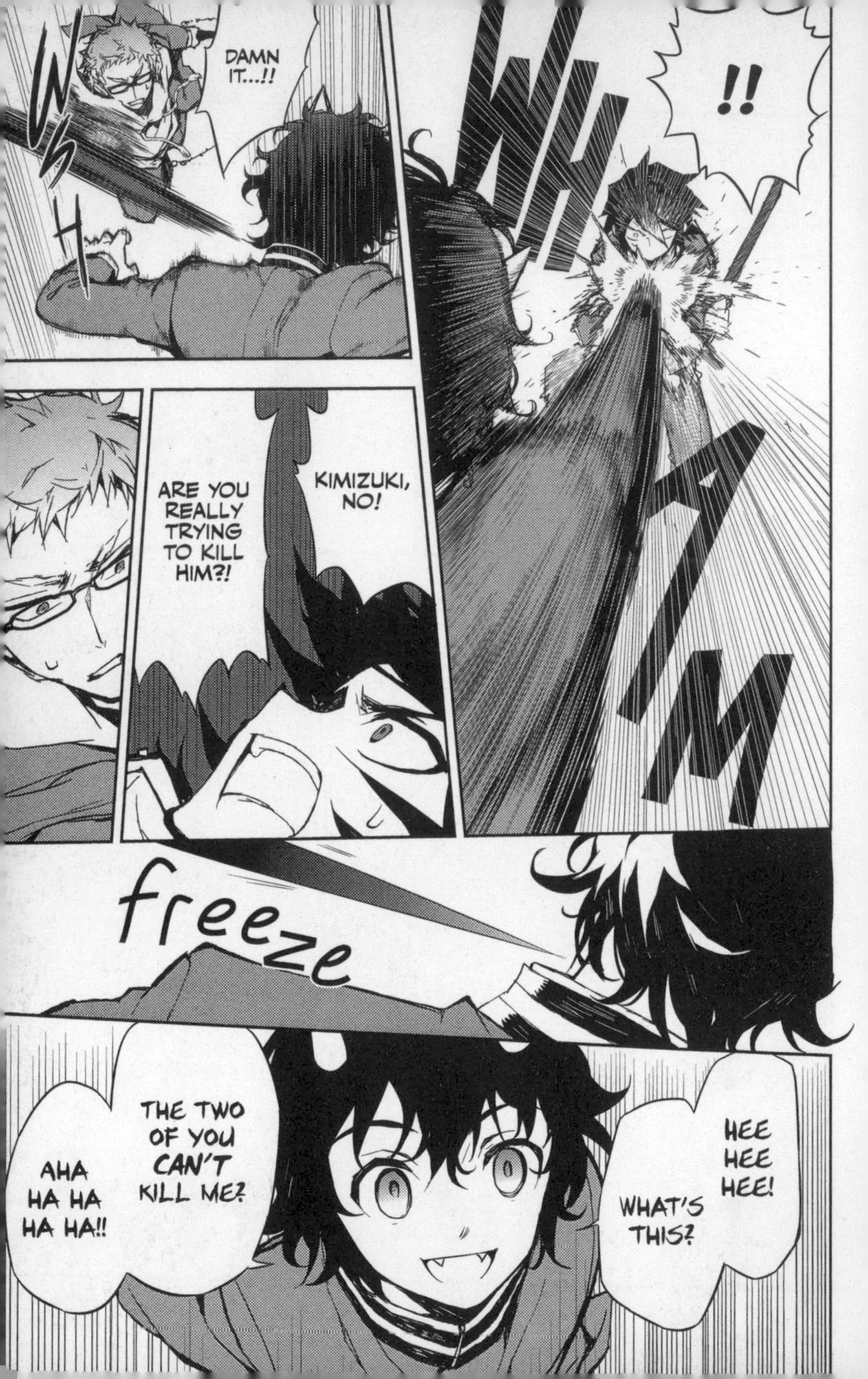
!!
WHAM
DAMN IT...!!
KIMIZUKI, NO!
ARE YOU REALLY TRYING TO KILL HIM?!
freeze
HEE HEE HEE!
WHAT'S THIS?
THE TWO OF YOU CAN'T KILL ME?
AHA HA HA HA HA!!

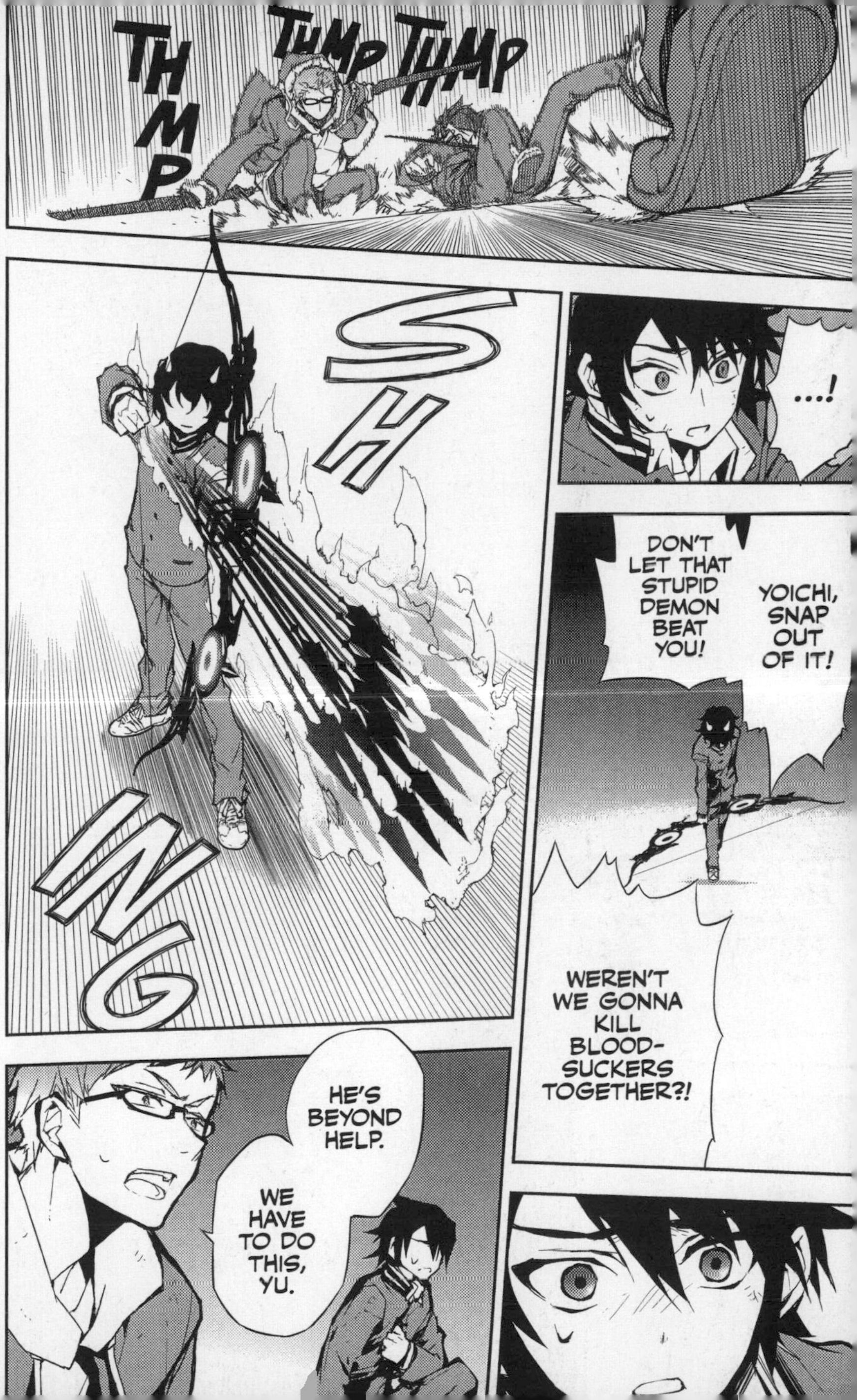
THUMP THUMP
THUMP
...!
YOICHI, SNAP OUT OF IT!
DON'T LET THAT STUPID DEMON BEAT YOU!
WEREN'T WE GONNA KILL BLOOD-SUCKERS TOGETHER?!
SHING
HE'S BEYOND HELP.
WE HAVE TO DO THIS, YU.

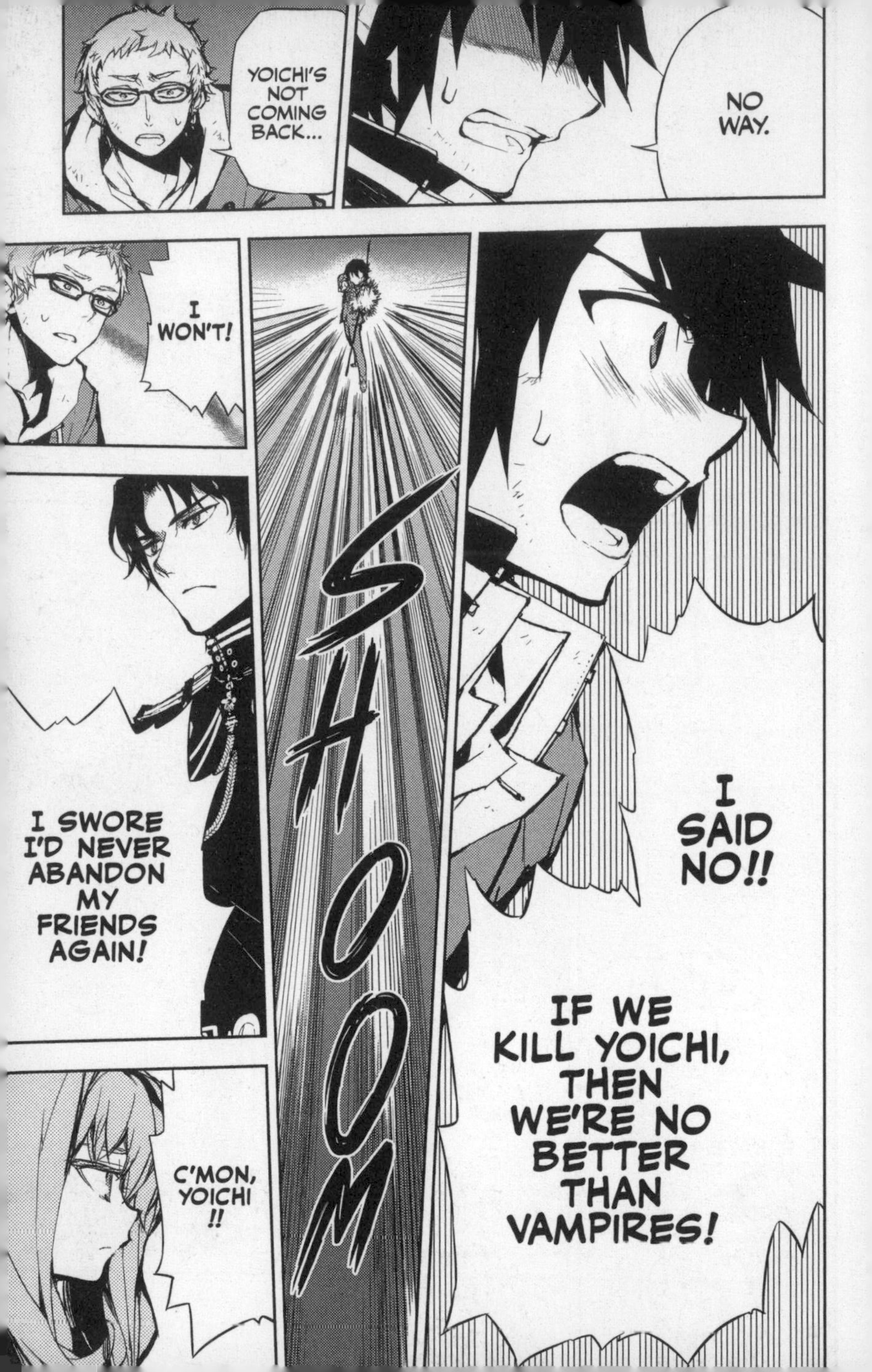
NO WAY.
YOICHI'S NOT COMING BACK...
I SAID NO!!
IF WE KILL YOICHI, THEN WE'RE NO BETTER THAN VAMPIRES!
SHOOM
I WON'T!
I SWORE I'D NEVER ABANDON MY FRIENDS AGAIN!
C'MON, YOICHI!!

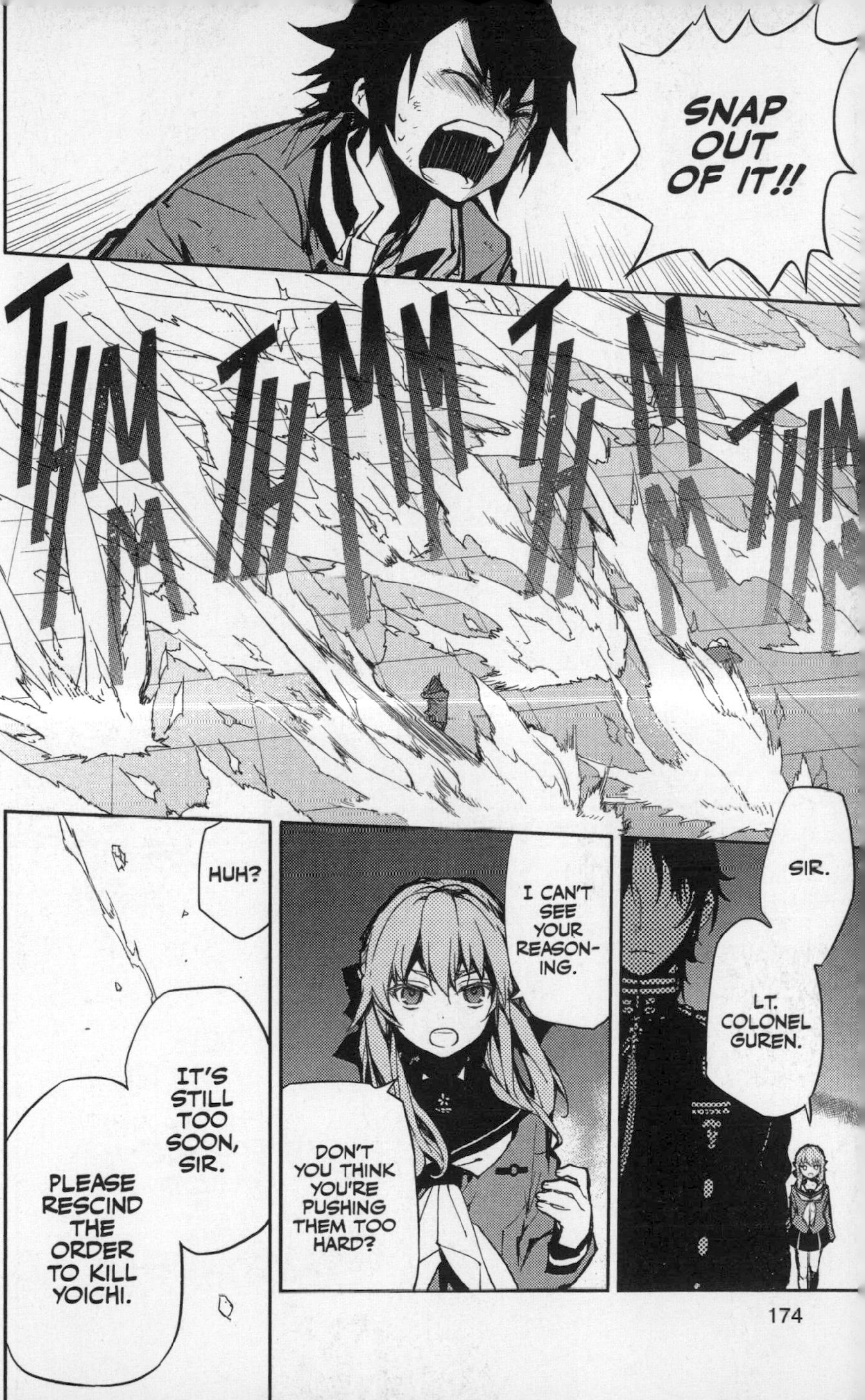
SNAP OUT OF IT!!
THUMM THUMM THUMM
SIR.
LT. COLONEL GUREN.
I CAN'T SEE YOUR REASON-ING.
DON'T YOU THINK YOU'RE PUSHING THEM TOO HARD?
HUH?
IT'S STILL TOO SOON, SIR.
PLEASE RESCIND THE ORDER TO KILL YOICHI.

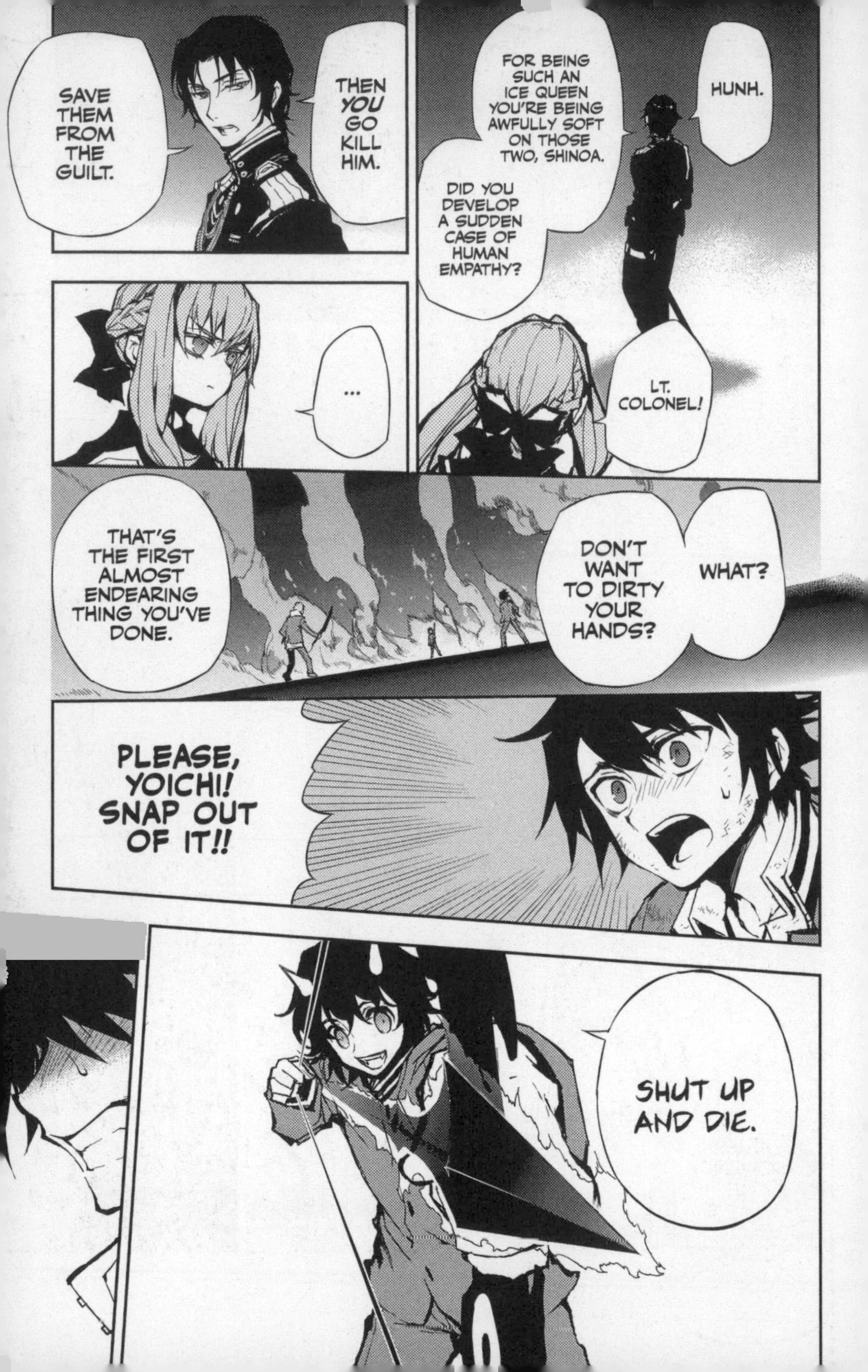
HUNH.
FOR BEING SUCH AN ICE QUEEN YOU'RE BEING AWFULLY SOFT ON THOSE TWO, SHINOA.
DID YOU DEVELOP A SUDDEN CASE OF HUMAN EMPATHY?
LT. COLONEL!
THEN *YOU* GO KILL HIM.
SAVE THEM FROM THE GUILT.
...
WHAT?
DON'T WANT TO DIRTY YOUR HANDS?
THAT'S THE FIRST ALMOST ENDEARING THING YOU'VE DONE.
PLEASE, YOICHI! SNAP OUT OF IT!!
SHUT UP AND DIE.

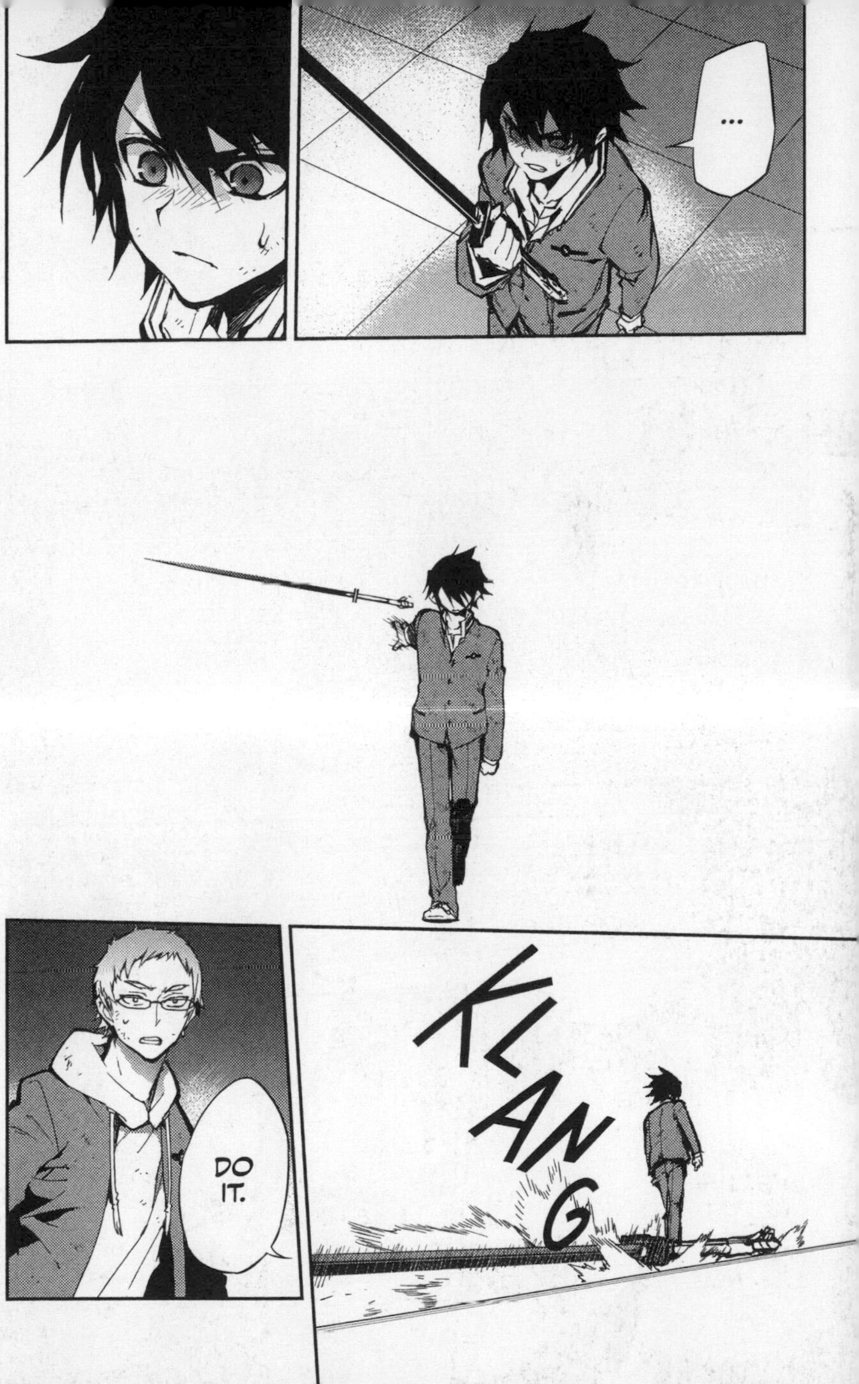
...
KLANG
DO IT.

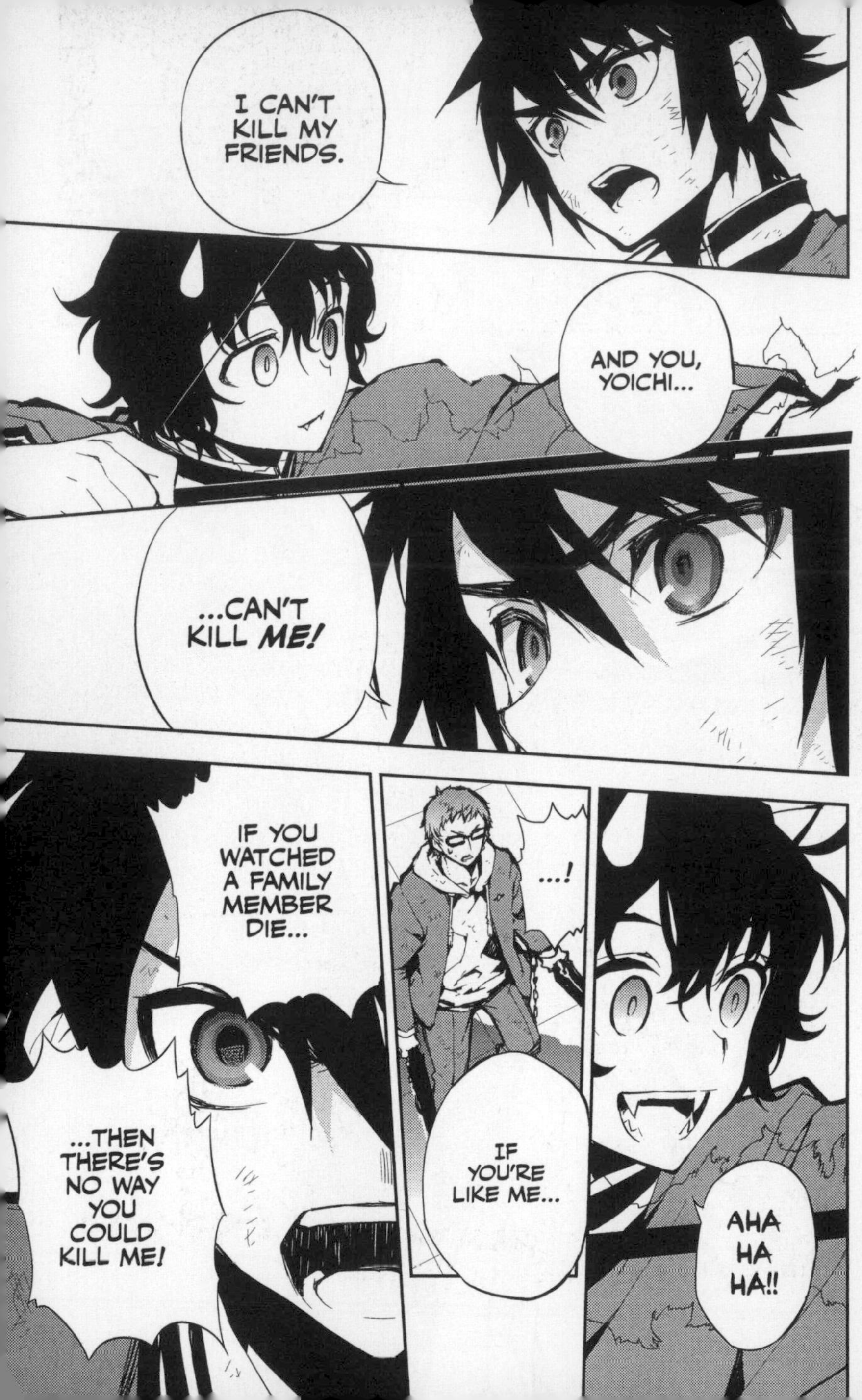
I CAN'T KILL MY FRIENDS.
AND YOU, YOICHI...
...CAN'T KILL *ME!*
IF YOU'RE LIKE ME...
AHA HA HA!!
...!
IF YOU WATCHED A FAMILY MEMBER DIE...
...THEN THERE'S NO WAY YOU COULD KILL ME!

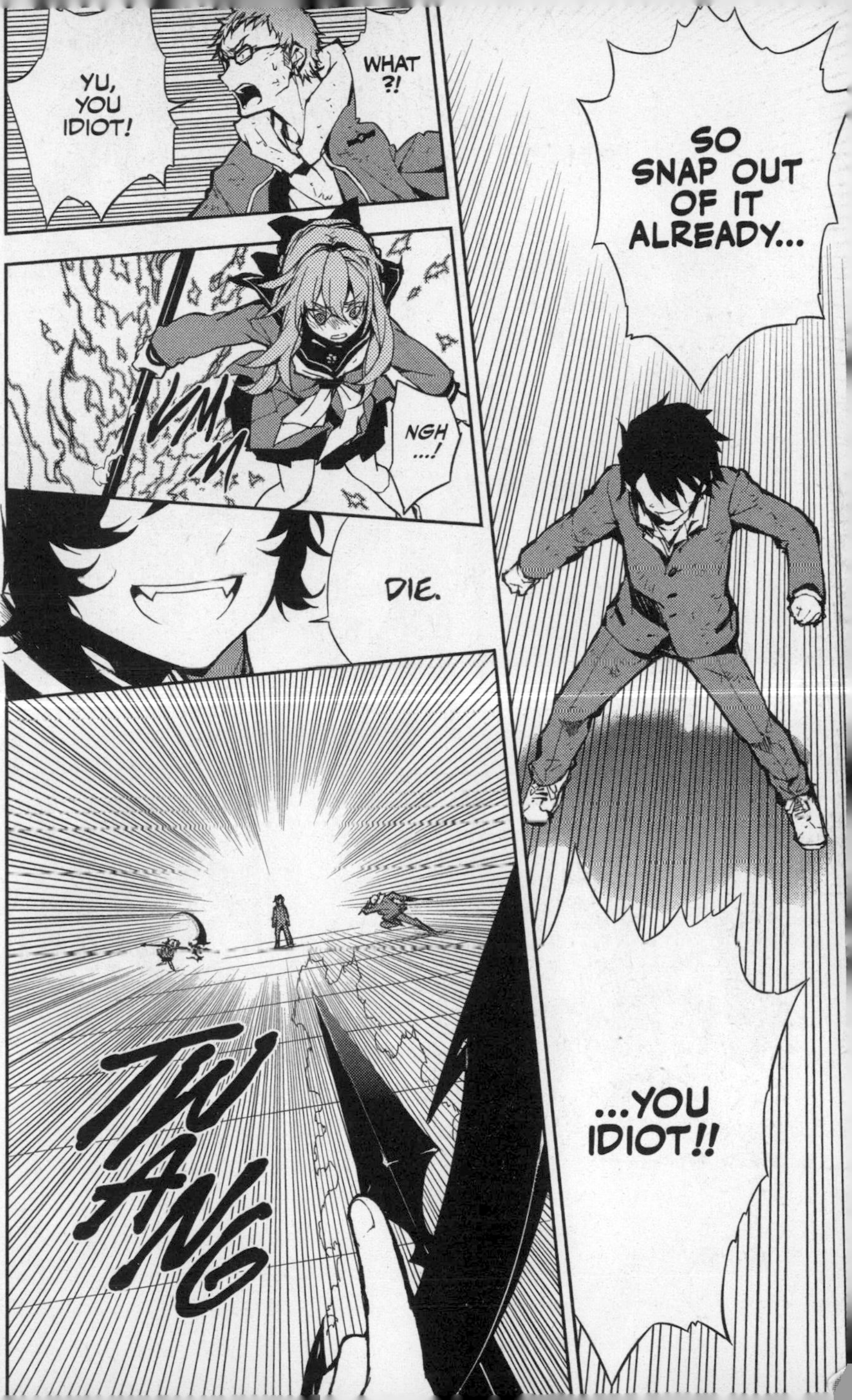
SO SNAP OUT OF IT ALREADY...
...YOU IDIOT!!
WHAT ?!
YU, YOU IDIOT!
NGH ...!
VMMM
DIE.
TWANG

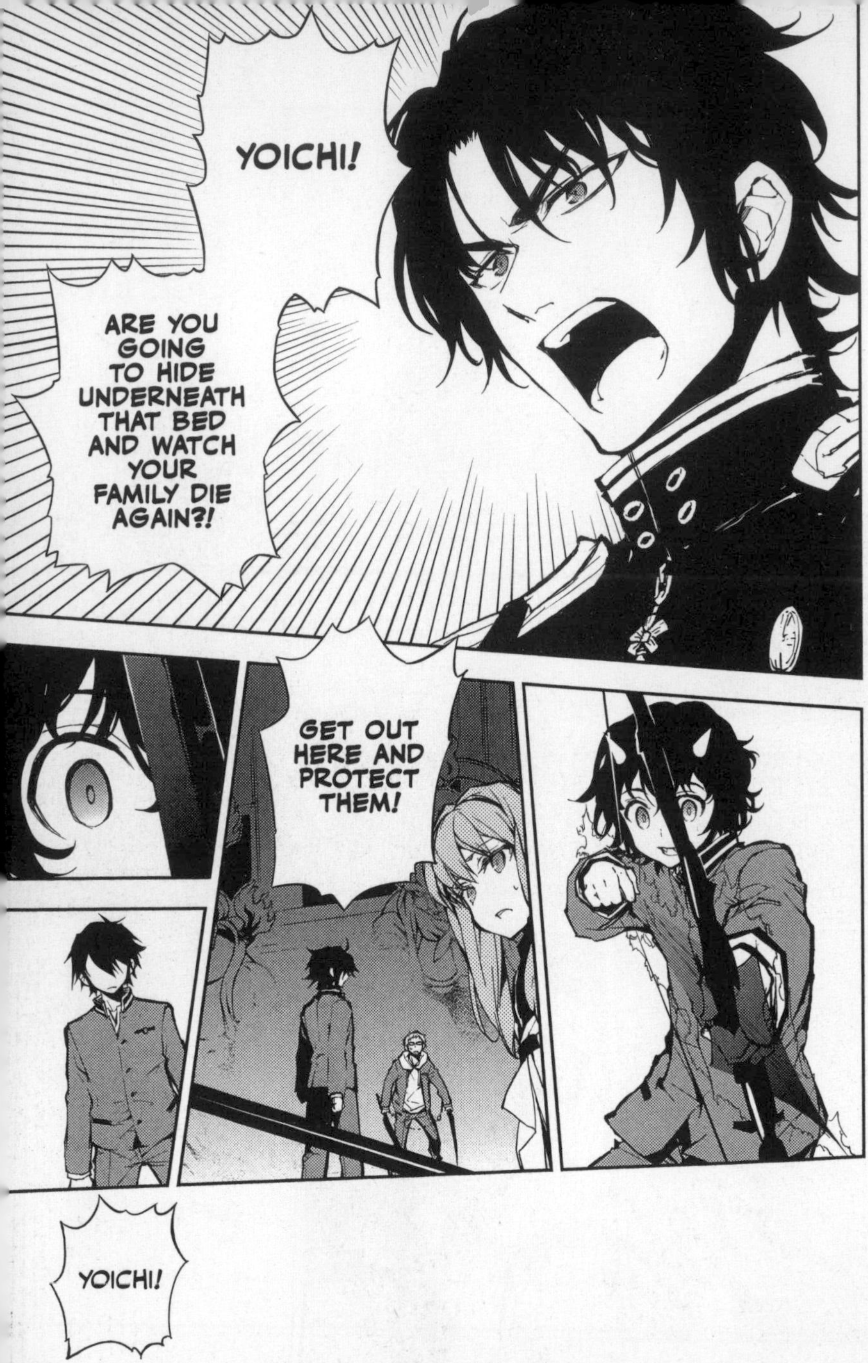
YOICHI!
ARE YOU GOING TO HIDE UNDERNEATH THAT BED AND WATCH YOUR FAMILY DIE AGAIN?!
GET OUT HERE AND PROTECT THEM!
YOICHI!

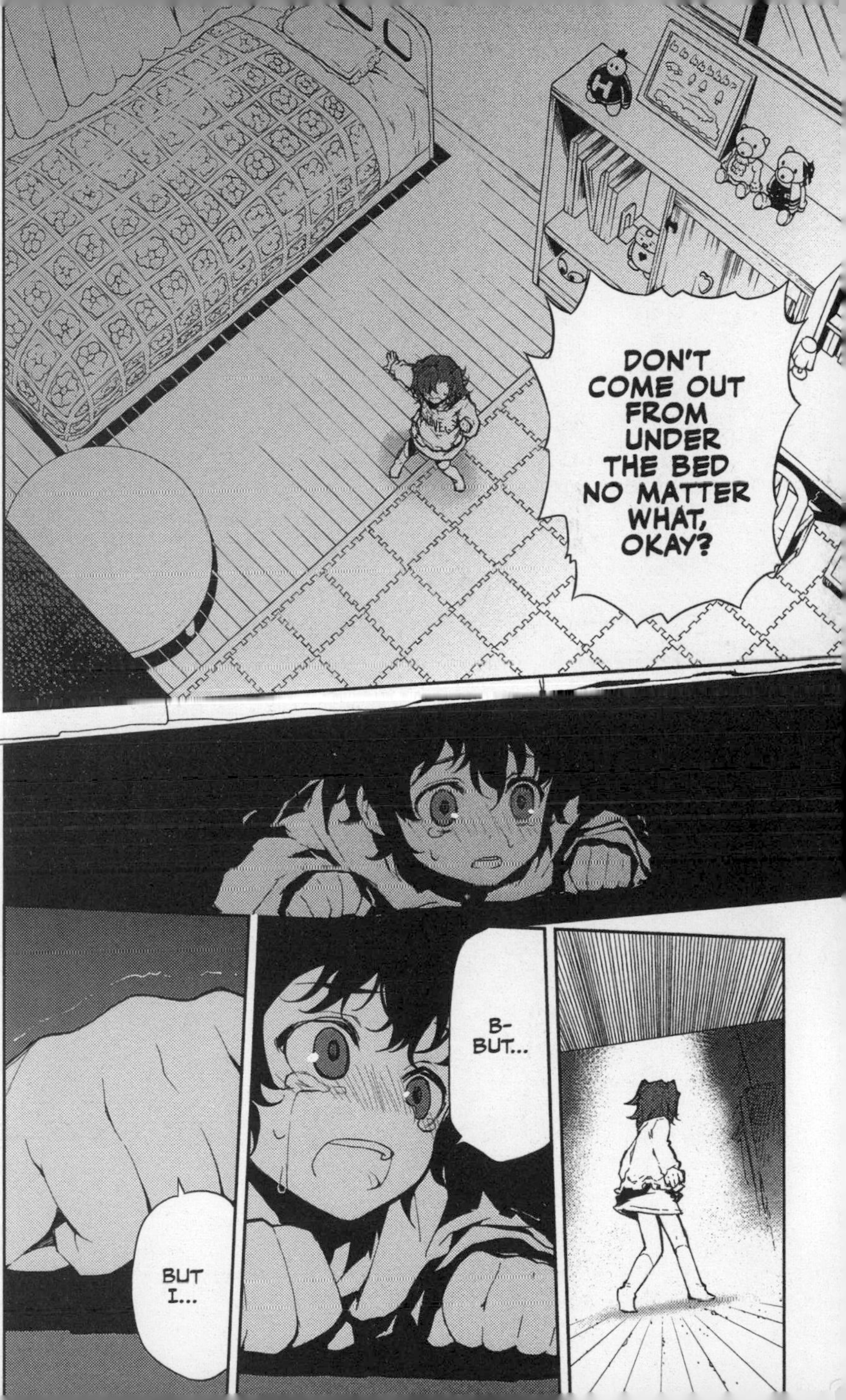
DON'T COME OUT FROM UNDER THE BED NO MATTER WHAT, OKAY?
B-BUT...
BUT I...

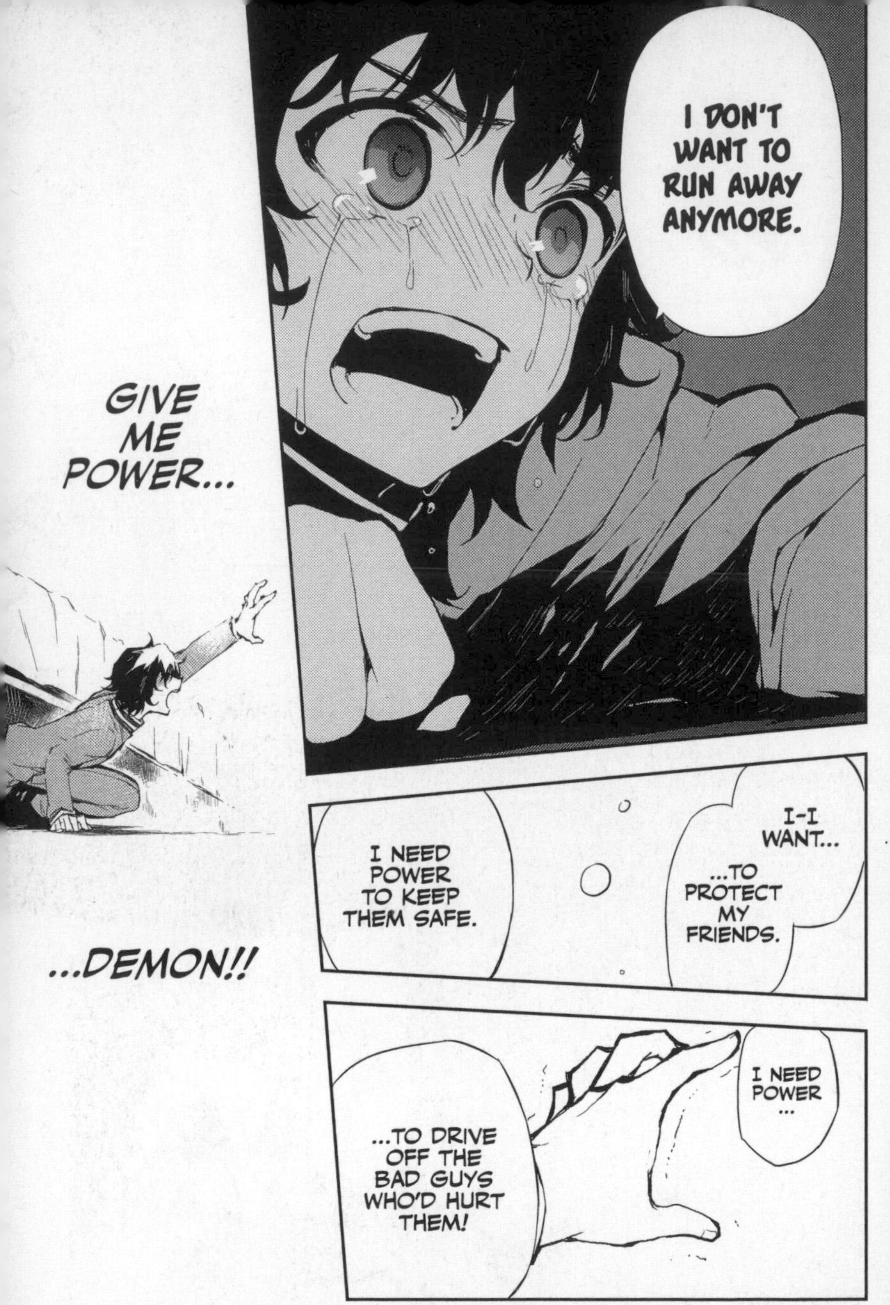
I DON'T WANT TO RUN AWAY ANYMORE.
GIVE ME POWER...
...DEMON!!
I-I WANT...
...TO PROTECT MY FRIENDS.
I NEED POWER TO KEEP THEM SAFE.
I NEED POWER ...
...TO DRIVE OFF THE BAD GUYS WHO'D HURT THEM!

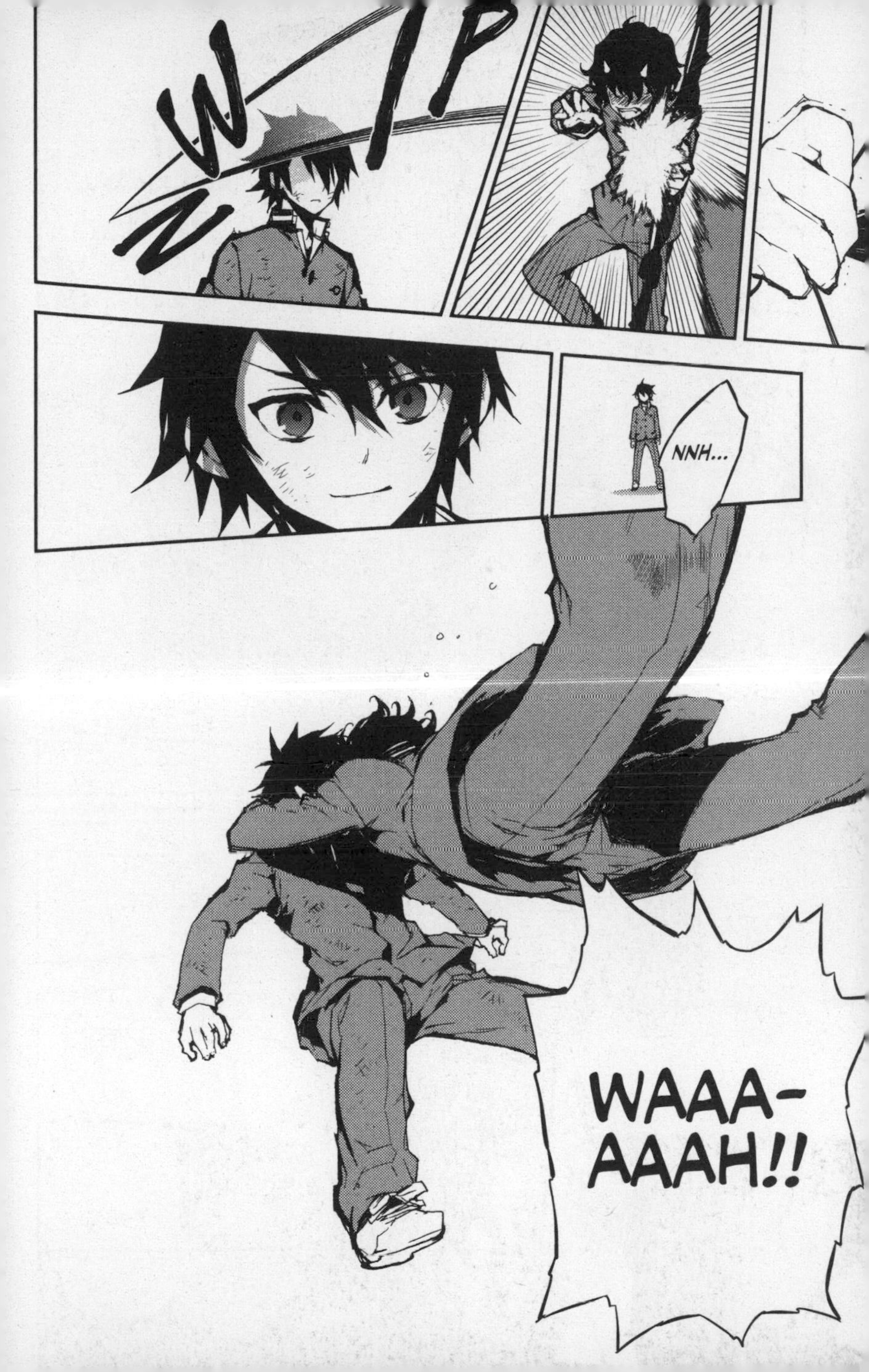

NNH...
WAAA-AAAH!!

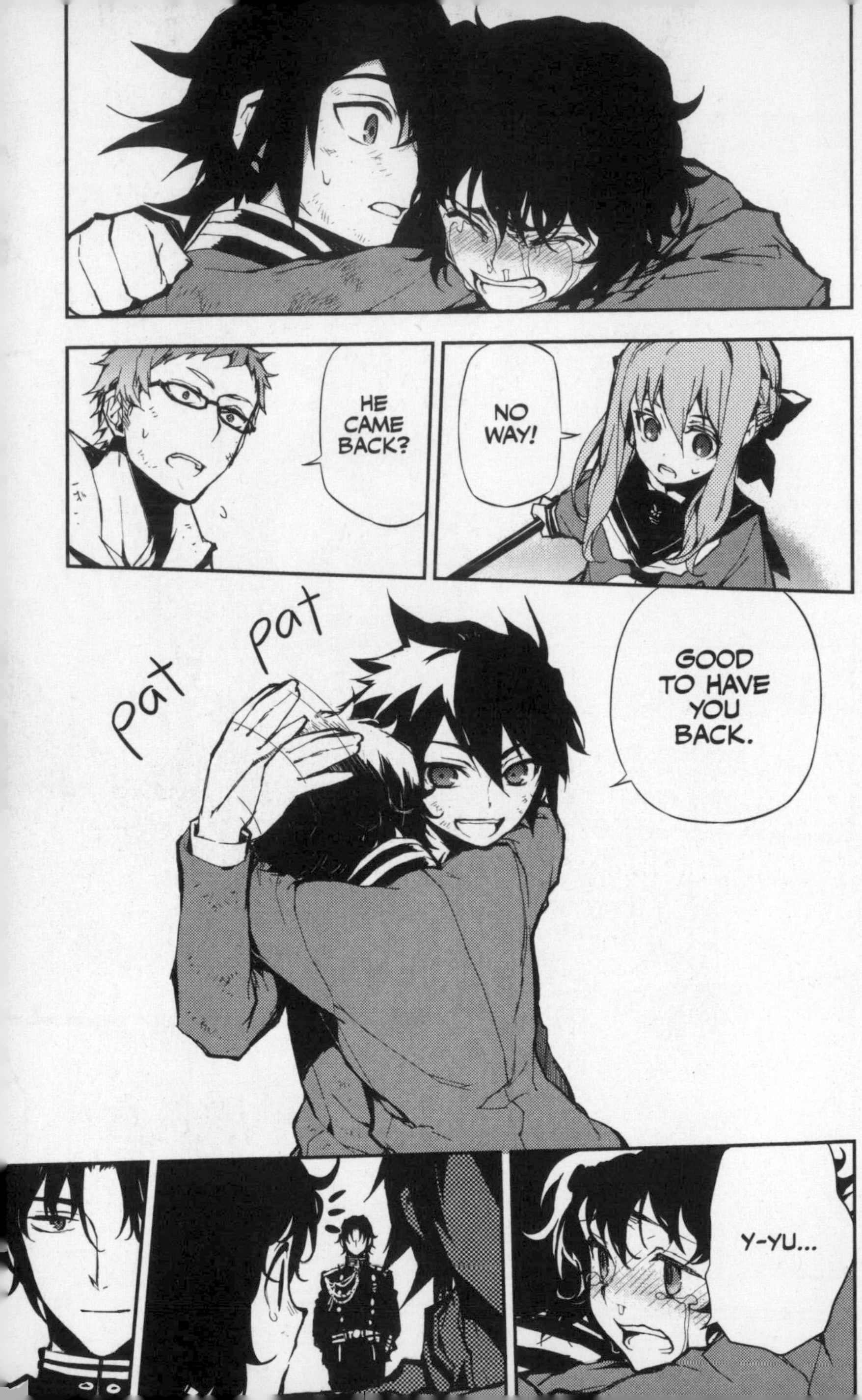
NO WAY!
HE CAME BACK?
GOOD TO HAVE YOU BACK.
pat pat
Y-YU...

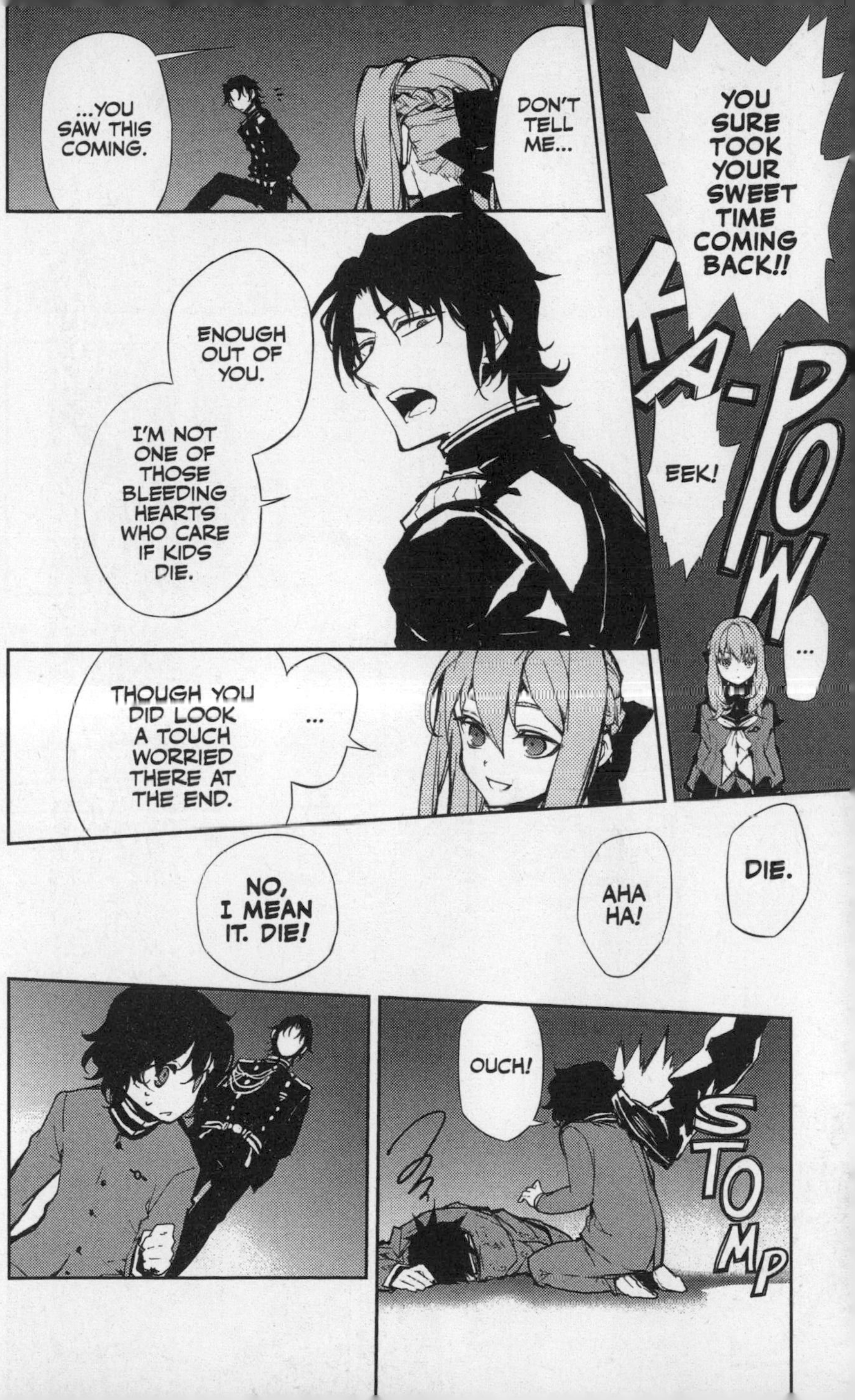
YOU SURE TOOK YOUR SWEET TIME COMING BACK!!
KA-POW
EEK!
...
DON'T TELL ME...
...YOU SAW THIS COMING.
ENOUGH OUT OF YOU.
I'M NOT ONE OF THOSE BLEEDING HEARTS WHO CARE IF KIDS DIE.
...
THOUGH YOU DID LOOK A TOUCH WORRIED THERE AT THE END.
DIE.
AHA HA!
NO, I MEAN IT. DIE!
OUCH!
STOMP

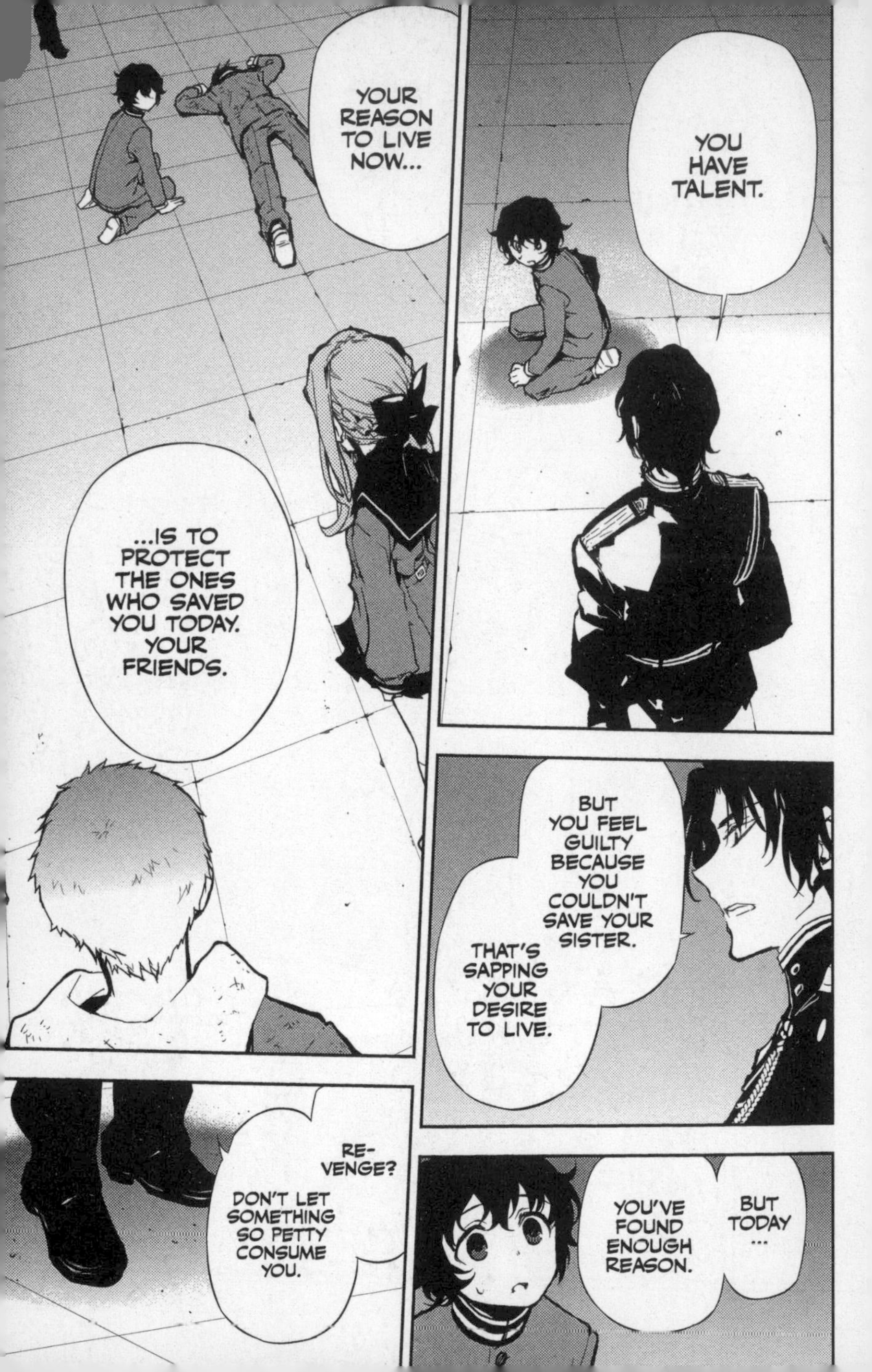
YOU HAVE TALENT.
BUT YOU FEEL GUILTY BECAUSE YOU COULDN'T SAVE YOUR SISTER.
THAT'S SAPPING YOUR DESIRE TO LIVE.
YOUR REASON TO LIVE NOW...
...IS TO PROTECT THE ONES WHO SAVED YOU TODAY. YOUR FRIENDS.
BUT TODAY...
YOU'VE FOUND ENOUGH REASON.
RE-VENGE?
DON'T LET SOMETHING SO PETTY CONSUME YOU.

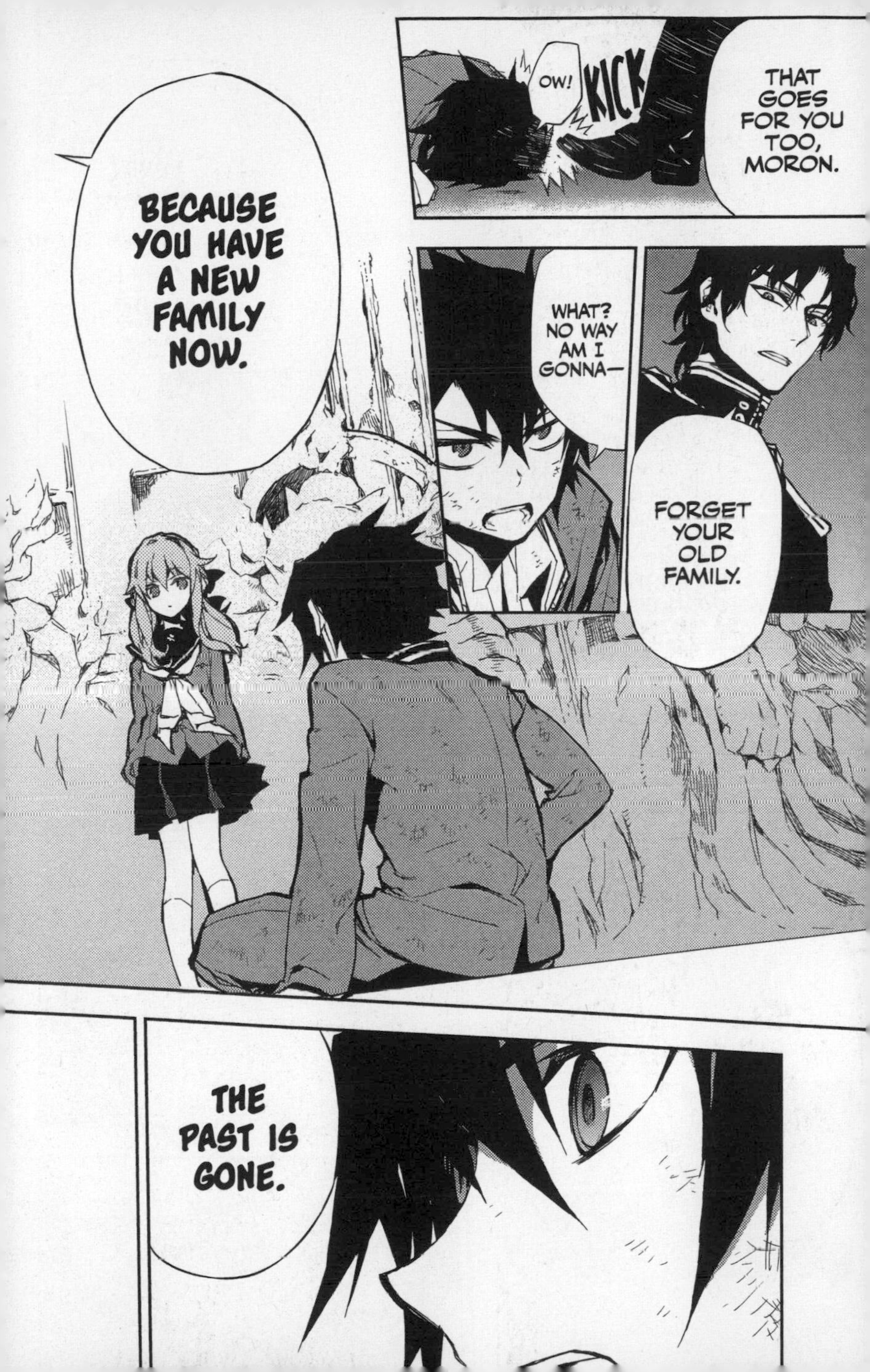
THAT GOES FOR YOU TOO, MORON.
KICK
OW!
FORGET YOUR OLD FAMILY.
WHAT? NO WAY AM I GONNA—
BECAUSE YOU HAVE A NEW FAMILY NOW.
THE PAST IS GONE.

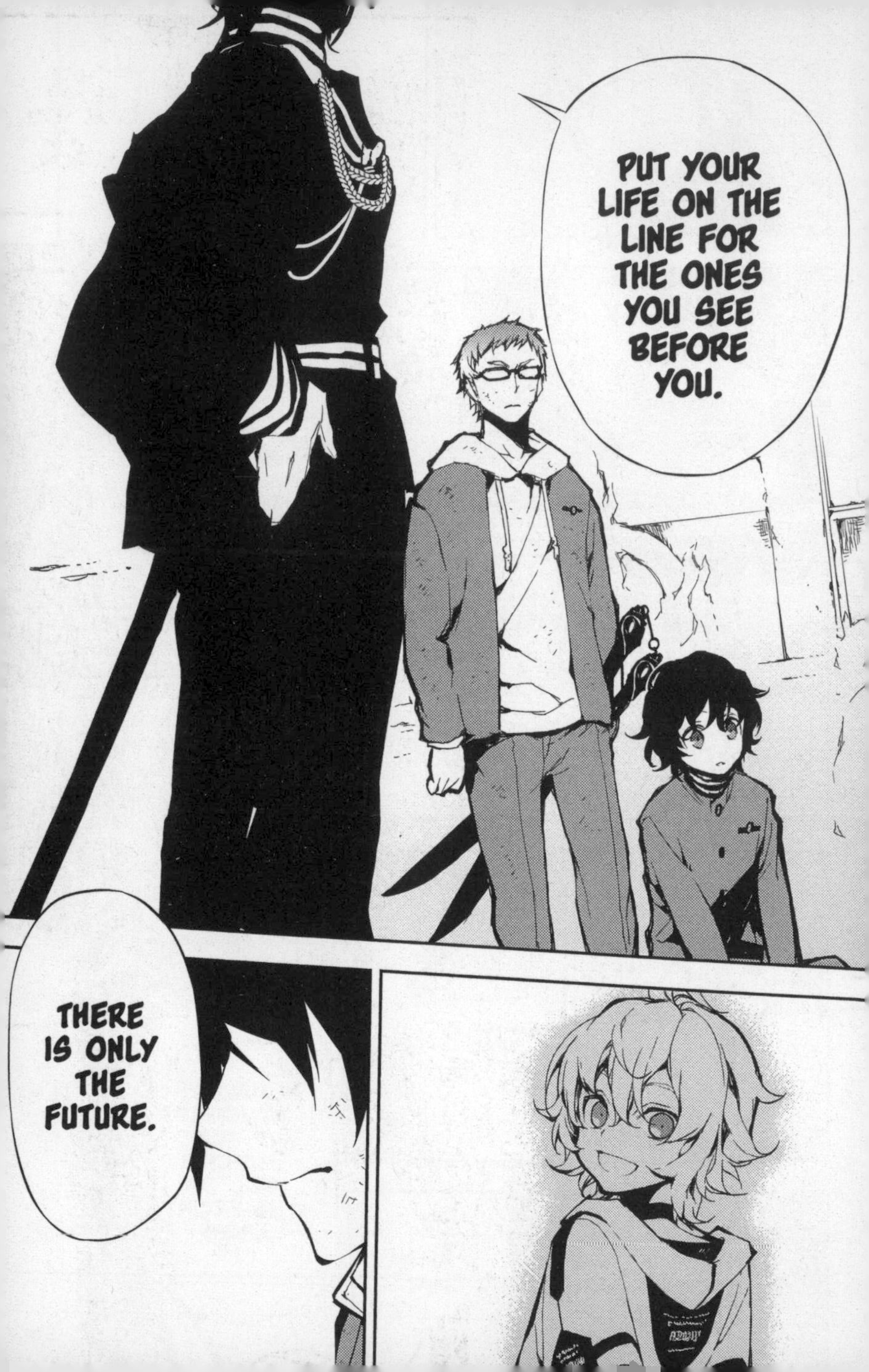
PUT YOUR LIFE ON THE LINE FOR THE ONES YOU SEE BEFORE YOU.
THERE IS ONLY THE FUTURE.

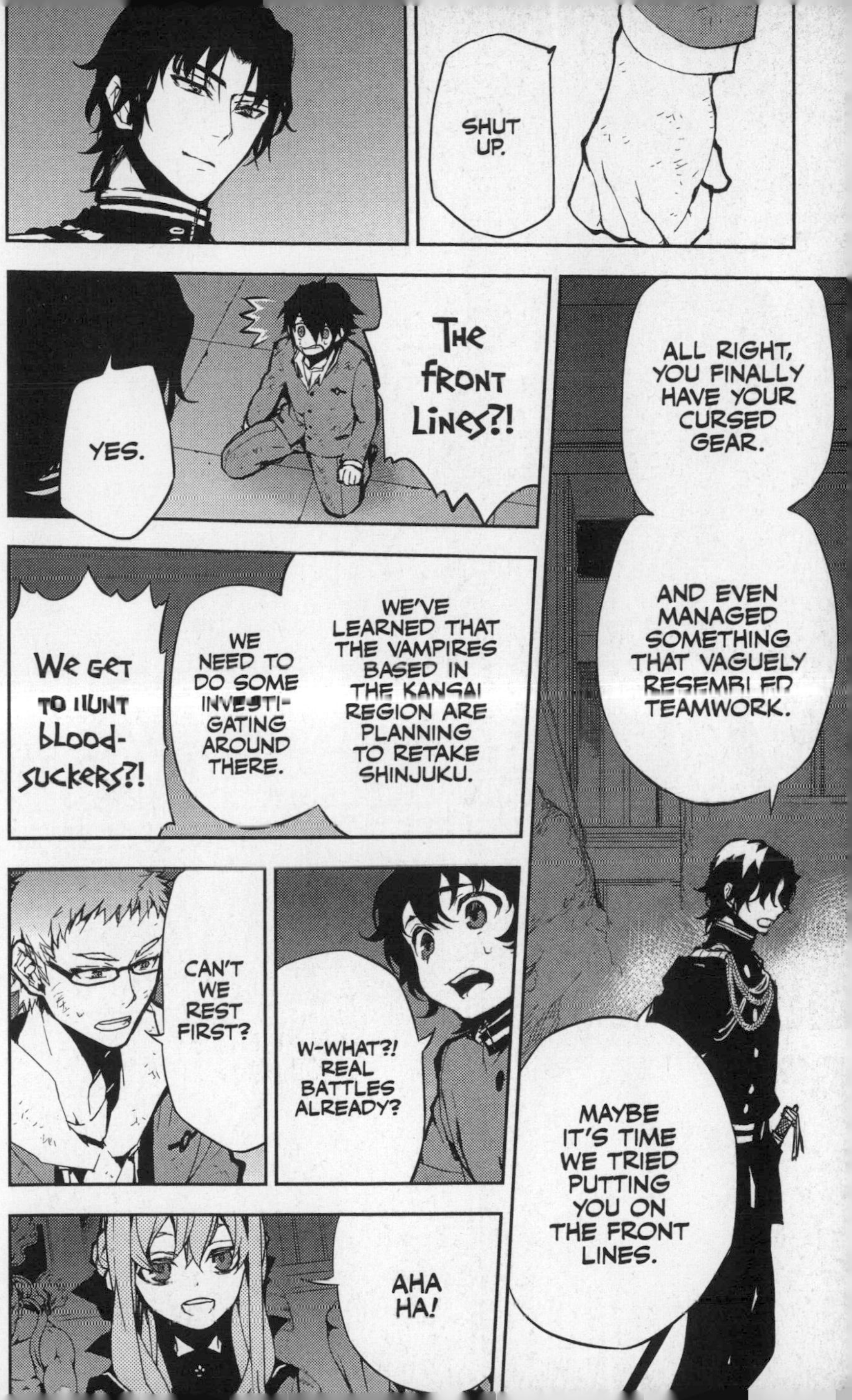
SHUT UP.
ALL RIGHT, YOU FINALLY HAVE YOUR CURSED GEAR.
AND EVEN MANAGED SOMETHING THAT VAGUELY RESEMBLED TEAMWORK.
MAYBE IT'S TIME WE TRIED PUTTING YOU ON THE FRONT LINES.
The front Lines?!
YES.
WE'VE LEARNED THAT THE VAMPIRES BASED IN THE KANSAI REGION ARE PLANNING TO RETAKE SHINJUKU.
WE NEED TO DO SOME INVESTI-GATING AROUND THERE.
We get to HUNT blood-suckers?!
W-WHAT?! REAL BATTLES ALREADY?
CAN'T WE REST FIRST?
AHA HA!

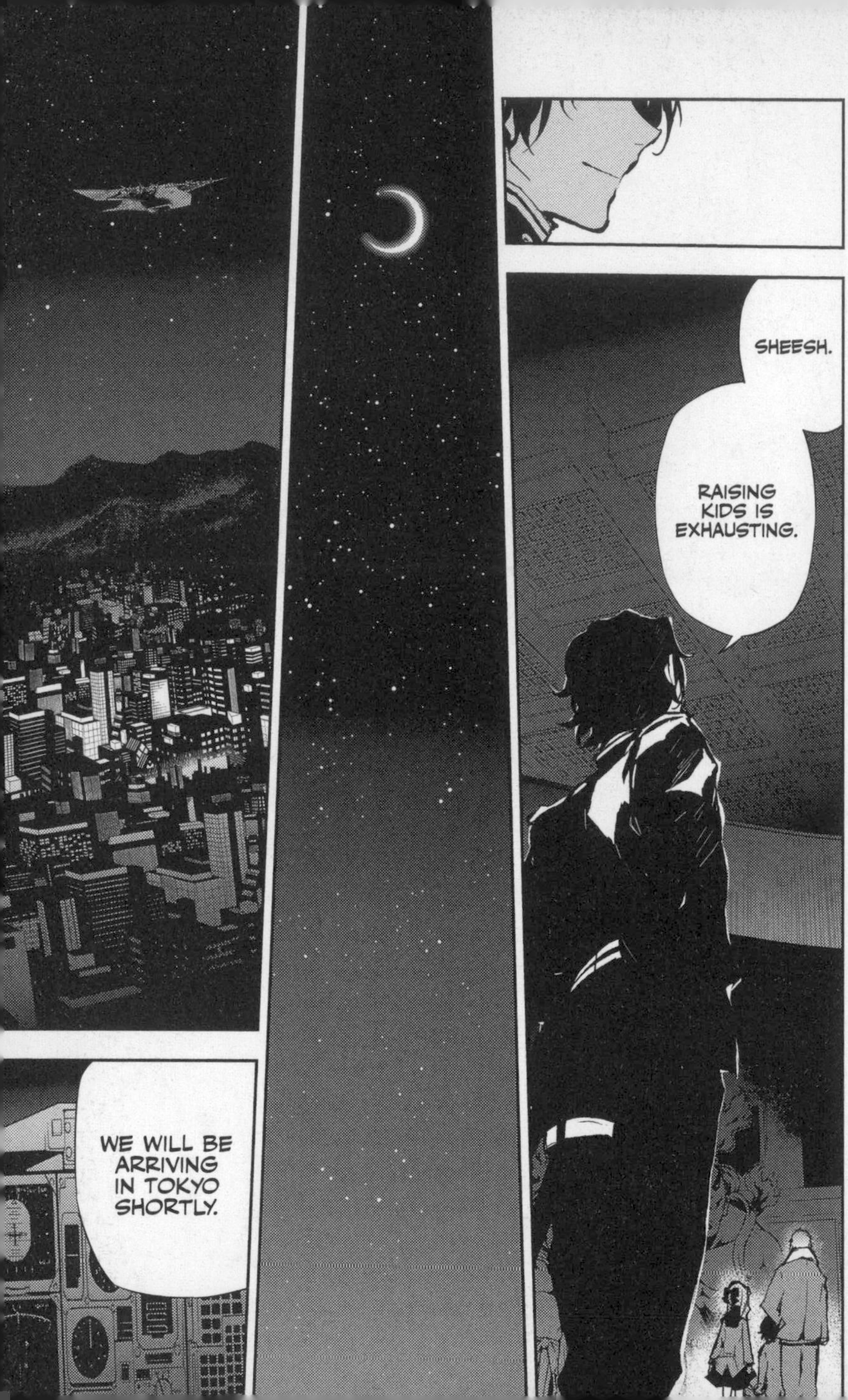
SHEESH.
RAISING KIDS IS EXHAUSTING.
WE WILL BE ARRIVING IN TOKYO SHORTLY.

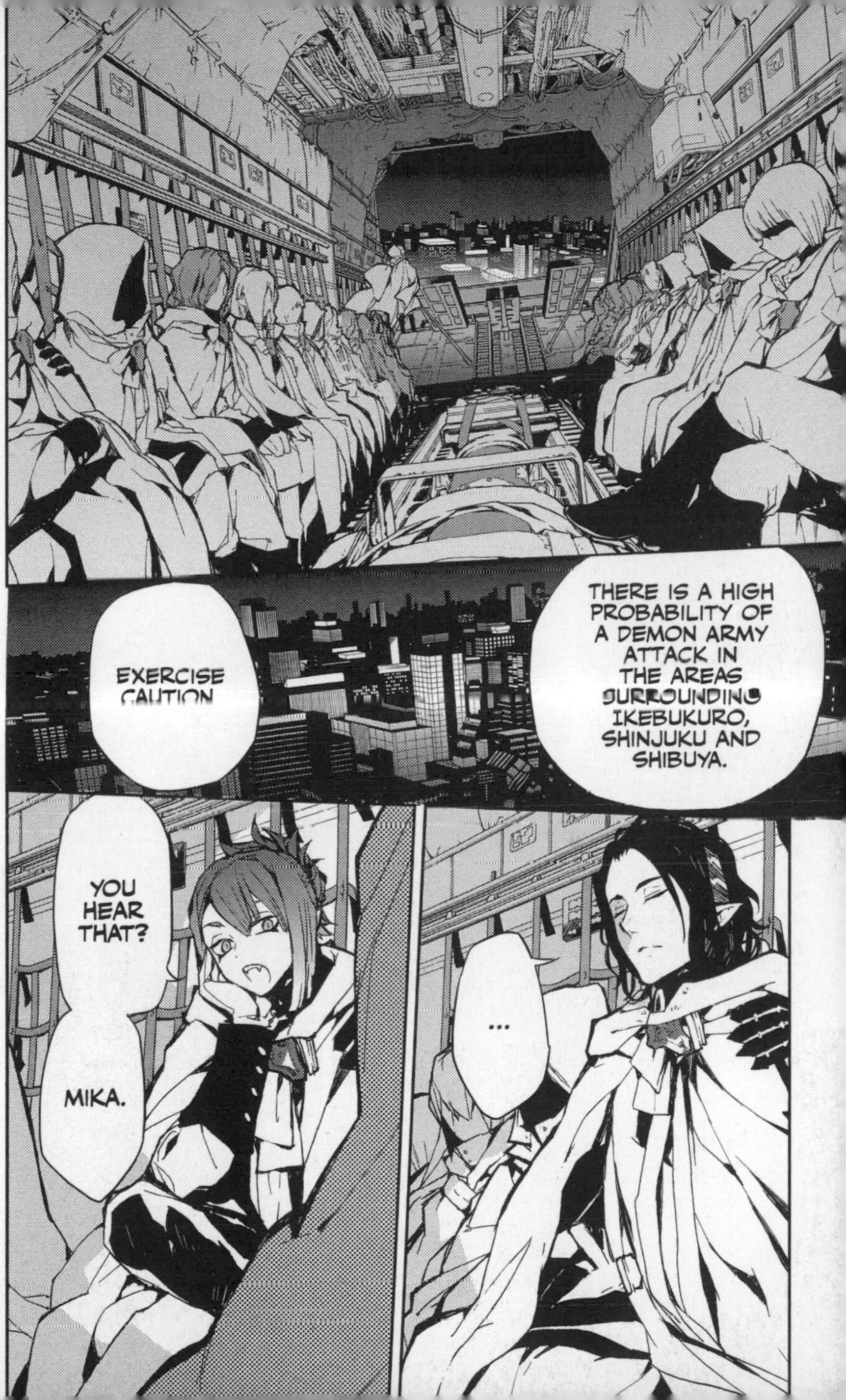
THERE IS A HIGH PROBABILITY OF A DEMON ARMY ATTACK IN THE AREAS SURROUNDING IKEBUKURO, SHINJUKU AND SHIBUYA.
EXERCISE CAUTION
...
YOU HEAR THAT?
MIKA.

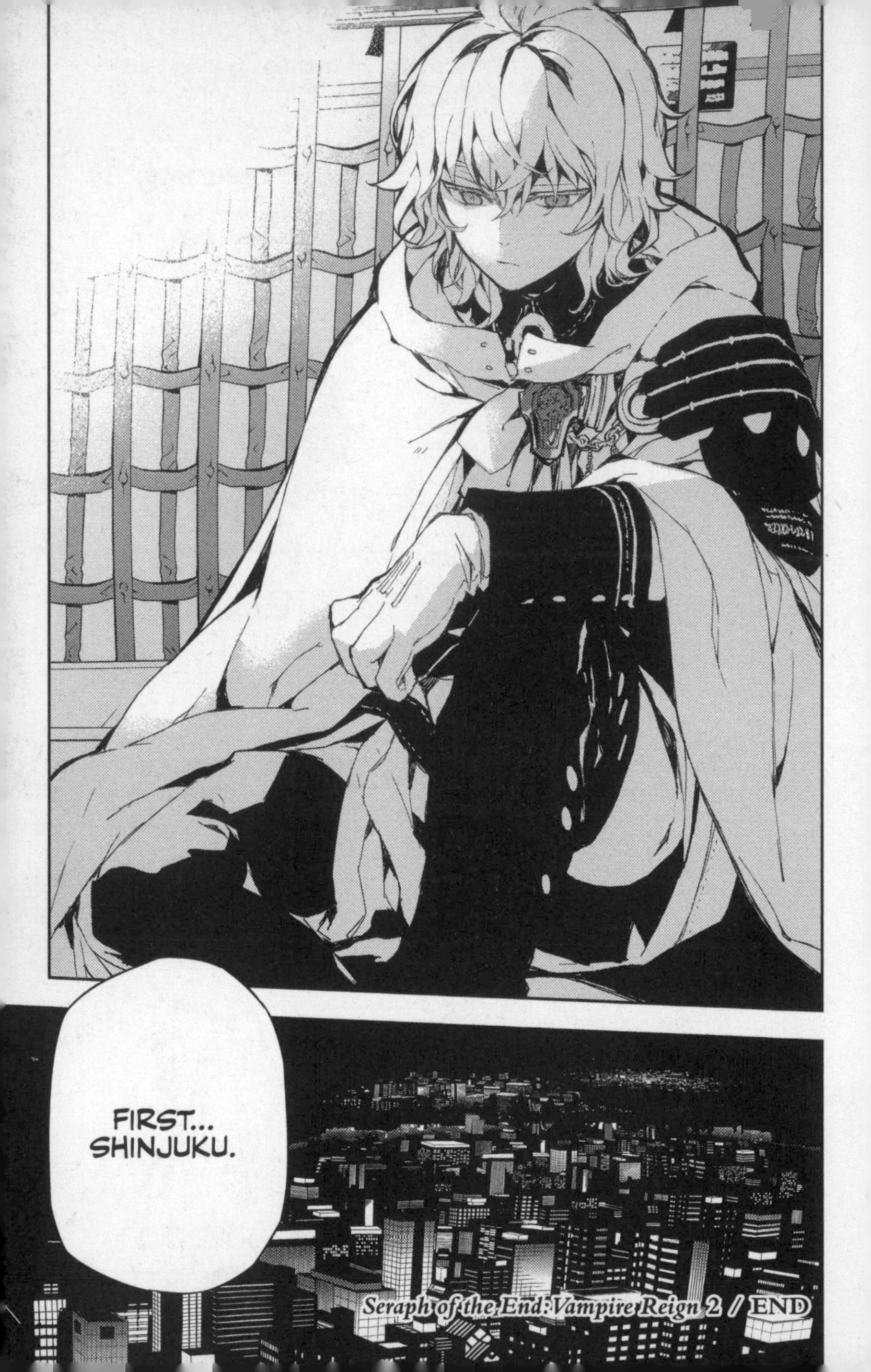
FIRST... SHINJUKU.
Seraph of the End: Vampire Reign 2 / END

Character Materials Collection by Takaya Kagami

HELLO. I'M TAKAYA KAGAMI. LET'S START UP WHERE VOLUME 1 LEFT OFF. THIS TIME WE HAVE THESE TWO CHARACTERS!

YOICHI SAOTOME

No saying "And he's an archer too? Ugh!"

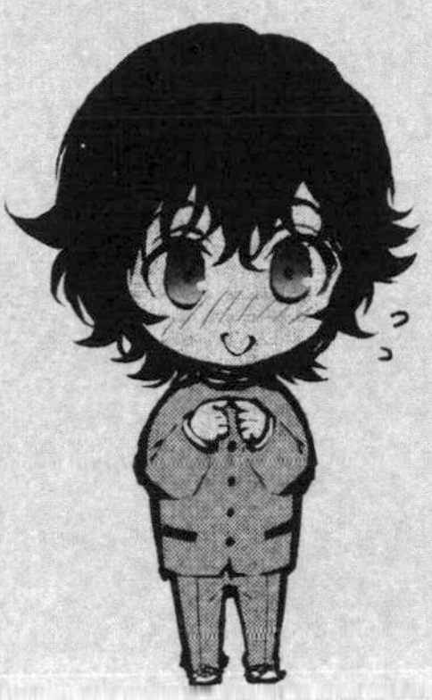

YOICHI:
"HUH? WHAT'S THAT MEAN?"

In Japanese entertainment like manga and video games, the name "Yoichi" is practically synonymous with "bow," from the famous historical Japanese archer Nasu no Yoichi. But actually, this Yoichi didn't get his name from that. There's a different reason, but it's a secret! (So then what's the point of this Collection, if not to spill those secrets?)

SHIHO KIMIZUKI

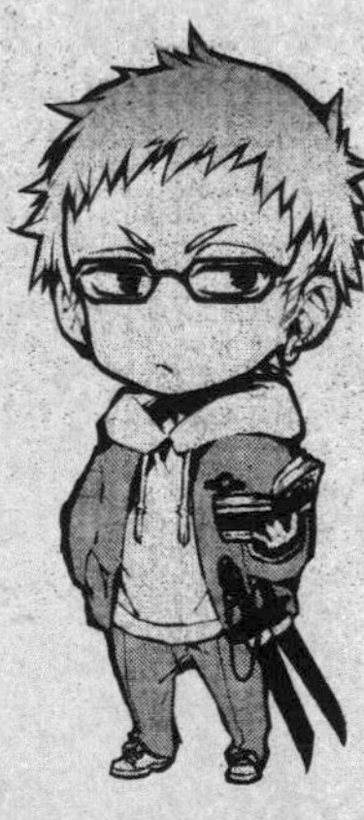

His original character design didn't have glasses. However, when Mr. Yamamoto saw him, he was like "Oooh! This guy needs glasses! Totally! Can I give him glasses?! I gave him glasses!" He sent over two sketches, one with and one without glasses. When we saw the sheer skill, coolness and glasses-power invested in the second option, my editor and I were like "Whoooa!! So cool! He's gotta have glasses!!" And that's how he got glasses. What do you think of that, Kimizuki?

KIMIZUKI: "LIKE I CARE!"

THIS REALLY ISN'T TURNING INTO A GOOD COLLECTION, IS IT?

GLOSSARY

The Overseas World After the Fall— Japan is not the only country with surviving human organizations. Various spellcaster unions are bringing together the remaining population in America, Europe, Russia, the Middle East and China. However, few of them are as organized and capable of confronting vampires head-on as the Japanese Imperial Demon Army.

Demon— Creatures that serve as a source of magic. Created when certain people, under certain circumstances, became them.

Black Demon Series— The highest rank of demons. Many have aggressive personalities, though the abilities they imbue into their weapon forms tend to be simple power magnifiers. Other demon series exist, such as the "Yasha Series" and "Bodhisattva Series." The Black Demon Series, however, is so powerful almost no one can handle one.

On Storing Cursed Gear— In the case of most Cursed Gear, the demon's power can be sealed into a small item, making it easily portable when not in combat form. However, the greater the demon's destructive power, the larger that passive-state item becomes. Currently Guren, Yu and Kimizuki have Cursed Gear with such destructive potential that they cannot seal them into smaller items. Support and magic-based Cursed Gear, such as Shinoa's and Yoichi's, can almost always be sealed into smaller, more portable forms.

AFTERWORD

HELLO. I'M TAKAYA KAGAMI, AUTHOR OF *SERAPH OF THE END: VAMPIRE REIGN*. IT SEEMS WRITING THE AFTERWORD HAS FALLEN TO ME AGAIN.

ED: IF WE DON'T HAVE SOMEONE DO AN AFTERWORD, WE WON'T HAVE ANY BONUS CONTENT AT ALL THIS VOLUME.

TK: WHAT? YEAH, THAT'S NOT GOOD...

ED: SO GET TO IT, OKAY? WE NEED TWO BONUS PAGES AND THREE PAGES OF AFTERWORD.

TK: YIKES! THAT'S A LOT!

AND THAT'S HOW I WOUND UP WITH IT. WHAT DO YOU ALL THINK ABOUT HAVING A NOVEL-LIKE AFTERWORD STUCK AT THE END OF A MANGA? WOULDN'T YOU RATHER NOT READ PAGES FULL OF NOTHING BUT WORDS? THAT'S WHAT I THOUGHT, AT LEAST, BUT I HOPE YOU'LL STICK WITH ME.

STILL, WHEN I'M NOT WORKING ON *SERAPH*, I DO OTHER NORMAL AUTHOR THINGS, SO I'VE WRITTEN TONS OF AFTERWORDS (IF YOU PUT EVERY ONE I'VE WRITTEN TOGETHER, I THINK IT WOULD BE ABOUT TWO FULL BOOKS' WORTH).

BUT DESPITE HOW MANY OF THEM I'VE DONE, THEY'RE STILL HARD FOR ME. SOMETIMES, I THINK I'LL WRITE ABOUT WHAT'S HAPPENING IN MY DAILY LIFE, BUT ALL I DO IS WRITE AT HOME OR WRITE AT A RESTAURANT, SO NOTHING INTERESTING THERE. BUT I WANT TO WRITE INTERESTING THINGS! I THOUGHT IF I WROTE AN AFTER-WORD ABOUT SOMETHING INTERESTING, THEN MAYBE PEOPLE WOULD THINK I WAS A GREAT CREATIVE WRITER! THAT THOUGHT HAD ME MOTIVATED FOR ABOUT FIVE MINUTES. THEN I REALIZED I PROBABLY COULDN'T DO IT, SO I GAVE UP. I MEAN, THE DEADLINE WAS LOOMING AND ALL.

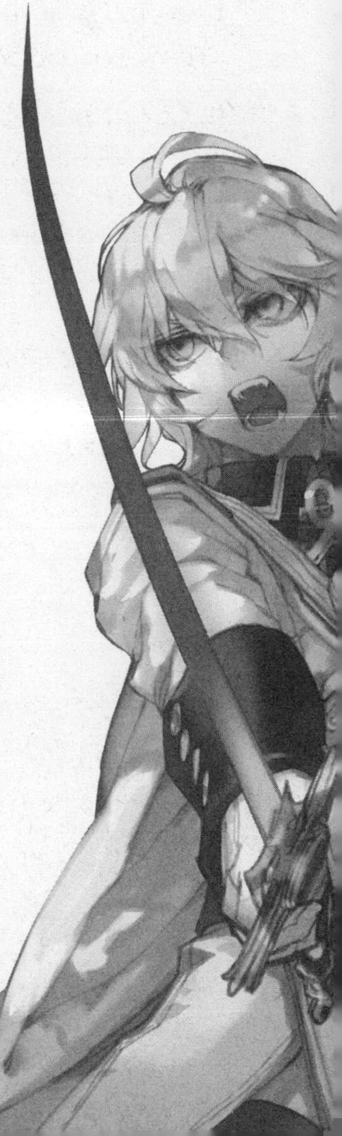

BY THE WAY, I'VE LEARNED THAT *WEEKLY SHONEN JUMP* WILL BE RUNNING A ONE-SHOT CHAPTER OF *SERAPH OF THE END: VAMPIRE REIGN* SOON. FOR REAL! ISN'T THAT AWESOME?! IT WAS, OF COURSE, DIRECTLY AFTER THAT SUDDEN OFFER THAT THIS AFTERWORD CAME UP AND, WELL, FOR DAISUKE FURUYA, YAMATO YAMAMOTO AND I, OUR SCHEDULES JUST KINDA EXPLODED. WE WERE ALL LIKE...

DF: WHAT, WAIT...YOU'RE GOING TO TRY TO WRITE AN AFTERWORD WHEN YOU HAVE THIS KIND OF SCHEDULE?!

ED: AAAAH!! CAN YOU DO IT, MR. KAGAMI?! CAN YOU MANAGE IT?!

TK: AUUGH!! HOLD IT! HANG ON! LEMME GO TALK TO MY OTHER EDITORS FOR MY OTHER BOOKS AND TRY TO SHIFT MY SCHEDULE...!!

YY: BY THE WAY, JUST SO YOU KNOW, I'M TOTALLY SWAMPED. I'VE HIT MY LIMIT!

TK: OH NO NO NO! I CAN'T FILL IT ALL OUT WITH JUST MY WRITING! I NEED SOME CHIBI CHARACTERS! JUST FOUR! CAN YOU GIVE ME FOUR?!

YY: FOUR?! YIKES! MAKE IT TWO! ONLY TWO!

TK: GAAAAH!!

ED: C'MON, EVERYONE! WE'LL PULL THROUGH THIS!

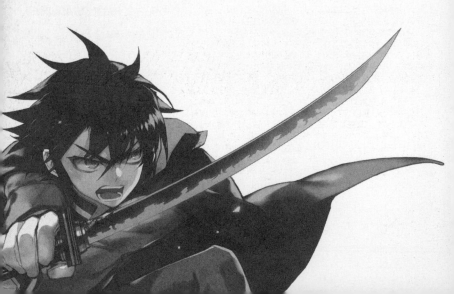

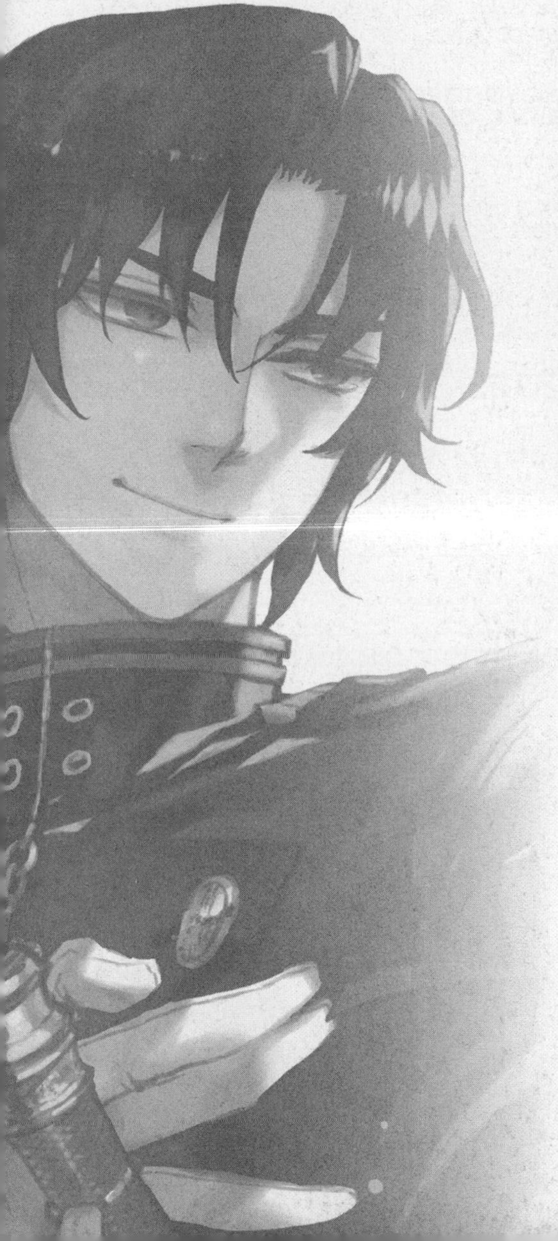

SO YEAH. I'M SORRY FOR THE LONG AND WORDY AFTERWORD, BUT WE HAD SPACE TO FILL. BUT IT DOES MEAN THERE'S MORE MANGA COMING FOR YOU TO READ ELSEWHERE. I HOPE YOU'RE LOOKING FORWARD TO IT!

OH, AND ONE MORE THING! I SHOULD PROBABLY SAY SOMETHING AS NOVEL-WRITER ME, AND NOT MANGA-SCRIPT WRITER ME. I HOPE YOU'RE ALSO ENJOYING THE NOVEL *SERAPH OF THE END: GUREN ICHINOSE'S CATASTROPHE AT 16!*

SEE YOU IN VOLUME 3!

P.S. - I HATE DEADLINES.

TAKAYA KAGAMI

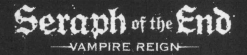

Seraph of the End
—VAMPIRE REIGN—

VOLUME 2
SHONEN JUMP ADVANCED MANGA EDITION

STORY BY **TAKAYA KAGAMI**
ART BY **YAMATO YAMAMOTO**
STORYBOARDS BY **DAISUKE FURUYA**

TRANSLATION **Adrienne Beck**
TOUCH-UP ART & LETTERING **Sabrina Heep**
DESIGN **Shawn Carrico**
EDITOR **Hope Donovan**

OWARI NO SERAPH © 2012 by Takaya Kagami,
Yamato Yamamoto, Daisuke Furuya
All rights reserved. First published in Japan in 2012 by SHUEISHA Inc., Tokyo.
English translation rights arranged by SHUEISHA Inc.

The stories, characters and incidents mentioned in this
publication are entirely fictional.

Printed in the U.S.A.

Published by VIZ Media, LLC
P.O. Box 77010
San Francisco, CA 94107

10 9 8 7 6 5 4 3 2 1
First printing, September 2014

www.viz.com

www.shonenjump.com

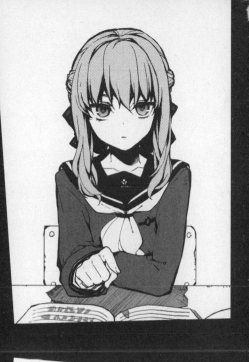

YOU'RE READING THE

WRONG WAY!

SERAPH OF THE END reads from right to left, starting in the upper-right corner. Japanese is read from right to left, meaning that action, sound effects, and word-balloon order are completely reversed from English order.

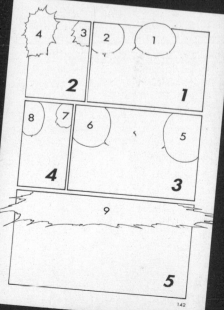

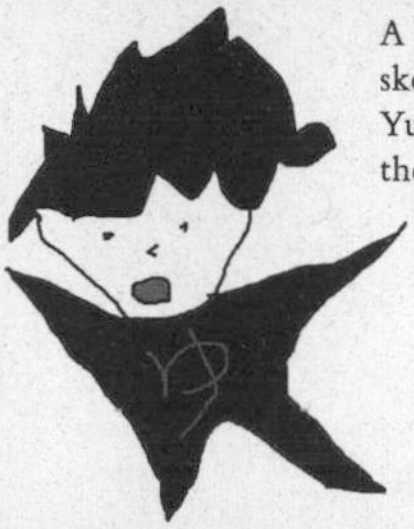

A brilliant sketch of Yuichiro by the author!

TAKAYA KAGAMI is a prolific light novelist whose works include the action and fantasy series *The Legend of the Legendary Heroes*, which has been adapted into manga, anime and a video game. His previous series, *A Dark Rabbit Has Seven Lives*, also spawned a manga and anime series.

“Lately, I’ve been doing all my writing at family restaurants. Now it feels like I’ve hurt my back. I think family restaurants should be required to provide ergonomic sofas. Anyway, here’s volume 2.”

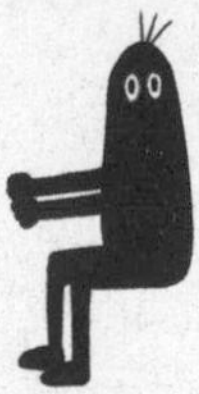

YAMATO YAMAMOTO, born 1983, is an artist and illustrator whose works include the *Kure-nai* manga and the light novels *Kure-nai*, *9S -Nine S-* and *Denpa Teki na Kanojo*. Both *Denpa Teki na Kanojo* and *Kure-nai* have been adapted into anime.

“Yuichiro has more friends. I’m sure they’ll grant him even greater power. I hope you enjoy it.”

DAISUKE FURUYA previously assisted Yamato Yamamoto with storyboards for *Kure-nai*.